TORPEDOES

AND

TORPEDO WARFARE:

CONTAINING A

COMPLETE AND CONCISE ACCOUNT OF THE

RISE AND PROGRESS OF SUBMARINE WARFARE:

ALSO A

DETAILED DESCRIPTION OF ALL MATTERS APPERTAINING THERETO,
INCLUDING THE LATEST IMPROVEMENTS.

BY

C. W. SLEEMAN, Esq.,

LATE LIEUT. R.N., AND LATE COMMANDER IMPERIAL OTTOMAN NAVY.

*WITH FIFTY-SEVEN FULL-PAGE ILLUSTRATIONS, DIAGRAMS,
WOODCUTS, &c.*

PORTSMOUTH:
GRIFFIN & CO., 2, THE HARD,
(Publishers by Appointment to H.R.H. The Duke of Edinburgh.)
LONDON AGENTS: SIMPKIN, MARSHALL, & CO.

1880.

PREFACE.

In the following pages the Author has endeavoured to supply a want, viz. a comprehensive work on Torpedo Warfare, brought down to the latest date.

The information has been obtained while practically engaged in torpedo work at home and abroad, and from the study of the principal books which have already appeared on the subject, and to the authors of which he would now beg to express his acknowledgments, viz.: "Submarine Warfare," by Lieut.-Commander Barnes, U.S.N.; "Notes on Torpedoes," by Major Stotherd, R.E.; "Art of War in Europe," by General Delafield, U.S.A.; "Life of Fulton," by C. D. Colden; "Torpedo War," by R. Fulton; "Armsmear," by H. Barnard; "Treatise on Coast Defence," by Colonel Von Scheliha; Professional Papers of the Royal Engineers; "The Engineering"; "The Engineer"; "Scientific American"; "Iron"; &c., &c.

The Author is also desirous of thanking the following gentlemen, to whom he is indebted for much of the valuable information contained herein :—

Messrs. Siemens Brothers, Messrs. Thornycroft and Co., Messrs. Yarrow and Co., Captain C. A. McEvoy, 18 Adam Street, W.C., Mr. L. Lay, Messrs. J. Vavaseur and Co.

London, 1879.

CONTENTS.

———•◦•———

LIST OF PLATES.

———•◦•———

Torpedoes and Torpedo Warfare.

CHAPTER I.

THE EARLY HISTORY OF THE TORPEDO.—REMARKS ON THE EXISTING STATE OF TORPEDO WARFARE.

THE earliest record we have of the employment of an infernal machine at all resembling the torpedo of the present day, was in 1585 at the siege of Antwerp. Here by means of certain small vessels, drifted down the stream, in each of which was placed a magazine of gunpowder, to be fired either by a trigger, or a combination of levers and clockwork, an Italian engineer, Lambelli, succeeded in demolishing a bridge that the enemy had formed over the Scheldt.

So successful was this first attempt, and so tremendous was the effect produced on the spectators, by the explosion of one of these torpedoes, that further investigation of this new mode of Naval warfare was at once instituted.

But it was not until some two hundred years after that any real progress was effected, though numerous attempts were made during this period, to destroy vessels by means of sub-marine infernal machines.

It was owing to the fact, that the condition which is now considered as essential in torpedo warfare, viz., that the charge must be submerged, was then entirely ignored, that so long a standstill occurred in this new art of making war.

Captain Bushnell, the Inventor of Torpedoes.—To Captain David Bushnell, of Connecticut, in 1775, is most certainly due the credit of inventing torpedoes, or as he termed them submarine magazines. For he first proved practically that a charge of gunpowder could be fired under water, which is incontestably the essence of submarine warfare.

Submarine Boat.—To Captain Bushnell is also due the credit of first devizing a submarine boat for the purpose of conveying his magazines to the bottom of hostile ships and there exploding them.

Drifting Torpedoes.—Another plan of his for destroying vessels, was that of connecting two of his infernal machines together by means of a line, and throwing them into the water, allowing the current to carry them across the bows of the attacked ship.

Mode of Ignition.—The ignition of his magazines was generally effected by means of clockwork, which, when set in motion, would run for some time before exploding the machines, thus enabling the operators to get clear of the explosion.

Captain Bushnell's few attempts to destroy our ships off the American coast in 1776 and 1777, with his submarine boat, and his drifting torpedoes were all attended with failure, a result generally experienced, where new inventions are for the first time subjected to the test of actual service.

Robert Fulton.—Robert Fulton, an American, following in his footsteps, some twenty years after, revived the subject of submarine warfare, which during that interval seems to have been entirely forgotten.

A resident in France, in 1797, he is found during that year making various experiments on the Seine with a machine which he had constructed, and by which he designed "to impart to carcasses of gunpowder a progressive motion under water, to a certain point, and there explode them."[*]

Fulton's Failures.—Though these first essays of his resulted in failure, Fulton thoroughly believed in the efficacy of his schemes, and we find him, during that and succeeding years, vainly importunating the French and Dutch Governments, to grant him aid and support in carrying out experiments with his new inventions, whereby he might

---

[*] C. D. Colden's "Life of Fulton."

perfect them, and thus ensure to whichever government acceded to his views, the total destruction of their enemy's fleets.

Bonaparte aids Fulton.—Though holding out such favourable terms, it was not until 1800, when Bonaparte became First Consul, that Fulton's solicitations were successful, and that money was granted him to carry out a series of experiments.

In the following year (1801), under Bonaparte's immediate patronage, Fulton carried out various and numerous experiments in the harbour of Brest, principally with a submarine boat devised by him (named the *Nautilus*), subsequently to his invention of submarine carcasses as a means of approaching a ship and fixing one of his infernal machines beneath her, unbeknown to the crew of the attacked ship.

First Vessel destroyed by Torpedoes.—In August, 1801, Fulton completely destroyed a small vessel in Brest harbour by means of one of his submarine bombs, then called by him for the first time, torpedoes, containing some twenty pounds of gunpowder. This is the first vessel known to have been sunk by a submarine mine.

Bonaparte's patronage withdrawn.—Notwithstanding the apparent success, and enormous power of Fulton's projects, on account of a failure on his part to destroy one of the English Channel fleet, at the end of 1801, Bonaparte at once withdrew his support and aid.

Disgusted with this treatment, and having been previously pressed by some of England's most influential men, to bring his projects to that country, so that the English might reap the benefit of his wonderful schemes, Fulton left France, and arrived in London, in May, 1804.

Pitt supports Fulton.—Mr. Pitt, then Prime Minister, was much struck with Fulton's various schemes of submarine warfare, and after examining one of his infernal machines, or torpedoes, exclaimed, " that if introduced into practice, it could not fail to annihilate all military marines."*

Though having secured the approval of Mr. Pitt, and a few other members of the Government, he was quite unable to induce the English to accept his schemes in toto, and at once employ them in the Naval service.

---

* C. D. Colden's " Life of Fulton."

Twice Fulton attempted to destroy French men-of-war, lying in the harbour of Boulogne, by means of his drifting torpedoes, but each time he failed, owing as he then explained, and which afterwards proved to be the case, to the simple mistake of having made his machines specifically heavier than water, thus preventing the current from carrying them under a vessel's bottom.

Destruction of the "Dorothea."—Though in each of the above-mentioned attempts Fulton succeeded in exploding his machines, and though on the 15th October, 1805, in the presence of a numerous company of Naval and other scientific men, he completely demolished a stout brig, the *Dorothea*, off Walmer Castle, by means of his drifting torpedoes, similar to those employed by him at Boulogne, but considerably improved, still the English Government refused to have anything further to do with him or his schemes.

England, at that time, being mistress of the seas, it was clearly her interest to make the world believe that Fulton's schemes were impracticable and absurd.

Earl St. Vincent, in a conversation with Fulton, told him in very strong language, "that Pitt was a fool for encouraging a mode of warfare, which, if successful, would wrest the trident from those who then claimed to bear it, as the sceptre of supremacy on the ocean." *

Wearied with incessant applications and neglect, and with failures, not with his inventions, but in inducing governments to accept them, he left England in 1806, and returned to his native country.

Application to Congress for Help.—Arrived there, he lost no time in solicitating aid from Congress to enable him to carry out experiments with his torpedoes and submarine boats, practice alone in his opinion being necessary to develop the extraordinary powers of his invention, as an auxiliary to harbour defence.

By incessant applications to his government, and by circulating his torpedo book + among the members, in which he had given detailed accounts of all his previous experiments in France and England, and elaborate plans for rendering American harbours, etc., invulnerable to British attack, a Commission was appointed to inquire into and practically test the value of these schemes.

---

* C. D. Colden's "Life of Fulton."

† "Torpedo Warfare," by R. Fulton, 1810.

They were as follows :—

1.—*Drifting Torpedoes.*—Two torpedoes connected by a line floated in the tide at a certain depth, and suffered to drift across the bows of the vessel to be attacked ; the coupling line being arrested by the ship's cable would cause the torpedoes to be forced under her bottom ; this plan is represented and will be readily understood by Fig. 3.

2.—*Harpoon Torpedo.*—A torpedo attached to one end of a line, the other part to a harpoon, which was to be fired into the bows of the doomed vessel from a piece of ordnance mounted in the bows of a boat, specially constructed for the purpose ; the line being fixed to the vessel by the harpoon, the current, if the vessel were at anchor, or her progress if underweigh, would carry the torpedo under her bottom. Fig. 2 represents this type of Fulton's submarine infernal machine.

3.—*Spar Torpedo.*—A torpedo attached to a spar suspended by a swivel from the bowsprit of a torpedo boat, so nearly balanced, that a man could easily depress, or elevate the torpedo with one hand, whilst with the other he pulled a trigger and exploded it.

4.—*Block Ship.*—Block ships, that is vessels from 50 to 100 tons, constructed with sides impervious to cannon shot, and decks made impenetrable to musket shot. A spar torpedo *a, a, a,* to be carried on each bow and quarter Fig. 4 represents this curious craft.

Stationary Mines.—Stationary buoyant torpedoes for harbour defence, to be fired by means of levers attached to triggers. This kind of mine is shown at Fig. 1.

5.—*Cable Cutters.*—Cable cutters, that is submarine guns discharging a sharp piece of iron in the shape of a crescent, with sufficient force to cut through ship's cables, or other obstructions. *

Practical Experiments.—Various and exhaustive experiments were carried out in the presence of the Commissioners, tending generally to impress them with a favourable view of Fulton's many projects.

---

* C. D. Colden's " Life of Fulton."

As a final test, the sloop *Argus* was ordered, under the superintendence of Commodore Rodgers, to whom Fulton had previously explained his mode of attack, to be prepared to repel all attempts made against her by Fulton, with his torpedoes.

Defence of the " Argus."—Though repeated attempts were made, none were successful, owing to the energetic, though somewhat exaggerated manner in which the defence of the sloop had been carried out. She was surrounded by numerous spars lashed together, nets down to the ground, grappling irons, heavy pieces of metal suspended from the yard arms ready to be dropped into any boat that came beneath them, scythes fitted to long spars for the purpose of mowing off the heads of any who might be rash enough to get within range of them.

As Robert Fulton very justly remarked, " a system, then only in its infancy, which compelled a hostile vessel to guard herself by such extraordinary means could not fail of becoming a most important mode of warfare."

Three of the Commissioners reported as favourably as could be expected, considering its infancy, on the practical value of Fulton's scheme of torpedo warfare.

Congress refuse aid.—But on the strength of Commodore Rodgers's report, which was as unfair and prejudiced, as the others were fair and unprejudiced, Congress refused Fulton any further aid, or to countenance any further experiments that he might still feel inclined to prosecute.

Though undeterred by this fresh instance of neglect, and still having a firm belief in the efficacy of his various torpedo projects, yet other important matters connected with the improvement of the steam engine occupied his whole time and prevented him from making any further experiments with his submarine inventions.

Mode of Firing, 1829.—Up to 1829, that is to say for nearly sixty years after the invention of torpedoes, mechanical means only were employed to effect the ignition of the torpedo charges, such as levers, clockwork, and triggers pulled by hand; with such crude means of exploding them, it is not extraordinary to find, that all the attempts made to destroy hostile ships, resulted in failure.

Briefly reviewing the history of the torpedo during its first period of existence, viz., from Captain Bushnell's invention of submarine magazines in 1775, down to the introduction of electricity, as a means

PLATE I

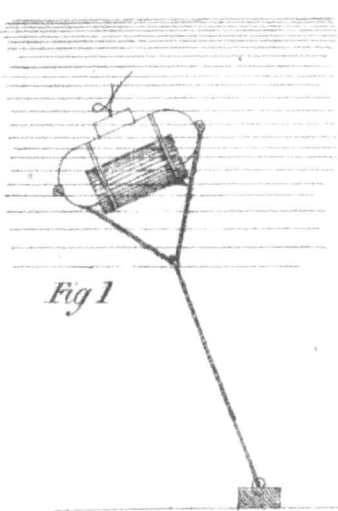

Fig 1

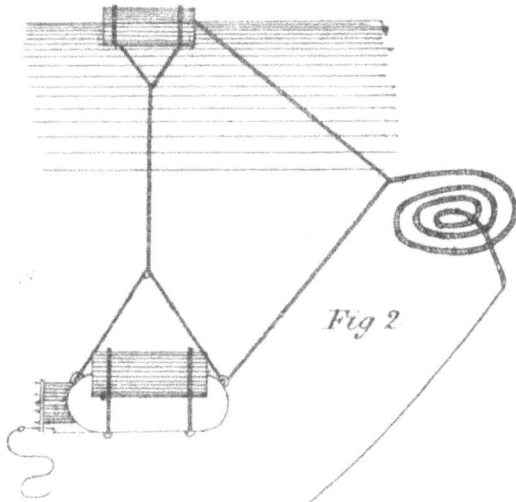

Fig 2

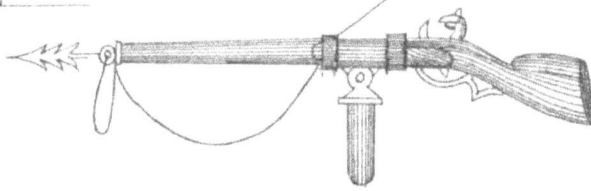

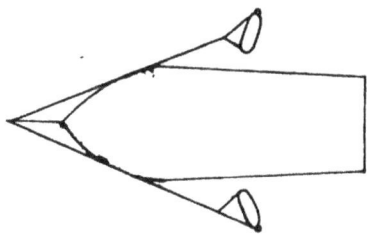

Fig 3

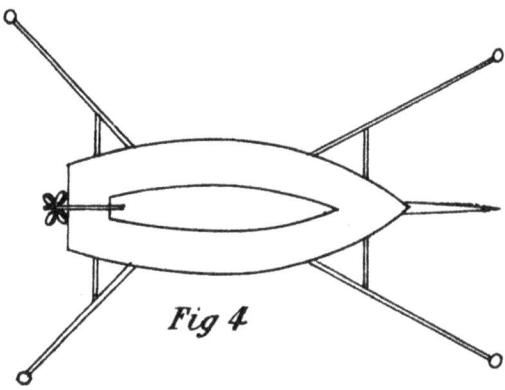

Fig 4

of exploding submarine mines, by Colonel Colt, in 1829, we find that due to the unwearied exertions, and numerous experiments carried out by Captain Bushnell, Mr. R. Fulton and others, the following very important principles in the art of torpedo warfare were fully proved :—

1.—That a charge of gunpowder could be exploded under water.
2.—That any vessel could be sunk by a torpedo, provided only the charge were large enough.
3.—That it was possible to construct a boat which could be navigated, and remain for several hours under water, without detriment to her crew.
4.—That a ship at anchor, by means of drifting torpedoes, or by a submarine or ordinary boat, armed with a spar torpedo.
5.—That a vessel underweigh could be destroyed by means of stationary submarine mines, and by the harpoon torpedo.

These principles, which at the time were fully admitted, laid the foundations of the systems of torpedo warfare, that are at the present day in vogue, all over the world.

Second Epoch.—The second epoch in the life of the torpedo dates from 1829, when Colonel Colt, then a mere lad, commenced experiments with his submarine battery.

Colt's Experiments.—His first public essay, was on the 4th June, 1842, when he exploded a case of powder in New York harbour, while himself standing at a great distance off.

Having by numerous successful experiments satisfactorily proved that vessels at anchor could be sunk by means of his electrical mines, Colonel Colt engaged to destroy a vessel underweigh by similar means, which feat he successfully accomplished on 13th April, 1844.

Colt's Electric Cable.—The electric cable as used by Colonel Colt, was insulated by cotton yarn, soaked in a solution of asphaltum and beeswax, and the whole enclosed in a metal case.

Colt's Reflector.—On examining Colt's papers after his death, one was found illustrating one of his many devices for effecting the explosion of a submarine mine at the proper instant.

Description of Reflector.—One set of conducting wires from all the mines is permanently attached to a single pole of a very powerful firing battery, the other wires lead to metal points which are attached to marks on a chart of the channel in front of the operator and which marks correspond with the actual positions of the mines in the channel. A reflector, is arranged to throw the image of a hostile vessel on the chart, and as this image passes over either of the wire terminations on it, the operator with the other battery wire, completes the circuit, and explodes the torpedo, over which by her image thrown on the chart, the vessel is supposed to be at that precise moment.* In his experiment with a vessel under weigh, Colt had probably taken the precaution of laying down several circles of mines, and thus aided by cross staffs, ensured the experiment being a success.

With regard to the invention of the word torpedo, for submarine infernal machines, Dr. Barnard in his life of Colt says, " that Fulton used the word torpedo, probably on account of its power of stunning or making torpid, and that a long way through the water,—in so naming it, he buildeth better than he knew, for Colt's torpedoes being fired by electricity may with special fitness take its name from the electric eel."†

Theoretical Knowledge.—Though many opportunities have occurred during the last thirty-five years for practically testing the effectiveness of torpedoes when employed on actual service, especially during the American Civil War (1861—65) and the late Turco-Russian War (1877 —78), yet in so far as the offensive and electrical portion of submarine warfare is concerned, our knowledge of them is still principally theoretically.

Failure of Offensive Torpedoes.—The manipulation of the ordinary spar or outrigger torpedo boats, and of the various automatic torpedoes, appears simple enough, when practice is made with those submarine weapons during peace time, also the results of such practice is without doubt uniformly successful, yet when the crucial test of actual service is applied, as was the case during the war of 1877, with the Whitehead and spar torpedoes, then a succession of failures had to be recorded.§

The cause of this want of success in war-time with offensive torpedoes, lies in the fact, that during peace time the experiments and

---

* Johnston's Cyclopædia.   † Armsmear.   § See Chapter VII.

practice carried out with them, are done so, under the most favourable circumstances, that is to say in daylight, and the nerves of the operators not in that high state of tension, which would be the case, were they attacking a man-of-war on a pitch dark night, whose exact position cannot be known, and from whose guns at any moment a sheet of fire may be belched forth, and a storm of shot and bullets be poured on them, whilst on actual service, this would in nine out of ten instances be the case.

Some uncertainty must and will always exist in offensive torpedo operations when carried out in actual war, where, as in this case, the success of the enterprise depends almost wholly on the state of a man's nerves, yet this defect, a want of certainty, may to a considerable extent be eradicated were means to be found of carrying out in time of peace, a systematic practice of this branch of torpedo warfare, under circumstances similar to those experienced in war time, and this is not only possible, but practicable.

Moral Effect of Torpedoes.—We now come to the moral effect of torpedoes, which is undoubtedly the very essence of the vast power of these terrible engines of war. Each successive war that has occurred, in which the torpedo has taken a part, since Captain Bushnell's futile attempt in 1775 to destroy our fleet by drifting numerous kegs charged with gunpowder down the Delawarre, teem with proofs of the great worth of torpedoes in this respect alone.

That such a dread of them should and always will be met with in future Naval wars, at times creating a regular torpedo scare or funk, is not extraordinary, when it is remembered that these submarine weapons of the present day, are capable of sinking the finest ironclad afloat, and of launching into eternity without a moment's warning or preparation, whole ships' crews.

The torpedoes existing at the present day have, without doubt, reached a very high degree of excellence, in so far as their construction, fuzes, cables, &c., both electrically and mechanically, is concerned, but much has yet to be done to develop their actual effectiveness.

The result of the numerous and exhaustive experiments that have of late years been carried out by England, America, and Europe prove that the necessary distances between stationary submarine mines are by far greater than those within which the explosions are effective.

Therefore it will be found necessary to supplement those submarine harbour defences, by automatic torpedoes that can be controlled and directed from the shore, as well as by specially constructed torpedo boats.

Automatic Arrangements.—And to ensure certainty, which is the desideratum in torpedo warfare, circuit closers, or other automatic arrangements for exploding the submarine mines, must be employed, as the system of firing them by judgment is not at all a sure one.

Ship Defence.—The problem, which occupies the attention of Naval and other scientific men, at the present day, is how best to enable a ship to guard herself against attacks from the fish and other automatic torpedoes, and this without in any way impairing her efficiency as a man-of-war.

The means of such defence, should most certainly be inherent in the vessel herself, outward methods, such as nets, booms, etc., are to great extent impracticable, besides one of the above mentioned torpedoes, being caught by such obstructions would, on exploding, most probably destroy them, thus leaving the vessel undefended against further attacks.

Mechanical Mines.—Several ingenious methods have of late been devised for the purpose of obviating one of the principal defects common to all kinds of mechanical submarine mines, the most efficient and practical of which will be found fully described in the following pages, viz., the great danger attendant on the mooring of such mines; but as yet, no really practical mode of rendering mechanical mines safe, after they have once been moored and put in action, has been discovered, were such to be devised, a very difficult and extremely important problem of defensive torpedo warfare would be solved.

Electrical Mines.—In regard to electrical submarine mines, much has been done by torpedoists in general to simplify this otherwise somewhat complicated branch of defensive torpedo warfare, by adopting the platinum wire fuze, in the place of the high tension one, by the employment of Le'clanché firing batteries, by the simplification of the circuit closer, and discarding the use of a circuit breaker, by altering the form of torpedo case, and whenever possible by enclosing the circuit closer in the submarine mine.

The necessity of a very elaborate system of testing should, if possible, be overcome, for a system of submarine mines that requires the numerous and various tests that are at the present day employed, to enable those in charge of them to know for certain that when wanted the mines will explode, cannot be considered as adaptable to actual service.   It must be remembered that the safety of many ports, etc., will in future wars depend almost entirely on the practical efficiency of electrical and mechanical mines.   As yet, in actual war, little or no experience has been gained of the real value of a mode of coast defence by electrical mines, excepting from a moral point of view, though in this particular they have most undoubtedly been proved to be exceedingly effective.

A submarine mine much wanted on active service, is one that can be carried on board ships, capable of being fitted for use at a moment's notice, and of being easily and rapidly placed in position by the ordinary boats of a man-of-war.   It should be a self-acting electrical mine, with the circuit closing apparatus enclosed in the torpedo case, and capable of carrying about 100lbs. of guncotton.   This form of mine would be found extremely useful to secure the entrance to a harbour, etc., where ships might happen to be anchored for the night, or which might have been wrested from the enemy, etc.

They should be capable of being placed in position and picked up again, in the shortest possible space of time.

Offensive Torpedoes.—Coming to the question of offensive torpedoes there still seems to be a great difference of opinion as to the real value of the Whitehead fish torpedo, and this point will never be finally settled until that weapon has been more thoroughly tested on actual service ; from a specially built torpedo boat, by which is meant a Thornycroft or Yarrow craft, the spar torpedo would seem to be the most effective weapon.   Torpedo vessels for the special purpose of experimenting with the Whitehead torpedo have been built by England, America, and several continental governments, so that we may soon hope to get some more decided opinion as to the utility of that weapon.   When manipulated from the shore, or large ships, the Lay torpedo boat, if only its speed be increased will prove an exceedingly effective submarine weapon, for the purposes of offence, active defence, or clearing harbours, etc., of mines, in fact, it may be more truly said of this weapon, than of the Whitehead, "that it can do everything but speak."   Captain Harvey has greatly improved his towing torpedo, but it is still a somewhat complicated and difficult weapon to manipulate by ordinary persons, that is, those not specially trained for the work.

Drifting torpedoes under certain circumstances should prove invaluable, but little or no improvement has been effected in this direction. Submarine boats have also remained *in statu quo*, though for the purpose of clearing an enemy's harbour of mines, it seems impossible to devise any better method.

Electric lights are now universally adopted for use on board ship, and will play a very important part in the defence of ships against torpedo attacks in future wars. Glancing back on what has been effected in the matter of improving the system of torpedo warfare in all its branches during the last few years, with the exception of the vast improvements in the form and construction of steam torpedo boats, their engines, etc., very little has been done, owing principally to the want of that practical knowledge which unfortunately can only be gained from their employment in actual war.

The late Turco-Russian war afforded a splendid opportunity for applying the crucial test of actual service to both the offensive and defensive branches of torpedo warfare, yet little or no light was thrown on the somewhat shadowy subject of submarine warfare. The present struggle between Peru and Chili may furnish some experience, but it will not be very satisfactory, as hardly any knowledge of manipulating torpedoes is possessed by either side.

CHAPTER II.

DEFENSIVE TORPEDO WARFARE.—MECHANICAL MINES.—MECHANICAL
FUZES.—MOORING MECHANICAL MINES.

BY defensive torpedo warfare is meant the protection of harbours,
rivers, etc., by means of various descriptions of torpedoes
moored beneath the surface of the water.

Submarine, or sea mine, is the term that has been generally
adopted to designate this particular species of torpedo.

Submarine Mines.—Defence in Future Wars.—The very conspicuous part played by submarine mines, in the many wars that have
taken place since the introduction of the torpedo as a legitimate mode
of Naval warfare, when their manipulation was comparatively little
understood, and construction very imperfect, proves that, with the
experience so gained, and the vast improvements that have been, and
are daily being effected, in all that appertains to the art of torpedo
warfare, the protection of harbours, etc., will in future wars depend
in a great measure on the adoption of a systematic and extensive
employment of submarine mines.

The utility and power of this mode of coast defence has been
fully exemplified in actual war, more especially during the Franco-
German war (1870—1) and the late Turco-Russian war (1877—8).

Torpedoes in the Franco-German War.—In the former instance, the
superiority of the French over the Germans, in the matter of ships, was
more than neutralised, by the use on the part of the latter of electrical,
mechanical, and dummy mines for the protection of their harbours, etc.
In regard to the utility of the latter, it is on record that a certain German
port was entirely defended by dummy mines, the Burgomaster of that
place having been unable to obtain men to place the active mechanical
ones in position, owing to the numerous and serious accidents that had
previously occurred in other German ports at the commencement of
the war, in mooring the latter kind of submarine mine.

The effect, so far as keeping the French fleet at a distance was concerned, was precisely the same, as though active instead of dummy mines had been employed, thus still further proving the vast moral power possessed by torpedoés.

Torpedoes in the Russo-Turkish War.—In the war of 1877, the Turks, though possessing a powerful fleet in the Black Sea and flotilla on the Danube, made little or no use of their superiority over the Russians in this respect. They failed to even attempt to destroy the bridges formed by the Russians over the Danube, nor did they make any attempt to capture Poti, re-take Kustendje, or to create diversions on the Russian coast in the Black Sea. Had the latter service alone been effectually carried out, by which means, a large force of the enemy would have been held in check, immense help would have been afforded to the Ottoman armies in Europe and Asia. Again, during the whole of the war, the Russian port of Odessa was never sighted, and Sebastopol only once by the Ottoman fleet.

Cause of Failure of the Ottoman Fleet.—The cause of this repeated neglect on the part of the Turkish fleet may be traced almost entirely to the assumption (which in nine out of ten cases was an erroneous one) on the part of the Naval Pashas and Beys that every Russian harbour, etc., was a mass of submarine mines, and this in several instances extending many miles to seaward.

So also, some of the many failures experienced by the Russians in their numerous boat torpedo boat attacks, were due in a great measure to an erroneous supposition on the part of the captain of the Russian steamer, *Constantine* (employed to convoy the torpedo boats), that the Turks had defended the entrance, to a distance of some miles to seaward, of their harbours, etc., and thus the torpedo boats were dispatched to the attack some miles off the entrance, causing them, owing to the darkness, to enter the harbour in which the Turkish vessels were lying, in a very straggling manner. And to a similar reason the failure of the Russians to capture Sulina, in the attack made on that place in October, 1877, was principally owing to their not daring to send their Popoffkas to attack from the sea.

One of the chief points of usefulness of an extensive and systematic employment of submarine mines, will be to minimise the number of vessels necessary for the protection of harbours, etc., thus enabling, a far larger number of ships to operate at sea against those of an enemy, this especially applies to countries like England and America possessing a large extent of seacoast, numerous harbours, rivers, etc., which it would be necessary to defend in the event of war.

Science of Torpedo Warfare.—The science of defensive torpedo warfare may be considered to consist of :—

1.—The arrangement of the mines in positions, such that it would not be possible for a hostile vessel attempting to force a passage into a harbour, etc., defended by such means, to pass more than one line of them, without coming within the destructive radius of some one or other of the remaining mines.

Note.—The difficulty of attaining the above effect, lies in the fact that the destructive radius of a submarine mine, is considerably less than the distance that must be maintained between them, to prevent injury by concussion to the cases, circuit closers, electric cables, etc., of such mines on the explosion of an adjacent one.

As an illustration of the above, take the case of a 500lb. guncotton submarine mine. Now the destructive radius of a sea-mine is found by the formula $R = \sqrt[3]{32.C}$. where R is the destructive radius in feet of a mine moored at its most effective depth, and C is the charge (guncotton) in lbs.

In the above case R would be about 24 feet, which in so far as the actual destruction of a ship is concerned, may be taken as correct, but if injury to a vessel's engines, boilers, etc., be also taken into consideration, and as the vessel would most probably be underweigh on such an occasion, this would be a very vital and important consideration, R would under those circumstances be more than doubled. Now the necessary interval for safety between such mines, according to torpedo authorities, is equal to 10 R, and should certainly be not less than 8 R, which in this case would give about 200 feet, therefore assuming the radius of destruction to be 50 feet, it is seen that there would be under those conditions a clear undefended space of about 100 feet between each couple of 500lb. mines in the same line.

2.—The combined arrangement of submarine mines with forts and batteries, in such a manner, that every one of the former shall be well covered by the guns of the latter, and also that it would be impossible for an enemy's ships to get within effective range of the forts, or batteries, without moving over ground where mines were laid.

Note.—This applies to the defence of the more important harbours, etc., in which case the submarine mines (which would be chiefly electrical ones) would only act as auxiliaries to the land defences. To effectually carry out the above, there can be no question but that they who plan the forts, etc., should also plan the systems of submarine defence.

A harbour, river, etc., which it is necessary to protect by electrical submarine mines, etc., and where no land defences exist, should have its mines supported by a powerful ship or ships, as may be thought desirable.

Success in Torpedo Warfare.—The two most important conditions essentially necessary to the successful employment of torpedoes, both offensive and defensive, are :—

    1. Certainty of Action.

    2. Simplicity of Manipulation.

Without the former this mode of Naval warfare is comparatively useless, while without the latter the former condition is rarely obtained, more especially in the case of offensive torpedoes.

Submarine mines are divided into separate classes, viz. :—

    1. Mechanical Mines.

    2. Electrical Mines.

Mechanical Mines.—By this description of submarine mines, is meant those whose charges are fired by mechanical means alone.

Mechanical Mines in the American Civil War.—During the civil war of America (1861—5), the Confederates depended almost entirely on mechanical submarine mines for the protection of their harbours, rivers, etc., and to this extensive use of such mines may be traced nearly the whole of the Federal disasters afloat.

In the principal wars that have subsequently occurred, though this form of submarine mine has been to a certain extent used, it has generally been only as an auxiliary to the more effective electrical torpedo, and owing to the deterrent effect produced by the numerous torpedo successes that characterised the American Civil War, on Naval Commanders, etc., few vessels have been destroyed by their means, the effect of the employment of defensive torpedoes having been almost wholly a moral one.

Mechanical Mines for Coast Defence.—The experience hitherto gained, with regard to the employment of mechanical mines for coast defence in actual war, proves that they will be found exceedingly valuable in the following positions :—

1.—In combination with booms or other obstructions placed in defence of narrow channels, etc., which are intended to be completely blocked up.

2.—In shallow water on the flanks of electrical mines.

3.—In protecting unfrequented bays, channels, etc., and a long line of seacoast, which may otherwise be entirely undefended.

NOTE.—In this latter instance, though the mines may not be covered by any guns, still they will be of great use, in so far, that being mechanical ones, they cannot be rendered useless by the process of cutting cables, etc., but must be destroyed, which in time of peace is a work of considerable labour and danger, and, therefore, would in the time of war, cause at the very least, serious delay to an enemy desirous of effecting a landing, etc., at a point so protected.

There are numerous objections against their employment, the principle ones being :—

1.—That they are all, more or less dangerous to place in position.

2.—That they cannot be tested when moored.

3.—That they are as dangerous to friend as to foe, when once placed in action.

4.—That an exploded, or known damaged mine cannot be replaced.

NOTE.—The above objections, especially 2 and 3, constitute without doubt very serious defects in a system of defence by mechanical mines, and in the case of purely mechanical ones, it seems almost impossible to eradicate any of them, though, notwithstanding, under the particular circumstance before-mentioned, these species of defensive torpedo will be found extremely useful.

The Advantages of Mechanical Mines.—They possess a few advantages, which are as follows :—

1.—They are comparatively cheap.

2.—They can be kept in store and ready for use at a moment's notice.

3.—They do not require specially trained men to manipulate them.

4.—Extempore ones can be easily and readily made.

Best Kinds of Mechanical Mines.—Among the very numerous and various kinds of mechanical submarine mines that have been devised the following may be considered as the most effective, and practicable of them all :--

      1.—FRAME TORPEDOES.

      2.—BUOYANT MINES.

This includes :—

          a.—BARREL MINE.

          b.—BROOK'S MINE.

      3.—SINGER'S MINE.

      4.—McEVOY'S IMPROVED MINE.

      5.—EXTEMPORE MINE.

Frame Torpedoes.—This form of defensive mine is shown at Fig. 6. It consists of a frame work which is formed of four strong timbers *a, a, a, a*, these being kept parallel and only a few feet apart by means of cross timbers *b, b*. A cast-iron torpedo *c, c, c*, in the shape of a shell, is bolted to the head of each of the timbers *a, a, a*, containing about thirty pounds of fine grained gunpowder, and fitted with a percussion fuse, which is so placed that it would come into contact with a vessel striking against the frame-work, directly or not, One end of the frame is securely anchored, the other, that on which the torpedoes are fixed, is kept at its proper distance below the surface of the water by means of chains, *d, d*, and anchors. To prevent the frame from sinking when sodden with water, the uprights *e, e*, are provided.

This form of mechanical mine, which performs the double function of torpedo and obstruction, was much used by the Confederates, and found extremely useful, no passage was attempted to be forced by the Federals where these torpedoes were known to be placed.

Stake Torpedo.—Fig. 7 represents another form of the frame torpedo.

It consists of a piece of timber, *a*, its heels secured by a heavy metal shoe *b*, working in a universal joint in the mooring, *c*. At the head of the piece of timber is secured a torpedo *d*, containing about fifty pounds of gunpowder, and fitted with four or five sensitive fuzes· The proper angle of inclination is obtained by securing the upper end of the timber to an anchor as shown at *e*. As a proof of the efficiency of this species of mechanical mine, even though having been in position for a great length of time, the U.S. gunboat, *Jonquil*, was nearly destroyed whilst attempting to remove some similar torpedoes which had been in position for two years.

PLATE II.

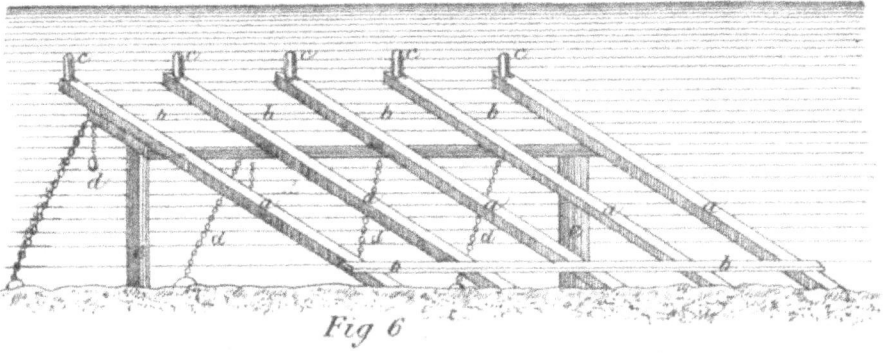

Fig 6.

Fig 7.

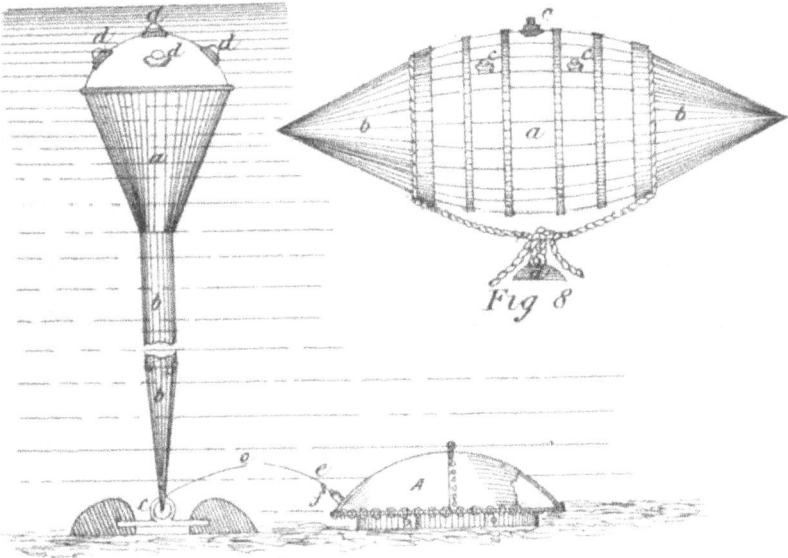

Fig 8.

Fig 9.

GRIFFIN & C°

PORTSMOUTH.

The Barrel Torpedo.—One description of this form of mechanical submarine mine is shown at Fig. 8. It consists of a barrel *a*, to the ends of which are attached two cones of pine *b, b*, for the purpose of preventing the current from turning the mine over.

To ensure its being watertight, pitch is poured into the interior through the bunghole, and the barrel rolled about, so that the inside may be evenly covered. The outside was also thoroughly coated with pitch. These mines usually contain about 100lbs. of gunpowder, and are exploded by means of percussion or chemical fuzes *(c,c,c,)* generally five in number, screwed into sockets on each side and on the top of the bilge of the barrels. To keep them upright a weight *d* is hung below the mine.

This kind of mechanical mine was much used by the Confederates, and to some extent by the Turks in their late war with Russia.

They are cheap, convenient, and under certain circumstances very effective. One of the objections to their use is the difficulty of mooring them securely in strong currents, as otherwise they are very liable to shift their positions. Three Confederate vessels were "hoisted by their own petards," from this cause.*

Brook's Torpedo.—Another form of buoyant mechanical mine is represented at Fig. 9. It was designed for the express purpose of preventing its discovery by dragging, etc., by the enemy. It consists of the torpedo case *a*, formed of copper, which is attached to a spar *b*, the lower end of which is secured to an universal joint in its anchor *c*. Five percussion or chemical fuzes *d, d, d*, are screwed into the head of the copper case.

Turtle Torpedo.—To increase the danger and uncertainty of any attempt to remove this form of buoyant mine, a turtle torpedo *A*, is attached to it by a wire *e*. This torpedo contains about 100lbs. of gunpowder, and is exploded by means of a friction primer which passes through a watertight joint *f*, and is attached to the wire *e*.

Whether this combination would prove effective, has yet to be seen, but the buoyant mine alone was considered one of the most dangerous used by the Confederates.

Singer's Mechanical Mine.--An elevation and section of this form of mechanical mine is shown at Fig. 10. It consists of an air chamber *a*, and a powder chamber *b*; in the latter is fixed a rod of iron *c*, one

---

* "Submarine Warfare," by Commander S. Barnes, U.S.N.

end of which rests in a cup formed in a lug d, where there is a screw
by means of which the rod c may be screwed against the bottom of
the torpedo case, on the interior. In the cup is placed the fulminating
substance. A heavy cast iron cap A B rests upon the top of the case
and is prevented from falling off by a low rim of tin, which enters an
aperture in the cap as at $e:$ a wire f connects this cap with a pin g,
which keeps a plunger h at rest. The head of this plunger h is
directly beneath the bottom of the rod c, within the case; by means of
a spring i, directly the pin g is drawn out, which is done by a hostile
vessel striking against the mine and knocking off the cap A B, the
plunger h is forced against the bottom of the case and drives the rod
c into the cup containing the fulminate, and so explodes the torpedo.
The case of these mines, as used by the Confederates, was formed of
tin, and they contained from 50 to 100lbs. of powder. A safety pin k
is provided to prevent a premature explosion due to the pin g being
accidentally withdrawn.

This form of submarine mine was one of the most successful and
most extensively employed of all, on the part of the Confederates.

Though no accidents are stated to have occurred in placing this
mine in position, yet the fact of the iron rod c having to be fixed for
action, and that close against the interior of the bottom of the case,
before the charge of powder has been put in, is an element of great
danger, for a comparatively slight blow beneath it, which might easily
occur in transport, etc., would explode the torpedo prematurely.

McEvoy's Improved Singer's Mine.—To obviate this defect Captain
McEvoy has designed an improved mode of ignition for Singer's mine.
This is shown at Fig. 11. The form of case, and arrangement of heavy
cap are similar to those in Singer's mine. The mode of ignition is as
follows:—In the powder chamber b is fixed a friction fuze f, which by
means of a piece of wire secured to a length of chain k, k, is connected
with the heavy cast iron cap A B. The piece of wire passes through
a diaphragm of thin metal h, which is soldered all around, thus forming
a complete watertight joint. Premature explosion is prevented by
passing a link of the chain, through a slot in the bolt c, securing it
there by a pin of bent wire l. The dotted line of chain k, k, shows its
position during the process of mooring this form of Singer's torpedo.
The manner of lowering this and also Singer's mine is shown at Fig.
12. A buoy r, is attached by means of a line, in the former case to

PLATE III.

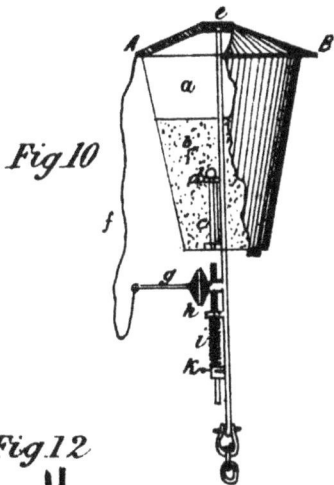

Fig 10

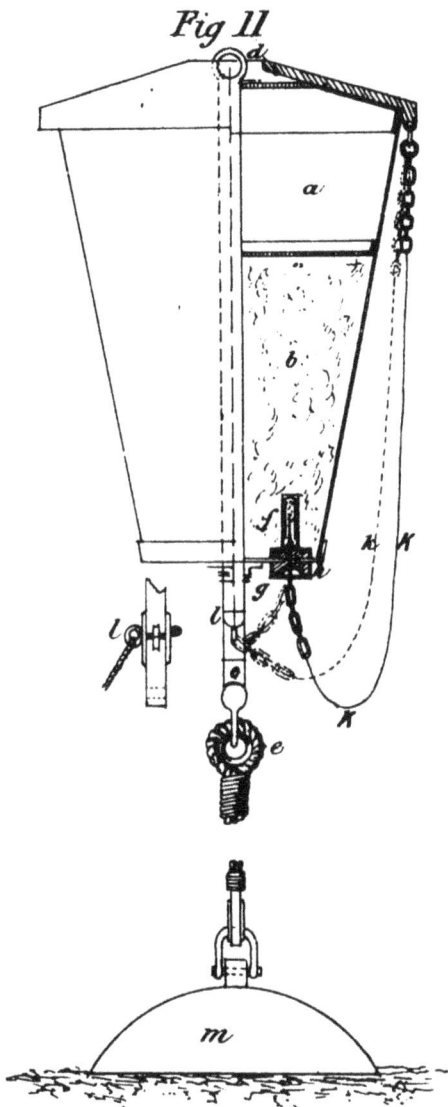

Fig 11

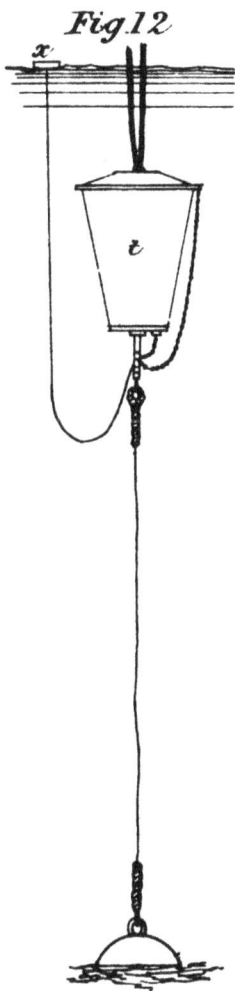

Fig 12

the pin *l*, Fig. 12, in the latter case to the pin *k*, Fig. 10, the pulling out of either, sets their respective mines in action.

Mathieson's Cement Safety Plug.—In the place of the safety pin *l*, Fig. 11, employed by Captain McEvoy in his improved form of Singer's mine, Quartermaster-Sergeant Mathieson, late Royal Engineers, employs a plug or disc of soluble cement, so arranged that the action of the sea-water after the mine has been placed in position destroys the plug or disc, and so frees the chain which is connected with the fuze and the heavy cap of the torpedo. This plan does away with the necessity of using a buoy and line as shown in Fig. 12, and also affords ample time for the men engaged in mooring the mine to get far away before it is ready for action.

Mechanical Mine.—The extempore mechanical submarine mine, shown at Fig. 13, will be found to possess all the qualities which are necessary to a perfect mine of that description.

It is extremely simple, it can be readily and quickly made, all the materials of which it is constructed are at hand on board every man-of-war, and it is certain in its action.

It consists of a barrel *a*, which is thoroughly coated inside and out with hot pitch, etc., to make it watertight, a block of wood *b*, secured to the top of the cask *a*, and having a recess cut in it to receive a round shot *c*, also a hole through which a strop *d*, is passed, and another hole to receive a toggle *e*. At the bottom of the cask on the inside, is fixed a wooden frame work *f, f*, to the top of which two ordinary gun friction tubes are fixed *g, g*. A piece of wood *h*, is secured to the bottom of the cask on the outside, bored with two holes, one to receive a thin iron rod *i*, the other for the safety pin *k*. Wires *x, x*, secure the gun tubes *g, g*, to one end of the iron rod *i*, the other end of which is connected by means of a rope lanyard to the shot *c*. Weights are slung beneath the barrel to keep the mine upright. The principle of action of this form of mechanical mine is precisely similar to that of Captain McEvoy's improved Singer's mine, and need not, therefore, be described.

McEvoy's Mechanical Primer.—A sectional view of this apparatus is represented by Fig. 14. It consists of two brass tubes fitting accurately one within the other, of which *a, a*, is the inner one. To this inner tube are affixed two brass diaphragms *b, b*. A brass spindle *c*, carries a weight *d*, which is regulated by a spring, *e*. A locking rod, *f*, moves in a ball and socket joint at *g*. A hammer *h*, which is shown in Fig. 14, at full cock, is kept in that position by the rod *f*. A vessel, striking the mine, in which this apparatus is placed causes the weight, *d*, to cant over, allowing the rod, *f*, to be forced upwards by means of the spring *e*, and so frees the hammer *h*, which falls on a nipple *i*, on which is placed the percussion substance, and so explodes the mine.

McEvoy's Papier Maché Safety Plug.—To prevent a premature explosion during transport, etc., of a mine in which this apparatus is placed, a plug of papier maché, which is soluble in water, is inserted in the two spaces *p, p*, by which the spindle *c*, is prevented from moving to one side or the other. The use of a papier maché, instead of a cement plug for the purposes of safety, is a great improvement, as by the simple process of pressure, any period of time that it is necessary should elapse before the complete destruction of the plug, can be readily and certainly obtained, which when a cement plug, formed of different ingredients is used, is not always the case.

McEvoy's Mechanical Mines.—Captain McEvoy has also devised a plan, whereby a mechanical mine of the foregoing form may be placed in a state of safety, even after it has been rendered active. In the place of the aforesaid papier maché wad at *p*, Fig. 14, he uses a plunger which fits into the cavity *p*, of the heavy weight *d*. This plunger is always kept in a position clear of the weight by means of a spiral spring, unless it is desired to render the mine inactive when the plunger is forced into the aforesaid cavity and kept there by means of a pin inserted above it. Above this there is another plunger, acted on by a spiral spring sufficiently powerful to enable it to force the previous mentioned plunger into the safety position; this upper plunger is rendered inactive by means of a pin. The mine being placed in position, that pin which is keeping the lower plunger inserted in the cavity *p*, of the weight *d*, is withdrawn and the mine rendered active. To the pin of the upper plunger is attached a line which is anchored some distance from the mine in a known position. Then to render the mine inactive for the purpose of picking it up, etc., it is only necessary to raise the aforesaid line, and draw out the pin of the upper plunger, which by means of the strong spiral spring will force the lower plunger into the safety position, and render the mine inactive.

Whether this invention is a practicable one or not, remains to be proved, but anyhow it is a step in the right direction.

PLATE 4

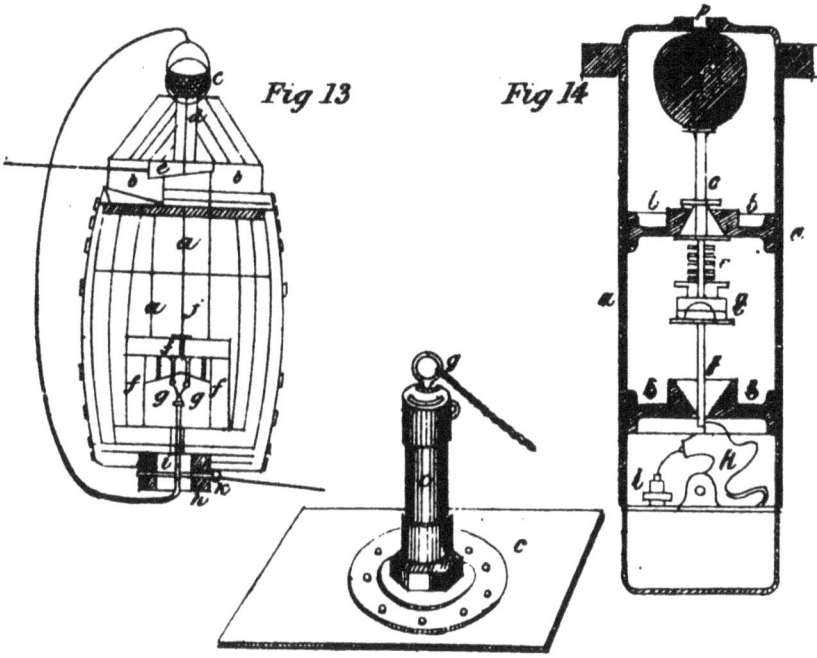

Fig 13   Fig 14

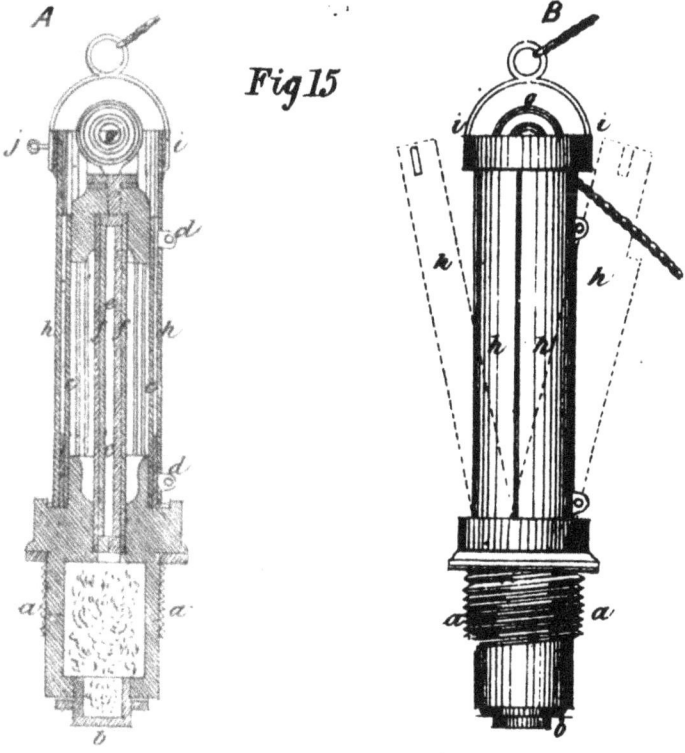

Fig 15

A   B

Abel's Mechanical Primer.—This is shown in section and elevation at Fig. 15 (A and B). *a, a*, is the powder chamber in which the priming charge is placed; *b* is a screw plug to close the chamber; *c* is a flexible india rubber tube; *d, d*, are screw bands; *e* is a glass tube containing oil of vitriol enclosed in a lead tube; *f* which contains the explosive mixture; *g*, an eye at the head of the primer to receive the firing line; *h, h* are segmental guards; *i* is the guard ring; and *j* the safety screw pin. This apparatus is screwed into a socket in the upper part of the torpedo case, as shown at Fig. 15 (C).

Mode of Action.—When placed in position, to render the primer ready for action, the guard ring, *i*, is pulled off, first having removed the safety pin *j*, when the segmental guards *h, h*, will fall away, leaving the india rubber tube *c, c*, exposed.

A sufficient strain being brought on the rope secured to the ring *g*, the lead tube *f* bends, causing the fracture of the glass tube *e*, thus igniting the priming charge and exploding the mine.

A submarine mine so fitted may be fired at will, by bringing a line, from the ring *g*, to the shore, or it may be made self-acting by connecting two of them together, etc.

Percussion and Chemical Fuzes.—Many forms of this mode of mechanical ignition have been from time to time devised, of which the following are the most important ones :—

Sensitive Fuze.—It consists of an inner cylinder *a, a*, Fig. 15, of composition metal, 1½″ diameter, and 2½″ long, having a thread cut on its outside, and a bouching *b*, 2¼″ diameter and 2″ long with a sexagonal projection *c*, for applying a wrench, also with an external and internal thread. The upper end of the inner cylinder *a*, is solid for 1″, and is perforated by three holes *d, d, d*, in each of which a percussion primer is placed *e, e*. A piece of thin, soft and well annealed copper *f* is soldered to the upper end of the bouching *b*, to keep moisture from the primers, and is so thin that a slight blow will crush without breaking it. A safety cap can be screwed on to the external thread above the projection *c*.

Rain's Detonating Composition.—The detonating composition employed in this and many other forms of percussion fuzes by the Confederates, etc., consisted of a combination of fulminate of mercury and ground glass, and was invented by, and is named after, General Rains, Chief of the Torpedo Bureau, at Richmond, during the Civil

War (1861-5). So sensitive was this composition that seven pounds pressure, applied to the head of one of the primers, would explode it.

When required for use the internal cylinder *a*, containing the primers *e, e*, is screwed up until contact between them and the copper cap *f* is secured.

McEvoy's Percussion Fuze.—Fig. 16 represents a longitudinal section, full size, of the mechanical percussion fuze, used by Captain McEvoy in connection with his drifting torpedo, which latter will be hereafter described. *a* is a piece of metal, having an external and internal thread, and a projection *b*, to which is applied the spanner for screwing it into the torpedo case. This piece *a* is hollow at its upper end, and is closed by means of a thin copper dome *c*, which is soldered to it. Screwed into the piece *a* is the plug, or nipple *d*, with a hole through it from end to end, it is rammed full of mealed powder, and then a fine hole is drilled through the composition. A cavity *e* at the head of the plug, or nipple *d*, is filled with a fulminating substance. A spiral spring *f*, encircles the plug *d*, on which a cap *g* rests ; *h* is a needle in this cap. The action of this fuze will be readily understood from the plan of the fuze at Fig. 16. A safety cap is provided, which fits into the slots *i, i*, and is fixed there by means of a set screw.

Improved Form of Jacobi's fuze.—The section shown in Fig. 17 is an improved form of the chemical fuze, invented by Professor Jacobi, and used by the Russians in their land and sea mines during the Crimean war (1854-5). It consisted of a small glass tube *a*, containing sulphuric acid, enclosed in a lead cylinder *b*. A mixture of chlorate of potash and white sugar surrounds the tube and holds it in position ; *c* is a primer filled with mealed powder in connection with the charge of the mine. The action of this fuze is as follows :—On a vessel striking against the lead cylinder *b*, it is crushed in, breaking the glass tube containing the sulphuric acid, and thus causes it (acid) to flow into the mixture of chlorate of potash and white sugar, producing fire, which by means of the primer *c*, passes into the charge, and explodes the mine.

Defect of Chemical Fuze.—The defect of the chemical fuze just described is its slow rate of ignition when compared to gunpowder. This may be remedied by adding a small quantity of sulphuret of antimony or perro cyanide of potassium.

Both the Turks and the Germans employed, as a mode of ignition

PLATE V.

Fig 15ᵃ

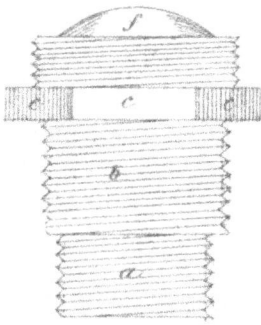
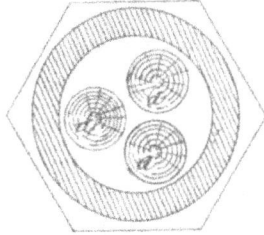
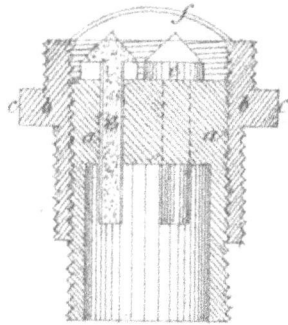

Fig 16

Fig 17

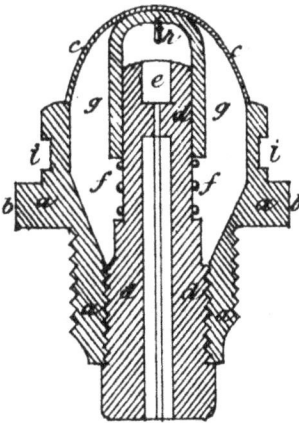
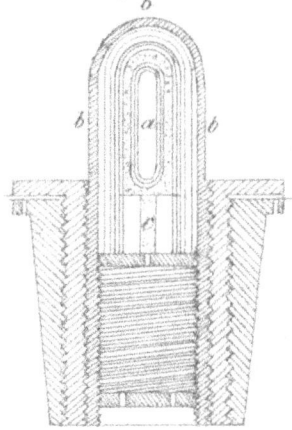

Fig 18

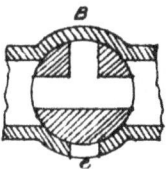
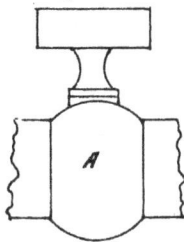
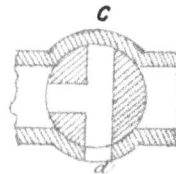

for their mechanical submarine mines, the chemical fuze described above, with but slight modifications in the shape of the lead cylinder and manner of fixing the fuze into the torpedo case.

Mechanical fuzes, both percussion and chemical, which require a blow to effect their ignition, are to a certain extent defective when applied to submarine mechanical mines (which are always buoyant ones) in so far that a hostile vessel passing over ground supposed to be defended by torpedoes of any description, would do so at as slow a rate of speed as it would be possible to proceed at, and would, under those circumstances, *push away* rather than strike a buoyant mine, with which she might come in contact. During the American civil war and the Russo-Turkish war, especially in the former, there are several instances on record of vessels passing over buoyant mechanical mines unharmed, whilst similar vessels have afterwards been destroyed by those self-same mines; and the only cause for such apparent inconsistency being the above-mentioned one, viz., the pushing rather than striking effect produced on a buoyant mine by a vessel under weigh proceeding at a very slow speed, or merely drifting with the current.

Steward's Safety-Cock Arrangements.—To obtain security to a certain extent in placing mechanical submarine mines in position, which, as has been previously stated, is one of the defects common to all forms of such torpedoes, many ingenious methods have been devised, such as safety caps to their fuzes, safety pins, soluble plugs, &c. Another method, suggested by Captain Harding Steward, R.E., which it is intended should be used in connection with the other safety arrangements, is shown at Fig. 18. It consists of a stop-cock *A*, which, in connection with a tube, is introduced between the fuze and the charge. It is so arranged that when the cock is turned in the direction of the tube, as shown in section *B* at *e*, the gas on formation can pass easily through and explode the charge; but when the cock is shut off, the gas on formation escapes through the side *d*, as shown in section *C*. To prevent destruction of the charge through leakage under the pressure of the water, the cone in connection with the stop-cock should fit very accurately, and, as an additional preventive, the escape hole should be covered with a waterproof plaster, which at a moderate depth would keep the water out and yet offer no material resistance to the escape of the gas if the stop-cock were shut off, as at *C*. The efficiency of this arrangement, as far as relates to its cutting off the gas from the charge, has been satisfactorily proved by practical experiments.

Mooring Mechanical Mines.—This description of defensive torpedo will rarely be used in deep-water channels, &c., and on account of the impossibility of ascertaining whether such a mine has drifted or otherwise, it should not be moored in a very rapid current. Such being the case, an ordinary mushroom anchor, heavy stone, &c., and single steel wire mooring-rope, will be generally found quite sufficient to keep such mines in position.

When only a few mechanical submarine mines are moored in position, and at some distance apart, it would be found a useful plan to moor them each with three anchors, one anchor being up-stream. By this method, at low water, on the up-stream anchor being raised, the mine would show itself, and might in that position be approached and rendered inactive. Were this plan to be adopted when several such mines are in position, there would be the danger of the up-stream anchor on being raised, bringing up to the surface, and probably in contact with the boat at work, a mine to which that particular anchor does not belong, an explosion being the result.

CHAPTER III.

DEFENSIVE TORPEDO WARFARE—*continued.*

BY electrical submarine mines is meant those whose charges are ignited by the agency of electricity.

Submarine Mines during the Crimean and American Wars.—It was during the Crimean war (1854-6) that this description of defensive torpedoes was for the first time employed on actual service. Several of the principal Russian harbours were protected by this form of submarine mine, but owing to the smallness of their charges, and to the want of electrical knowledge on the part of the Russian officers and men in charge of them, none of the ships of the Allies were sunk, or even rendered *hors de combat* by this mode of harbour defence, though in several instances ground known to be covered with submarine mines was passed over by both English and French vessels of war.

Subsequently the Confederates, during the American civil war, employed electrical submarine mines in considerable numbers for the defence of their numerous harbours, rivers, &c.; but though in so far as the size of the torpedo charges was concerned, they did not make the same mistake as the Russians, yet, owing to the absence of proper electrical apparatus, and the want of any practical knowledge of the manipulation of electrical sea mines, on the part of the Confederate torpedoists, they were almost entirely unsuccessful in destroying the Federal warships; the *Commodore Jones* being the sole instance, out of the large number of vessels belonging to the Northerners which were sunk and severely injured by torpedoes, of a war steamer being sunk by means of electrical submarine mines.

In the Franco-German and Russo-Turkish wars which have lately occurred, electrical sea mines were very extensively used in coast defence, but with the exception of the loss of the gunboat *Suna* to the Turks, during the latter struggle, by this form of defensive torpedo, no other damage to vessels resulted from their use, yet owing to the vast moral power possessed by these submarine weapons, they were enabled to most effectually carry out the work of defence entrusted to their care.

Of late years many important discoveries have been made in the science of electricity, and vast improvements have been effected in electrical apparatus, to which causes may be traced the vastly improved system of electrical submarine mines as adopted by the English, American, and principal European governments at the present day, as compared with those that have hitherto been employed.

The certainty of action when required of electrical submarine mines, which is of course the desideratum of all torpedoists, has, by the improved mode and manner of ascertaining the exact electrical condition of each particular mine, and of the system as a whole, which is at present in vogue, been made almost absolute.

Advantages of Electrical Submarine Mines.—This form of defensive torpedo possesses numerous important advantages, the principal of which are as follows :—

1.—They are always absolutely under control.

Note.—By detaching or connecting the firing battery, which is effected by means of a plug, key, &c., they may be respectively rendered harmless, or dangerous. Thus friendly ships may pass over them in safety, whilst those of the enemy are debarred from so doing. On this account harbours, &c., protected by such mines are termed " Harbours of refuge."

2.—Fresh mines may be added to a system of such defensive torpedoes, thereby allowing an exploded mine to be replaced.

Note.—This is a very important point in connection with a system of defence by submarine mines, as in the case of a deep water channel, a hostile vessel being sunk by one of them, would not become an obstruction, as, were the channel a comparatively shallow one would most probably be the result, and therefore it would be necessary to put a fresh mine in the place of the exploded one; this would also apply were a mine to be prematurely ignited, or if any portion of its firing apparatus were injured.

3.—At night, or in a fog, no vessel can pass through a channel, &c., so protected without affording a means of ascertaining her presence.

Note.—This is also a very important advantage of a system of defence by electrical sea mines, affording as it does a complete safeguard against surprise.

4.—The power of obtaining proof, without going near it, by a system of testing that the electrical condition of the mine, &c., is perfect.

NOTE.—This again is an extremely important point. For were a charge to become wet, one of the electric cables of the mine broken, or damaged, &c., it would instantly be made apparent at the firing station, and could be at once remedied.

5.—They can be raised for examination, or removed when no longer required, with ease and safety.

Such are some of the chief advantages of employing the agency of electricity to effect the ignition of the charge in a system of defence by submarine mines.

Defects of Electrical Submarine Mines.—The following are the chief defects connected with the use of electrical mines :—

1.—The number of wires that are required to be used with them.

2.—The necessity of employing specially trained men in their manipulation.

In time there seems little doubt but that the former obstacle will be to a considerable extent overcome, but the latter must always be a flaw in an otherwise perfect system of coast defence by submarine mines.

Rules to be observed in using Electrical Submarine Mines.—In connection with a system of electrical submarine mines the following rules should be carefully observed :—

1.—They should be moored in deep channels, that is to say, where the larger class of vessels would in attempting to force a passage be obliged to go.

NOTE.—Mechanical submarine mines should never be used under these circumstances, as the difficulties of mooring them and keeping them in position would be very considerable, also a vessel being sunk in a very deep channel would not necessarily block it, and as a mechanical mine cannot be replaced, a gap would be left in the defence.

2.—They should be placed in the narrowest parts of the channel.

NOTE.—The object of this rule is evident, fewer mines being required, and consequently in the case of electrical ones, a far less number of wires are needed, which gives an increase of simplicity, and consequently more effectiveness. This point should be observed in connection with mechanical, as well as electrical submarine mines.

3.—They should where practicable be moored on the ground.

Note.—The advantages attendant on an observance of this rule are :—

a.—Increased vertical effect.

b.—Avoidance of mooring difficulties.

c.—Less liability of shifting from its original position.

d.—Less chance of its being discovered and rendered useless by an enemy.

e.—By far heavier charges may be conveniently employed.

4.—Where possible, no indication whatever should be given of the position of the mines by their circuit closers, or in the case of small buoyant ones, by the mines themselves.

Note.—In some instances this will be almost impracticable, as for example, where there is a very great rise and fall of tide. For instance, at Noel Bay in the Bay of Fundy, the rise is over fifty feet. Here, when circuit closers, or small buoyant mines are used, both of which ought never to be more than twenty feet below the surface, long before low water they would be found floating on the surface in full view. Many attempts have been made to overcome this difficulty, but as yet no really practicable means have been devised.

5.—The stations where the firing batteries, &c., are placed, should be in the defensive work likely to be held the longest, thus enabling the mines to be commanded up to the last moment.

6.—The electric cables should be laid in positions such that their discovery by the enemy would be extremely difficult, and almost impossible.

Note.—This may be to a certain extent effected by leading them from the mines to the firing and observing stations by circuitous routes, and by burying them in trenches.

7.—They should not be thrown away on boats.

Notes.—As they can in all cases be fired by will, even when circuit closers are used, this rule is easily observed. But to prevent an enemy's boats from rendering the mines useless, a line of small torpedoes might be placed in advance of the large ones, or the circuit closers themselves might be charged.

At night, or in foggy weather it will be necessary to employ guard-boats, electric lights, &c., to protect them against damage by an enemy's boats, &c.

In the foregoing pages of this chapter will be found the requirements and conditions essential to a perfect system of electrical submarine mines for the defence of a harbour, river, &c.; in the following pages a general description of the component parts of such defensive torpedoes, under the following heads—Form and Construction of Case; Electrical Fuzes; Electric Cables: Watertight Joints; Junction Boxes; and Mode of Mooring, will be considered.

Form and Construction of Torpedo Case.—The case of a submarine mine should be capable of fulfilling the following conditions :—

1. It must be able at great depths to withstand a great pressure of water, and remain perfectly watertight.

NOTE.—This in the case of a charge of gunpowder being an imperative necessity.

2. As a buoyant mine, it must be capable of affording a considerable excess of buoyancy, by which it may be rendered stationary when moored.

NOTE.—This is generally obtained by having an air space within the torpedo, thus requiring a much larger case in which the charge is enclosed than would otherwise be necessary, causing increased difficulties in transportation, mooring, and raising them for examination, &c.

3. When explosive agents which require a certain time for thorough combustion are used as the charge, such as gunpowder, picric powder, gun-cotton (not fired by detonation), &c., a much stronger case is necessary to obtain the full explosive effect than would be the case were detonated charges, under the same conditions, employed.

NOTE.—This is an extremely important point, for if a weak case is employed with a charge of gunpowder, &c., fired by a fuze primed with powder only, a portion of it on being fired would generate a sufficient quantity of gas to burst the case, thus blowing out the remainder of the charge before its ignition had been effected.

4. It should be of such a form that the complete ignition of the charge is obtained by the employment of the least number of fuzes possible to effect this result.

Note.—This point is especially to be observed when gunpowder is the explosive agent.

The various forms of defensive torpedo cases may be classed under the following heads :—

1.— Spherical shape.

2.— Cylindrical shape.

3.— Conical shape.

Spherical Shape.—This form of case is theoretically the very best one possible to devise, but on account of the difficulty of constructing it, and its comparative costliness, such a form may be put aside as being impracticable.

Cylindrical Shape.—Torpedoists in general have hitherto adopted the cylindrical form of case as being the best adaptable for both ground and buoyant mines containing a heavy charge.

The Confederates employed exclusively this shape for their electrical submarine mines, which were ground ones, and the Austrians in the war of " 66 " approved of this form of case for their electrical submarine mines, which were buoyant ones. Figs. 19 and 20 represent respectively the American and Austrian mines.

In England the cylindrical shape has up to quite lately found most favour with her torpedoists for both buoyant and ground mines. At Fig. 21 is represented a 100-lb. buoyant electrical mine, surrounded by a wooden jacket, *e*, and having its circuit closer, *C*, enclosed within it; and at Fig. 22 is shown a 250-lb. electrical mine, which may be used either as a buoyant or ground one.

For large ground mines, the best form of torpedo case seems to be that of the turtle mine, which is shown at Fig. 9. A heavy charge may be contained in it; it forms its own anchor; and it would withstand an explosion of an adjacent mine without sustaining any injury. At present the cylindrical shape is the form generally used, though as far as retaining its position on the ground in a strong tide, it cannot be compared to the turtle form.

The Conical Shape.—Hitherto this shape of submarine mine case was only used in connection with mechanical mines, but now it is the form considered most suitable for all buoyant mines, electrical or mechanical. At Fig. 23 is shown the conical shaped mechanical mine, employed by the Confederates for use with sensitive fuzes. The conical form of torpedo case lately approved of by the English torpedo

FORM OF CASE OF SUBMARINE MINES.

PLATE VI.

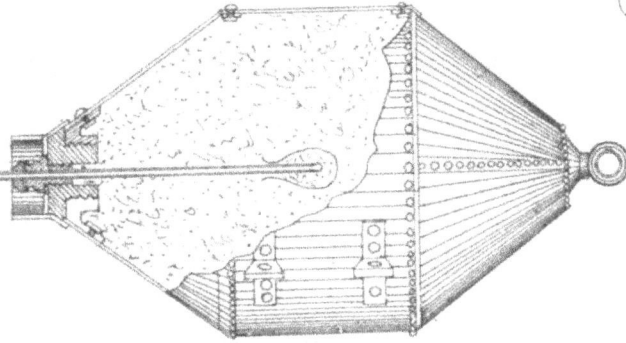

Fig 19

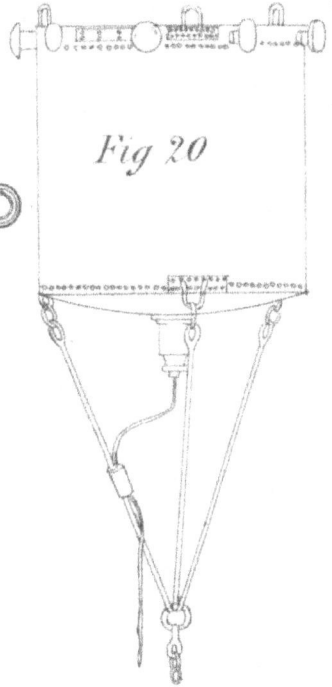

Fig 20

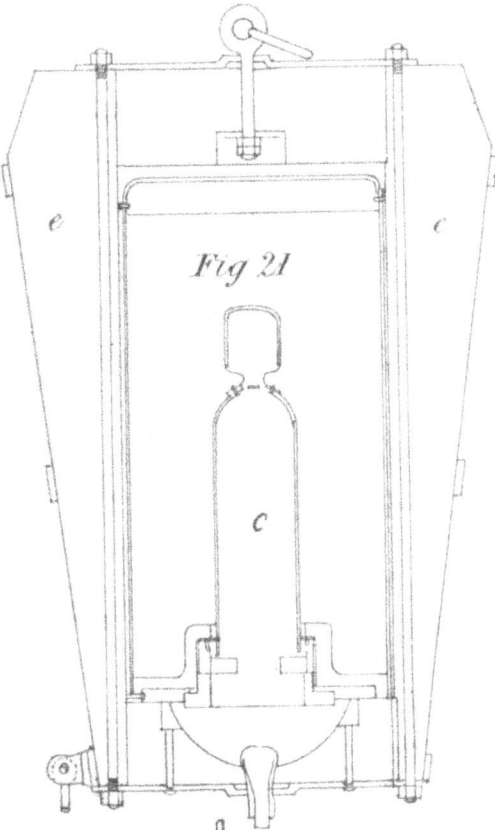

Fig 21

e

c

c

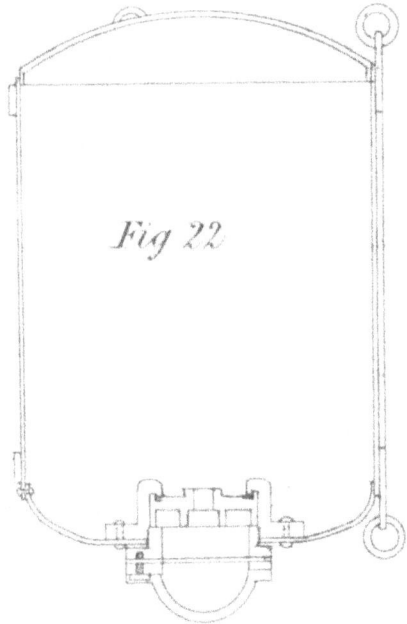

Fig 22

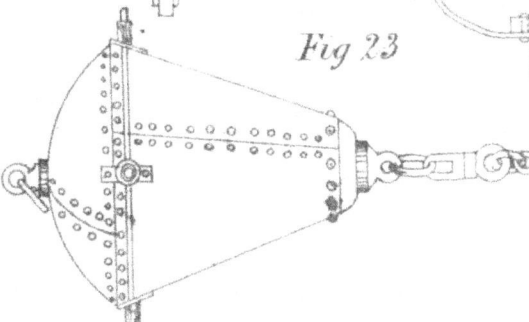

Fig 23

authorities is somewhat similar to that one, the charge being contained in a kind of box hung from the top of the case, and the circuit closer is screwed into the bottom of the case; surrounding the upper part of the case is a thick buffer of wood, by which damage to the mine is prevented by the passage of friendly ships. This is altogether a very neat and serviceable form of torpedo case. This form of case is also more difficult to discover by dragging, and easier to retain in position.

Electrical Fuzes.—The fuzes employed in connection with electrical submarine mines may be divided into two classes :—

1. Platinum wire bridge fuzes.

NOTE.—That is where the evolution of heat is caused by a large *quantity* of the electric force flowing through a good conductor of large section, such as the copper core of electric cables, being suddenly checked by a very thin wire composed of a metal which compared with the conductor offers a very great resistance, such as *platinum.*

2. High tension fuzes.

NOTE.—That is where the evolution of heat is caused by the electric spark, or by the electric discharge taking place through a substance which offers very great resistance to the passage of the electric force.

Platinum Wire Fuze.—This is the form of electrical fuze most commonly used, and which will most certainly supersede altogether the high tension fuze.

There are numerous advantages accruing from the use of platinum wire fuzes, the chief of which are here enumerated :—

a.—Great facilities for, and entire safety whilst testing the circuit.

b.—Extreme simplicity of manufacture.

c.—Non-liability to deteriorate.

d.—Perfect insulation of the electric cables used in connection with submarine mines not necessary.

English Service Platinum Wire Fuze.—The following is a description of the platinum wire fuze of the form adopted in the English service, a section of which is shown at Fig. 24. It consists of a head of ebonite *a*, hollowed out, in which a metal mould is fixed, the wires which have been previously bared are inserted into holes in this mould, and firmly fixed thereto by means of a composition poured into the mould, whilst hot ; this is shown at *b*. The two bared ends of the wires which project beyond the metal mould, as c, c, are connected by a bridge of platinum-silver wire ·0014″ in diameter and weighing ·21 grs. per yard. This is effected as follows :—

A very fine shallow groove is made in the flat ends of the bare wires c, c, and the platinum-silver wire is laid across in the incisions, and fixed there by means of solder. The length of the bridge d is ·25.″

A tube e, made of tin, and soldered to a brass socket f, is fixed by means of cement to the ebonite head a; in this tube is placed the fulminate of mercury, the open end of the tube g being closed with a pellet of red lead and shellac varnish; around the bridge of the fuze is placed some loose gun-cotton.

McEvoy's Platinum Wire Fuze.—Another form of platinum wire fuze, which has been devised by Captain McEvoy, formerly of the Confederate Service, is shown at Fig. 25. It consists of the head a, formed of a mixture of ground glass, or Portland cement, worked up with sulphur as a base : this mixture when hot is poured into a mould, in which the two insulated copper wires, b, b, have been previously placed; when cold, the mixture with the wires affixed is removed from the mould, and the platinum wire bridge c being secured to the bare ends of the copper wires, the whole is firmly fixed in a brass socket d, by means of cement; the space e is filled with loose dry gun-cotton, so as to surround the bridge c; a copper tube f, closed at one end, is partly filled with fulminate of mercury, and when the fuze is required for service, this tube is secured to the brass socket d by means of cement.

In this form of low tension fuze there is no liability whatever of any injury being caused to the bridge by the working of the wires in the head, or by damp even after lying in the water for a month or more. One peculiarity of this fuze is that the composition is run over the insulated wires without materially softening the dielectric, or affecting in the slightest degree the insulation of the wires.

High Tension Fuzes.—The high tension fuze was devised for use with electrical submarine mines, in the place of the platinum wire fuze, on account of the little knowledge possessed, in the early days of submarine warfare, in regard to the manipulation of Voltaic batteries.

Platinum wire requires a temperature of some 500° F. to heat it to incandescence, and therefore necessitates the use of a powerful Voltaic battery, both in intensity and power, to effect the ignition of gunpowder by this means at considerable distances.

The Grove and Bunsen pile were the only suitable form of Voltaic battery known at the period of the introduction of high tension fuzes, both of which possessed the defects of uncertainty and inconstancy, and also were by far too cumbersome and too difficult to keep in effective working order to be of any real practicable value.

High tension fuzes may be ignited by means of either an electro-magneto machine, an electro-dynamo machine, a frictional machine, or by a Voltaic battery, generating an electric current of high intensity. Various kinds of this form of electrical fuze have been designed, the principal of which are as follows :—

1.— Statham's fuze.
2.— Beardslee's fuze.
3.— Von Ebner's fuze.
4.— Abel's fuze.
5.— Extempore fuze.

Statham's Fuze.—A section and elevation of this electric fuze are shown at Fig. 26 ; *a, b* is a gutta percha tube, with an opening cut in it, as shown in figure. The interior of this vulcanised gutta percha tube is coated with a thin layer of sulphide of copper, which coating is obtained by leaving a bare copper wire for some time in connection with the above-mentioned tube. The extremities of two insulated copper wires *c, c*, considerably smaller than the conducting wires, are uncovered, scraped, and then inserted into the tube *a, b*, with an interval of ·15 inch between them. The wires are then bent as shown in the figure, and the priming placed between the terminals. The whole is covered with a gutta percha bag, which is filled with fine grained gunpowder. The priming substance is composed of fulminate of mercury worked up with gum water. The objection to this fuze, which was used by the Allies in their destruction of the Russian fortifications at Sebastopol, is the want of sensitiveness of sulphide of copper, and the consequent necessity of a very powerful firing battery.

Beardslee's Fuze.—This high tension fuze is shown at Fig. 27. It consists of a cylindrical piece of soft wood *a*, which is about three-quarters of an inch in length and in diameter ; two copper nails, *b, b*, are driven through this piece of wood *a*, in such a way that while the two heads come together as close as possible without absolutely touching, the pointed ends are some distance apart from each other, and project through the wood *a*; two insulated copper wires, *c, c,* are firmly soldered to these projecting ends, and a piece of soft wax, *d,* is pressed around the junction points.   In a groove, across the heads of the copper nails, is placed a little black lead, to which is added a minute quantity of some substance, the nature of which is known only to Mr. Beardslee.   Several folds of paper are wrapped round the wooden cylinder, forming a cylinder about 2½ inches long, one end of which is tightly fastened round the insulated wires as at *e.* The other end of the cylinder is then filled with powder, *f,* and closed by a piece of twine.   The whole fuze is then coated with black varnish. Though not highly sensitive, Beardslee's fuze is exceedingly efficient, and extremely simple.

Von Ebner's Fuze.—This form of fuze was devised by Colonel Von Ebner of the Austrian Engineers.   A section and elevation of it is shown at Fig. 28.   It consists of an outer cylinder, *a,* of gutta percha, and an inner one of copper, *b,* which latter encloses a core formed of ground glass and sulphur, *c,* which core is cast round the two conducting wires *d, d* in such a way that they are completely insulated from one another.   In the first instance the wire is in one continuous length, the opening *e* being subsequently made, and carefully gauged, so as to ensure a uniform break, or interval in the conductor of each fuze.   The priming composition, which consists of equal parts of sulphide of antimony and chlorate of potash, is placed in the hollow *f,* to which is added some powdered plumbago, for the purpose of increasing the conducting power of the composition.   This mixture is put into the hollow, *f,* of the fuze under considerable pressure, the terminals being connected with a sensitive galvanometer, in circuit with a test battery, and the pressure applied so as to obtain, as far as possible, uniformity in the electrical resistance of each fuze.

The Austrians employed this form of high tension fuze in connection with a frictional machine for the electrical mines used in their defence of Venice, &c. during the war of 1866.

Abel's Fuze.—Mr. Abel devised a high tension fuze, which in 1858 was extensively experimented with ; the Beardslee and Von Ebner fuze being based upon the principles applied for the first time in Abel's fuze.

Many modifications of it have been from time to time devised by Mr. Abel ; a section and elevation of the more recent form of his fuze is shown at Fig. 29.   It consists of *b, b,* a body of beech wood, hollowed

PLATE VII

Fig 24

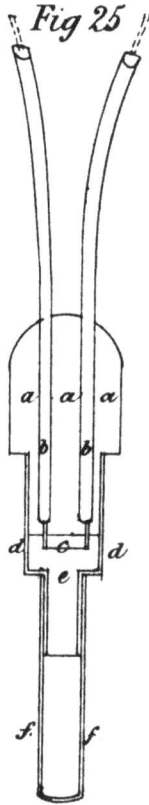

Fig 25

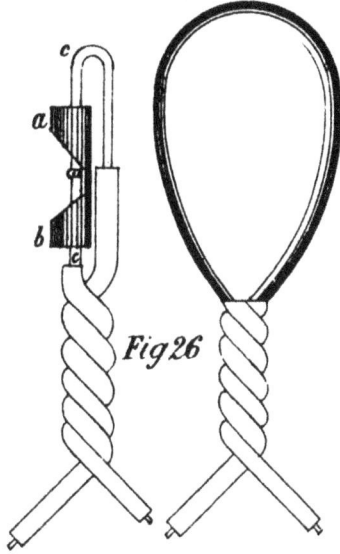

Fig 26

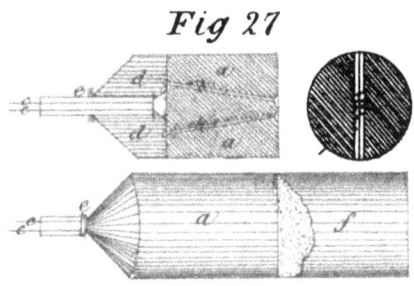

Fig 27

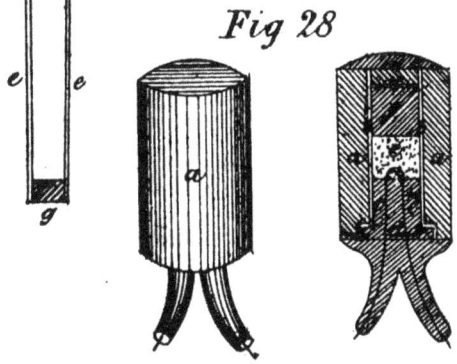

Fig 28

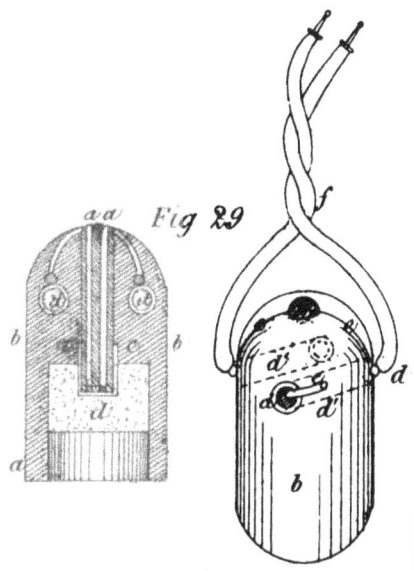

Fig 29

for half its length, in which space the priming charge is placed; it is also perforated by three holes, one vertical for the reception of the capsule of sensitive mixture, the other two horizontal, in which the conducting wires are placed; *a, a* are two insulated copper wires, passing into the vertical hole, and resting on the sensitive mixture; in a cavity, *d,* of the body of the fuze is placed some mealed powder, which is fired by the ignition of the sensitive mixture on the passage of the electrical current.

The insulated wires used in connection with this fuze consist of two copper wires, about 2 inches long, and ·022 inch in diameter, enclosed in a covering of gutta percha ·13 inch in diameter, and separated about ·06 inch from each other.

At one end the wires are bared to 1·25 inch, at the other they are merely cut across by a very sharp pair of scissors. This end of the double covered wire is inserted into a paper cylinder *c, c,* which holds a small quantity of the priming mixture. This capped end of the wires is inserted into the wooden body of the fuze through the vertical hole *i,* and projects ·15 inch into the cavity *d.* The bare ends of the double covered wires are pressed into small grooves in the head of the cylinder *e e,* and each extremity is bent into one of the small channels *d' d',* which are at right angles to the vertical perforation. *d' d'* are two small copper tubes driven into these channels over the wire ends, to keep the wires in position, and to form the opening into which the conducting wires *f* are inserted and bent round, as at *e'.*

The priming mixture of Abel's original fuze, which was the one used by the Confederates, was composed of 10 parts of subphosphide of copper, 45 parts of subsulphide of copper, and 15 parts of chlorate of potash. These ingredients reduced to a very fine state of division, and intimately mixed, in a mortar, with the addition of a little alcohol, are dried at a low temperature and preserved in bottles until required for use. The sensitive mixture used by Mr. Abel more recently for his submarine electrical high tension fuzes, is composed of an intimate mixture of graphite and fulminate of mercury. By the process of ramming, the electrical resistance of the fuze is regulated.

Extempore Fuzes.—It may be necessary in some cases, when a specially manufactured fuze is not attainable, to make a fuze on the spot. The following is a neat and simple method of constructing an extempore high tension fuze.

Fisher's Extempore Fuze.—This form of fuze was devised by Lieutenant now Captain Fisher, R.N. It consists of a small disc of gutta percha, through which the ends of two wires are inserted about $\frac{1}{4}$ inch apart, their ends terminating in small copper plates formed by hammering down the wire. These flat ends should be fixed parallel, and in the first place in contact with one another, also should be level with the surface of the gutta percha. The other two extremities of the wires are then placed in circuit with a sensitive galvanometer and a test battery; the needle of the former deflects violently, there being a complete metallic circuit; the flat ends of the wires or poles of the fuze are then separated very carefully, until the needle just ceases to deflect. In the space thus formed, a little scraped charcoal is placed, and rammed in by a piece of wood. By the application of pressure, any degree of sensitiveness may be attained, merely observing the deflection of the galvanometer needle. Over the charcoal a little powdered resin is shaken, and pressed down, by which means the charcoal is fixed in position, and owing to the inflammability of the resin, the ignition of the gunpowder priming is ensured. The disc of gutta percha is then placed in an empty Snider ball cartridge, &c., and by the application of a little warm gutta percha applied externally, the holes where the projecting ends of the wires pass are closed, and the disc is fixed and insulated. The case is then filled with some mealed powder and fine grained powder, on the top of which is placed a little cotton wool, and the whole pressed down tightly with the finger, the open end of the case being then choked, as in Beardslee's fuze and Abel's extempore one. The apex is then covered with some warm gutta percha, and the whole of the fuze coated over with red sealing-wax dissolved in methylated spirits.

Insulated Electric Cables —For the work of defence by electrical submarine mines, the wires along which the electric current flows have, on account of their being led underground and through the water, to be covered with some substance which shall prevent the current during its passage from escaping to earth, or in other words, they (the wires) must be insulated.

The substances in general use for such purposes are as follows :—

1.—Gutta percha.

2.—Ordinary india rubber.

3.—Hooper's material.

Gutta Percha —This substance was used by Messrs. Siemens in the cables manufactured by them for the Austrian government in 1866, and is to some extent still employed, though Hooper's material, or vulcanised india rubber, has been found to be more suitable. The dielectric, gutta percha, possesses the following advantages :—

a.—It can be put on the conducting wire, as an unbroken tube.

b.—It only absorbs 1 per cent. of water.

c.—It has the property of clinging to the metallic conductor, by which is meant, that should it (conductor) be cut through, and any strain be brought on the cable, there is a tendency on the part of the gutta percha to cling to the conducting wire, thereby not increasing the fault.

The defects of such an insulator are :—

a.—Its liability to become hard and brittle when exposed to dry heat, and consequently it requires to be stored under water.

b.—It becomes comparatively a bad dielectric at 100° F.

c.—It becomes plastic at high temperatures, which causes the conducting wire to alter its position.

In some particulars ordinary india rubber is a better insulator than gutta percha, but this substance is equally inferior to Hooper's material, &c. The advantages possessed by this substance are :—

a.—It is not easily affected by a dry heat.

b.—It is a very excellent dielectric.

The defects of this mode of insulation are :—

a.—It must be put on the conducting wires in a series of jointed pieces.

b.—It does not cling to the conducting wire, so that if the electric cable be cut, and any strain be brought on it (cable), the previous fault is increased.

c.—It absorbs 25 per cent. of water.

Hooper's Material.—This insulating material consists of an inside coating of pure india rubber, then another similar coating in conjunction with oxide of zinc, which is termed the separator, and an outside coating of india rubber combined with sulphur. The use of the separator is to prevent any damage to the conducting wires by the action of the sulphur. The three coatings are then baked for some hours at a very high temperature, which fuses the whole into a solid mass, and vulcanises the outer coating. The properties of the pure india rubber which is in contact with the metallic conductor are thus preserved, while any decay of the outer covering is prevented by the vulcanising process.

The advantages claimed by Mr. Hooper for this mode of insulating electric submarine cables, are :—

a.—High insulation.

b.—Flexibility.

c.—Capability of withstanding the bad effects of dry heat.

The qualifications essential to a perfect insulated electrical cable for use with submarine mines are as follows :—

1.—Capacity to bear a certain amount of strain without breaking.

2.—Perfect insulation, or at least as nearly so as it is possible to obtain, and composed of a substance capable of being readily stored, and kept for a considerable length of time without being injured.

3.—Pliability so that it may be wound on, or paid out from, a moderately sized drum without injury.

4.—Provided with an external covering capable of protecting the dielectric from injury when used in situations where there ꞏis a rocky or shingly bottom, &c.

The insulated wire of a submarine cable is technically spoken of as its *core.*

By a *cable* is meant to be understood any piece of covered wire.

Several forms of submarine electrical cables have been devised, all of which more or less possess the qualifications enumerated above. The following are some of the most effective :—

1.—Siemens's cable.

2.—Hooper's cable.

3.—Gray's cable.

4.—Service cable.

Siemens's Cable.—This form of cable is represented at Fig. 30. It consists of a strand *a*, which is composed of three or more copper wires formed by laying up the several single copper wires spirally several layers of gutta percha, or india rubber, *b*, two coverings of hemp, saturated with Stockholm tar, *c* and *d*, and several plies of copper tape *e*, wound on, so that each strip overlaps the preceding one, as shown at Fig. 30. The conductivity of the copper employed for the strand is equal to at least 90 per cent. of that of pure copper.

This exterior covering of copper tape is a patent of Messrs. Siemens

Brothers, and when once laid down, the cable so covered is very efficiently protected, and of course it is little affected by the action of the sea water. This mode of protection has one great defect, viz., that in the event of a kink occurring in paying out the line, and at the same time a sharp strain being applied, the copper tape at that point is extremely likely to destroy the insulation by being drawn in such a way as to cut through the dielectric. On this account great care must be observed in handling this form of cable.

In practice precautions must be taken to prevent the copper tape covering from being brought into contact with any iron, for were such to happen, electrical action would at once ensue, causing the iron to corrode with enormous rapidity.

In some of Siemens's cables, vulcanised india rubber replaces the gutta percha insulation. Iron covered cables, either galvanised or plain, are manufactured as well as the copper tape covered ones by that firm.

Hooper's Cable.—This form of cable is represented at Fig. 31. It consists of a metal conducting wire, generally copper, *a*, covered with an alloy to protect it from chemical action, the insulating substance *b*, known as Hooper's material, previously described at page 39, a covering of tarred hemp *c*, and an outer covering of iron wires (No. 11 B. W. G.), each of which is separately covered with tarred hemp and wound on spirally, *d*.

Gray's cable is very similar to the one just described, the chief difference in it as compared with Hooper's being the absence of the separator.

Silvertown Cables.—The following is a description of the core of an electrical submarine cable, which is used by the English government, and is supposed to contain all the advantages of the foregoing, and none of their defects. It consists of a strand conductor of four copper wires (No. 20 B. W. G.) of quality not less than 92 per cent. of pure copper, and possessing an electrical resistance of not more than 14 ohms per nautical mile. This strand is tinned and insulated with vulcanised india rubber to a diameter of ·24 inch, and then covered with a layer of felt, and the whole subjected to a temperature of 300° F. under steam pressure. This forms the core of the various kinds of cables employed in connection with a system of defence by electrical submarine mines, which are enumerated as follows :—

E

1.—Single core armoured cable.

2.—Multiple cable.

3.—Circuit closer cable.

4.—Single core unarmoured cable.

5.—Special cables for firing by cross bearings.

Single Core Armoured Cable.—This form of cable is used in connection with each mine of a group or system, and also to connect forts, &c. across an arm of the sea. Over the core, which has been fully described, is laid a spiral covering of tanned, picked Russian hemp, over this are laid ten galvanised iron wires (No. 13 B. W. G.), each one of which is covered with a similar hemp, which is laid in an opposite spiral to the former similar covering, with a twist of one revolution in about thirteen inches; in order to prevent these wires from gaping when the cable is kinked, a further covering of two servings of hemp passed spirally in opposite directions is laid, and the whole passed through a hot composition of a tar and pitch mixture. Exterior diameter of this cable is $\frac{7}{8}$ inch. Its weight in air is $27\frac{50}{113}$ cwt., and in water $14\frac{40}{113}$ cwt. per nautical mile. The breaking strain of a cable thus manufactured is $62\frac{1}{2}$ cwt., and its cost about £47 per nautical mile. A diagram of this cable is shown at Fig. 32.

Multiple Cable.—This form of cable is employed in cases where it is necessary to carry a large number of cables into the firing station, &c. It consists of seven single cores formed into a strand, over which a padding of hemp fibres is laid longitudinally, and over this again is laid an armouring of sixteen (No. 9 B. W. G.) galvanised iron wires, each one of which is covered with a layer of tarred tape put on spirally with a twist of one revolution in 15 inches. The exterior covering consists of two layers of hemp and composition, which is laid on with a short twist, and in opposite directions. The external diameter of this cable is $1\frac{1}{4}$ inch. Its weight in air and water is $78\frac{40}{113}$ cwt., and $45\frac{34}{113}$ cwt. respectively per nautical mile. Its breaking strain is 135 cwt., and cost about £357 per nautical mile. This form of cable is used in connection with a junction box, from which the single armoured cables leading to the different mines radiate, and is shown at Fig. 33.

Circuit Closer Cable.—This cable, which connects the mine and circuit closer, has been found to be subjected to exceptional wear and tear, and therefore requires a special form of exterior protection. The core of this cable is the same as the one described at page 41, also it is covered with a similar padding of hemp, but instead of the iron wires as in the case of the multiple cable, &c., nine strands, each of which is composed of fourteen No. 22 Bessemer Steel Wires, are wound on, each such strand being covered with hemp, which is put on with a twist of one revolution in every $7\frac{1}{2}$ inches, the external covering being the same as in other cables.

This form of armouring for an electric cable possesses the qualifications of pliability, lightness, and great tensile strength. Its weight in air is $52\frac{106}{112}$ cwt., and in water $28\frac{4}{112}$ cwt. per nautical mile. Its breaking strain 65 cwt., and cost about £127 per nautical mile.

Single Core Unarmoured Cable.—This form of cable is used in a system of defence by submarine mines to connect the detached works of a maritime fortress, &c., for the purpose of telegraphing.

It consists of the ordinary service core, over which are laid two servings of tarred hemp, put on spirally. The weight of this cable in air is $4\frac{13}{112}$ cwt., and in water $1\frac{36}{112}$ cwt. per nautical mile; its breaking strain is $7\frac{1}{2}$ cwt., and its cost per nautical mile is about £35.

Special Cables.—In firing electrical submarine mines by means of cross bearings, a special cable is employed. As a general rule there would be three lines of mines placed to converge on one of the stations.

Each of these lines would be provided with a conducting wire in connection with the firing arrangements, while one line of wire in connection with the firing station would be required for telegraphing. For the purpose in question a four cored cable is used.

Land Service Cable.—The cable employed for this service consists of a core formed similar to that of the multiple cable, described at page 41; over which is laid a padding of hemp, and finally two servings of tarred hemp laid spirally in opposite directions are wound on. Its weight in air is 16 cwt., and in water $4\frac{40}{112}$ cwt. per nautical mile. Its breaking strain $17\frac{1}{2}$ cwt., and cost per nautical mile about £137.

Sea Service Cable.—This consists of a similar core to the land service cable, and padding of hemp, over which is laid an armouring of fifteen No. 13 galvanised iron wires, each one being covered with tarred tape, and finally the ordinary servings of tarred hemp. Its weight in air is $49\frac{41}{112}$ cwt., and in water $25\frac{99}{112}$ cwt. per nautical mile. Its breaking strain $65\frac{99}{112}$ cwt., and cost per nautical mile about £202.

When frictional electricity is used to fire high tension fuzes, it has been found by experiment that if several lines of insulated cables are laid in the same trench for a few hundred yards, the inductive effect of the electrical charge generated by a frictional machine is so great that its discharge through one cable is sufficient not only to fire the fuze in immediate connection with it, but by induction every other fuze in connection with the remaining wires laid in the trench. And this effect equally occurs when the electric cables are some feet apart, provided they run parallel for a few hundred yards, and whether the shore ends of the cables, the fuzes in connection with which are not intended to be fired, are insulated, or put directly to earth, the connections beyond the fuzes being to earth, or even insulated, provided a very few yards of conductor exist beyond the fuze.

The length of wire which it is necessary to use between the mine and its circuit closer would be quite sufficient for the purpose of effecting ignition by induction. With platinum wire fuzes there is no danger whatever of the above happening, nor in the case of high tension fuzes is there so much danger of ignition by induction, when a constant instead of a frictional electric battery is used to generate the current.

Another mode of protecting an insulated cable is to place it, as it were, in the core of a hempen cable. In forming the rope on the cable, great care is necessary to prevent any serious amount of torsion, or tension coming on the insulated wire, either of which would most assuredly result in injury to the cable. This form of cable might in connection with obstructions, &c., be of great use, as on account of its closely resembling an ordinary rope, it would be very unlikely to excite suspicion, and so would most probably be cut, the result of which, by previous arrangement, would be an explosion of a mine, or by means of a galvanometer, &c., an indication that the obstructions, &c., were being interfered with.

Jointing Electrical Cables.—This is a very important point in connection with a system of defence or offence by electrical torpedoes. In many instances it will be found necessary to join either two lengths of cable, or an insulated wire and a cable, together, in both of which cases, great care must be used in making the joints, so that the insulation and the continuity of the circuit may be perfect.

Many species of junctions have been from time to time devised, the most practical and generally employed of which are :—

PLATE VIII

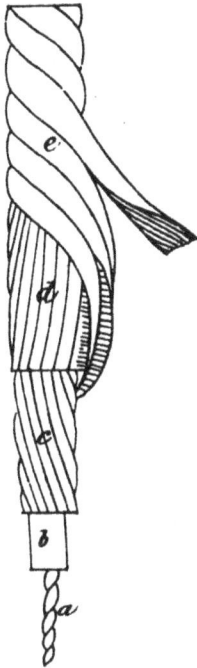

Fig 30

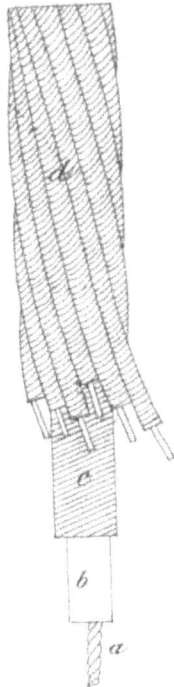

Fig 31

Fig 32

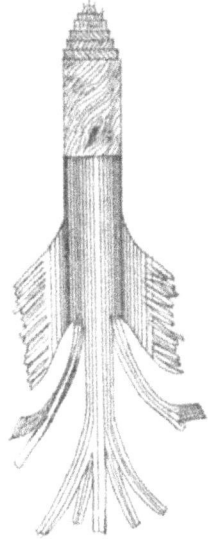

Fig 33

Fig 36

Fig 34

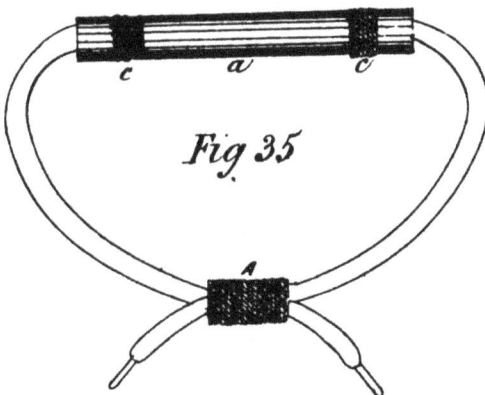

Fig 35

1.—India rubber tube joint.
2.—Mathieson's joint.
3.—Beardslee's joint.
4.—McEvoy's joint.
5.—Permanent junction.

India rubber Tube Joint.—This form of joint is a very useful one for extempore purposes, being easily and quickly made, and being very effective. At Fig. 34 is shown a sketch of such a junction. About 1·5 inches of the copper conductor of the two insulated cables are laid bare and connected together by means of Nicoll's metallic joint, as shown at Fig. 36, or by turning one of the conductors round the other, their ends being carefully pressed down by means of pliers, to prevent any chance of the india rubber tube being pierced ; over the splice thus formed serve some twine, and over the whole put a coating of india rubber cement, grease, &c., then draw the vulcanised india rubber tube, which has been previously placed on one of the insulated cables, over the splice *a*, as shown at *b*, and secure it firmly by means of twine, *c, c*, and then to prevent any strain being brought on the joint, form a half-crown as shown in Fig. 35 at *A*.

In forming the splice, it is very important that the metallic ends should be perfectly clean. The danger to this mode of jointing of the piercing of the tube by the ends of the conductors is entirely removed by employing the Nicoll metallic joint, which is formed as follows :—

Nicoll Metallic Joint.—One of the conducting wires, as *a*, Fig. 36, is formed into a spiral twist by means of a very simple instrument, and the other wire *b*, which is left straight, is inserted into the spiral, the whole being placed on an anvil, and pressed closely and securely together by a single blow of a hammer.

Mathieson's Joint.—This somewhat complicated, though very effective mode of jointing, which is adopted in the English torpedo service, is shown at Fig. 37, in elevation and section. It consists of two ebonite cylinders *a, a*, through which the cables to be connected are passed. Within these cylinders an ebonite tube *b, b* is placed, the ends of which are wedge-shaped, and which press against two vulcanite rings *c, c;* in the interior of this tube *b, b* is the metallic joint *d* of the two cables. The centre of the tube *b, b* is of square section, and fits into a hollow of similar form in the cylinders *a, a*, the object of this being to prevent any twisting of the wires during the process of screwing up, which would be liable to injure the metallic joint *d*.

The manner of making this joint will be easily understood from the figure. With this, as with all other temporary joints, it is advisable to form a half-crown in the cable, including the joint.

Beardslee's Joint.—This form of temporary joint when used with strand conductors, which are composed of a number of small wires, has been found to be exceedingly useful and effective, the only defect of such a joint being the liability of straightening the wires of the conductors should a direct strain be brought upon the wire extremities. Fig. 38 represents a section of this joint; it consists of an ebonite cylinder *a*, one end of which is solid, and the other open and fitted with a screw thread, into which is screwed a plug *b*; through both the plug *b*, and the solid end of the cylinder *a*, perforations are made just large enough to admit the insulated wires *c*, *c* ; about half an inch of the extremities of these wires are bared and cleaned, and then passed, the one through the plug *b*, a disc of vulcanised india rubber *d*, and a metal disc *e*, and the end of the strand conductor turned back on the face of this metal disc, the other through the perforation in the solid end of the cylinder *a*, then through similar discs *d* and *e*, and the end of the strand conductor treated in the same manner as the former one ; then by means of the screw plug *b*, the two metallic discs *b*, *b*, and consequently the bare extremities of the strand conductors are brought into close metallic contact.

McEvoy's Joint for Iron Wire covered Cable.—This form of joint is shown in section at Fig. 39. Two brass caps *a*, *a* are slipped over the ends of the cables required to be joined, then the iron wire and other coverings of the cables down to the insulating substance are removed, the former being bent back close against the bottom of the caps *a*, *a*, as shown in Fig. 39 at *b*, *b*; the cores of the cables are then joined by an india rubber temporary joint *c*, which has been described at page 45: the whole is then placed in the body of the joint, and the brass caps *a*, *a* screwed up, jamming the bent back iron wires against a solid piece of brass *d*, *d*, by which means a firm and perfect joint is made in the cables.

Fig. 40 represents a section of a McEvoy temporary joint for single cored unarmoured cables, which seems to fulfil all the conditions necessary to a perfect joint of that description. This joint is, with the

PLATE IX

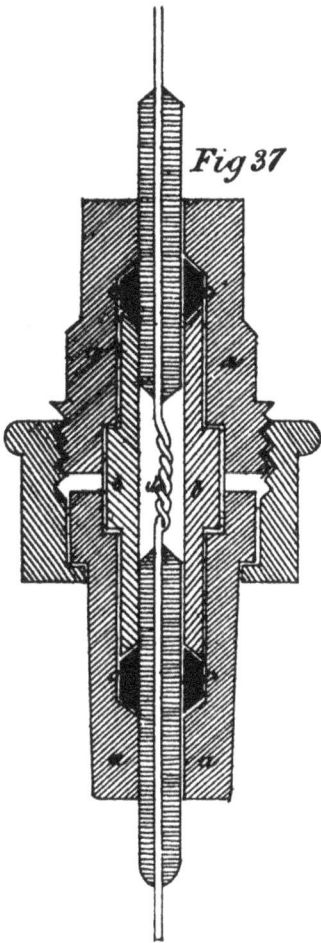

Fig 37

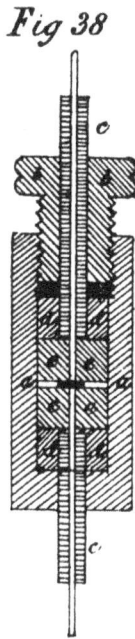

Fig 38

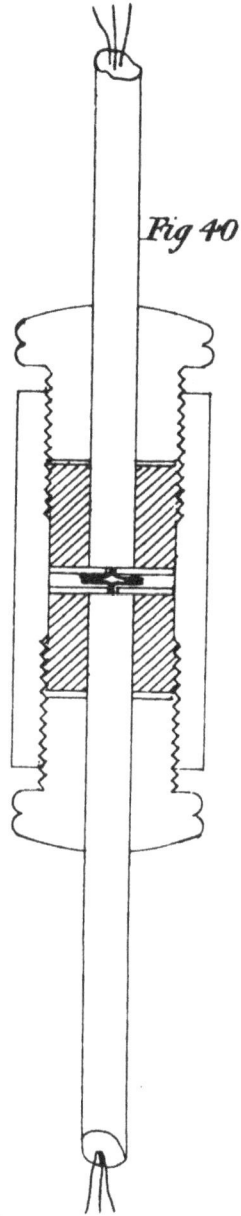

Fig 40

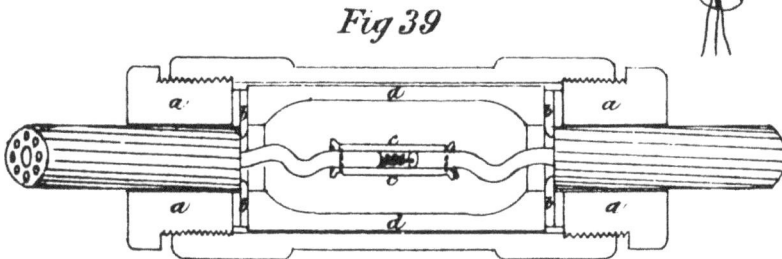

Fig 39

exception of there being two screw plugs instead of one, very similar to Beardslee's joint described at page 46; this alteration is a great improvement, remedying as it does the one defect of Beardslee's joint, viz., the liability of the cables to be drawn apart due to any great tension being brought on them.

A permanent joint in electrical submarine cables, which from its nature requires to be an exceptionally good one, is a somewhat difficult and troublesome operation, and also requires a considerable time to form a thoroughly reliable one.

Siemens's Methods of Jointing.—The following methods, and instructions for forming such joints, are those adopted by Messrs. Siemens Brothers in connection with their telegraph cables, and which will be found generally applicable to all insulated cables.

The Formation of a Joint in the Conductor of an Insulated Cable.—The conductor is either covered with a gutta percha or an india rubber dielectric. In both cases cut off the dielectric so as to bare the conductor-wire for a length of about three inches, taking care never to cut at right angles to the conductor-wire, for fear of injuring it with the cutting-knife or scissors.

Then clean the wires forming the strand with file-card and emery-paper, and solder them into a solid bar for a length of about one inch.

Having soldered the wires, forming the ends of the two lengths of conductors to be joined, into two solid rods, file each of them off in a slanting manner, so that they will form a scarf-joint when put together.

Place the two ends of strand in the two small vices on a stand which is supplied for the purpose, so that the two scarfed ends overlap each other, and bind them round with a piece of fine black iron wire, in the shape of a spiral, so as to keep the ends close together, then solder the two ends together by applying a hot soldering iron.

Then remove the iron binding wire and clean up the joint, filing off all unnecessary solder.

And make a band of four fine tinned copper wires, and bind them tightly side by side round the joint, covering the whole length of the scarf, and then solder the band and joint solidly together.

Then make another band of four fine tinned copper wires and bind them round the joint in the same manner as before, but extending about a quarter of an inch beyond each end of the other binding wire, the parts only of this second binding which project beyond the end of the first binding are to be soldered, so that the centre part remains loose and may keep up a connection between the two ends by forming a spiral between them in the event of the scarf giving way and the two ends of the conductor separating slightly.

This form of joint is called the " spring " joint.

The finished joint should be washed with spirit of wine and brushed, so as to take away all particles of soldering flux, and to avoid oxidation of the wire.   The washed joint should then be dried with a piece of cloth and exposed to the flame of a spirit lamp to dry it thoroughly.   A cable conductor ought never to be jointed with the help of soldering acid, but with that of resin, sal ammoniac, or borax only, so that any chance oxidation, and consequently destruction, of the conducting wire may be avoided.

There are other modes of jointing conductors, such as the twisting and scale joint, but the foregoing method will sufficiently explain this part of electric cable work.

The Formation of a Joint in an India rubber Insulated Cable.—In making a joint in any insulated cable, the very greatest care must be taken to keep the hands, tools, and materials clean and dry.

Remove the felt for about twelve inches from each end of the core by soaking it with mineral naphtha and then rubbing it off clean with the file-card.   The cleaned surface sear with a red-hot iron, to burn off all remaining fibres of the felt.   Wash these seared ends clean with naphtha.

Then cut off about four inches of the insulating material (taking care never to cut at right angles to the conducting wire for fear of injuring it) so as to leave enough of the conductor bare to join and solder in the manner described at page 47.

After the conductor is jointed and soldered, clean again the seared parts of the insulator with the glazed side of the squares of cloth moistened with mineral naphtha, so as to leave a clean adhesiveness only ; taper again the insulating material down to the conductor for about two inches on each side of the conductor-joint with a pair of curved and very clean scissors.

The tapering must be completed in such slanting way that the different layers of the dielectric are so far exposed as to enable a secure laying on of the new jointing material.

India rubber core consists chiefly of three layers of insulating material : the first layer next to the strand is called the pure or brown ; the second layer is the white or separating ; the third layer is the light red or jacket rubber.

Coat the conductor with a pure (brown) rubber tape tightly laid on in a spiral form, commencing at the spot where the separator (white) ends, across the corresponding place on the opposite side of the joint and back again in a contrary direction.   The ends are fastened down by pressing a clean, heated searing-iron or a heated knife on them. By doing so the band will stick ; the remaining portions of the band to be cut off with the scissors.

Lay on tightly the separating india rubber tape in the same manner, but beginning where the jacket or outer layer of rubber ends.   One lap will be sufficient.

Complete the insulation by lapping on tightly two layers of red india rubber tape : the last lap must cover each end of the core to four inches on each side of the conductor-joint, or extend to the searing or tackiness, but not beyond it.

Lay on three tight bindings of the cloth tapes, all in the same direction, care being taken to avoid wrinkles.   The ends of the cloth tapes are cemented down with a thin coating of india rubber cement.

Immerse the joint in the jointing-bath at 150° to 200° F. and gradually raise the heat so that in half an hour the temperature will be 320° F., at which temperature keep the joint for twenty minutes : then take it out and let it cool in the open air.

The Formation of a Joint in a Gutta percha Insulated Cable.—Having jointed the conducting wires in the manner described at page 47, clean and dry the joint well and cover the bare conductor with a thin layer of compound.   This is best done by heating a small stick of compound to nearly its melting point, and rubbing it over the bare conductor, which has been previously heated with the flame of a spirit-lamp.

Heat the gutta percha covering of both ends gently until it is quite soft, without, however, causing it to bubble or burn.   Draw, then, with the fingers, the gutta percha coverings of both ends down, tapering them off until they meet in the middle of the joint; heat them sufficiently to make them adhere together.

Apply a layer of compound on the tapered-off gutta percha in the same manner as described for coating the bare conductor, and cover it with a first coating of gutta percha sheet to about half the thickness necessary to finish the joint. This is done by heating a small sheet of gutta percha, of about one-eighth of an inch in thickness, until it is quite soft, and by pressing it in that state round the joint to the required size; the greatest care to be taken to expel all the air.

The projecting lips are then cut off with a pair of curved scissors. The seam thus produced is to be rubbed with a hot iron until it is completely closed and the joint well rounded off.

Apply another layer of compound and a second layer of gutta percha in exactly the same manner as described for the first layer; care, however, is to be taken to get the seam in this second layer of gutta percha not over, but as nearly as possible right opposite to, the seam in the layer underneath.

The whole to be worked as cylindrical as possible, and to a size not exceeding the original core. The joint, so far finished, is then to be cooled with water until the gutta percha is quite consolidated.

Another, the overlapping gutta percha joint, is made in the following manner :—

Cut off the two ends of the core, so that the gutta percha and the conductor-wire are flush. Warm the gutta percha for a distance of about three inches from each of the ends with the flame of a spirit lamp, and, when sufficiently soft, push it back until it forms an enlargement. The two ends of the conductor are then to be soldered according to instructions for making joint in conductors.

To have a perfectly clean surface of the two gutta percha enlargements, remove all impurities by the way of peeling them with a sharp knife. Warm gently both knobs and the copper joint, and cover the whole length of the bare wire with compound, planing it with a warm smoothing-iron.

Draw then with the fingers one of the warmed and softened knobs carefully up to the other knob or enlargement, leaving on its way a perfect tube of gutta percha upon the wire, decreasing gradually to the thickness of the copper strand towards the other knob. Any superfluous gutta percha is removed. This scarf is finished with a warm smoothing-iron, so as to unite it to the compound on the wire strand, and a thin layer of compound is also put over the scarf in the same manner as before.

The other knob is then warmed and drawn in the same way over the tube already formed, which is at the same time heated sufficiently to make the two adhere.

Apply a layer of compound on the second scarf of gutta percha, covering it in the same manner as described for coating the bare conductor, and cover it with a small sheet of gutta percha in the same manner as described above, so as to make the finished joint to the size of the core as manufactured.

Rules to be observed in forming Joints.—The following rules must be carefully observed in forming either a temporary or permanent joint :—

1.—In laying bare the conductor, the dielectric should be warmed and then pulled off, so preventing any chance of it being damaged, which might be the case were the dielectric to be cut off.

2.—For a perfect junction, soldering is necessary.

3.—The wires before connection should be carefully cleaned, and the hands of those performing the work must be dry.

4.—Gutta percha should not be given too much heat, for it then becomes oily and will not, in that state, properly adhere.

5.—Grease and dirt must be scrupulously avoided.

Great care is absolutely necessary in making junctions, as they are the principal sources of defect in the insulation of electrical submarine cables.

Junction Boxes.—When it is necessary to employ a multiple cable, a junction box is used to facilitate the connection of the several separate wires diverging from the extremities of such a cable. In one angle of such a box the multiple cable is introduced, while the separate cables make their exit on the opposite sides and pass to the different mines. Different views of a junction box are shown at Fig. 41, where A is a plan of the top or lid, B a plan of the bottom, with the lid off, C an elevation, and D a section of the box.

The manner of using the junction box is as follows :—

The multiple cable is put in at a, and secured there by means of a nipping hook, shown at Fig. 42, which hook passes through the bottom of the junction and is made secure by means of a nut. The single core cables radiating from the junction box pass through the openings b, b, b on the sides, and angle opposite to where the multiple cable *a* enters.   Each multiple cable is composed of seven cores, and each of these is connected by means of joints with the mine cables within the junction box, and each of these seven cables is secured by means of a nipper similar to, but smaller than, the one shown at Fig. 42, which are also secured by means of nuts, as in the case of the multiple cable nipping hook.   When all the connections are made, the lid *A* is placed so as to rest on the studs *c, c, c,* and firmly secured by a bolt *d,* which is made water-tight by means of a washer and nut.

By means of the nipping hooks, which take any strain that may be brought on the cables, the connections within the box are ensured against injury by such a cause.

To enable the whole to be lifted together for the purposes of examination of the cables, &c., a buoyed rope is connected to the eye-bolt *e.* For this service a dummy circuit closer is the best form of buoy, it having great buoyancy and resembling in appearance an active circuit closer.

A junction box should be placed in such a position as to be easily attained, even in the presence of an enemy, and its buoy should, if possible, not be seen.   It is also very essential that it should be in a safe and guarded position, for any injury to the junction box or multiple cable would be fatal to the group of mines in connection.

In the following cases, special junction boxes are used :—

1.—A seven cored armoured cable to be connected direct to another length of the same.

2.—A single armoured cable to be connected as in foregoing instance.

3.—A T junction box for the branch system of electrical contact mines.

Junction Box for Multiple Cables.—At Fig. 43 is represented a plan of lower half of this form of junction box.   It consists of a pair of cast iron plates of precisely similar form to the one shown at Fig. 43, and so made as to be capable of being fastened tightly together by means of four bolts and nuts passing through the holes *a, a.*   The grooves *b, b* at the two extremities are just large enough to grip the armoured cable firmly, when the upper and lower parts are screwed together.   A larger space is provided in the hollow for the joint.

Junction Box for Single Cored Cables.—For this purpose a junction box similar to, but smaller than the one above described is employed.

T Junction Box.—This form of junction box is employed when the system of electrical contact mines on branches from a single cable is used. This system is dependent on the use of a platinum wire fuze in connection with a platinum wire bridge in each branch close to its junction with the main cable.

This form of junction box, which is shown at Fig. 44 is very similar to the one used for the connection of two multiple cables, only differing in its shape, which is that of a T. *a* is a disconnector, which will be described further on; *b, b, b'* are the armoured electric cables, *b, b* being the main, and *b'* the branch cable in connection with the forked joint formed within the T junction box; *c, c, c* are Turk's heads formed to prevent any strain being brought on the forked joint. This form of Turk's head is made by turning back the wires of the cable armouring, and frapping them round with spun yarn until the necessary size and shape is attained.

McEvoy's Turk's Head.—Another form of Turk's head, devised by Captain McEvoy, is shown at Fig. 45. It consists of two separate pieces of brass, *a* and *b*, the former screwing over the latter. The mode of using it is as follows :—

Slip the piece of brass *b* over the cable *c*, and turn back the wires of the cable *d, d,* &c., so that they lie against the shoulder of the brass piece *b*, then slip the other piece of brass *a* over the cable and screw it on the piece *b*, firmly jamming the turned back wires *d, d,* &c. This is a very neat and quick method of forming a Turk's head, and it should be invariably used in preference to the foregoing method, which is clumsy, and which takes some time to form.

The section of a disconnector is shown at Fig. 46. It consists of an iron cover, or dome *a*, which is provided with a screw fitting on to another screw on the ebonite body *b* of the apparatus. When the dome *a* is screwed tightly down on the washer *i*, the whole is made perfectly watertight. *c, c* are insulated terminals for connecting the cores of the branch and main cables after their armouring has been removed, as shown at Fig. 44. *d, d* are two copper conducting wires (No. 16 B. W. G.) passing through the centre of the ebonite body *b*, and projecting into the interior of the apparatus. These wires are held in position and insulated by means of a composition formed of a mixture of pitch, tallow, beeswax and gutta percha. This composition is put on whilst hot and allowed to cool gradually, when it becomes hard and durable. Great care is necessary to ensure the cavity within the ebonite body b being completely filled, as otherwise a leakage might occur, owing to the great pressure of water at depths where the disconnection would be generally used. f is a boxwood cover which is slipped on, and fits fairly tight to the ebonite body b; g is a piece of thin platinum wire, weighing 1·6 grains to the yard, and being $\frac{4}{10}$ inch in length; h is an ebonite pin, which passes through two small holes in the boxwood cover f, into which it fits tightly, and in such a position as to be directly beneath the platinum wire bridge g, when the boxwood cover f is fixed on. The pin h is pushed through the holes in the cover f from the outside, so as to pass beneath the bridge g after the priming has been inserted, and the cover has been placed on.

When prepared for use, the platinum wire bridge g is surrounded by some loose gun-cotton priming, sufficient in quantity to blow off the boxwood cover f, without destroying the dome a; the cover f being blown off, carries the ebonite pin h with it, and through the platinum wire bridge g, thereby rupturing it, and breaking the continuity of the circuit. The object of so doing is to cut off the connection of an exploded mine, so that the full amount of the firing current is available for the other mines, and not suffered to be wasted by passing through the exposed wire of the broken circuit, which, were the disconnector not employed, would be the case.

When any particular mine of a system is struck, the current passes through the main cable b, the disconnector a (which is in connection with that mine), and branch cable b' to the fuze, and so explodes the mine, and destroys the platinum wire bridge g of the disconnector at practically the same instant. The effect of the latter operation would be to cut off and insulate the branch cable of the exploded mine, and so prevent any loss of the electrical current, when another mine of that system is required to be fired.

The platinum wire bridge g is $\frac{4}{10}$ inch long, while that of the fuze is $\frac{3}{10}$ inch, the object of this difference in length of the bridges being to ensure the former one g being fired, and thus the insulation made doubly sure. Many other forms of disconnectors have been devised, but none have proved in practice so effective as the one just described.

Mooring Electrical Submarine Mines.—This is one of the most

PLATE X

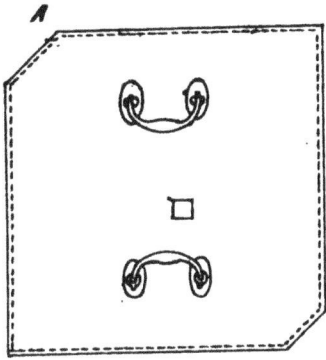

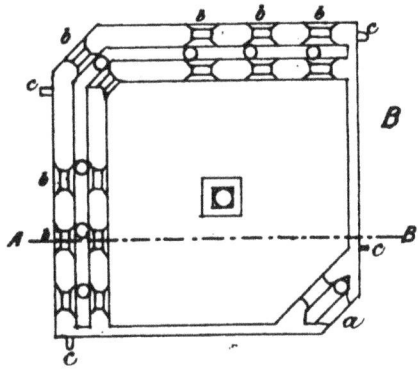

Fig 41

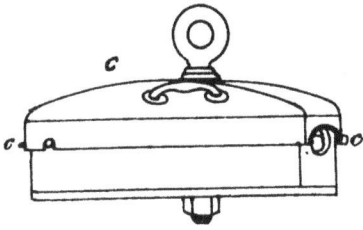

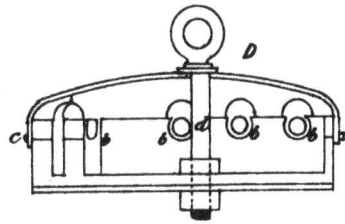

Fig 42

Fig 43

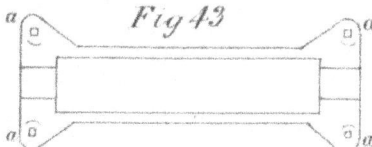

Fig 45

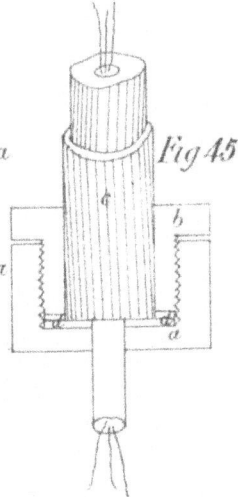

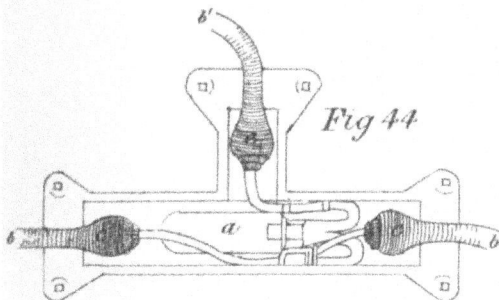

Fig 44

Fig 46

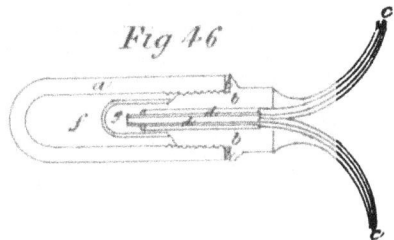

difficult problems to be solved in connection with a system of sub-marine mines. The objects to be attained in mooring are as follows:—

1.—The mines should preserve the exact positions in which they are laid down.

NOTE.—From the comparatively small radius of destructive effect, of even heavily charged submarine mines, it will be understood how absolutely essential, in the case of mines fired by judgment, it is that this object should be attained.

2.—The mooring chains, or ropes, must be so arranged that no twisting whatever should occur, as otherwise fracture of the insulated wire would be likely to happen.

3.—In the case of buoyant mines, their distance from the bottom must be so adjusted, that at no time shall a vessel passing over them be out of their vertical range of destruction, nor shall they be visible.

The difficulties attendant upon the efficient mooring of submarine mines are immense, as will be understood when the action of gales of wind, and strong tides, which latter vary continually in their direction and in their rise and fall, are taken into consideration.

The foregoing remarks apply more particularly to a system of buoyant submarine mines, as those placed on the ground are comparatively easy to moor.

Several modes of mooring buoyant submarine mines have been suggested, the most practicable of which are as follows:—

1.—Ladder moorings.
2.—Fore and aft moorings.
3.—Austrian method of mooring.
4.—Single rope mooring.

Ladder Mooring.—This is a method of mooring, which in places where it may be necessary to place the anchors far apart will be found useful.

The circuit closer is connected to the mine by two ropes which lead thence to two anchors, the ropes being separated by wooden rounds, or spreaders, 1 to 3 feet long, by which the tendency to twisting is prevented.

The anchors are placed some 12 feet apart.

The only defect of the ladder mooring is the quantity of sea-weed, &c., that is liable to be lodged on the rounds, thus causing the circuit closer to be drawn out of its proper position.

Fore and aft Mooring.—This mode may be advantageously employed in a tideway where the current runs very strong, that is to say, five knots per hour, or more. It consists simply of two anchors, one of which is moored up, and the other down the stream.

Austrian Method of Mooring.—This method of mooring, adopted by the Austrians during the war of 1866, is shown at Fig. 47. It consists of a wooden triangular platform on which several heavy weights a, a, a are placed; the mine is attached to this platform by means of three wire ropes b, b, b, connected to the angles of the latter, and fastened to three chains, which by means of a catch holds the mine at the position required.

This catch consists of a pulley attached to the extremity of the wire rope of the platform, through which the mooring chain of the mine is passed, and fastened by a key at the required depth by means of a self-acting arrangement.

This key, which is of considerable weight, slips down as the mine is being hauled into position, but the moment the chain is slacked, two arms catch into a link of· the chain, and so hold the mine in position. The weight of such a key is about 60 lbs. It is fitted with nuts, &c., to enable it to be taken to pieces.

This plan of mooring proved very effective in the harbours of the Adriatic, where there is hardly any tide or current to twist the mooring ropes, or otherwise disturb the mines. The Austrians have lately adopted the mushroom sinker in place of the wooden platform and weights, for their anchor.

Single Rope Mooring.—This simple method of mooring has after numerous exhaustive experiments been adopted as the most practicable and effective of all others. Whenever possible, a wire instead of hempen cable should be used to connect the mine and its circuit closer to the mooring anchor, as the former is less liable to twist, kink, or wear from friction than the latter.

A ground mine with circuit closer attached is represented at Fig. 48, where a is the wire mooring rope, b the electric cable leading from the mine to the circuit closer, C, and c the cable leading from the firing station to the mine; d is the oblong sinker attached to the mine, and e the tripping chain leading to the shore, to which the cable c is attached at intervals, so that by underrunning the electric cable, the tripping chain may be easily picked up, and the mine raised.

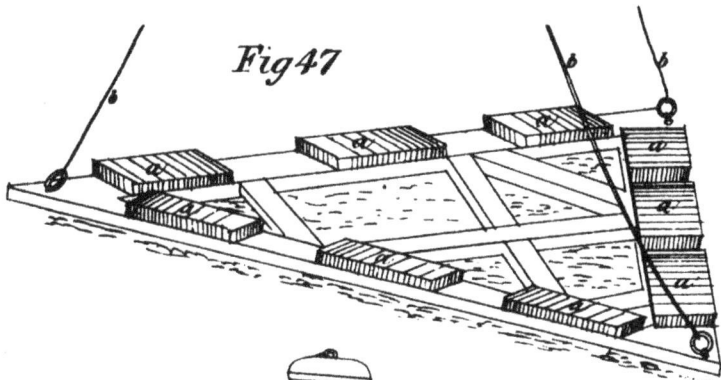

Fig 47

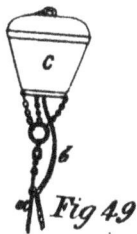

Fig 49

Fig 48

Fig 50

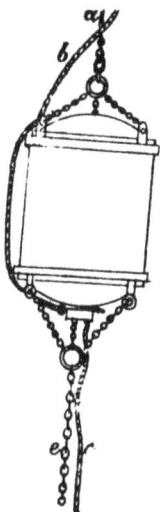

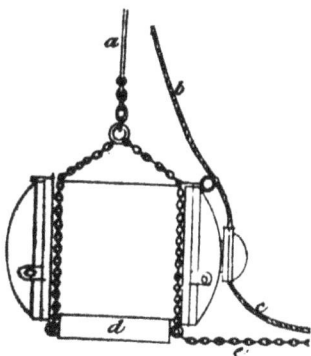

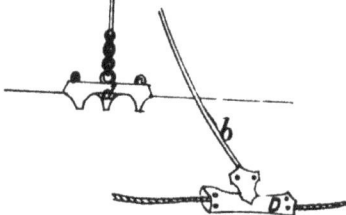

Fig 51.

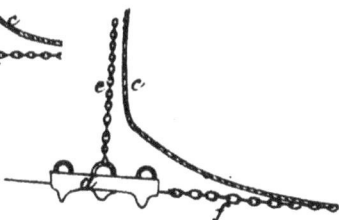

At Fig. 49 is shown a buoyant mine. The only difference in the mooring of this and the one before described, is that instead of resting on its anchor on the ground, it is moored at a certain distance above its anchor *d*, to which it is secured by a chain *e*.

Fig. 50 represents an electro contact mine. *M* is the mine with circuit closer enclosed, *a* the wire mooring rope, *d* the mushroom anchor, and *b* the electric cable leading from the mine to the disconnector *D*.

The mushroom sinker or anchor, which is undoubtedly the most effective of all other forms of mooring anchors used for the purposes of anchoring submarine mines, is shown at *e*, Fig. 49 ; the legs are added for use on rocky or hard bottoms, under which circumstances the weight of the anchor should also be increased.

For ground mines the form of sinker shown at *d*, Fig. 48 is employed ; it is of an oblong shape, and hollowed out in the centre to allow of its being lashed close up to the mine.

Large blocks of stones with their bases slightly hollowed are useful as extempore moorings, so also is the one shown at Fig. 51, which consists of a strong heavy wooden shaft *a*, with a number of wooden arms *b, b* attached to its base; this form of extempore sinker was considered very efficient by the American authorities.

The wooden weighted platform, which was described at page 56, is also a very useful form of extempore sinker.

For dead weight moorings, pigs of ballast, heavy stones, &c., may be used.

The weight of the anchor or sinker for mooring submarine mines is a very important consideration. It will depend on the amount of buoyancy of the mine, on the strength of current, and on the nature of the bottom, also whether the mines are to be hauled down to, or moored with the anchor.

Stotherd uses the following formula :

$$W = 2 \sqrt{B^2 + P^2}$$

where B is the excess of the flotation over the weight of the charge of a given submarine mine ;

P is the pressure exerted by any given current on the same buoyant mine ;

W the weight of sinker necessary to overcome the tendency of the mine to move. In still water P becomes nothing, and therefore W equal to 2 B, that is, in still water double the buoyancy of a mine is a sufficient weight for its anchor.

The value of P may be found from the formula $P = 4.085 \times V^2$, where V is the velocity of the current in miles per hour.

From this equation P will be found in terms of pressure in pounds per square foot of flat surface, which is nearly double that on the curved surface of a cylinder.

In regard to the amount of buoyancy of a submarine mine, it has been found by actual practice that in the case of a mine moored in still water it should certainly be not less than the weight of the charge, whilst if subjected to the lateral pressure due to a current, it should be not less than three times the pressure exerted by the current.

It is always necessary to allow an excess of buoyancy over the calculated amount to counteract any leakage, or other disturbing cause which might otherwise materially affect the efficiency of the mine.

There are two modes of placing a mine in position; either by attaching the anchor, with the cable necessary for the depth of water, to the mine, and lowering both together, or by placing the anchor first, and then hauling the mine down to it, and by means of a catch, fastening it at the required depth.

The first mode is exceedingly simple, but except under very favourable circumstances cannot be relied on when firing by observation is the means adopted to explode a system of submarine mines. The second plan is practically easy to carry out, and by it a mine may be placed more accurately. To enable either of the above methods to be properly carried out, specially fitted steamboats, &c., are requisite.

At Fig. 52 is represented a 42 feet launch fitted for laying down a submarine mine by the first of the two modes enumerated above.

a is the mine; b is the electric cable carried from the drum c to the charge, and connected for use; d is the circuit closer, which is attached to the mine by its electric cable and mooring rope; f is the mushroom sinker attached by means of its mooring chain to the mine, it is suspended by a slip rope g, which passes over a small crutch fitted with a sheave h; i is a hollow iron derrick, and k the tackle and fall for lifting mine into boat; this derrick is formed of an iron tube about 3 inches diameter, $\frac{3}{8}$ inch thick, and 10 feet 6 inches long; it is attached

PLATE XII.

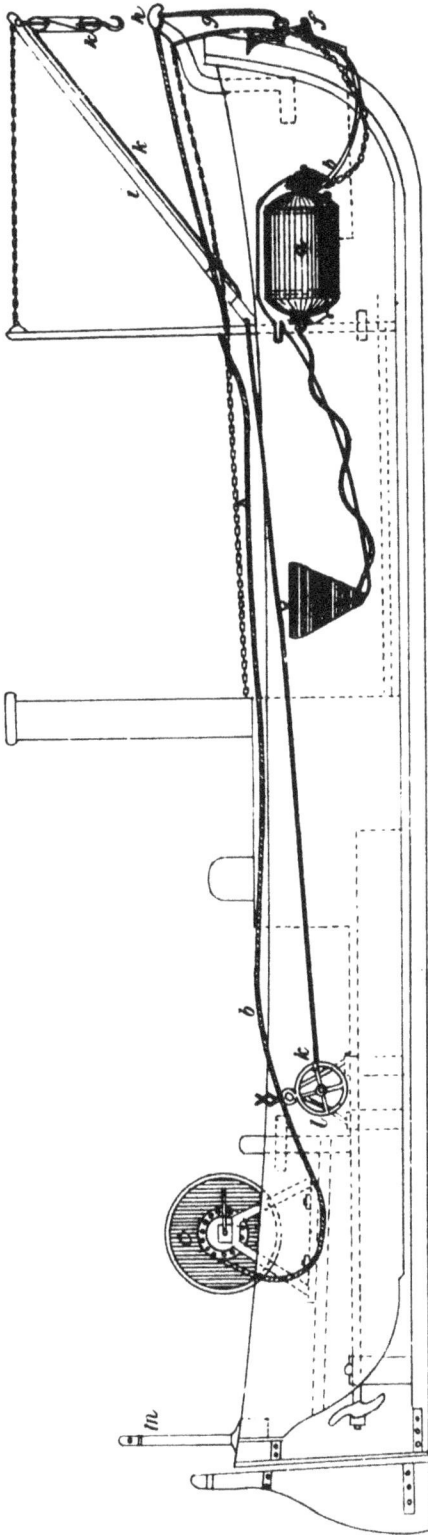

Fig 52

to an iron tube mast of similar diameter and thickness to the derrick, but 12 feet 3 inches long, an iron chain 6 feet 6 inches long and $\frac{3}{4}$ inch diameter, connects the derrick to the mast; m is a leading sheave to keep the cable clear whilst it is being paid out; l is a crab, for working the tackle k, &c., and c is the drum on which the electric cable is wound.

In connection with the defence of a harbour by a system of electrical submarine mines of large size, it will be necessary to employ a service of steamtugs, steamboats, mooring-barges, &c., specially fitted for such work. One of the great advantages of the hauling down method of placing mines in position, is, that the anchors, with the cables connected thereto, may be carefully and accurately got into position during the time of peace, and the mines themselves, which should be kept in store ready fitted for immediate use, need not be placed in position until they are actually required. The drums used for reeling a multiple cable on, are capable of holding half a nautical mile in length. That used for a single core armoured cable is similar to but smaller than the aforesaid drum, and is capable of stowing one nautical mile of such a cable. For transportation wooden drums are ordinarily used.

CHAPTER IV.

DEFENSIVE TORPEDO WARFARE—*continued.*

C LOSING the Electric Circuit.—In connection with the system of coast defence by means of electrical submarine mines, there are two distinct methods of effecting the closing of the electric circuit, and consequently, the firing battery being connected, the explosion of the mine or mines, which methods may be used separately, or in combination, and are as follows :—

1.—The self-acting method.
2.—The firing by judgment, or observation method.

During the early days of submarine defensive warfare, the latter method alone was used, owing to the absence of anything like a practicable form of self-acting apparatus; but within the last few years, the former has almost entirely superseded the latter method, except in very exceptional cases ; this revolution being due to the vast improvements that have been, and still are being effected in the system of firing electrical submarine mines automatically.

Use of Circuit Closers.—Electrical submarine mines may by means of an apparatus, termed a *circuit closer,* be rendered self-acting ; that is to say, by the action of a vessel coming in contact with such an apparatus, which may be either within the mine itself, or within a buoy attached to the mine, the electric circuit is closed, and the mine in connection with the circuit closer so struck, exploded. The essential feature of such a mode of closing the electric circuit is, that electrical submarine mines may be rendered either active or harmless, at the will of the operator, which is effected by the putting in, or taking out of a plug, by which means the firing current is either thrown in, or out of the circuit.

Circuit closers.—Many different forms of circuit closers have been devised, among which the following seem the most suitable and are those generally used :—

1.—Mathieson's inertia circuit closer.

2.—Mathieson's spiral spring circuit closer.

3.—Austrian self-acting circuit closer.

4.—McEvoy's mercury circuit closer.

5.—McEvoy's weight magneto circuit closer.

Mathieson's Circuit Closer.—This form of circuit closer has been adopted by the English government in connection with their system of defence by electrical submarine mines.

The details of this apparatus are shown at Pl. xiii.

Fig. 53, *a* is a gun-metal dome screwed on to a metal base *b*, its foot resting on a gutta percha washer *c*, so as to exclude any water ; *d* is a cap screwed on to the top of the dome, and made watertight by the leather washer *e* ; *f* is a guard cap screwed into the cap *d*, this is to keep the spindle of the circuit closer steady during transport, and would be removed when the apparatus is prepared for service ; *g* is the ebonite base plug through which pass the insulated wires *E* and *L* ; *h* is an hexagonal collar, working in the metal base plate *b*, by means of which, and the brass collar *i*, and the leather washer *k*, the base plug is secured, and water is excluded from the interior of the circuit closer ; *l, l, l* are brass columns supporting a circular ebonite piece *m* ; *n* is a metal bridge screwed on to the base plate *b*, into which is screwed the spindle *p*, both of which are prevented from moving after being screwed up by the set screws *r* and *s*.

The spindle *p* carries a leaden ball *t*, which is supported upon the rest *v*, and is secured in position by the screw nut *w* ; *x* is an india rubber ring, the object of which is to prevent any damage being done to the spindle should the ball when set in action by a heavy blow from a passing vessel be brought into contact with the dome ; 2 is a brass disc attached to the spindle carrying an ebonite disc 4, connected to it by screws ; 6 is a brass contact ring also fixed to the ebonite disc 4, provided with a screw 8, for the attachment of one of the base plug wires, and with platinised projections 3, 3, 3, Fig. 56. The contact ring 6 is completely insulated from the spindle and brass disc 2. Three contact springs 5, are attached to the circular ebonite piece *m*, and the faces opposite to the platinised projections of the disc 2 are also platinised. 7 shows the contact screws of the connecting pieces, which serve also as adjusting screws to regulate the sensitiveness of the apparatus, the points of which as well as their bearings on the springs are platinised.

The springs are connected together by means of the wires 9, Fig. 55, one end of which is secured to the connecting piece by the screw 10, and the other passes through to the top of the ebonite piece, and is attached to the top of the spring next in succession to that to which it is fixed below.

One terminal of a coil of 1000 ohms resistance (which is used for testing purposes) is attached to the line L, terminal of the ebonite base plug, which latter is also connected to the screw 8, on the circumference of the contact ring 6; the other terminal of the resistance coil is connected to the earth, E terminal of the base plug.

A bare copper wire of No. 16 B. W. G. connects the top of the last contact spring with the set screw s; a piece of similar wire jointed to it is passed round one of the brass collars and connected to the screw r. As a precaution against bad contact, the contact springs are connected together by bare wires A, B, C. This completes the connections for the signalling circuit, the earth being formed by the body of the instrument; D is a hole left in the metal base for the passage of the insulating wire which connects the earth plate to the earth E terminal of the base plug.

Testing Current.—For testing purposes the current from the test battery arrives by the line wire L, and passes thence through the resistance coil to earth by means of the wire E, which is attached to a zinc earth plate placed in a recess in the jacket of the circuit closer.

Action of the Circuit.—The action of the apparatus is as follows :—

Closer.—On the circuit closer being struck, the weight of the lead ball t causes the steel rod p to be deflected and brings the brass ring 6 in contact with one of the springs 5; the signalling current which up to this moment has been passing through the 1000 ohms coil to earth, then passes to the contact ring 6 (avoiding the resistance coil) thence to the spring which is in contact with it, and from there by means of the wire connections to the set screws s and r, and so to earth through the metal body of the apparatus; the effect of the resistance coil being thus eliminated, is to strengthen the signalling current, and thus enable it to work the shutter apparatus, by which means the firing current is thrown into circuit and the mine exploded.

Circuit Breaker.—By altering the mode of connecting the wires, the above apparatus may be used as a circuit breaker, that is to say, the signal may be given, and the mine exploded by the cessation of a

PLATE XIII

Fig 53

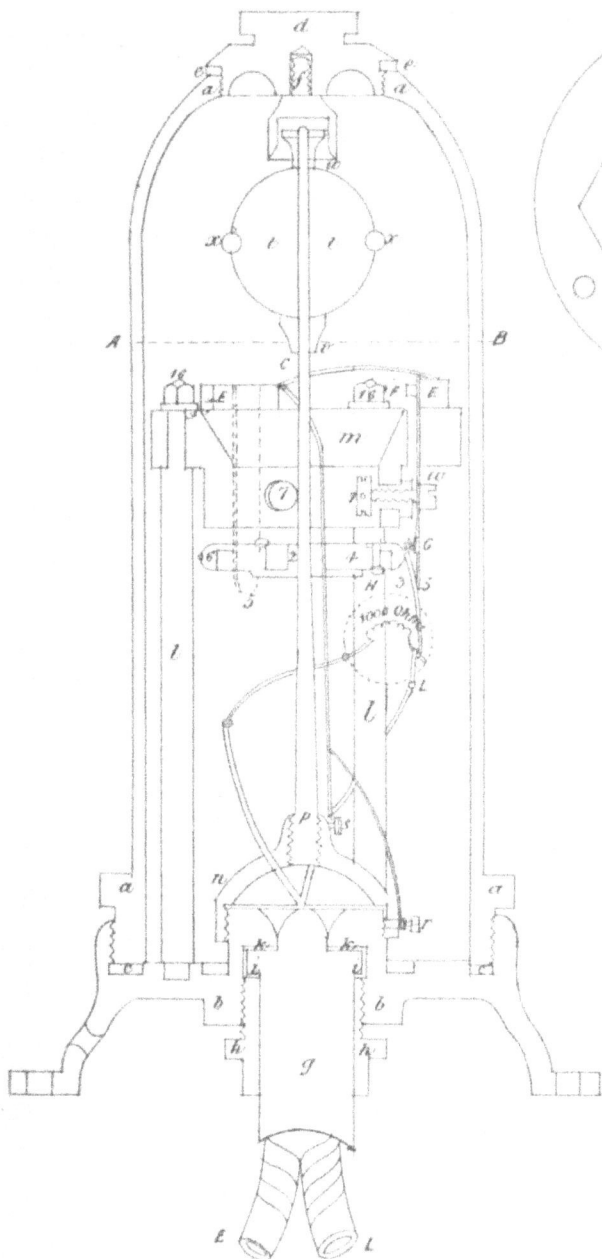

Fig 54

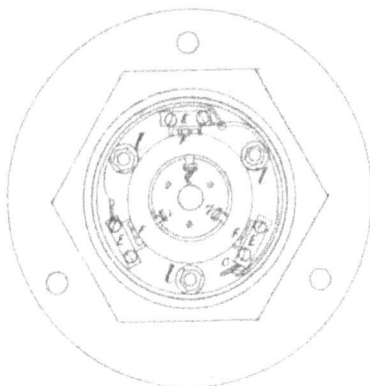

Fig 55

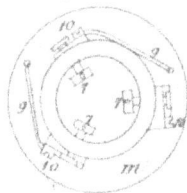

Fig 56

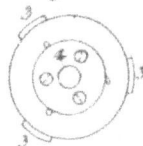

passing current, instead of by the closing of the electric circuit. This system was specially designed for use with platinum wire fuzes, but is rarely used.

Circuit Closer of Electro Contact Mines.—When the inertia circuit closer is employed in connection with electro contact mines, the circular ebonite piece *m* is replaced by a similar shaped piece of brass, and which is in metallic connection through the brass pillars *l, l, l* with the mass of the metal of the apparatus which forms the earth plate.

The insulated wire of the base plug is connected to one pole of a platinum wire fuze, the other pole of which is connected by another wire to the outer metal rim of the disc of the spindle. As long as the circuit closer remains undisturbed, a break will remain in the circuit, which is due to the ebonite insulation between the spindle and the outer metal rim of the disc; but the moment the apparatus is struck, which causes the spindle to vibrate, the outer metal rim will come in contact with one of the springs completing the circuit, through the circular metal portion and the pillars of the circuit closer to earth.

Adjustment of Circuit Closer.—The sensitiveness of Mathieson's inertia circuit closer is determined by the distance between the disc 4 and the springs 5, 5, 5, which is regulated by means of the adjusting screws 7, 7, 7, which press against the inner faces of the springs. Owing to the great weight of the leaden ball, when by any cause the circuit closer is inclined for a length of time, a permanent set is given to the spindle, thereby destroying the adjustment of the instrument.

Improvements in the Inertia Circuit Closer.—To remedy this very serious defect, a cylinder of india rubber is substituted for the leaden ball; a circuit closer so fitted is also less affected by the action of counter mines, which is a very important advantage.

Mathieson's Spiral Spring Circuit Closer.—A sectional elevation of this form of circuit closer is shown at Fig. 57. It consists of a brass base *a*, provided with a grooved flange for carrying a gutta percha washer, and it has also an hexagonal projection for the purpose of screwing the circuit closer into the gun-metal mouth of its air-tight cylinder, or buoy; *b* is a brass dome enclosing the apparatus for the purpose of protecting it from injury, and also by means of india rubber washers to prevent an ingress of water, should the circuit closer case become injured, and leak; *c* is a brass collar to which the brass contact springs *i, i* are attached, and which are regulated by the set screws *j, j*; a brass spiral spring *d* carries a metal rod *e*, which supports a brass ball *f*, surrounded by an india rubber band *h*.   A contact disc *g* is secured to the base of the spindle *e*, but insulated from it by an ebonite boss; *k* is an ebonite base plug with two channels in it, through which the wires *m, m¹* pass.

An Improvement on the Inertia Circuit Closer.—This instrument is a vast improvement on the inertia apparatus previously described, being more simple and more certain in its action, a desideratum in all circuit closers; but notwithstanding, up to the present time Mathieson's inertia apparatus has been used by our government, to the exclusion of all other instruments of a similar nature, some of which were proved to be far superior when subjected to the crucial test of actual practice.

Austrian Self-acting Circuit Closer.—This form of circuit closing apparatus, which is purely a self-acting one, that is to say, a mine so fitted cannot be fired at will, is shown at Fig. 58.

It consists of several buffers *a, a, a*, which by means of strong springs are held in position, their heads projecting outside the torpedo case *b*; on being pressed in by the contact of a passing vessel, the ends of these buffers would be forced against a ratchet wheel *c*, which is also kept in position by means of a spring.   Several strong pieces of wood *d, d* within the case keep the buffers and their attached arms in the proper direction, and also afford rigidity to the torpedo case. The brass ratchet wheel *c* being put in motion carries round with it a central arrangement *e*, the lower part of which is shown at Fig. 58, *A*.

This portion consists of a cylinder of brass *f* divided into two parts insulated one from the other by a piece of ebonite *g*; on one side of this cylinder there are three arms of brass, *h, i,* and *k,* and on the other there are two arms, *l* and *m*, all of which are insulated from each other.

The arm *h* is close to, but insulated from a metal plate *n*, which latter is permanently connected with the conducting wire leading from the firing battery, and thus while in a state of rest is electrically charged; beyond the arm *i* is a spring *o*, which is connected with the earth, and in such a position that when the central portion is moved round, this spring *o* comes in contact with the arm *i*, and the plate *n* with the arm *h* simultaneously, and the circuit is thus completed through earth to the battery, but the current of electricity does not pass through the fuze.   The arms *k, l* on the opposite sides

PLATE XIV

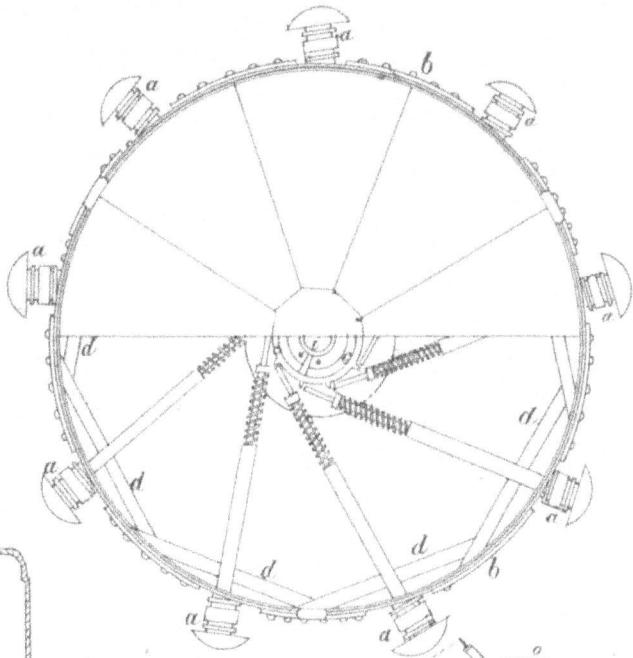

Fig 57

Fig 58

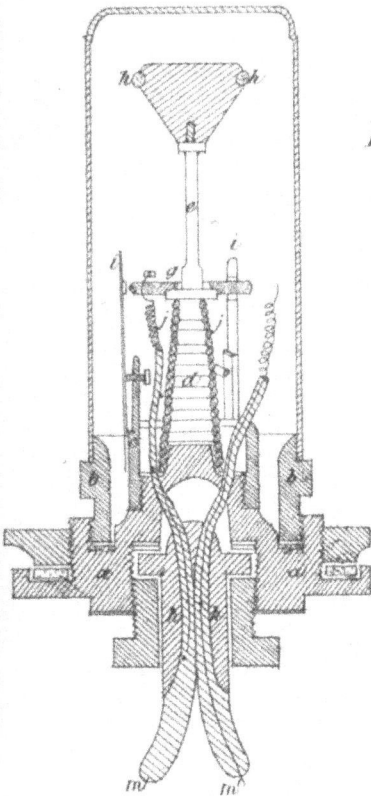

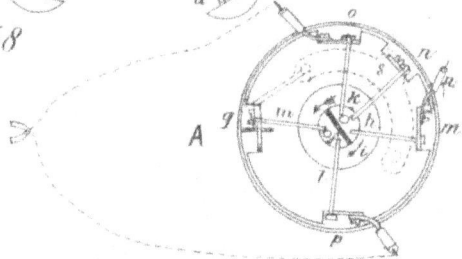

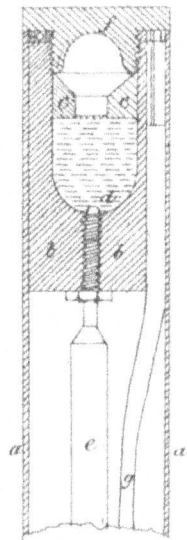

Fig 59

of the cylinder, and consequently insulated one from the other, are connected with the fuze, and the arm *m* is connected with the earth.

On a further pressure of the vessel on the buffer, the arm *i* is pushed beyond the spring, and in contact therewith, and consequently the circuit by earth to the battery is broken, while the contact of the arm *h* and plate *n* is still retained, and the current is passed by the arm *k* through the fuze to the arm *l*, and then to earth through the arm *m*, thus completing the electric circuit of the firing battery through the fuze, and to exploding the mine.

The spring acts as a circuit breaker, and by means of an intensity coil in connection with the firing battery, the current is only passed through the fuze when at the point of greatest intensity.

By detaching the firing battery, the channel defended by such submarine mines may be rendered safe.

Fuze only in Circuit at Moment of Firing it.—One of the principal objects to be gained by the employment of such an arrangement for the closing of the electric circuit in connection with submarine mines, is the prevention of premature explosion from induction which might be caused by the proximity of any atmospheric electricity, the fuze in this system being entirely cut out of circuit until the moment when it is necessary to fire it.

The Austrians employed this form of circuit closing instrument during the war of 1866, and still continue to use it in connection with their coast defence by submarine mines.

McEvoy's Mercury Circuit Closer.—At Fig. 59 is represented a longitudinal section of a circuit closer of this construction.

It is placed in the mine in such a manner that when undisturbed it maintains an approximately upright position.

It consists of a metal tube *a* into which the cup *b* of vulcanite, or other insulating material is fixed. The cup is contracted at some distance from the top by the perforated plug *c*, which is also of insulating material; *d* is a metal pin fixed into the bottom of the cup *b*, it is connected with the wire *e*, which is insulated and passes to the battery; *f* is a metal plug closing the tube *a* and the cup *b* at the top; *g* is a wire attached to the plug *f*, and passing from it to an earth connection. The cup *b* is filled with mercury up to the level of the plug *c*. By the contact of a passing vessel the instrument would be tilted sufficiently to cause the mercury to flow into contact with the metal plug f, thus completing the electric circuit and exploding the mine.

This form of circuit closer, though not generally adopted, would, on account of its being less liable to derangement by the motion of the waves, or by the explosion of an adjacent or counter mine, seem to fulfil the many requirements of a circuit closer for general service.

McEvoy's Weight Magneto Circuit Closer.—This form of circuit closer, which is shown in section and plan at Figs. 60 and 61, is one of the most important improvements that has ever been effected in such apparatus, and bids fair to become universally adopted.

A heavy metal conical shaped weight a (Fig. 60), hollowed out in its base and working in a ball and socket joint b, rests on a solid brass base c, and is so arranged that on the apparatus being struck, the weight a will fall over, pivoting on one of its supports d, d; e is a band of india rubber, encircling the weight a, for the purpose of preventing a jar on its falling against the sides of the brass cylinder f, which contains the weight a and joint b. A brass rod g, connected to the ball and socket joint, passes through the base c, through a strong spiral spring h (which latter rests on an adjusting screw k), through a piece of ebonite l, which supports the bobbins and core m, m^1; then between these bobbins m, m^1 through an armature n, which is pivoted at p; and lastly through a slight spiral spring o, which is kept in position by the adjusting screw i.

The armature n is fitted with a small piece of brass r, so arranged that when it (the armature) is in the position shown in Fig. 60, this piece of brass r does not make contact with the two strips of metal, s, s, between which it, r, works; but when the armature n is in contact with the cores of the bobbins m, m^1, then the piece of brass r makes contact with the metal strips s s, and so makes a short circuit for the electric current. An ordinary telephone t, Fig. 61, in which some small shot, bells, &c., are placed, is fixed to the top of the brass cylinder f.

Action of Circuit Closer.—The action of this apparatus is as follows :—

On the mine carrying this form of circuit closer being struck by a passing vessel, the weight a is caused to fall over towards the side of the brass cylinder f, thus allowing the strong spiral spring h to act on the brass rod g in an upward direction, by which means the armature n is brought into contact with the soft iron cores of the bobbins m, m^1.

PLATE XV

Fig 60

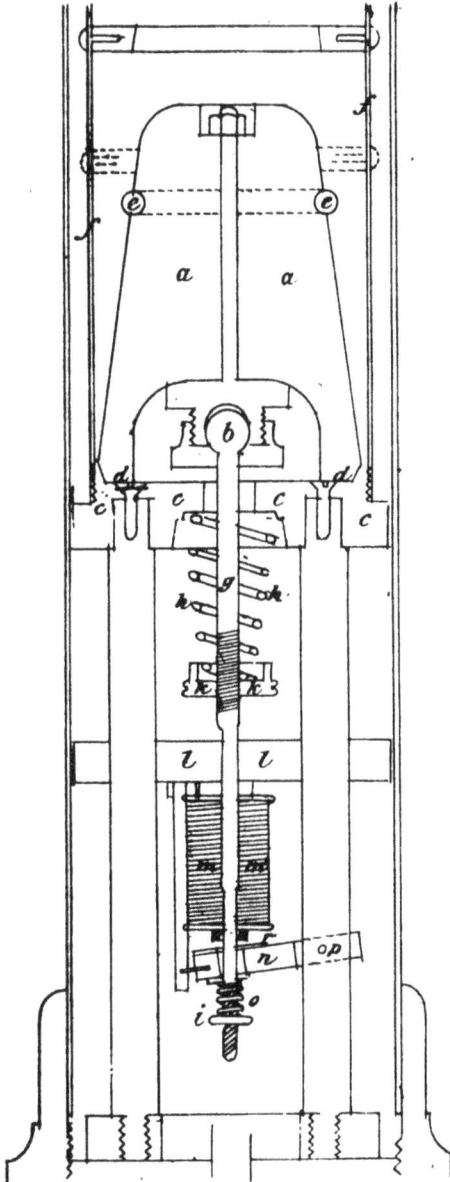

Fig 61

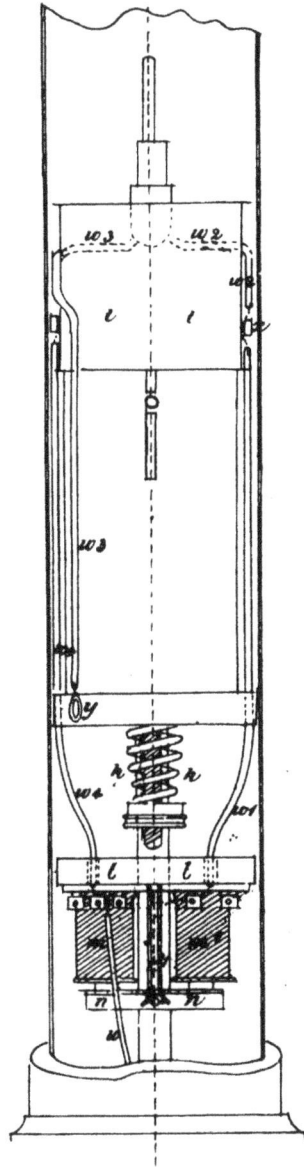

The connections of the wires are made as follows :—

The line wire w is led through the base of the apparatus and connected to a piece of brass under the ebonite support l, in connection with one of the wires of the bobbin m, the other wire of which is attached to the metal strip s; the wires of the bobbin m^1 are connected, the one to the metal strip s_1, the other to a piece of brass under the ebonite support l; from this latter piece of brass a wire w_1 is led to the brass screw x. The wires w_2, w_3, from the fuzes are led, the one to the brass screw x, the other to a screw y, which forms through the metal of the apparatus the earth plate. One of the wires of the telephone t is connected to the brass screw x, the other w_4 is connected to the piece of brass to which the line wire w is also attached. While the circuit closer remains in a state of rest, the current from the signalling battery flows along the line wire w, up the telephone wire w_4, through the telephone which has a high resistance, then by the wire w_2 through the fuzes, and to earth by the wire w_3.

On the circuit closer being struck, by which cause the armature n is brought up to the cores of the bobbins m, m^1, and the piece of brass r in contact with the metal strips s, s_1, the signalling current, instead of circulating through the high resistance of the telephone t, passes round the bobbin m, down the metal strip s, across the brass piece r, up the metal strip s_1, round the bobbin m_1 (thus forming an electro magnet of m, m_1), and by the wire w, direct through the fuzes to earth, and so explodes the torpedo. The effect of the telephone resistance·being cut out, is to strengthen the signalling current, and enable it to work the shutter apparatus and so throw the firing battery in circuit and explode the mine.

The advantages of this circuit closing apparatus are :—

1.—Simplicity.

2.—Compactness.

3.—Increased certainty of action, due to the sustained contact of the armature n, on the apparatus being struck.

4.—Additional means of testing a system of electrical submarine mines, which is afforded by the telephone : —

When this form of circuit closer is put in action by a friendly vessel coming in contact with it, or when experiments are being made, the signalling current must be reversed, so that no doubt may exist as to the armature n having dropped, on the apparatus coming to rest.

The telephone test indicates whether the circuit closer is in position or not, the shot, &c., within the telephone being shaken about by the movement of the buoyant circuit closer, the noise so created is readily distinguished by the receiving telephone at the station.

Another form of submarine mine is that known as the "Electro Mechanical" mine. The difference between this form and an ordinary mechanical mine is, that the exploding agent is electricity, and that it may be converted into an electro contact mine if desirable.

Description of a Russian Electro.—The electro mechanical mine, used by the Russians during the late Turco-Russian war, is shown in elevation and section at Figs. 62 and 63.

Mechanical Submarine Mine, used by them during the late Turco-Russian War.—A is the conical shaped case; B the loading hole; C the base plug; D, D, &c., are five horns, screwed into the head of the case A; these are composed of a glass tube A, containing a chlorate of potash mixture, enclosed in a lead tube B, over which is screwed a brass safety cylinder C; when ready for action this latter tube C is removed; directly beneath each of the horns A, on the inside of the case, as at E, is a thin brass cylinder, closed at one end by a piece of wood d, and containing several pieces of zinc and carbon, arranged in the form of a battery, the zinc and carbon wires z and x being led through the piece of wood d; F is a copper cylinder containing the priming charge of gun-cotton g, and detonating fuse f; the terminals of the fuze are connected to two insulated wires, w and w_1, the former of which is led direct to the loading hole B, and attached on the inside to the five zinc connecting wires z, &c.; the latter is attached to one end of a safety arrangement S, the other end of which is connected to the wire w_2, which is attached on the inside to the carbon wires x, &c.; the safety arrangement S consists of an ebonite cylinder, containing a brass spiral spring fixed to one end of it, and pressing against a brass plate at the other, thus preserving a metallic connection between the wires w_1, and w_2; the mine is rendered inactive by pressing the spring down, and inserting a piece of ebonite between it and the plate.

Its Action.—The action of this form of electro mechanical sub-marine mine is very simple; the brass safety cylinders c, c, &c., being removed on a vessel striking either of the horns, D, D, &c., the lead tube b is bent, causing the glass tube a to be broken, and the mixture contained therein to flow into the cylinder E, instantly generating a current of electricity in the zinc carbon battery, and exploding the mine.

Mode of Converting into an Electro Contact or Observation Mine.— To convert this mine into an electro contact one, it is only necessary to connect the wires w_1, and w_2 to other wires leading from the shore ; also by replacing the horns D, D by solid brass screw plugs, the mine may be converted into an ordinary observation one. In this case the two wires w and w_1 attached to the fuze f, terminals would have to be connected to the observation instruments on shore.

Turkish Vessel sunk.—It was by means of one of these electro mechanical mines, that the Turkish gunboat *Suna* was sunk at Soulina.

Firing by observation, that is to say, effecting the ignition of an electrical submarine mine at the precise moment of a hostile vessel being vertically over it, through the agency of one or two observers stationed at a very considerable distance from the mine, should, with the very perfect self-acting circuit closers that exist at the present time, be resorted to only in very exceptional cases, or in connection with the self-acting system.

There are two defects, which are common to all methods of firing submarine mines by observation, and these are :—

1.—At night time, or in foggy weather, it cannot be employed.

2.—It is necessary to employ at least two observers, at a considerable distance apart, who to effect a proper action at the right moment, must work in perfect unison. These defects alone are sufficient to explain the preference given to a self-acting method of closing the electric circuit at the precise moment of a vessel being in position over a mine by those governments who have adopted electrical submarine mines as a means of coast defence.

Methods of Firing by Observation.—There are several methods of firing by observation, of which the following are the ones principally used :—

1.—By pickets or range stakes.

2.—By cross bearings.

3.—By intersectional arcs fitted with telescopes.

4.—The Prussian system.

Intersection by Pickets or Range Stakes.—In narrow channels and at short distances, this system of ascertaining the relative position of a hostile vessel and a submarine mine may be used, provided that skilled and careful men are employed to work it. Two or more pickets or stakes are arranged in front of the firing station in such a manner that a vessel passing up the channel on the prolongation of these stakes will be over a mine. This arrangement should of course always be considered as an extempore one; it was used on several occasions by the Confederates during the American civil war.

Firing by Cross Bearings.—The simplest method of so determining the relative position of a vessel and a submarine mine, and exploding it at the right moment, is that in which observers are placed on the prolongation.of the mines. This mode is shown at Fig. 64, where m_1, m_2, m_3, &c., and n_1, n_2, n_3, &c., are the mines; A and B, the points in prolongation of the mines where the observers are stationed; D the firing battery, and s, and s_1 two hostile vessels.

At the stations A and B firing keys are placed, at the former one for each separate mine, perfectly distinct and insulated from each other, at the latter a single key. The pivot points of the series of keys at A are connected by separate wires to one pole of the firing battery D, the other pole of which is connected by a single cored insulated cable to the pivot point of the key at B; the contact points of the series of keys at A are connected by separate line wires as $A\ m_1$, $A\ m_2$, $A\ m_3$, &c., to the different mines, while the contact point of the key at B is put to earth. Thus it will be seen that, in the case of the row of mines, m_1, m_2, &c., unless the key at B, and the key at A, of either of those mines are both pressed down at the same instant, no current can pass, and therefore none of those mines can be exploded.

In the case of the vessel S, though at C, she is on the prolongation of the line $A\ m_3$, C, and therefore the key of the mine m_3, is pressed down at A, yet not being on the prolongation of the line B, E, the key at B is not pressed down, therefore the firing battery is not thrown in circuit, or the mine m_5 exploded, but when the vessel s reaches the position N, that is over the mine m_3, she being on the prolongation of the lines $A\ m_3$, and $B\ E$, the key (m_3) at A, and the key at B would both be pressed down, and therefore the mine m_3 exploded, and the ship destroyed. In the case of a vessel passing through an interval between any two mines at such a distance as to be out of the radius of destructive effect of either of the mines belonging to the first row (which is shown at s_1,) only the key at B would be pressed down, and thus the vessel enabled to pass safely through, but only to come

PLATE XVI

Fig 62

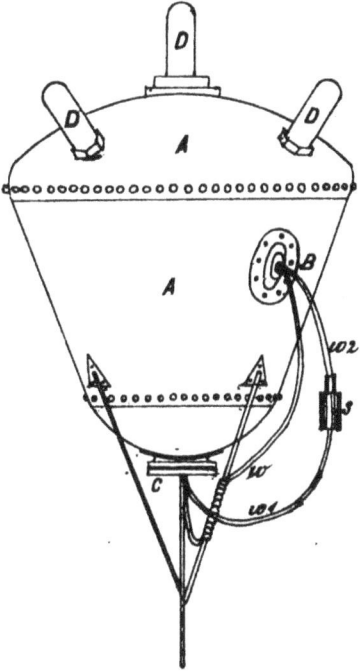

Fig 63

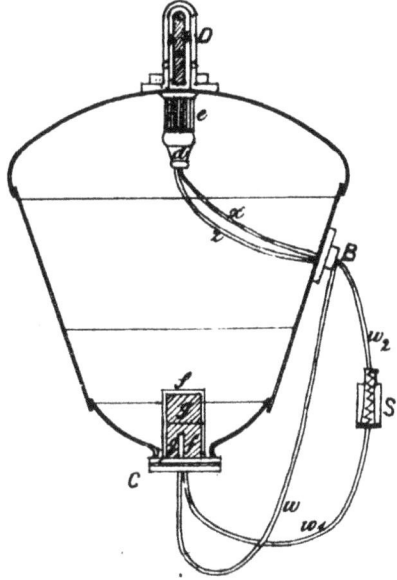

Fig 65

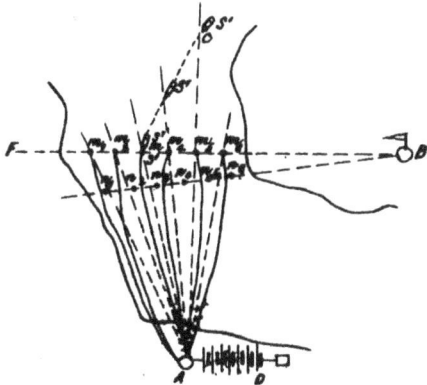

Fig 64

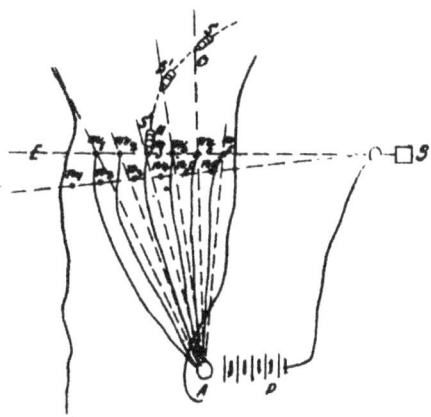

to grief at the second or third row of mines, provided they have been properly placed, and separate though similar arrangements as in the case of the line of mines, m_1, m_2, &c. have been made.

Firing by a Preconcerted Signal.—At Fig. 65 is represented a some-what similar, though a much simpler plan of the foregoing system, by employing a preconcerted signal at the station B in the place of the firing key and insulated cable, as in the former case. The only material difference in the arrangement of these two methods, is that in the latter case the pole of the firing battery at A, which in the former case was connected to the firing key at B, is put direct to earth. As will be readily understood, this latter system requires great coolness and nerve on the part of the operator at A, who has not only to watch the vessel passing across his intersections, but also to be on the alert to receive the signal from the observer at B. Should it ever be necessary to adopt this latter system, it will be found advisable to employ two men at station A, one to watch station B, the other to attend to the firing key and intersections. A separate signal-flag for each line of mines, and also a separate firing arrangement, would be required. As in many cases it would not be practicable to have a station in such an advanced position as at B, in Figs. 64 and 65, on account of the danger of its being cut off by an enemy, another com-bination becomes necessary. In this instance the station B is placed on the opposite side of the river, &c., to that on which the station A is placed, and a series of firing keys, instead of a single one, is here used, necessitating a multiple cable between the stations A and B, in the place of single cored cable ; the manner of manipulating this method is very similar to that previously described.

Firing by Intersectional Arcs fitted with Telescopes.—The foregoing methods of firing by cross bearings are replete with many serious defects, to remedy which, to a considerable extent, special arrange-ments have been devised, that is, the employment of intersectional arcs fitted with telescopes at the stations A and B.

Figs. 66 and 67 show the arrangements of these arcs, the former being the one used at the firing station A, the latter at the converging station B. At each station one arc is provided for each row of mines placed in position. The firing arc Fig. 66 consists of a cast iron frame a, with three feet b, b, b, these being provided with levelling screws.

To ascertain when this frame is level, a circular spirit level is attached thereto, a telescope d provided with one horizontal and three vertical cross wires, supported on Y's, admitting of vertical motion and attached to an upright e.   A mill-headed screw f enables the telescope d to be raised or lowered; the telescope, which is rigidly connected to a vernier g, traversing over a graduated arc h, can be moved rapidly in a lateral direction by means of a rack and pinion arrangement i, and it can be clamped in any position by means of the screw h. Sights are fixed on the telescope in a vertical plane passing through its axis. To the outer rim of the frame of the arc, which is smooth, are secured the sights $l\,l$ (shown on a large scale at Fig. 68), to give the direction of the mines. These sights are provided each with a brass point of V form, m, and a binding screw, n, in metallic connection with each other, but insulated by means of an ebonite plate from the rest of the metal of the sight. One end of a short piece of insulated wire is attached to the binding screw n, and the other passes through a hole in the base of the sight and projects below it ; o is a brass tube rigidly connected to and moving with the upright carrying the telescope d, and projecting in front of this latter. A brass spring p (see Fig. 69) is attached to, but insulated from the outer extremity of this tube, and is so arranged as to make contact with the V point m on the sight, by means of a corresponding projection fitted to its under side. An insulated wire passing the tube o, the outer end of which is connected to a screw on the spring p, forms a metallic connection between this projection and the firing key.

At Fig. 68 is shown an enlarged view of the front of the sight ; in addition to the V projection m, and binding screw n, it is fitted with a capstan-headed screw to bear against the inner rim of the frame, and a thin wire upright t for giving the alignment of the mine, to which a disc is attached, on which the number of the mine is affixed.

When the distance between the station and the mine is only about one mile, an ordinary eyepiece is used in the place of the telescope d.

At Fig. 67 is represented the arc employed at the converging station, which with the exception of there being no tube o, and only one sight, is precisely similar in construction to the one used at the firing station, and which has been described.

Application of the Intersectional Arc Method.—The application of the method of firing by observation, by means of intersectional arcs fitted with telescopes, is shown at Fig. 70. C, D, and E are three of the

PLATE XVII

Fig 66.

Fig 67

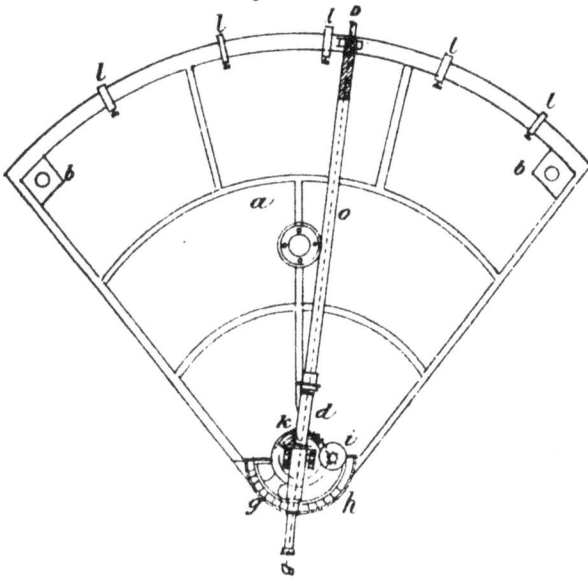
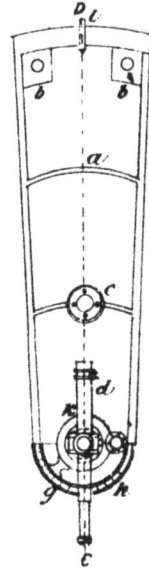

Fig 68

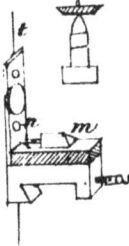

Fig 69.

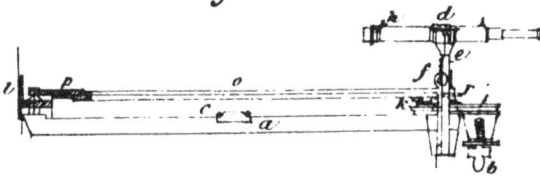

larger kind of arcs, one being used for each row of mines at the firing station *A*. At the converging station *B*, one of the smaller arcs is used for each row of mines, as shown at *F*, *G*, and *H*. *S*, S_1, S_2, are the signalling apparatus, the *F* terminals of which are connected to the sights *l*, *l*, *l*, Fig. 69, of arcs *C*, *D*, *E*. Firing keys *a*, *a*, *a* at station *A* are connected to each arc, and to three of the cores of the cable connecting the two stations *A* and *B*, respectively. At the converging station *B*, three firing keys *b*, *b*, *b* are connected to earth and to three cores of the connecting cable respectively. The remaining core of this cable is connected to the recording instruments *d*, *e*. The action of the arcs, &c., will be readily understood from the diagram at Fig. 70.

This arrangement does not interfere with the action of the circuit closer, as all that is effected by the observing arc circuit is to put the signalling battery current at the converging station *B* to earth instead of at the circuit closer.

Prussian System of Firing by Observation.—The principle on which this system is based, depends upon the proposition that if *c d*, in the triangle shown in Fig. 71, be always kept parallel to *H B*, then *A c*, *c d*, *d A* bear exactly the same proportion to each other as *A B*, *B H*, *H A* do to one another ; so that by means of the small triangle *A d c*, the lengths of the sides of the large triangle *A B H* can be obtained, and hence the position of the point *H*, the base *A B* being of course known. In Fig. 71 at *A* there is a slate table representing the roadstead, and upon it the exact position of every torpedo is laid down, corresponding to their position in the roadstead. At *A* and *B*, 500 yards apart, telescopes having cross wires are placed ; at *A* a long narrow straight-edged strip of glass *A d* is arranged to move in unison with the telescope at *A*; and by the application of dynamo electricity, a similarly constructed piece of glass *c d* moves in exact unison with the telescope at *B*, and having its pivot at *C*; that is to say, *C d* keeps parallel with *B H*, the line of sight of the observer at *B*.

Then if the observers at *A* and *B* have got a ship in their telescopes, the point of intersection *d* of the two pieces of glass *A d* and *C d* gives the position of the ship on the slate table at *A*, and when this point *d* comes over the position of any one mine on the slate, it is known that the ship is over that particular mine in the harbour, and she may be destroyed accordingly, by throwing the firing battery into circuit.

By the employment of electricity and a mirror, the great defect of this method, viz., the necessity of employing four people to manipulate it, would be remedied. The foregoing is a modification of Siemens's method of ascertaining distances at sea, &c.

Rules observed in Planting Mines.—In placing a system of submarine mines in position, the following are some of the chief points to be attended to, this work depending in a great measure on local circumstances, and on the method that is to be adopted in exploding and mooring them :—

1.—The plan of defence must be carefully laid down on a chart, on a scale of not less than six inches to the mile, and on this plan are to be marked the sites of the observing stations, the positions of each mine, circuit closer, and junction box, with their corresponding numbers, and also of the electric cables.

2.—The position of each mine having been determined, should be marked off by buoys.

3.—The utmost care should be taken to lay the electric cables, so that they shall be as far as possible away from the mines in the vicinity of which it may be necessary to take them, so as to lessen the liability of injury to them, by the explosion of the latter.

4.—The electric cables should be laid parallel, and never be allowed to cross directly over each other, otherwise the operation of underrunning them will be much complicated, also a certain amount of slack should be allowed to facilitate in picking the cables up for repair, &c.

5.—Every manner of device is to be used to conceal the electric cables, such as laying dummies, making detours inland, &c.

6.—All marks indicating position of the mines to be removed, after the mines have been placed in position.

7.—The identity of each cable and mine to be very carefully preserved throughout, by means of a number.

8.—A number of electro contact mines should be placed in advance of the leading line of mines, at irregular intervals, to prevent the enemy, having once ascertained the position of one mine of a line, from knowing within limits the position of the others of that line.

PLATE XVIII

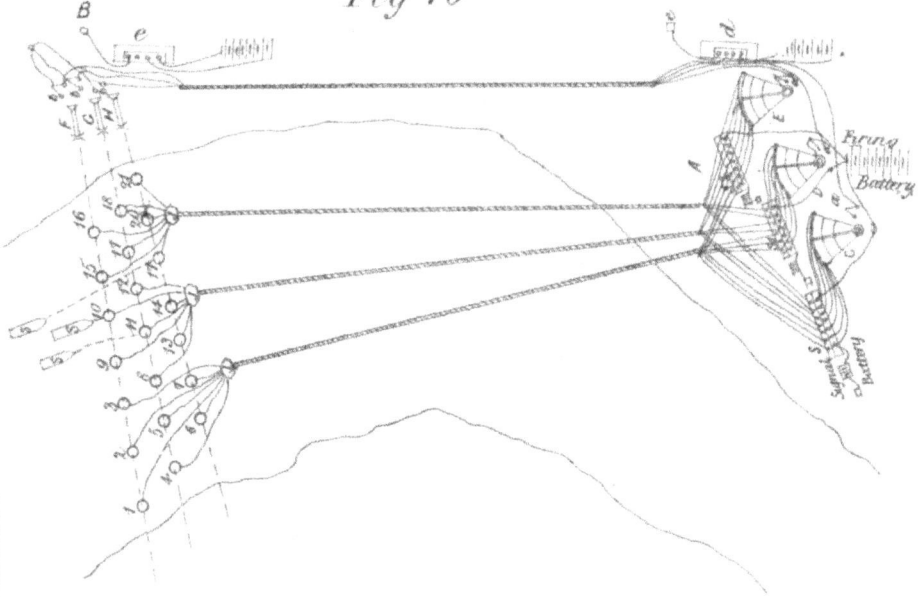

Fig 70

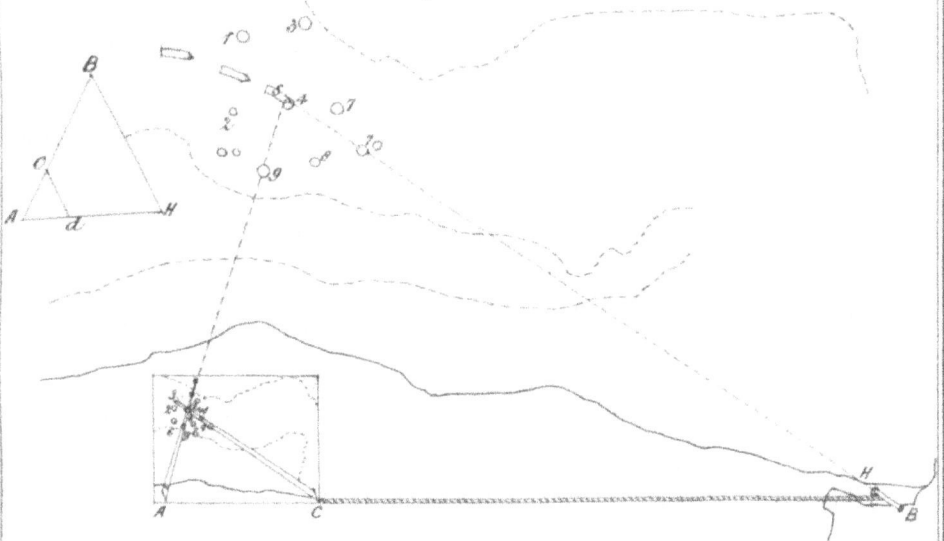

Fig 71

In connection with a system of defence by electrical submarine mines, the following batteries are required :—

1.—Firing battery.

2.—Signalling, or shutter battery.

3.—Testing battery.

4.—Telegraph battery.

Firing Battery.—The firing battery should be suited to the nature of the fuze employed, and should possess considerable excess of power to enable it to overcome accidental defects, such as increased resistance in the various connections, or defective insulation in the line wire, &c.

As platinum wire or low tension fuzes are now universally adopted as the mode of ignition for submarine mines, it will be only necessary to describe those electrical batteries which are most suitable as an exploding agent in connection with such fuzes ; these are as follows:—

1.—Siemens's dynamo low tension machine.

2.—Von Ebner's Voltaic battery.

3.—Chromic acid or Bichromate Voltaic battery.

4.—Leclanché's Voltaic battery.

Siemens's Low Tension Dynamo Electrical Machine.—This instrument consists of an electro magnet and an ordinary Siemens armature, which, by the turning of a handle, is caused to revolve between the poles of the electro magnet. The coils of the electro magnet are in circuit with the wire of the revolving armature, and during rotation the residual magnetism of the soft iron electro magnet cores at first excites weak currents which pass into the electro magnet coils, increasing the magnetism of the core, thus inducing still stronger currents in the armature wire. This accumulation by mutual action goes on until the limit of magnetic saturation of the iron cores of the electro magnets is reached.

By the automatic action of the machine, the powerful current so produced is sent into the leading wire or cable to the fuze to be exploded.

In this apparatus the electric current passes continuously through the line wire until a sufficiently powerful current is generated to heat or fuze the bridge of the fuze, and so ignite the gun-cotton priming. The coils of the armature and electro magnets are wound with wire of large diameter, to a total resistance of 8 to 10 Siemens units, or 7·6 to 9·5 ohms, in about 2,000 windings.

With a platinum wire weighing 1·65 grains per yard, 6½ inches can be fuzed on short circuit, and 14 inches can be heated to redness.

The total weight of this machine, which is manufactured by Messrs. Siemens Brothers, is about 60 lbs.

Advantages of Siemens's Dynamo Electrical Machine.—The advantages of such a machine over Voltaic apparatus are :—

1.—The absence of chemical agents.

2.—There is less liability to get out of order.

3.—No special knowledge is required to work them, or to keep them in order.

4.—Greater durability.

The great defect of this and all similar machines is that the electric force has to be developed by turning a handle for a certain time before it is possible to generate a current sufficiently powerful to ignite a fuze, which defect, in connection with a system of defence by self-acting submarine mines, particularly at night, renders them inferior to Voltaic batteries, as under such circumstances, an apparatus is required that will cause an electric current to flow at any moment when the circuit is completed.

The application of steam power would to a certain extent remedy the above-mentioned defect, but the cost of such a method, compared to that of a Voltaic arrangement, would be far too great to allow of its superseding the latter arrangement.

Von Ebner's Voltaic Battery.—This form of Voltaic battery, which may be considered as a modification of that known as Smee's, was designed by Baron von Ebner, colonel of the Austrian imperial corps of engineers, for use in connection with the Austrian system of submarine defence, by self-acting electrical mines.

A section of one of these cells is shown at Fig. 72. It consists of a glass vessel *a*, to contain the diluted sulphuric acid, within which is suspended a plate *b* of platinised lead, which is bent round into a cylindrical form to fit close around the inner surface of the glass vessel. In the centre of this latter is hung a porcelain perforated cup *c*, containing some cut-up zinc and mercury to keep it (the zinc) amalgamated. The top of each cell is furnished with a porcelain cover, through which the wires attached to the positive and negative poles of the cell project.

Due to the large quantity of liquid contained in the cell, the tendency to alter its internal resistance is retarded; also by the arrangement of the porcelain cup, above detailed, the consumption of zinc and mercury, which in an ordinary Voltaic battery is very considerable, is materially diminished.

Chromic Acid or Bichromate Battery.—This form of battery is very similar to Grove's, the difference being that, in the place of the nitric acid as the exciting liquid, either chromic acid, or a solution of bichromate of potash, sulphuric acid and water is substituted.

A form of this battery, as designed by Dr. Hertz, is used in connection with the German system of torpedo defence.

Leclanché Voltaic Battery.—This form of Voltaic battery was invented by M. Leclanché, some twelve years ago. At Fig. 73 is shown a cell of this battery in its original form. The positive pole *a* consists of a plate of graphite in a porous pot *b*, and surrounded by a mixture of peroxide of manganese and graphite. The negative pole *c* is a rod or pencil of amalgamated zinc. The whole is enclosed in an outer vessel of glass *d* containing a solution of sal ammoniac.

A modified form of the Leclanché cell as used in a firing battery is shown at Fig. 74. It consists of an ebonite trough or outer vessel *a* about 16' long, 9" deep, and 2¾" wide. The negative pole or zinc plate *b* is of similar shape to the trough *a*, but with its base removed, and does not fit the trough exactly, the space between it and the trough being left to ensure the former being completely surrounded by the sal ammoniac solution; the positive pole, or carbon element, consists of four gas carbon plates *c* attached together at their head by means of lead, and enclosed in a flannel bag, in which they are firmly embedded in the peroxide of manganese mixture; the positive element is of such a shape that it fits loosely between the sides, and is nearly of the same height as the zinc plate.

The object of such a form of cell was to obtain an electric current of large *quantity*, with as few cells as possible, by which means the loss of power which might occur from the employment of a great number of small cells is avoided.

Advantages of a Leclanché Firing Battery.—The advantages of the Leclanché firing battery are : —

1.—The absence of chemical action when the battery circuit is not complete, and consequently there is no waste of material.
2.—Requires little or no looking after.

3.—It may be kept ready for action in store without in any way
deteriorating.

4.—It is comparatively very cheap.

These advantages combine to make a Leclanché battery the most
suitable of any other form of electrical battery for use as the exploding
agent for electrical submarine mines, and it is now universally used
for such purposes.

Signalling Battery.—The signalling battery should be so constituted
as to be capable of working the electro magnet of the shutter apparatus effectually when the circuit is closed direct to earth, and yet
not so powerful as by the continuous passage of the current generated
by it to fire the fuze in the mine. In the case of a platinum wire
fuze being in the circuit, plenty of power may be given to the battery
without fear of a premature explosion from this cause, but in the case
of a high tension fuze it is necessary to be very careful in order to
guard against such a contingency.

As in the case of a signalling or shutter battery, the electric
current will be continually flowing, it is necessary to employ a constant
battery, or one that requires least trouble and expense to maintain it
in working order, and it is for this reason that a modified form of
Daniell battery has been adopted to work the shutter apparatus.

Daniell Signalling Battery.—At Fig. 75 is shown the manner of
arranging a Daniell cell. A glass or porcelain vessel *a* contains a
saturated solution of sulphate of copper, in which is immersed a copper
cylinder *b* open at both ends and perforated by holes; at the upper
part of this cylinder there is an annular shelf *d*, also perforated by
holes, and below the level of the liquid; this is for the purpose of
supporting crystals of sulphate of copper for the replacing of that
decomposed as the electrical action proceeds. Inside the cylinder *b*
is a thin porous vessel *c* of unglazed earthenware; this contains either
water, or a solution of common salt, or dilute sulphuric acid, in which
is placed the cylinder of amalgamated zinc *e*. Two strips of copper
p and *n*, fixed by binding screws to the copper and to the zinc, serve
for connecting the elements in series, or otherwise.

For the purposes of testing, either the Leclanché or Daniell battery
specially arranged, or the Menotti battery, which is really a modification of the Daniell, may be used.

Description of a Menotti Cell.—A Menotti cell, shown at Fig. 76,

PLATE XIX

Fig 72

Fig 73

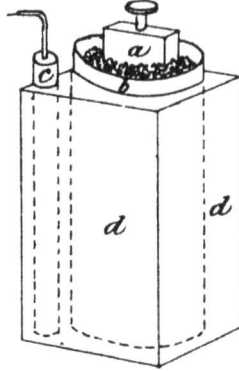

Fig 74

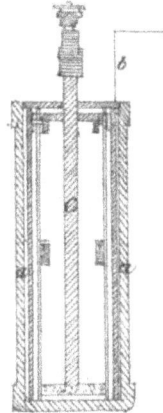

Fig 75

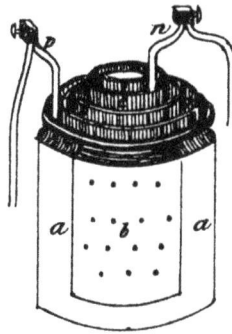

Fig 76

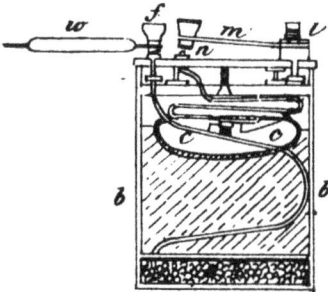

Fig 77

consists of a copper cup containing some crystals of sulphate of copper and covered with a fearnought diaphragm *a*, placed at the bottom of an ebonite cell *b* ; over this cup is put some sawdust, and resting on top of this is a disc of zinc *c* on another piece of fearnought. The upper portion of the zinc and its connection with the insulated wire are carefully insulated. Fresh water poured on the sawdust renders the battery active.

Description of a Menotti Test Battery.—Fig. 77 represents a plan of the top of such a test battery with a 20-ohm galvanometer attached thereto. The connections are made as follows :—

One of the wires *w* of the object to be tested is attached to the terminal *f*, which is also connected by an insulated wire to the copper cup *a* ; the other main wire w_1 is attached to the terminal *g* of the galvanometer ; *h*, the other terminal of the galvanometer, is connected by a short piece of wire *k* to the terminal *l* of the contact key *m* ; and the contact point *n* is in connection with the zinc plate *c* ; thus the current from the battery flows along the wire *w* through the object to be tested, back along the wire w_1, through the coils of the galvanometer, along the wire *k* to the contact key *m*, and if this is pressed down to the zinc plate *c*, so completing the circuit.

To steady the needle of the galvanometer a bar magnet is used, which is inserted in the space *r*. The whole of the apparatus is enclosed in a leathern case fitted with a cover and strap.

This is a very compact and simple form of test battery, and will be found extremely useful in boats, &c., when placing mines in position.

Telegraph Battery.—For the purposes of telegraphing between torpedo stations, &c., a form of Leclanché battery, known as No. 3 commercial pattern, is generally used.

Voltaic Batteries.—The following points in connection with the use of voltaic batteries, which are taken from Beechey's ' Electro Telegraphy,' should be carefully observed : —

1.—Each cell of a battery should be carefully insulated.

2.—The floors and tables in the battery room should be kept scrupulously clean and dry, so as to prevent the least leakage or escape of the current.

3.—The plates of a battery should be clean.

4.—Porous cells should be examined, and cracked ones replaced.

5.—No sulphate of zinc or dirt should be allowed to collect at the lips of the cells.

In the case of a Daniell battery—

1.—The solutions should be inspected daily, and crystals of sulphate of copper added as required.

2.—The zinc plate must not touch the porous cell, or copper will be deposited on it (the zinc).

3.—The battery should be charged with sulphate of zinc from the first.

4.—The copper solution must be watched and prevented from rising over the edge of the porous jar, the tendency of such solutions being to mix with each other by an action termed *osmosis*.

These being in addition to foregoing general directions for Voltaic batteries.

Defects in a Voltaic Battery on its Current becoming Deficient.—On the electric current of a Voltaic battery becoming deficient, the following defects should be looked for :—

1.—Solutions exhausted; for instance, sulphate of copper in a Daniell's entirely or nearly gone, leaving a colourless solution.

2.—Terminals or connections between the cells corroded, so that instead of metallic contact there are oxides of almost insulating resistance intervening in the circuit.

3.—Cells empty, or nearly so.

4.—Filaments of deposited metals stretching from electrode (pole) to electrode (pole).

Also intermittent currents are sometimes produced by loose wires or a broken electrode, which alternately makes and breaks contact when shaken. Inconstant currents are also sometimes produced when batteries are shaken. The motion shakes the gases off the electrodes, thus increasing temporarily the electro-motive force of the battery.

Firing Keys and Shutter Apparatus.—The following is a description of the various firing keys and shutter signalling apparatus, which is used in connection with a system of electrical submarine mines. By means of the former the firing or other batteries may be thrown into circuit at will, whilst by means of the latter the firing battery is thrown in circuit without the aid of an operator, and a signal at the same instant given, indicating that a certain mine of the system has been struck.

Description of a Series of Firing Keys.—At Fig. 78 is shown a plan and section of a series of firing keys as arranged for firing several mines by observation.

It consists of a strong wooden frame *a*, of a convenient form for the purpose of attaching it to the firing table by screws through the holes *b, b*. On this frame a series of keys *c, c, c* are fixed at convenient intervals. These consist of a strong brass spring firmly screwed to a series of brass plates *d, d, d* on the front of the wooden box *a*. From these latter short copper wires pass through the woodwork, and of such a length that, when required, the mine wires may be easily attached by means of binding screws, as shown at *f*. The inner end of each key is fitted with an ebonite knob (which is shown at *c* in the section) to insulate the hand of the operator when using the key. On the frame, and directly under each of the ebonite knobs, are arranged a series of metallic points *g, g, g*, so placed that on either of the keys *c* being pressed down, a perfect contact is made between it and its respective metallic point; *h, h, h* are copper wires leading from the metallic points *g, g, g* through the box, and of such a length that binding screws *f, f, f* can be easily attached to them when necessary.

A single firing key of an improved form is shown at Fig. 79. It consists of a strong wooden box *a a*, weighted at the bottom with lead in order to steady the key on the table, &c., on which it may be placed; on the inside of the bottom of the box is fixed a piece of ebonite, by which means the metallic point *b*, and the terminal of the firing key *c*, are insulated from each other; *d d'* are two terminals at the end of the box, to which the circuit wires are attached, one of these terminals is connected in metallic circuit to the firing key at *c*, the other one to the metallic point *b*; a wooden cover *h*, fitted with a catch *k*, protects the connections of the wires; by means of a plate, and catch *e e*, the key can be rendered inactive, thus preventing the danger of a premature closing of the electric circuit; by means of a spring *s* a break is always established between the key and the metallic point. It is immaterial to which of the two terminals *d d'* either wire is connected.

The Morse Firing Key.—This form of key is so well known in connection with the Morse telegraph, that it is not necessary to describe it.

It is usually employed in torpedo work in connection with a testing and firing table.

The Shutter Apparatus.—The shutter signalling and firing apparatus was devised to enable the firing battery current to be thrown in circuit without the aid of a personal operator, the signalling current (which is always kept in circuit) at the same instant ringing a bell, by which is known the particular mine that has been struck.

At Fig. 80 is represented a diagram of such an apparatus. *a* is an armature working on a pivot between the two horns of an electro magnet *b b*, and held in position by a spiral spring *c*; the latter is in connection with a regulating screw, by which more or less pressure may be brought to bear in an opposite direction to that of the attractive action of the electro magnet. A stud *i* regulates the distance to which the armature may be drawn back; *d* is a shutter on which a reference number for each mine should be indicated, attached to a lever pivoted at the point *e*, the inner arm of which is just long enough to catch under the point of the armature *a*; when a current of sufficient strength is passed through the coils *b b* of the electro magnet, the armature *a* is attracted, releasing the lever attached to the shutter *d*, which by its own weight falls into the position shown by the dotted lines. *f* and *g* are two mercury cups, the former being in connection with the signalling current, and the latter with the firing current. When the lever is horizontal and the shutter drawn up and ready for action, the circuit of the signalling battery *s* is completed through the mercury cup *f*, along an arm *h* of the lever to the pivot *e*, and thence to the mine by the line wire *w*. When the circuit closer is struck by a passing vessel, and consequently the shutter thrown into the position shown by the dotted lines, another arm *k*, a prolongation of the lever, falls into the mercury cup *g*, which latter is in connection with the firing battery *F*. The armature *a* is prevented from coming into actual contact with the horns of the electro magnet by two small studs. The object of this is to prevent any effect of residual magnetism which might otherwise interfere with the rapidity of action of the armature when released and drawn back by the spring *c*.

PLATE XX

Fig 78

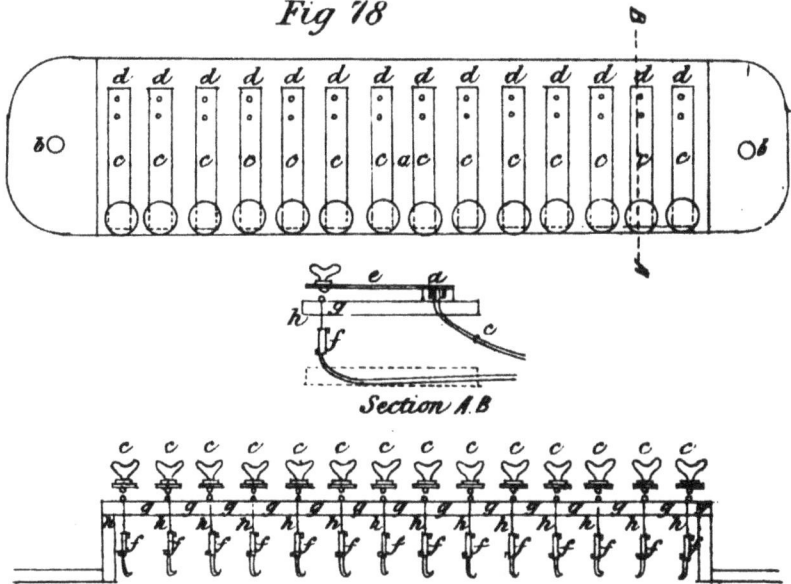

Section A.B

Fig 79

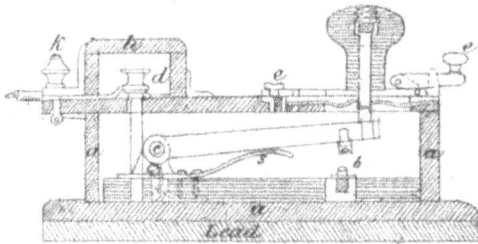

Fig 80.

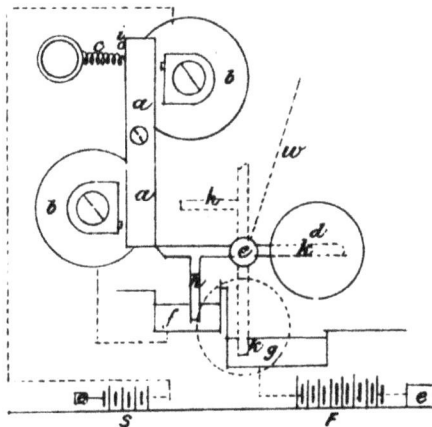

The object of employing Mercury Cups.—Mercury cups were devised in the place of the springs used in connection with the original design of a shutter apparatus, for the reason that electrical circuits dependent on the pressure of springs are always liable to interruption from dirt or oxide intervening between the points of contact.

Shutter Apparatus used with a Circuit Breaker.—When the circuit breaking system is used with the shutter signalling apparatus, the action of the armature in releasing the lever must be reversed; that is to say, that when the current is passing and the armature a attracted to the electro magnet b b, the shutter d must be held up, and when the current ceases, and the armature a drawn back by the spring c, the lever must be released, and the shutter allowed to fall. This is effected by altering the end of the lever, so that it hooks into, instead of abutting against the armature a.

To each shutter apparatus an electric bell is fitted, by which notice is given when a circuit closer has been struck. For general service, a box containing seven such shutter signalling and firing apparatus has been adopted, a plan of which is represented at Figs. 81, 82 and 83. The connections of the different circuits are as follows:—

The insulated wire of the upper bobbin of the electro magnet is connected to the spring of the armature; the pivot of the lever is connected with the right-hand terminal B, or main line connection on the top of the box; the insulated wire from the lower bobbin is connected to the middle brass plate k in the front ledge of the apparatus, the circuit from B to k being thus completed. The front adjoining brass plate A, provided with a terminal, is connected with the negative pole of the signalling battery, the positive pole being put to earth.

On a brass plug being put in the hole l, the signalling current will flow to the plate k, thence through the lower and upper bobbin to the spring of the armature, along the latter to the shutter lever, and from the pivot through the main line wire to the mine. The innermost brass plates H H are all connected in the same metallic circuit, and to them are attached by means of the binding screw D the test battery and galvanometer. Thus on the brass plug being removed from l, and placed in m, the signalling battery is cut out of circuit, and the test battery thrown in. In this way the condition of each individual mine may be ascertained while the connections of the remaining mines are left undisturbed. The positive pole of the firing battery (the negative being to earth) is connected to the terminal S at the right-hand corner of the lower ledge of the box; the plate to which the terminal S is fixed is divided at G, the left-hand portion being connected to a bar which runs horizontally the whole length of the box, and in metallic connection with each mercury cup g, Fig. 80. A brass plug is placed in the hole G, and when from any cause the lever drops, the firing battery will be thrown into circuit, and the mine to which the lever that has fallen is attached will be exploded.

Shutter Instrument and Observing Telescope.—Each mine is given a number, which is put on the disc of the shutter instrument connected to it, and also on the corresponding tablet C. From the brass plate in connection with the spring c, Fig. 80, a wire is taken to the terminal f, Fig. 81, on top of the box. From this terminal a wire is led to the connections of the observing telescope, and thus the mines can be fired by judgment if required, without the aid of the circuit closer.

The signal battery current is always circulating, even when the system is in a state of rest, but in consequence of the resistance placed in this circuit, which may be either a resistance coil in the circuit, added to the resistance of the fuzes, when high tension fuzes are used, or only the former resistance in the case of low tension fuzes, this current is too feeble to form an electro magnet; directly, however, a circuit closer is struck, this resistance is cut out, and thus the signal battery current becomes sufficiently powerful to work the electro magnet of that particular mine.

The circuit of the signal battery, and that to the observing telescope, are broken the instant the lever commences to fall.

To enable the apparatus to be used on the circuit breaking system, a spare lever E is provided for that purpose with each box.

The object to be gained by a system of testing is to ascertain the condition of the electrical submarine mines placed in the defence of a harbour, &c., and should there exist any fault, not only to detect its exact position and cause, but also its magnitude, so that it may be at once determined whether it is necessary to remedy the fault, or whether the electrical apparatus is sufficiently powerful to overcome the defect.

Tests.—There are two distinct kinds of tests, viz. :—

1.—Mechanical tests.

2.—Electrical tests.

SHUTTER APPARATUS.

PLATE XXI

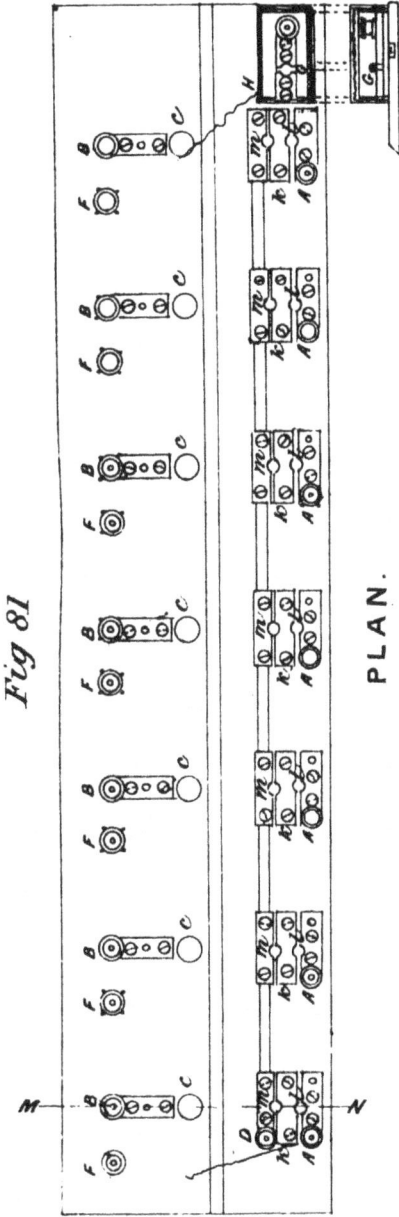

Fig 81

PLAN.

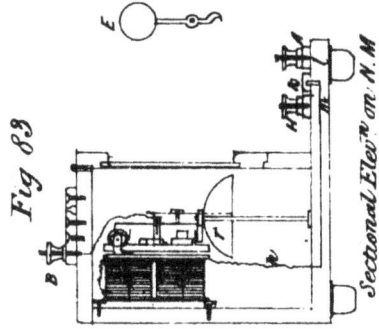

Fig 83

Sectional Elev:ᵒⁿ on N.M.

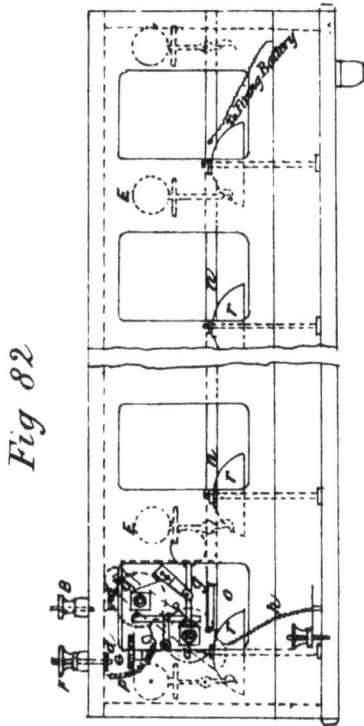

Fig 82

Mechanical tests are applied to ascertain that the mechanical arrangements of the shutter apparatus, circuit closers, and all similar appliances work efficiently and easily ; that the several parts of the mine case when put together for service are thoroughly watertight ; that the chains, wire cables, and ropes in connection with the mooring apparatus are of sufficient strength to perform the work required of them ; that the weights of the anchors, or sinkers, are such as to keep the mines in position after submersion ; and that the case of the mine be sufficiently strong to enable it to bear the external pressure due to the depth at which it may be submerged for a considerable time without any leakage.

The foregoing tests of the mine case and moorings would of course be performed during the process of manufacture, but to prevent any chance of failure they should be repeated before being employed on actual service.

Electrical Tests.—Electrical tests are those which are applied to the several component parts of the system, to ascertain that the electrical conditions necessary to a successful result exist.

The importance of being able to carry out the above in its entirety is understood when it is remembered that a submarine mine becomes practically valueless unless it acts efficiently at the single instant of time that it would be required so to do.

List of Instruments used in Testing.—The following are some of the instruments that are employed in connection with a system of electrical tests :—

1.—Thomson's electrometer.
2.—Thomson's reflecting galvanometer.
3.—Astatic galvanometer.
4.—Differential galvanometer.
5.—Detector galvanometer.
6.—Three coil galvanometer.
7.—Thermo galvanometer.
8.—Siemens's universal galvanometer.
9.—A shunt.
10.—Commutator.
11.—Rheostat.
12.—Resistance coils.
13.—Wheatstone's balance.

Electrometers indicate the presence of a statical charge of electricity, by showing the force of attraction or repulsion between two conducting bodies placed near together. This force depending in the first place on the quantity of electricity with which the conducting bodies are charged, ultimately depends on the difference of potential between them; an electrometer is therefore strictly an instrument for measuring difference of potential.*

Sir William Thomson's quadrant electrometer is the most perfect form of electrometer yet constructed, and the one usually employed in cable testing. It consists of a very thin flat aluminium needle spread out into two wings, and hung by a wire from an insulated stem inside a Leyden jar, which contains a cupful of strong sulphuric acid, the outer surface of which forms the inner coating of the Leyden jar. A wire stretched by a weight connects the aforesaid needle with this inner coating. A mirror, rigidly attached to this needle by a rod, serves to indicate the deflection of the needle by reflecting the image of a flame on to a scale. The needle hangs inside four quadrants, which are insulated by glass stems: each pair of opposite quadrants are in electrical connection. Above and below the quadrants two tubes, at the same potential as the needle, serve to screen it and the wires in connection with it from all induction except that produced by the four quadrants. Suppose the needle charged to a high negative potential (—), then if the quadrants are symmetrically placed, it will deflect neither to the right nor to the left, so long as the near quadrants are at the same potential. If one of these be positive relatively to the other, the end of the needle under them will be repelled from the negative quadrant to the positive one, and at the same time the other end of the needle will be repelled from in the opposite direction. This motion will be indicated by the motion of the spot of light reflected by the mirror, and the number of divisions which the spot of light traverses on the scale measures in an arbitrary unit the difference of potential between the + and — quadrants.

The reflecting electrometer being a very delicate instrument, requires careful handling, and should only be used by a practised electrician. Its use would therefore be restricted to important stations, and special tests of a delicate nature.

---

* 'Electricity and Magnetism,' by Professor F. Jenkins.

Thomson's Reflecting Galvanometer.—A galvanometer is an instrument intended to detect the presence of a current and measure its magnitude.

The most sensitive galvanometer as yet constructed is the reflecting galvanometer of Sir William Thomson, a diagram of which is shown at Fig. 84.

A small piece of magnetised steel watch spring, $\frac{3}{8}$ths of an inch long, is fastened with shellac on the back of a little round concave mirror, and of about the size of a fourpenny piece. This is suspended by a piece of unspun silk thread in the centre of a coil of many hundred turns of fine copper wire insulated with silk, and well protected between the turns with varnish. The two ends of the coils are soldered to terminal screws *a*, *b*, so that any conducting wire can be joined up to it as required. The little mirror hangs in the middle of its coil, with the magnet lying horizontally. By means of a lamp *L* placed behind the screen, the light of which passes through a slit *M*, and is thrown on the face of the mirror, a spot of light is reflected on the scale *N*.

When a current passes through the coil, the little magnet is deflected, and since the magnet is attached to the mirror, which is very light, both are deflected as forming one body, and the spot of light moves accordingly along the scale *N*.

A powerful steel magnet *S* is placed above the coil, and can be moved up or down, whereby the directive force of the earth may be increased or weakened. This magnet *S* is used to steady the spot of light, which otherwise would shake about, and there would be no certainty about the measurement. A second magnet *T* is placed perpendicular to the magnetic meridian, to adjust the zero of the instrument, i.e., to bring back the spot of light to a fiducial mark at the centre of the scale when no current is passing.

This instrument should only be used at important stations, and when special tests of a delicate nature are required to be applied.

Astatic Galvanometer.—An astatic galvanometer is that in connection with which an astatic needle is employed, by the use of which the sensitiveness of a galvanometer is greatly increased.

An astatic needle is a combination of magnetised needles *with their poles turned opposite ways*.

At Fig. 85 a diagram of such an instrument is shown. Two

magnets D and C are joined, with the north pole of one over the south pole of the other, forming one suspended system. In the ordinary form of astatic galvanometer the needles D and C are about two inches long, and are each covered by a coil, these latter being so joined that the current must circulate in opposite directions round the two so as to deflect both magnets similarly. The deflection of the needles D and C is observed by means of a pointer or glass needle A, B, rigidly connected with the astatic system by a prolongation of the brass rod connecting the needles D and C. The coils are flat and of the shape indicated in Fig. 85, and are also made in two halves, placed side by side with just sufficient space between them to allow the rod to hang freely.

This form of galvanometer, though less delicate than the preceding one, is still a very sensitive one, and should only be applied in the case of fine and delicate tests.

Differential Galvanometer.—A differential galvanometer consists of a magnetic needle surrounded by two separate coils of equal length and material carefully insulated from each other and wound in opposite directions. In using it one circuit acts against the other. If a current of equal strength were passing through each there would be no deflection of the needle, because the influence in both directions is equal. If one current were stronger than the other, the needle would be deflected by the stronger.

This form of galvanometer will be found extremely useful in connection with a system of electrical tests.

Latimer Clark's double shunt differential galvanometer is the instrument best adapted for submarine mine tests.

Detector Galvanometer.—A detector galvanometer is usually made with a vertical needle, and is employed to detect and roughly estimate the strength of a current where no particular accuracy is required.

It consists of a magnetic needle pivoted in the centre of a coil of insulated wire, and having an index needle attached to move with it, the latter appearing on a dial, divided into 360 equal arcs or portions : a diagram of such an instrument is shown at Fig. 86.

This instrument should be of small size and portable form, and as sensitive as it is possible to make it, under such conditions.

Three Coil Galvanometer.—The three coil galvanometer is provided with a vertical needle, and is in other respects very similar in appearance to the detector galvanometer before described.   It is formed with three coils of 2, 10, and 1000 ohms resistance ; each coil is connected with a brass plate on the top of the box which encloses the whole, and may be switched into circuit by means of a plug at will.   The object of the three resistances is to suit the different resistances that may occur, with a perfect, or imperfect state of the electrical combination in connection with each mine.   A diagram of this instrument is shown at Fig. 87, the dotted portions are inside the case.

Thermo Galvanometer.—A thermo galvanometer is an instrument used to ascertain the power of a firing battery which is employed to ignite platinum wire or low tension fuzes.

The form of thermo galvanometer generally used in connection with a test table, is arranged as follows :—

Two ebonite studs, fitted with brass connecting screws, are fixed to the lid of a box containing some resistance coils, and placed in circuit with them ; these studs, placed about ·3 of an inch apart, are arranged to receive a piece of platinum wire which is stretched from one stud to the other; the firing battery being placed in circuit with the platinum wire, and the resistance coils, its working power would then be tested by the fusion of the wire through a given electrical resistance, as indicated by the resistance coils put in circuit.

Another form of thermo galvanometer, which is very compact and portable, is shown at Fig. 88.   It consists of a wooden box *a*, with a cover of ebonite *b*, within the box is placed a resistance coil *c* ; *d* and *e* are two ebonite standards ·3 " apart, the former of which is connected by a copper wire with the terminal *f*, the latter to the terminal *g* ; the terminal *h* is similarly connected to the contact piece *k*, and the terminal *l* to the firing key *m*, at *n* ; the resistance coil *c* is connected to the terminal *g* and to the copper wire *n* ; the platinum wire (of which several lengths are used, according to the resistance of the coil *c*) is placed between the standards *d* and *e*.   To test a battery, it is only necessary to connect it to the terminals *f* and *h*, when by pressing down the key *m* the power of the battery, according as to its fusing or not the platinum wires, will be ascertained ; the use of the terminals *g* and *l* is to cut out the resistance, which is effected by connecting them by means of a copper wire.

Siemens's Universal Galvanometer.—Siemens's universal galvano-

H

meter is an instrument combining in itself all the arrangements necessary for the following operations :—

1.—For measuring electrical resistances.

2.—For comparing electromotive forces.

3.—For measuring the intensity of a current.

The instrument which is shown in elevation and plan at Pl. xxiii., Figs. 1 and 2 respectively, consists of a sensitive galvanometer which can be turned in a horizontal plane, combined with a resistance bridge (the wire of which bridge instead of being straight is stretched round part of a circle).   The galvanometer has an astatic needle, suspended by a cocoon fibre, and a flat bobbin frame wound with fine wire.   The needle swings above a cardboard dial divided in degrees ; as however, when using the instrument the deflection of the needle is never read off, but the needle instead always brought to zero, two ivory limiting pins are placed at about 20 degrees on each side of zero.

The galvanometer is fixed on a graduated slate disc, round which the platinum wire is stretched.   Underneath the slate disc three resistance coils of the value of 10, 100, and 1000 Siemens' units are wound on a hollow wooden block, which protrudes at one side, and on the projection carries the terminals for the reception of the leading wires from the battery and unknown resistance.   The adoption of three different resistance coils enables the measuring of large as well as small resistances with sufficient accuracy.

The whole instrument is mounted on a wooden disc, which is supported by three levelling screws, so that it may be turned round its axle.   On the same axle a lever is placed which bears at its end an upright arm, carrying a contact roller.   This roller is pressed against the platinum wire round the edge of the slate disc by means of a spring acting on the upright arm, and forms the junction between the A and B resistances of a Wheatstone's bridge, which resistances are formed by the platinum wire on either side of the contact roller, one of the three resistance coils forming the third resistance of the bridge. G is the galvanometer, k a milled head from which the needles are suspended, and by turning k they can be raised or lowered, m is the head of a screw which arrests or frees the needle when in motion. h_1, h_2, h_3, h_4, are the terminals of the respective ends of the three resistance coils, viz., 10, 100, and 1000 units, which are wound on the wooden block C; these terminals may be connected to each other

PLATE XXII

Fig 84

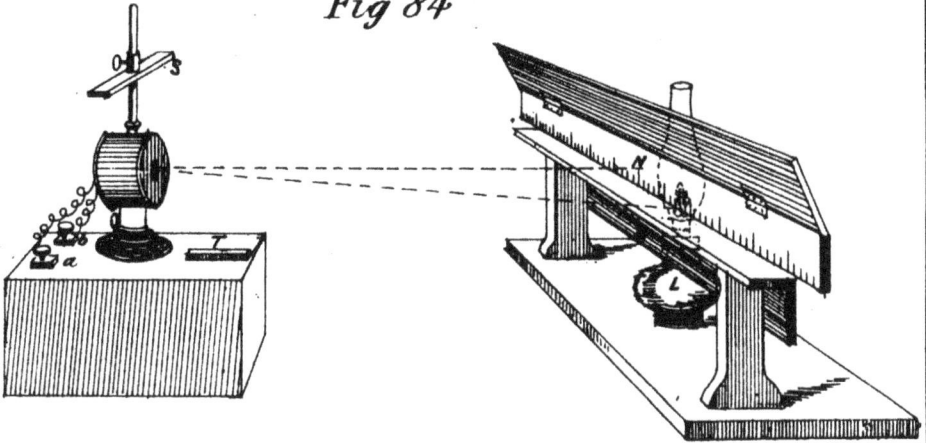

Fig 85

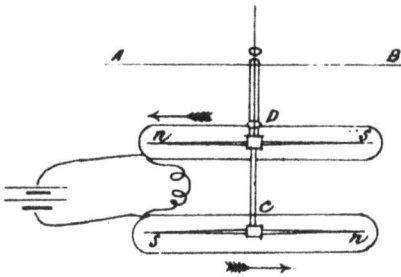

Fig 86

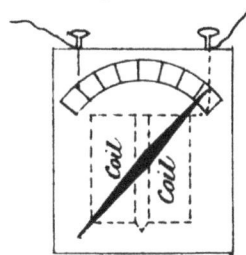

Fig 87

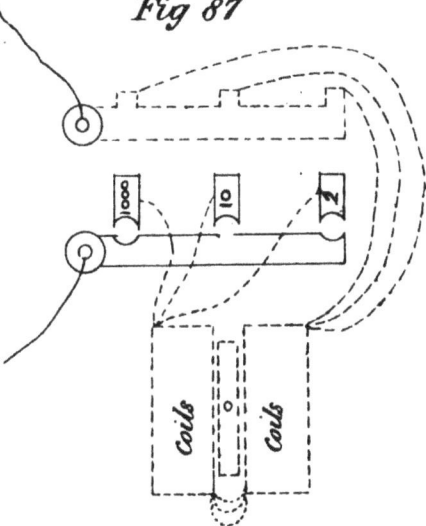

Fig 88

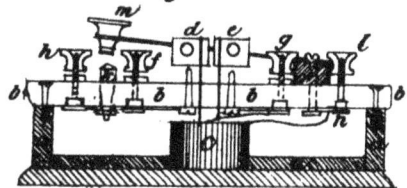

by means of stoppers, and therefore one or more of the resistances may
be brought into circuit as desired, and to the ends of these terminals
the wires of the artificial resistances are connected as shown on
diagrams Pl. xxiv., Figs. 1, 2, 3a and 3b; f is the graduated slate disc,
round which the platinum wire is stretched in a slight groove at the
edge of the disc, and is inserted in such manner that about half its
diameter protrudes beyond the slate. The ends of the platinum wire
are soldered to two brass terminals l and l^1, which are placed at the
angles formed by the sides of the gap in the slate disc, and which
form the junctures, as in the ordinary resistance bridge, between A,
n, and the galvanometer on one side, and B, X, and the galvanometer
on the other side, of the parallelogram. The terminal l is permanently connected by a thick copper wire or metal strip to terminal
h_1, and the other terminal l^1 is connected in a similar manner to
terminal III.

Slate is adopted for the material of which to make the disc f,
because it is found by experience to be the material which is the least
sensitive to variations in the weather or temperature.

The slate disc is graduated on its upper edge through an arc of 300
degrees, zero being in the centre, and the graduations figured up to
150 on each side at the terminals l and l^1 of the bridge wire.

In the centre of the circular plate E of polished wood, supported
upon three levelling screws b, b, b, a metal boss is inserted, in which
turns the vertical pin a which carries the instrument. This pin, being
well fitted to the boss, supports the instrument firmly, but at the same
time allows it to be turned freely round its vertical axis without losing
its horizontal position when once obtained.

On the arm $D\ D$, which turns on the pin a, and somewhat behind
the handle g, there is a small upright brass arm d turning between two
screw points r, and carrying in a gap at its upper end a small platinum
jockey pulley e turning on a vertical axis. This pulley forms the
movable contact point along the bridge wire, against which it is
kept firmly pressed by means of a spring acting on the arm d. The
arm $D\ D$, which is insulated from the other parts of the apparatus, is
permanently connected with the terminal I. On the top of d a pointer
Z or a vernier is fixed, which laps over the upper edge of the slate disc
and points to the graduations.

To the pin a is attached a circular disc of polished wood C, about

H 2

one inch thick, and having a groove turned in its edge for the reception
of the insulated wires composing the resistances. The disc C has a
projection c, which carries the five insulated terminals marked I., II.,
III., IV., V., as shown on Figs. 1 and 2, Pl. xxiii. Terminals III.
and IV. can be connected by a plug, II. and V. by the contact key K.
Terminal I. is in connection with the lever $D\ D$.

Figs. 3 and 4, Pl. xxiii. show the shunt box supplied with the
galvanometer if specially desired ; the copper connecting arms a, a are
screwed to the terminals II. and IV. By inserting a plug at c (Fig. 4,
Pl. xxiii.), the galvanometer is put out of circuit altogether, whilst
by plugging either of the other holes shunts of the value of $\frac{1}{9}$, $\frac{1}{99}$, or
$\frac{1}{999}$, are introduced into the circuit, and the effect upon the galvanometer is reduced to $\frac{1}{10}$, $\frac{1}{100}$, $\frac{1}{1000}$, respectively of what it would
have been without the insertion of the shunt.

Figs. 5 and 6, Pl. xxiii., show a battery commutator allowing to
bring into the circuit four different amounts of battery power. It is
placed in the battery circuit whenever consecutive tests with different
batteries are desired to be made, it being only necessary to change the
place of the stopper in the battery commutator, the terminal screw a
of the battery commutator being connected to terminal V. of the
galvanometer, and the screws b, b, b, b to various sections of the battery :
see diagram of connections, Fig. 4, Pl. xxiv.

The application of the universal galvanometer will be clear from
the diagrams on Pl. ii. ; instructions, however, for its practical use
are added further on, and also tables for use when measuring conducting resistances.

As will be seen from diagram, Fig. 1, Pl. xxiv., the proportion
between the unknown resistance X, and the artificial resistance n is,
when the deflection is read off on the side of the slate disc marked A :

$$X : n = 150 + a : 150 - a$$
$$\text{or,}\quad X \quad = \frac{150 + a}{150 - a} \cdot n \ .$$

but if read off on the B side of the disc—

$$X \quad = \frac{150 - a}{150 + a} \cdot n \ .$$

The values of these two fractions, for every half degree, will

PLATE XXIII

Fig 1.

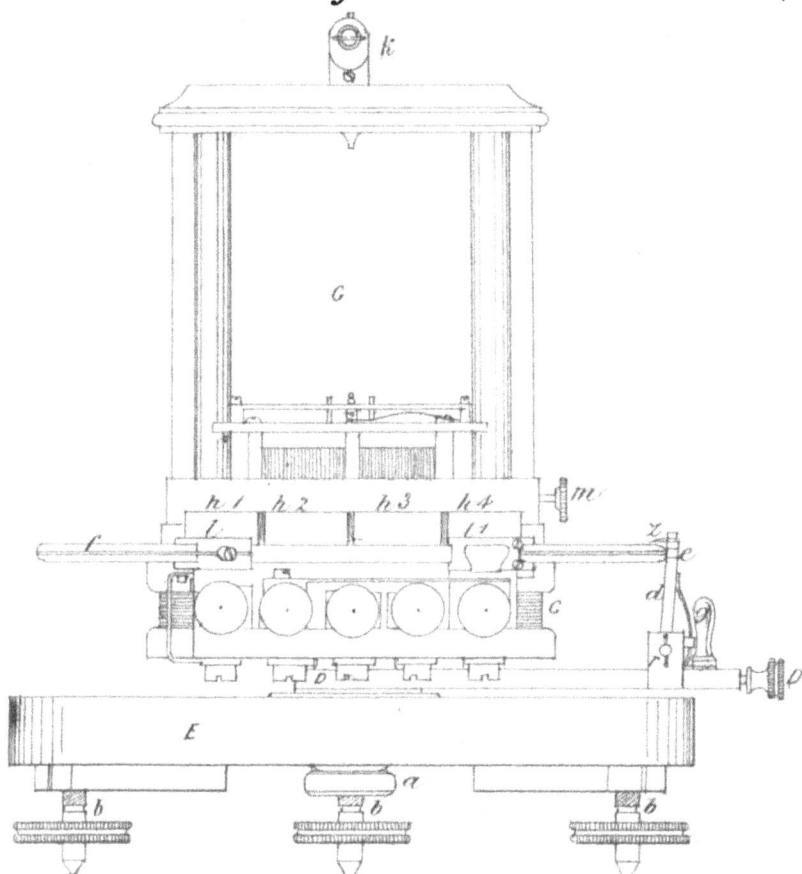

Fig 3.

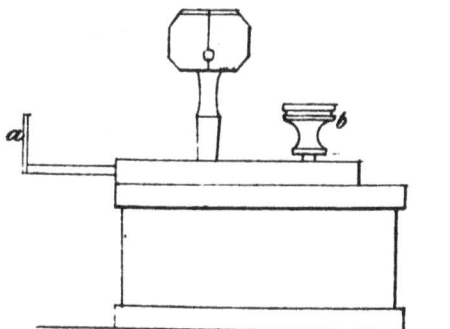

Fig 4

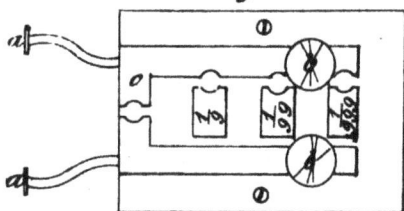

PLATE XXIIIᴬ

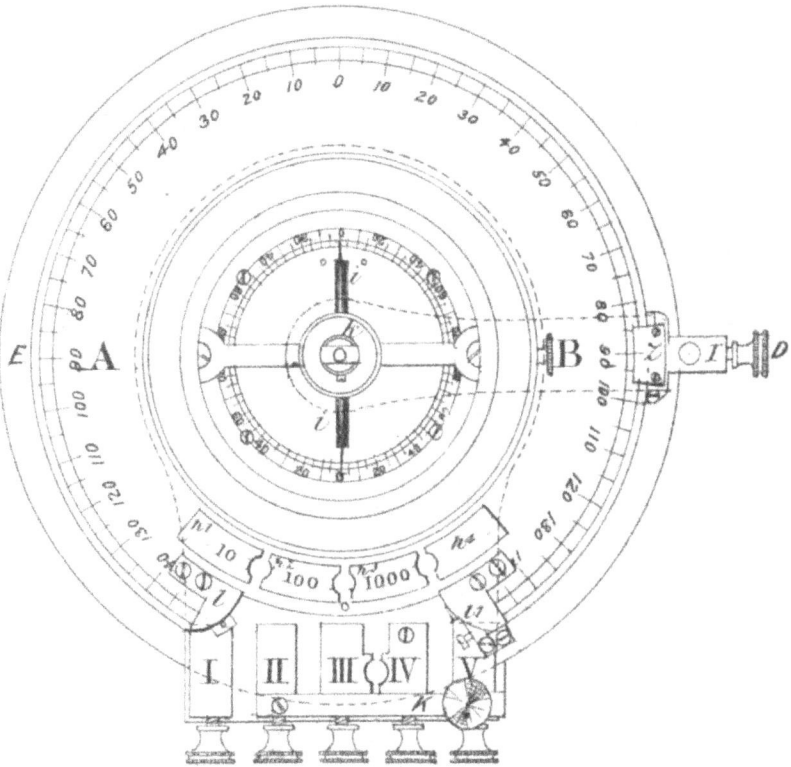

Fig 2.

Fig 5.

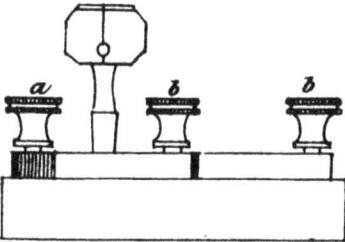

Fig 6

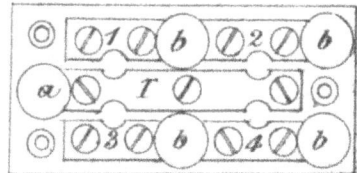

PLATE XXIV

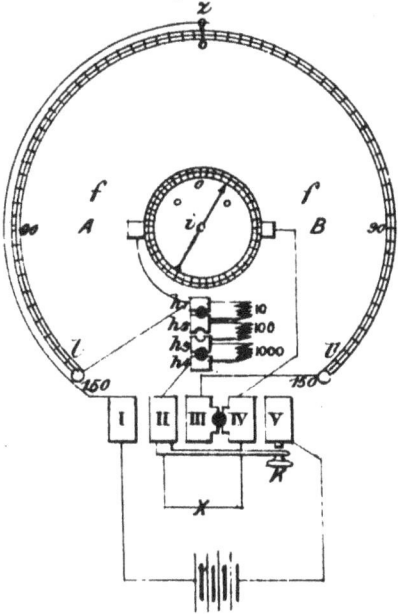

Fig 1

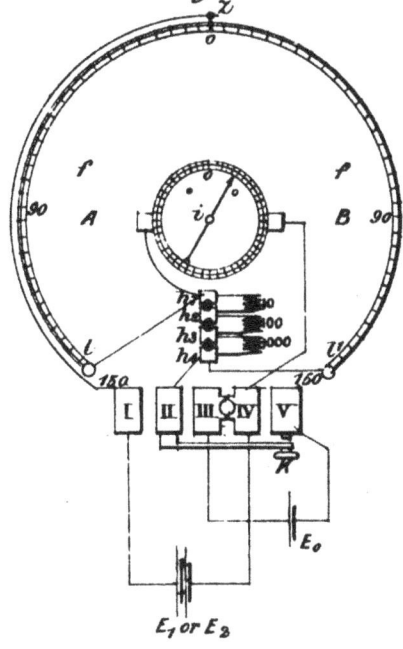

Fig. 2.

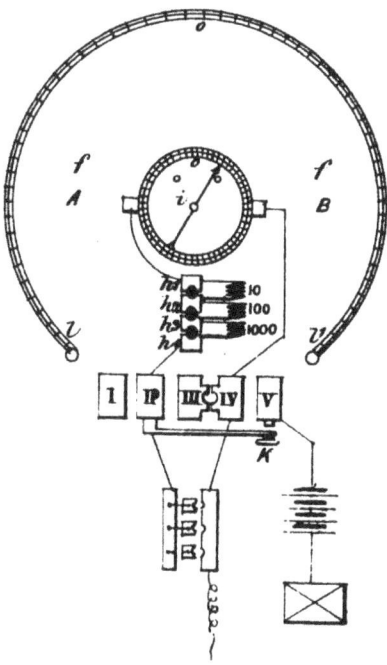

Fig 3.ᵃ

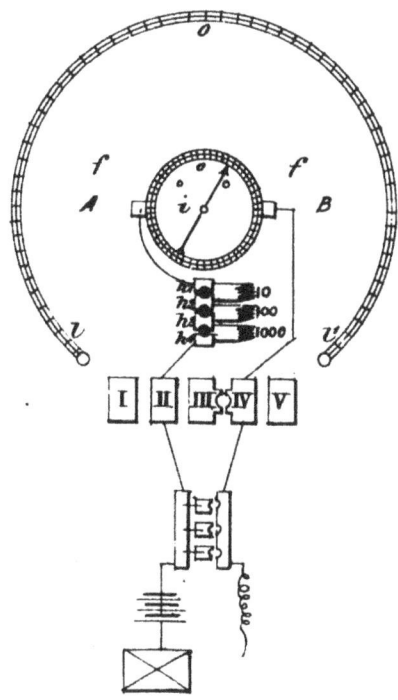

Fig 3ᵇ

PLATE XXIV A

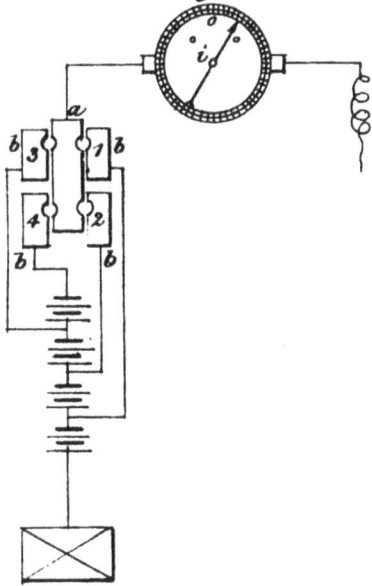

Fig 4.

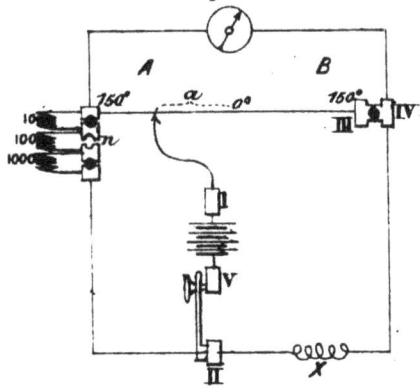

Fig 5.

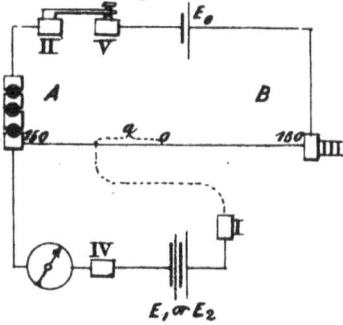

Fig 6.

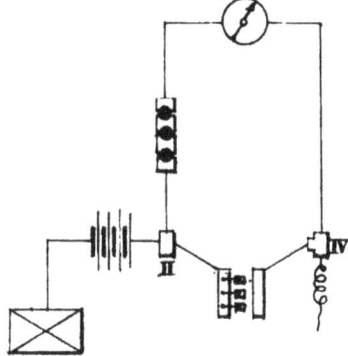

Fig 7.

be found in the columns headed *A* and *B* of the table in the Appendix.

Measuring Electrical Resistances.—For this purpose the instrument is arranged as a Wheatstone's balance. The connections are made as shown at Pl. xxiv., Figs. 1 and 5, where *X* is the unknown resistance.

a.—The needle *i* is to be brought to the zero point of the small cardboard scale by turning the galvanometer *G* round its vertical axis, taking care that the needle moves with perfect freedom.

b.—The pointer or vernier *Z* is to be brought, by means of the handle *g*, to the zero point of the large scale on the slate disc.

c.—A plug is to be inserted between the terminals marked III. and IV.

d.—The holes 10, 100, and 1000 are, two of them, to be plugged, and one left open, according to the extent of the unknown resistance to be measured ; either 10 or 100 must be left open if the resistance is small, and 1000 if it is large.

e.—The two ends of the unknown resistance are to be connected to terminals II. and IV.

f.—The two poles of some galvanic battery are to be connected to terminals I. and V.

When the above-mentioned connections have been made, and on depressing the key *K*, the battery current is sent into the combination and deflects the needle, say, to the right-hand or *B* side of the instrument, the pointer or vernier *Z* must then be pushed, by means of the handle *g*, to the *B* side of the instrument. If this is found to increase the deflection of the needle *i*, the pointer *Z* should be pushed to the other or *A* side of the instrument beyond the zero point of the large scale until the needle remains stationary when the key *K* is depressed.

The number indicated by the vernier *Z* should be read off carefully, and notice taken whether it is on the *A* or *B* side of the large scale. This number must then be referred to the galvanometer table,* when the figure opposite to the number, multiplied by the resistance unplugged, is the resistance of *X*. The value of the resistance to be determined will be thus found by a single operation.

---

* See Appendix.

Supposing the reading to be 50 on the A side of the large scale, the resistance n unplugged having been 100 units, we get according to the before-mentioned law of resistance bridge the following proportion (see Fig. 5, Pl. xxiv.) :—

$$X \ : \ 100 = 150 + 50 \ : \ 150 - 50$$
$$X = \frac{150 + 50}{150 - 50} \cdot 100$$
$$X = 200 \quad \text{units.}$$

For measuring very small resistances a single cell will be found sufficient ; but for large resistances more should be used, say, 15 to 20. If very accurate measurements of small resistances are to be taken, the screw at the end of the moving arm $D\,D$ should receive one battery wire, terminal V. receiving the other.

Comparing Electromotive Forces.—For this purpose Professor E. du Bois-Reymond's modification of Poggendorff's compensation method is used.

The connections are made as shown at Pl. xxiv., Figs. 2 and 6.

For comparing two electromotive forces E_1 and E_2, a third electromotor of higher electromotive force E_0 is used, and two separate tests taken.

The manipulations a and b are to be the same as before.

c.—The hole between III. and IV. to be left unplugged.

d.—Plugs to be inserted in 10, 100 and 1000.

e.—The two poles of the electromotor of an electromotive force E_0 are to be connected to the terminals III. and V.

f.—The poles of the battery whose electromotive force E_1 is to be compared are connected to terminals I. and IV. in such a manner that the similar poles of the two electromotors are joined to terminals I. and III., and to IV. and V. respectively.

When depressing the key K the galvanometer needle will be deflected and can be brought back to zero by turning the pointer Z either to the right or to the left. Should for instance the pointer have to be brought to 30° on the A side we have the following equation—

$$E_1 = E_0 \frac{150 - 30}{300 + n} \quad \cdots \cdots \cdots \cdots (1),$$

where n is the resistance of the battery E_0.

The electromotor E_2 is now to be inserted in the place of E_1, and the galvanometer needle, when it deflects, again brought back to zero by moving the pointer Z. If for instance the pointer has to be pushed to $40°$ on the B side to obtain equilibrium we have—

$$E_2 = E_0 \frac{150 + 40}{300 + n} \quad \ldots \ldots \ldots \ldots \ldots (2).$$

By eliminating n from equations 1 and 2 we have

$$E_1 : E_2 = (150 - 30) : (150 + 40) = 12 : 19 \ldots \ldots (3).$$

The two electromotive forces are in the same proportion as the two observed distances of the pointer Z from $150°$ on the A side of the instrument.

For measuring the Intensity of a Current.—For this purpose the instrument is simply used as a sine galvanometer. The connections are made as shown at Pl. xxiv., Figs. 3a and 7.

The manipulations a, b, c, and d same as in the second case.

    e.—Connect one pole of a battery to terminal II. and put the other pole to earth.

    f.—Connect the line to terminal IV.

The galvanometer is then to be turned in the same direction as the needle is deflected until the needle coincides with the zero point. Whilst this is being done the large scale on the slate disc will move under the pointer Z, which must be left stationary; the sine of the angle indicated by Z will thus give the value proportionate to the strength of the current. Should the shunt box be required, it has to be connected with terminals II. and IV.

Fig. 4 shows the same connections as Fig. 7, but without the shunt box, and with the battery commutator. Fig. 3_a shows diagram of the same connections but with the key K, and Fig. 3_b the same without the key.

A Shunt.—A " Shunt " is a second path offered to a current traversing a given circuit, or portion of a circuit, so as to diminish the amount of the current flowing through that portion of the circuit. In the diagram shown at Fig. 89 the shunt diminishes the amount of the current flowing along the circuit between A and B.

If only $\frac{1}{N}$th of the current is to pass along the circuit between A and B (of resistance R) then the resistance of the shunt must equal $\frac{R}{N-1}$.

By the aid of shunts it is quite possible to make use of very sensitive instruments to measure powerful currents.

Commutators or Switch Plates.—A commutator or switch plate is an apparatus by which the direction of currents may be changed at will, or by which they may be opened or closed. Bertin's commutator, which is represented at Fig. 90, consists of a small base of hard wood on which is an ebonite plate, this by means of the handle m is turned about a central axis between two stops c and c'. On the disc are fixed two copper plates, one of which o is always positive, being connected by the axis and by a plate $(+)$ with the binding screw P, which receives the positive electrode of the battery; the other copper plate i, e, bent in the form of a horse-shoe, is connected by friction below the disc with a plate $(-)$, which plate is connected with the negative electrode N. On the opposite side of the board are two binding screws b, and b', to which are attached two elastic metal plates r, and r'.

On the disc being turned as shown in the figure, the current coming by the binding screw P passes into the piece o, the plate r, and finally the binding screw b, which by means of a copper wire leads the current to the apparatus in connection with b; then returning to the binding screw b', the current reaches the plate r', the piece i, e, and so to the battery by the binding screw N.

If the disc is turned so that the handle m is half way between c and c', the pieces o and i, e, being no longer in contact with the plates r and r', the current will not pass. If m is turned as far as c, the plate o will then touch r', and the current pass to b', and return by b, thus reversing its direction.

"Peg" switches are also often used; they are arranged so that the removal or insertion of a brass peg or plug cuts out, or completes a circuit.

Rheostat.—A rheostat is an instrument used for the comparison of resistances.

Wheatstone's rheostat, which is shown in elevation at Fig. 91, consists of two cylinders A and B, one of brass and the other of non-conducting material, so arranged that a copper wire can be wound off the one on to the other by turning a handle C. The surface of the non-conducting cylinder B has a screw thread cut in it for its whole length, in which the turns of the copper wire lie,

PLATE XXV

Fig 89.

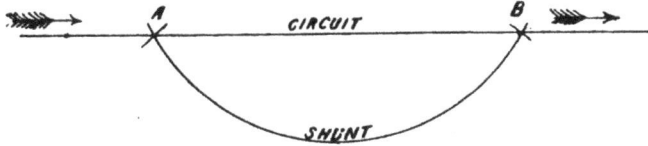

Fig 90

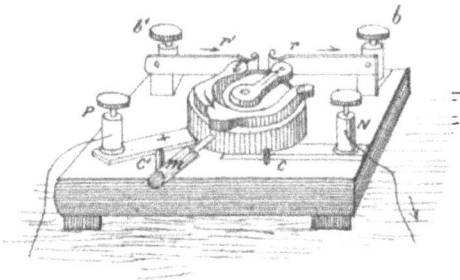

Fig 91

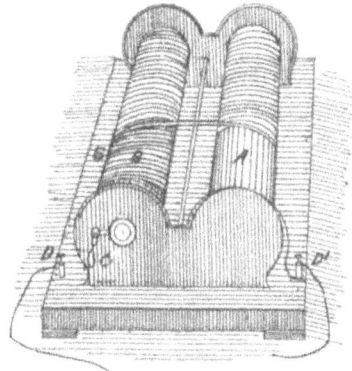

Fig 92

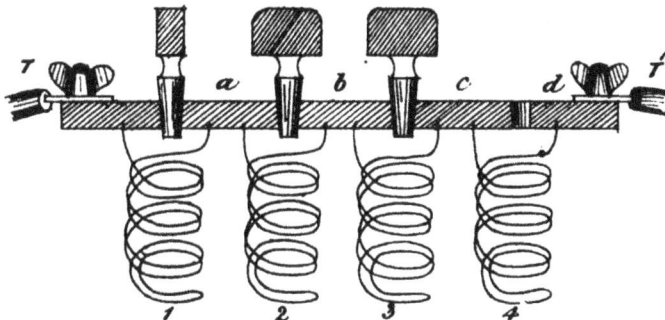

so that its successive convolutions are well insulated from each other. Two binding screws D, D' connected with the ends of the copper wire are provided, to which the circuit wires are connected. A scale is attached at E, by means of which the number of convolutions on B can be read off; and parts of a revolution are indicated on a circle at one end. The handle C can be shifted from one cylinder to the other.

Supposing the rheostat introduced into a circuit, and the whole of the copper wire wrapped on the metal cylinder A, then, on account of the large section of this metal cylinder, its resistance may be entirely neglected, but for every convolution of the wire on the non-conducting cylinder B, a specific resistance is introduced into the circuit. The amount of resistance can thus be varied as gradually as desired by winding on and off the cylinder B. This instrument is often used in connection with the thermo galvanometer.

Resistance Box.—The general arrangement of a resistance box is shown in the diagram Fig. 92.

Between two terminal binding screws T and T_1 secured on a vulcanite slab are fixed a series of brass junction pieces a, b, c, d; each of these is connected by a resistance coil to its neighbour, as shown at 1, 2, 3, and 4. A number of brass conical plugs with insulating handles of vulcanite are provided, which can be inserted between any two successive junction pieces, as between T and a, or a and b.

With all the plugs inserted, the electrical current will flow direct from T to T_1, the large metallic junction pieces directly connected by the plugs would offer no sensible resistance; but if all the plugs were removed, then the current would flow through each of the coils 1, 2, 3, and 4, and the resistance in the circuit would be the sum of the resistances of those four coils. With the plugs arranged as in the figure, the current would flow through coil 4 only, and the resistance in the circuit would be equal to the resistance of that coil.

Wheatstone's Balance.—The electrical conductivity of a body is determined by ascertaining the ratio between the resistance of a certain length of the conductor in question, having a given section, to that of a known length of a known section of some substance taken as a standard.

For this purpose Wheatstone's bridge in connection with a box of resistance coils is the most convenient method.

At Fig. 94 is shown Wheatstone's balance (Post-office pattern), and at Fig. 93 the apparatus is, reduced into the form of a parallelogram, which is the usual diagram of Wheatstone's bridge. The theory of the bridge is as follows :

Four conductors $A B$, $B C$, $A D$, and $D C$ are joined at A and C to the poles of a battery Z; the resistance between A and B is R; that between A and D is r; that between D and C is R_1; and that between B and C is x, the unknown resistance to be measured. A convenient constant ratio is chosen for R_1 and r, such as equality 1 to 10, 1 to 100, or 1 to 1000; and then R_1 is adjusted until no current flows through the galvanometer G; when this is the case we have $R : r = R_1 : x$, or $x = \dfrac{r}{R} R_1$; so that if $r = \dfrac{R}{100}$, x will be equal to $\dfrac{R_1}{100}$.

Two keys a and b are inserted ; the current is wholly cut off the four conductors until contact is made at a; and then after the currents in the four conductors have come to their permanent condition, contact is made at b to test whether any current flows through the galvanometer. The three resistances R, R_1 and r and the resistance of the galvanometer should be small if x is small, and great if x is great.

The conductors $A B$ and $A D$ of the bridge are each formed of three resistance coils having a resistance of 10, 100, and 1000 ohms respectively, inserted between the terminals B and D of the balance, Fig. 94.

The conductor $D C$ is formed of a set of resistance coils from 1 up to 4000 ohms, amounting altogether to 11,110 ohms, inserted between the terminals D and C of the balance; in the balance, a brass plug being inserted between the terminals D and D_1, they may be considered as one terminal D. The conductor $B C$ is the wire to be tested, and is connected to the terminals B and C of the balance.

Measurement of Resistances.—When a resistance is to be measured that is within the range of the coils in R_1, R and r are made equal. The needle of the galvanometer will move in a different direction, either to the right or to the left, according as the resistance in R_1 is greater or less than the line wire x. The needle remains at zero only when the resistance in R_1 is equal to that in x. For $r : R :: R_1 : x$.

When the resistance of x is greater than that of R_1, as in an

PLATE XXVI

Fig 93

Fig 94

insulation test, the resistance in r is made *less* than that in R, in order that r and R may have such a proportion one to the other as will enable the coils in R_1 to balance a resistance in x, greater than their own, that is to say, greater than 11,100 ohms; thus $r : R : : R_1 : x$, or $10 : 1000 : : 10,000 : 1,000,000$, the resistance in the line to be tested would be 1,000,000 ohms, supposing the values of r, R and R_1 to be respectively 10, 1000, and 10,000 ohms.

When the resistance to be tested is less than that of the least coil in R_1 (1 ohm), then the resistance in r is made greater than in R. Thus $r : R : : R_1 : x$, or $100 : 10 : : 2 : 0.2$; the resistance of the line to be tested would in this case be $\frac{1}{10}$ of an ohm.

Manipulation.—In all cases the key in connection with the battery should first be depressed, then the galvanometer key, making very short contacts by the latter, just sufficient to show the direction of the deflection, until the coils in R_1 are nearly adjusted, otherwise considerable time will be lost in making a series of tests, owing to the swing given to the needle, which will take some little time before it again remains steady at zero. When once the coils in R_1 are adjusted, and a balance obtained, it should be ascertained whether the needle will remain steady when contact is made and broken.

Test Tables.—In connection with a system of testing electrical submarine mines, for the sake of convenience and simplicity it is necessary to use a table (termed a "Test Table"), on which all the apparatus used for the purpose of testing are fixed. Several forms of tables have been designed for such a purpose. At Fig. 95 is shown the method of arranging such a table.*

A is an astatic galvanometer placed between two switch plates, B and C; ten other similar switch plates, 1, 2, 3, 4, D, 5, 6, 7, E, and 8, are arranged in front of the galvanometer A; F, G, and H are three terminal plates; K is a box of resistance coils used in connection with the thermo galvanometer M; L is a firing key, and N a battery commutator; O is a three-coil galvanometer; R is a Wheatstone balance (Post-office pattern).

The ten switch plates, 1, 2, 3, 4, D, &c., are used for the connection of any particular line to be tested, as well as for the earth connections and instruments employed in that operation.

---

* As constructed by Mr. J. Mathieson, late R.E., at the Silvertown Telegraph Works, Essex.

"Sea Cell" Tests.—The arrangement shown in the figure is that required in connection with the sea cell test, and Mr. Brown's method of keeping certain earth plates in a bucket instead of in the sea.

If two plates of suitable metal to form a Voltaic battery are placed in salt water and connected by a metallic conductor, a battery is at once formed capable of producing considerable deflection on a moderately delicate galvanometer. Testing by this arrangement has been termed the " sea cell " test.

Arranging Earth Plates.—Mr. Brown's, Assistant-Chemist to the War Department, method of arranging the earth plates is as follows :—

A series of earth plates, such as copper, carbon, tin, zinc, &c., are placed in a bucket filled with sea water, and which is placed in the testing room. The water in the bucket is put in connection with the water of the sea by means of a conducting wire, terminating at one end with a zinc plate in the bucket, and at the other with a zinc plate in the sea. By this means the tests made with the different earth plates in the bucket are identical with those made with corresponding earths placed absolutely in the sea, and therefore these latter may be done away with, the sea cell tests being entirely carried out by means of the bucket earth plates.

In addition to the bucket earth plates there will be several other earth plates in connection with the testing room, these being placed in the sea, such as the zinc earth for the firing battery, the zinc earth for the signalling battery, &c.

Connections of Switch Plates.—The switch plate *D* is used for the connection of any particular mine cable which it may be required to test. The switch plate *E* is connected with a zinc earth plate used for testing the firing battery. This must always be in the sea. The switch plate 1 is in connection with a zinc earth in the bucket; 2 is attached to a copper earth plate in the bucket; 3 is attached to a carbon earth plate in the bucket; 4 to a tin earth plate in the bucket; 5 is used for connection with the zinc signalling earth connection in the sea; 6 is attached to a copper earth plate used for the sea cell test, or any other purpose required, in the sea; 7 is attached to a zinc earth plate in the sea ; and 8 is a common zinc earth in the sea.

The terminal plates *G* and *H* are used for the connection, for testing purposes of the negative and positive poles, of the firing battery, and *F* is connected with a zinc earth in the sea, for a similar purpose. These plates are in connection with the resistance coils K and the thermo galvanometer M, employed for testing the firing battery, the circuit being closed by the firing key L. Other ways of using these plates may of course be adopted if desired. The resistance coils K range from 0·5 to 100 ohms, and are composed of wire adapted for the passage of a quantity current. A reversing key is generally used in connection with a testing battery and the three-coil galvanometer O. This reversing key would consist of two bridges completely insulated from each other, the upper one attached to the negative, the lower one to the positive pole of the test battery. In their normal position both keys press against the upper bridge, and until one or other of the keys is pressed down no current will pass, the direction of the current being altered by pressing down a different key. The point of each key is provided with a terminal and connected, the one to a zinc earth through the switch plate 8, the other to one terminal of the three-coil galvanometer when the tests are to be applied.

The Wheatstone balance R is used in finding the resistances of electrical cables, balancing fuzes, &c. By means of a commutator, N, the necessary number of cells for any particular test may be thrown in circuit when required.

Test of Platinum Wire Fuze for Conductivity.—The platinum wire fuze may be tested electrically as follows :—

If placed in circuit with a few cells of a Daniell or Leclanché battery and a detector galvanometer, before the platinum wire bridge of the fuze is fixed, there should be no deflection of the needle, for no metallic circuit exists; if it did, such would be fatal to the efficiency of the fuze. If similarly placed in circuit after the bridge has been fixed, a considerable deflection of the needle should result, such deflection being due to the current passing through the metallic bridge, which to be efficient ought to be the sole medium through which the circuit is completed.

Test of Resistance of Platinum Wire Fuze.—The electrical resistance of a platinum wire fuze is ascertained by means of the Wheatstone's balance R and galvanometer A, Fig. 95. The terminals of the fuze are connected to the binding screws of the balance, the commutator N and galvanometer A being connected up in circuit. The resistance of the coils is then adjusted by taking out plugs until the needle of the galvanometer A is brought to zero, when the sum of the resistances indicated by the unplugged coils will be equal to that of the fuze. The resistance of a platinum wire fuze might also be ascertained by means of a differential galvanometer instead of a Wheatstone balance.

The electrical resistance of $\frac{3}{10}''$ of fine platinum wire, weighing 1·9 grains to the yard, is $\frac{3}{10}$ of an ohm nearly (Schaw).

Testing High Tension Fuzes.—High tension fuzes require very delicate and careful management in testing them, due to the high electrical resistance of such fuzes, which ranges from 1500 to 2000 ohms, combined with the danger of premature explosion when testing even with a small number of battery cells. Very sensitive galvanometers, such as the reflecting galvanometer, should if possible be used, otherwise the mode of making the tests for conductivity and resistance of a high-tension fuze is similar to that already given for a platinum wire fuze.

Detonating fuzes should always be placed in an iron case during the process of testing.

Insulation Test for Electrical Cables.—To test an electrical cable for insulation, it should first be put in a tank of water, or in the sea, and allowed to soak for at least forty-eight hours. The object of this is to allow the water to penetrate the outer protection of hemp and iron wires, &c., and to search out and get into any weak places there may be in the insulation under the armouring. At Fig. 96 is shown the method of performing this test. A is a tank holding the electrical cable, which has been in soak for forty-eight hours; B is an astatic galvanometer; C, Z a Leclanché or Daniell battery of great power; and C is an ordinary firing key. One end of the electric cable D is connected to the galvanometer B through the firing key C; the other end of the cable is very carefully insulated; one pole of the battery is connected to the galvanometer B, the other is put to earth in the tank at F; should the insulation be perfect, no deflection of the needle should follow on the key being pressed down. A very slight deflection might be observed on a moderately sensitive galvanometer, due to the current passing through the insulation; its whole length being immersed, the surface through which such a current would pass would be large, and the sum of the infinitesimally small quantities escaping over the whole length, would in the aggregate be sufficient to deflect the needle to a small extent in completing the circuit of the battery. Should any considerable deflection occur, it would indicate a defect or leak in the insulation of the cable, the extent of which would be roughly measured by the amount of such deflection.

By using a reflecting galvanometer a very much more delicate test would be obtained, but for the comparatively short lengths of electric cables used in connection with submarine mines, such accuracy is hardly necessary.

To test an electric cable for conductivity, it would be only necessary to expose the metallic conductor G, and put it in the water of the tank. If the conductivity were good, then the whole of the current would pass through the cable and the needle of the galvanometer would be violently deflected. If the continuity were broken, no deflection would be observed.

Defects observed in the Conductivity of the Cable.—To ascertain the position of a defect in the insulation of a cable, as indicated by the tests above described, it would be only necessary to keep a continuous current flowing through the cable, and gradually take it out of the tank. If the fault existed at a single point, the deflection of the needle would be suddenly reduced at the moment of that point of the cable being lifted out of the water, and therefore its position would be determined with considerable accuracy. Should several defects exist as each was lifted out, a sudden reduction of the deflection would occur.

Discharge Test.—The conductor of an electrical cable may be broken without destroying the insulation, and on applying the foregoing tests, good insulation would be indicated, but no conductivity, and no information would be given as to the position of the fault. Under such circumstances the following test must be applied :—

Put one pole of a very powerful battery to earth, and charge one end of the defective cable, then immediately discharge it through a reflecting galvanometer, and note the extreme limit of the swing of the needle, then, charge the other end of the cable in a similar manner, and discharge it through the same galvanometer, noting as before the swing of the needle. This should be done three or four times, and the average of the deflections taken. Then the position of the fault would be indicated by the proportion between the average deflections in each case, and the cable might safely be cut at that point. Should the precise position of the fault not be discovered in thus cutting the cable, each section should be tested again for conductivity, and that in which a fault was still found to exist should be again tested by the discharge as before.

Test of Electrical Resistance of Cable.—This is effected by balancing it against the Wheatstone balance, in a similar manner to that explained for a fuze. The electrical resistance of the conductor of a cable affords a very correct indication of the quality of the metal of which it is composed. For a very delicate test the reflecting galvanometer should be used.

Electrical Test of Insulated Joints.—Insulated joints and connections, whether of a permanent or temporary nature, should be tested electrically, in a precisely similar manner to that explained for electric cables.

They should be soaked for forty-eight hours, and then tested for insulation, conductivity, and electrical resistance.

In testing permanent joints special tests are carried out, which are described by Mr. Culley in his 'Handbook of Practical Telegraphy.'

Voltaic batteries should be subjected to the following tests :—

1.—For potential.
2.—For internal resistance.
3.—For electromotive force.

For the purpose of testing the potential of a battery, one pole should be put to earth, and with the other one pair of the quadrants of a Thomson's reflecting galvanometer should be charged; when this is done, a certain deflection of the spot of light will occur, and the amount of such deflection, as compared with that produced by a standard cell applied to the instrument in a similar manner, would give the relative value of the potential of the battery.

The following method of determining the internal resistance of a battery is that recommended by Mr. Latimer Clark in his book on electrical measurements.

The instrument employed is a double shunt differential galvanometer, a diagram of which is shown at Fig. 97. Connect the battery and a set of resistance coils in circuit between the terminals A and D, and insert plugs in the resistance coils so that they give no resistance; insert plugs at A and C, and also both the shunt plugs at A and D. The current will now flow through one half of the galvanometer circuit only, being, however, reduced to $\frac{1}{100}$ of its amount by the shunt D; the deflection of the needle must be carefully read. The plug A must now be removed to B, which causes the battery current to flow through both halves of the galvanometer (each being shunted). The circuit will now be as shown in the figure, and the needle will of course be deflected somewhat more than before. Now unplug the resistance coils which are in circuit with the battery until the deflection of the needle is reduced to its original amount, and the resistances unplugged will be equal to the internal resistance of the battery.

The following is another method of ascertaining the internal resistance of a battery cell.

A circuit is formed, consisting of the battery cell, a rheostat, and a galvanometer, and the strength C is noted on the galvanometer. A second cell is then joined with the first, so as to form one of double the size, and therefore half the resistance, and then by adding a length l of the rheostat, the strength is brought to what it originally was, C.

Then if E is the electromotive force, and R the resistance of cell, r the resistance of the galvanometer, and other parts of the circuit, the strength C in the one case is $C = \dfrac{E}{R + r}$, and in the other $= \dfrac{E}{\frac{1}{2}R + r + l}$, and since the strength in both cases is the same, $R = 2\,l$, i.e., the internal resistance of the cell is equal to twice the resistance corresponding to the length l of the rheostat wire.

The comparative electromotive force of a battery may be determined by means of a double shunt differential galvanometer in the following method, as recommended by Mr. Latimer Clark.

" This can only be done relatively in terms of some other standard battery. First determine the resistance of the standard and of the other cells to be measured; then insert the shunt plugs at A and D, Fig. 97, and also at C and B, and join up the standard cell in circuit with a resistance coil to the terminals A and D, and unplug the resistance coils until a convenient deflection is obtained, say 15°; note the sum of the resistances in circuit, including that of the battery galvanometer, resistance coil and connecting wires; now change the battery for another, and by unplugging the resistance coils bring the needle again to the same deflection, 15°; having again found the total resistance in the circuit, the relative electromotive force will be directly proportional to these resistances."

The electromotive force of a battery may also be measured statically by means of Thomson's quadrant electrometer, the poles of the battery being connected with the two chief electrodes of the instrument, in which arrangement no current will pass, and the electromotive force will be directly indicated by the difference of potential observed.

In the case of a quantity battery, that is, a battery capable of fusing a fine platinum wire, its electromotive force and internal resistance may be determined by means of the resistance coils K, and thermo galvanometer M, shown at Fig. 95.

Tests after Submersion. —After an electrical submarine mine has been placed in position, it should be immediately tested to ascertain that all is right, and similar tests should be applied at intervals to ascertain that the charge remains dry ; that the insulation and conductivity of the electric cable remains the same ; and that its electrical resistance indicates a state of efficiency.

The nature of the tests applied to determine these points will depend upon the nature of the combination in which the mine is arranged.

The manner of applying the " sea cell " test, by which is ascertained the condition of a system of electrical submarine mines, will be readily understood from the following examples.

The arrangements for testing to ascertain whether a charge is dry, or wet, is shown at Fig. 98.

z is a plate of zinc introduced in the circuit within the charge, and between the fuze and the shore ; another earth plate of carbon x is connected with the electric cable beyond the fuze, forming the ordinary earth connection of the system at that point ; and at home a copper earth plate c is used.

First, in the case of a dry charge with the insulation and conductivity of the cable, good ; under these circumstances there would be formed a sea cell between the earth plates x, and c, which would produce a certain deflection of the needle of a galvanometer g, which is placed in the circuit, and in a certain direction.

Secondly, in the case of a charge becoming wet, through leakage, with the insulation and conductivity of the cable, good ; under these circumstances, a sea cell would be formed between the plates c and z, causing a different deflection of the needle in amount and in direction, by which it would be at once indicated that the charge had become wet.

" Sea cell " Test for Insulation.—Again, in the case of the insulation of the electric cable being damaged to such an extent as to expose the

PLATE XXVII

Fig 95.

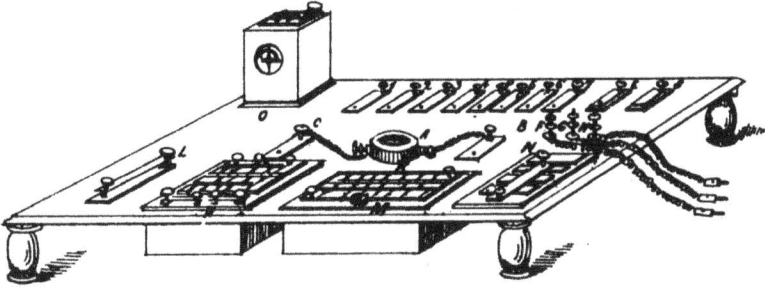

Fig 96

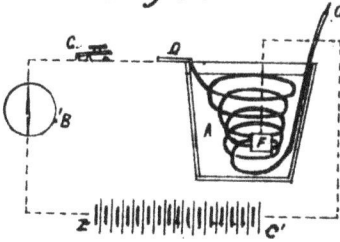

Fig 97.

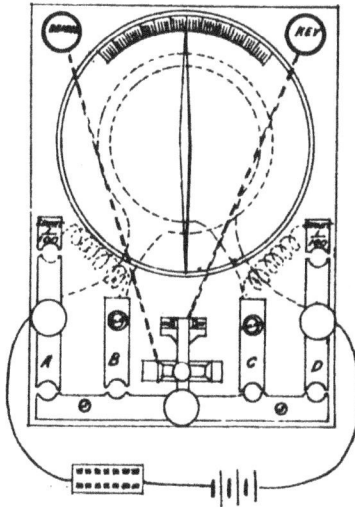

copper conductor. Under these circumstances there would be formed a sea cell between the copper earth plate c, and the exposed copper conductor of the cable, by which a certain definite deflection of the galvanometer would be observed, which deflection would differ in character from that produced by the copper carbon sea cell, when the insulation of the cable was good, and the system in working order, and therefore it would indicate that some change in the electrical conditions of the system had occurred. The fact that a leak existed in the insulation would be proved by changing the earth plate at home from copper to zinc, carbon, tin, &c.

In the case of no deflection being produced on the galvanometer, on applying the sea cell test, a want of continuity, or inefficient connections would be indicated.

The foregoing afford examples of the vast utility of the " sea cell " in connection with a system of electrical tests for submarine mines, numerous variations of which may be effected by employing a series of earth plates, of different metals, at the home end of the circuit, in connection with a carbon and zinc earth plate at the other end. And the mode of manipulating these tests may, by means of numerous switch plates, as shown at Fig. 95, be made extremely simple and efficient.

Armstrong's System of Electrical Testing.—A very simple method of testing electrical submarine mines, with which low tension fuzes are used, has been devised by Captain Armstrong, R.E., and is shown at Fig. 99. a is the electric cable leading from the shore ; b the cable attached to a polarised relay c, and connecting the charge through the fuze f to the earth ; b' the cable, attached to another polarised relay c', and connecting the mine with the circuit closer ; the polarised relay c, in the mine, is arranged to be worked by a positive current, that is to say, the wire surrounding the core is so wound as to increase the polarity of the electro magnet, near the armature d, when a positive current is passed through it, and to diminish the polarity when a negative current is passed through the wire surrounding the core; the polarised relay c' within the circuit closer is arranged to be worked by a negative current, the coil being so wound as to produce an influence exactly the reverse of c.

Then, a positive current passing along the line wire a, the armature d in the charge will be attracted, while d' will remain unaffected ;

again, if a negative current be circulated, the armature d' within the circuit closer will be attracted, while the armature d will remain unaffected. Two insulated wires forked together are wound round each electro magnet, one a thin wire (g and g') having a considerable resistance, about 1000 ohms, being connected direct to the earth plates e and e', and the other a thick wire (h and h') offering a very small resistance, and so arranged that when the armature is attracted, they may be in contact with and complete the circuit through the armature to earth.

The thin wire coils are so arranged that a certain number of Leclanché cells (ten or twelve, as may be desired) will make the electro magnets act, while with fewer cells the current would be too weak, and would therefore pass through them to earth without affecting the armature.

By means of the three-coil galvanometer, a table of the deflections, obtained by the foregoing system of testing, should be carefully recorded, when the circuit is known to be in good working order, so that any defect in the circuit would be at once indicated on the application of the various tests, by the results so obtained differing from those originally recorded. When a system of submarine mines is placed in position for the purposes of practice and experiment, every trouble should be taken to endeavour to fix the exact position of any defect that may exist, also to ascertain its magnitude, &c., but in time of war, should a defect exist in the system, no time must be lost in such operations, but the mine at once lifted, and the fault repaired, or a fresh one laid in its place, unless the presence of an enemy or other imperative cause should prevent such work being done.

Austrian Testing Table.—The following is a description of the Austrian testing table, and their mode of making electrical tests with it, in connection with their system of self-acting electrical submarine mines.

Its design is shown at Fig. 100 ; $c z$ represents the battery with one pole to earth at e, and the other in connection with an intensity coil a, through which the current passes to the contact plate b. When it is desired to put the system of mines in connection with the table, in a state of preparation to be fired by the contact of a vessel, a plug is inserted between the contact plates b and f, and the current passes through the galvanometer g, and electrically charges the conducting wires connecting the mines with the battery, through the several

PLATE XXVIII

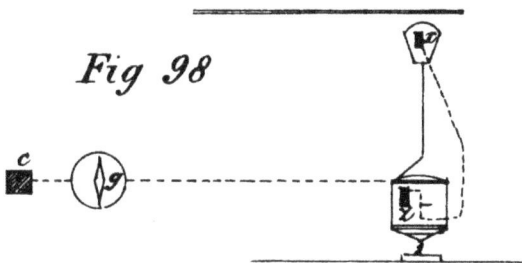

Fig 98

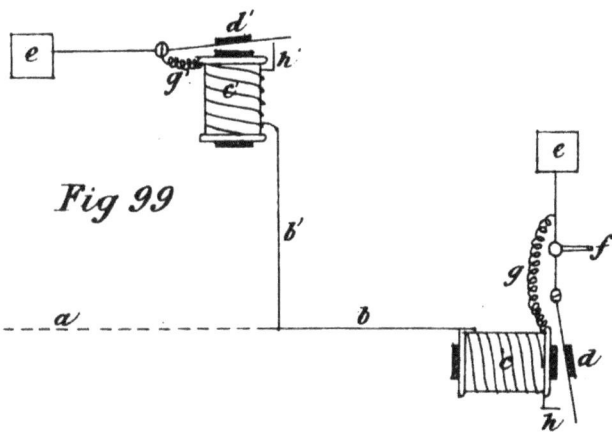

Fig 99

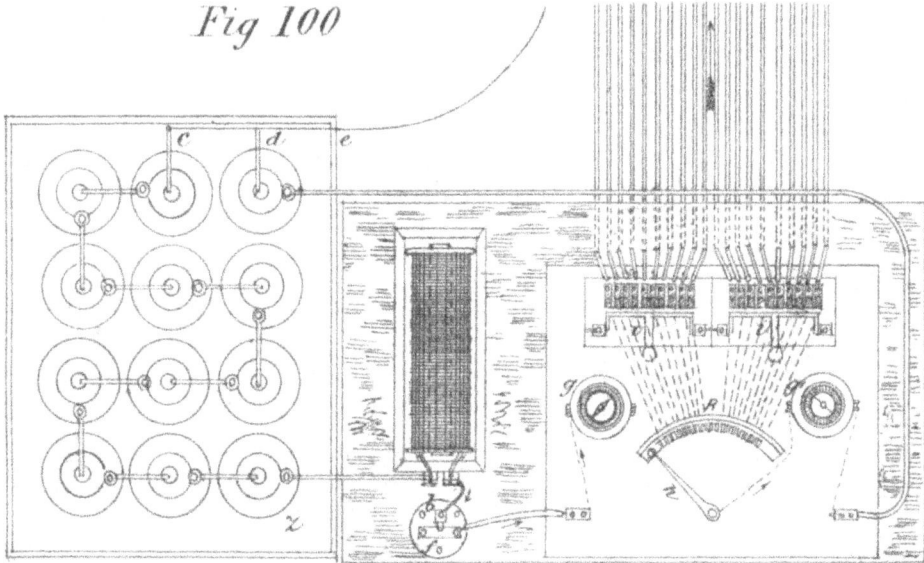

Fig 100

binding screws on the contact plates, numbering 1, 2, 3, &c. The fact that the charge has been fired is also at once indicated on the galvanometer g.

Test to discover an Exploded Charge.—It then becomes necessary to ascertain which particular mine of the system has been exploded; for this purpose a separate circuit in connection with a single cell d is employed. This cell is in connection through a galvanometer g' (a more sensitive instrument than the galvanometer g) with the pivot of the key h, and rheotome R, which latter is connected, as shown by the dotted lines, with each individual mine of the system attached to the contact plates numbered 1, 2, 3, &c. The handle of the rheotome is moved round, to each number in succession and directly it is placed in contact with that corresponding to the exploding mine, the electrical circuit is completed through the exposed end of the fractured wire, and this is indicated by the galvanometer g'. During the testing process the firing battery c z must be disconnected; this is done by raising one of the bridges i i with which each group of ten mines is provided.

Insulation Test.—The rheotome and testing galvanometer g' are also used to test the insulation of the electric cables connecting the mines to the testing table. This is done in precisely the same manner as testing for an exploded mine : the handle of the rheotome is turned round, and each cable connected in succession with the testing circuit as before; should the galvanometer g' remain stationary, the insulation is good; but should a defect of insulation exist, the current passing through it would act on and deflect the galvanometer, indicating the particular line in which it exists, and, roughly, its extent in proportion to the deflection shown; should the fault be considerable, the defective cable should be at once detached, as the current lost through it might so diminish the working power of the firing battery, as to prevent it exploding any of the fuzes attached to the group in connection with it. By the above arrangement, the insulation of each line can be tested at any moment required.

In making the delicate test for insulation, which should invariably be done at leisure, and, if possible, when an enemy's vessels are not in the vicinity of the mines, a large number of Daniell's or other cells of suitable form should always be used. To do this, it would only be necessary to connect such a battery in place of a single cell permanently arranged, as described, in the testing circuit, and to proceed with the details of the operation as before. As the cable would, in actual work, always be charged with the full power of a firing battery, the value of its insulation to resist an electrical charge at such a high potential would be an important point to determine. The fuzes being entirely out of the circuit till the moment of the action arrives, no danger of a premature explosion need be apprehended; if a fuze were in such a position as to be fired prematurely, it would be exploded, in connection with the firing circuit, independently of the operation of testing the insulation of the cables.

To render a Channel Safe.—In order to render the channel safe for a friendly vessel, it is only necessary to remove the plug from between the contact plates *b* and *f*; this disconnects the firing battery from the circuit.

Defence of Harbours by Booms, &c.—Booms or cables supported by rafts may also be employed in the defence of harbours, or rivers, either by themselves, or in combination with submarine mines; in the latter case, the booms, &c., may be moored either in advance of the mines, or in rear of the front row, this last method of mooring them being the most effective one.

There are a great variety of forms in which a boom may be constructed. The qualities essential for a good and practicable boom are:—

1.—Great strength.
2.—Great power of resistance.
3.—Convenience in handling.
4.—Easy to manipulate.
5.—Its materials easily procurable.

Construction of a Boom.—The general construction of a boom consists of a main cable, buoyed up at intervals by floats. The main cable may be either wire, chain, or rope, the former being very much superior for this purpose to chain or rope. The floats consist of balks of timber built round the main cable and bound together by means of iron hoops, &c. A space is left between each float, by which a certain amount of flexibility in the boom is obtained, without which it would be of comparatively little use, as it might be easily overrun.

It must be borne in mind, in constructing all such booms, that the smaller the proportion of timber used in forming the floats to the cable, consistent with buoyancy, the stronger will be the structure.

A very important feature in connection with such a mode of defence is the manner of mooring it; for if it be moored so as to be unyielding, then its sole power of resisting a vessel charging it is the actual strength of the materials composing the structure, but if it be moored so that it is capable of yielding to a sudden blow, this force will be to some extent absorbed, and resistance of the defence greatly increased.

The raft employed to support the main cable should be moored by means of very heavy chains (without anchors) in the direction of the attack, and with ordinary anchors and cables on the other side.

As a rule, the booms should be moored obliquely to the direction of the current, where there is any, as the tendency of the current to over-run the boom when so placed will be less, and also a ship ramming it must place herself athwart the current to attack the boom at right angles.

Clearing a Passage through the Torpedo Defences of an Enemy.—The subject of clearing a passage through the torpedo defences of an enemy is one fraught with innumerable difficulties, on account of the varied nature and impracticability of obtaining accurate and *certain* information of such defences, and thus it is impossible to lay down any fixed rule or plan for carrying out such an operation.

In fact, it will be only under the most favourable circumstances that such a service will be successfully accomplished, that is to say, in the case of a harbour or river defended by submarine mines but unsupported by guns, or guard boats, or where the electric light is used.

Numerous methods have been devised from time to time to effect the destruction of an enemy's submarine defences, among which are the following :—

1.—Projecting frames, &c., from the bows of a vessel.

2.—Creeping and sweeping by boats.

3.—Countermining.

Projecting Frames, &c., from the Bows of a Vessel.—This method was adopted by the Federals during the American civil war of 1861–5, and in many instances it was the means of saving their ships when proceeding up rivers which had been torpedoed by the Confederates, though notwithstanding this precaution several vessels were sunk. The submarine mines against which this mode of defence was used were in nine cases out of ten mechanical ones, and therefore the framework defence afforded a better means of protection then, than would be the case now that electrical ground mines and circuit closers are used, as the framework would catch the circuit closer only, and the vessel would probably be over the mine when the explosion took place. The Americans moor their circuit closers in rear of their mines, so that a vessel fitted with a bow frame or not, coming in contact with the former must be right over the charge at the instant of explosion.

Against ground electrical mines fired at will, the bow net, &c., is no protection whatever, still under certain circumstances it would be found extremely useful.

Sweeping for Submarine Mines.—This method of clearing a channel of submarine mines could not possibly be carried out under artillery fire, but in waters not so defended it would prove of some value.

Where only buoyant mines, or ground mines with circuit closers are to be cleared away, two or more boats dragging a hawser between them would be sufficient to discover them, and so lead to their destruction ; but where dummy mines and inverted creepers are moored in addition, another method of sweeping must be resorted to, viz., that of bringing an explosive charge of gun-cotton to act on the obstruction grappled, and thus destroy it. This is effected by lashing a charge to each end of the sweep, so that whatever is grappled may slide along it, until caught by hooks, which are attached for this purpose to the centre of the charge. On grappling an obstruction, the two boats drop their anchors, one hauling in, the other veering out the sweep, until the charge is hooked by the obstruction ; this being effected, the boats move out of range, and the charge is fired.

Creeping for Electrical Cables, &c.—Creeping is the method employed for picking up the electric cables of the enemy's submarine mines, and is effected by boats towing an ordinary grappling iron, or specially prepared creeper on the ground.

In both sweeping and creeping it would be found necessary to employ a diver, who would ascertain the nature of the grappled obstructions which could not be easily raised by the boats.

The Lay torpedo boat, which is fully described in the chapter on offensive torpedoes, is capable of being used for the foregoing purposes.

Countermining.—Countermining, that is, the destruction of submarine mines by the explosion of other mines dropped close to them, will under certain conditions prove of great use in clearing harbours of mines. This method could not be operated in waters properly guarded and swept by artillery fire.

There are two distinct methods of laying out countermines, viz. :—

1.—In a boat, which may be either towed, or hauled out to its destination, or may be steered, and controlled by electricity.

2.—By attaching them to buoys so that they are suspended at the proper depths, and then hauled out by means of a warp to an anchor which has been previously placed in position.

Both of the foregoing methods have been successfully manipulated in practice, the first method, where the boat carrying the countermines is towed either by a pulling or steam boat being the most practicable one. A large amount of material would be required for clearing a channel by means of countermines: for example, if the mines to be attacked require 500-lb. gun-cotton charges to be used, $7\frac{1}{2}$ tons of the explosive, besides cables, buoys, &c., would be required to clear a passage about one mile in length and 200 feet in width.

A ship's launch will carry about twelve of these 500-lb. countermines, with all the gear attached thereto.

Experiments to ascertain the effect of countermining have been carried out in England and Europe for the last five years, some of which are given at length in the chapter on "Torpedo Experiments." During the Turco-Russian war, a portion of the Danube was swept in the ordinary and most simple manner by the Turks, and five Russian electro contact buoyant mines were picked up; one other exploded during the process of dragging it to the surface, but no injury occurred to those at work.

Destruction of Passive Obstructions.—To clear away booms, or other passive obstructions, if not possible to cut them away, they may be destroyed by outrigger boats exploding their torpedoes underneath, and in contact, or by attaching charges of gun-cotton at intervals, and then exploding them simultaneously. When a chain is horizontal, and therefore somewhat taut, a charge of $3\frac{1}{2}$ lbs. of gun-cotton (this explosive, being the most effective and convenient for such purposes, should always be used) will be found sufficient to destroy it, no matter what size, and whether the chain is in or out of the water, the charge being of course placed in contact with it. Great uncertainty must

always attend the supposed clearance of a channel, or passage of
submarine mines, as was exemplified during the American civil war,
when most of the Northeners' vessels were destroyed while moving
over ground which had been previously carefully dragged, and buoyed,
and this fact, coupled with the tediousness and danger of performing
such a service, proves the enormous value of a system of defence by
submarine mines.

CHAPTER V.

OFFENSIVE TORPEDO WARFARE.

THE term "Torpedo" is applicable more particularly to offensive submarine mines than to those employed for the purposes of defence, and therefore by *torpedoes* will be understood every kind of submarine explosive weapon designed to be used for active attack against vessels, &c., no matter how they may be manipulated.

Offensive Torpedo Warfare still in its Infancy.—Though during the seventeen or eighteen years that torpedoes have been considered as a legitimate mode of naval warfare there have occurred three big wars, in each of which submarine weapons, offensive and defensive, have played an important part, still the subject of *offensive* torpedo warfare must be even now considered as in its infancy, and therefore any opinions expressed as to the merits and demerits of the various apparatus in connection therewith can but be based on the theoretical capabilities of each torpedo, and on the results of experiments carried out with them during peace time, which latter as a rule are conducted under far too favourable conditions to be relied upon.

Their Use during the Civil War in America.—During the American civil war, the only offensive submarine weapon that was used was the outrigger or spar torpedo, which in those days was a crude and imperfect machine, and manœuvred from boats possessing all the features which a torpedo boat should *not* possess. Still under these unfavourable conditions ships were sunk by such means by both Federals and Confederates, proving that in future wars this mode of attack, favoured by the vast and important improvements that have lately been effected both in connection with the torpedoes and torpedo boats, should play a prominent part, and prove a most destructive mode of attack.

Their Use in the Franco-German and Russo-Turkish Wars.—In the Franco-German war of 1870-1, offensive torpedo warfare was not resorted to by either side, the French fleet being deterred from entering German waters by the submarine mines placed, or at least supposed to be placed, in position.

From the Russo-Turkish war much light was expected by torpedoists to be thrown on the subject of torpedo warfare, but alas, .ittle or nothing was done to settle any of the many vexed questions which exist in regard to offensive submarine weapons. The torpedo experience of that struggle tended rather to prove that the vast importance hitherto attached to torpedo attack was much exaggerated.

One of the causes which led to the failure of offensive submarine weapons, when employed on active service, seems to be due to the fact that, owing to the extremely small radius of the destructive effect of such weapons, it is absolutely necessary for complete success to explode the mine in actual contact with the attacked vessel; to ensure which, at night time, in an unknown harbour, with the position of the vessel attacked somewhat uncertain, and even without the additional obstacles of guard boats, booms, electric lights, &c., is a service of infinite difficulty, and one which may easily terminate in a failure. The foregoing would more especially apply to the spar torpedo attack, but in an attack with the Whitehead fish, or towing torpedo, there would be an additional cause of failure, viz., the complicated nature of their manipulation.

Torpedoes may be divided into four classes, viz. :—

1.—Drifting or floating torpedoes.

2.—Towing torpedoes.

3. Locomotive torpedoes.

4.—Outrigger or spar torpedoes.

Drifting or Floating Torpedoes.—By " drifting" or " floating " torpedoes are meant all those submarine machines which are dependent on the tide or current of a stream for their action and motion.

During the American civil war this mode of attacking vessels was constantly employed by the Confederates, and though not successful in destroying any of the Federal ships, was the means of considerably hampering the movements of their river flotillas.

Drifting torpedoes might be advantageously used for the destruction of pontoon bridges, booms, &c., and in this way, had the Turks in their late war used them, the Russians would have found the crossing of the Danube a matter of infinite danger and difficulty; in fact, by a systematic use of such weapons, combined with a little dash on the part of the Ottoman flotilla on the Danube, that river should have been to the Russians an impassable barrier. To use these torpedoes most effectively, especially against a single vessel, a thorough know-ledge of the force and direction of currents should be gained before proceeding to undertake an operation in which these submarine weapons are used.

Another point to be remembered is, that if such a torpedo were started with the flood, for example, towards an enemy, and did not explode, there would be a chance of its being returned to the starting-place by the ebb tide.

In this class the following torpedoes seem the most practicable :—

1.—Lewis's drifting torpedo.

2.—McEvoy's drifting torpedo.

3.—American extempore drifting torpedo.

Description of Lewis's Drifting Torpedo. — "Lewis's" drifting torpedo, designed for the express purpose of destroying booms or other floating obstructions placed round a vessel at anchor for the purposes of defence, is shown at Fig. 101. It consists of a box *a*, containing the charge and fitted with several detonating fuzes. This box is attached to one side of a beam *b*, and within 6 inches of one extremity, the beam being about 20 feet long and 7 inches square ; to the opposite side of the same end of the beam *b* a heavy weight *c*, resting in a shoe *d*, is attached by a long iron rod *e*, which reaches to the other extremity of the beam, and is there connected to a bell-crank lever and spring *f*, a pressure on which detaches the weight *c*; a chain *g*, 18 feet long, connects the weight loosely with the upper end of the beam, and another chain *h*, 9 feet 6 inches long, connects it with a point more than 2 feet below the centre of the beam. The apparatus is so constructed that it floats nearly vertical with the top of the beam just above the surface of the water.

On the machine drifting against the boom or other obstruction, the spring or lever *f* at the upper extremity is pressed down, thus releasing the weight *c*, which falling, becomes suspended by the two chains *g* and *h*, and brings the ·beam into an inclined position. The weight of this mass of iron and the chain suspending it are suddenly brought to bear on the top of the beam, dragging it under water and clear of the boom, &c. At the same time the lower end, released from the weight, rises, and the whole apparatus is carried forward by the current against the side of the vessel, on striking which the torpedo is exploded.

Description of McEvoy's Drifting Torpedo.—"McEvoy's" drifting torpedo is intended to be floated, singly or in groups, by the aid of tides or currents against vessels at anchor, bridges, &c.

At Fig. 102 is shown a plan of this form of drifting torpedo.

It consists of the body of the torpedo *a*, which contains the charge, at the side of which is placed the loading hole *b*; *c* is the tube containing the priming charge; *d* is the framework surrounding and protecting the wheel or screw *e*; *f* is the fuze pillar, in the centre of which is a steel rod *g*, and on the top a thin steel plate *h* is placed; *i* is the nipple for the percussion cap; *k* is a horizontal bar, turning and resting on top of the fuze pillar *f*; *m* is the lever for supporting the hammer *n* when it is set; *l* is the screw barrel supporting the wheel or screw *e*; *o* is a safety pin; *q* is the supporting chain, and *p* the spring for working the hammer *n*.

By means of a buoy or log of wood, from which the torpedo is suspended, it can be adjusted so that the explosion shall occur at the requisite depth.

To prepare the torpedo for use, unscrew the fuze pillar *f*, take off the horizontal bar *k*, place a percussion cup on the nipple *i*, and screw it tightly against the end of the steel rod *g*. The fuze pillar is then ready for use, and should be screwed into the body *a*. Then fill the torpedo with the explosive and close the loading hole *b*. The hammer *n* is then set by drawing it back and bringing the end of the lever *m* against it, at the same time running the screw barrel *l* under the lever *m*, so that its end catches the screw of the barrel, as shown in the figure. The safety pin *o* is then put in its place and secured by a few parts of thread, which by a sharp jerk 'on the safety line will be easily broken.

The horizontal lever *k*, which carries the lever *m* and propeller *e*, rotates on the top of the fuze pillar *f*, and is prevented from rising by means of a screw. The torpedo being let go, the safety pin *o* is pulled out by means of a line which is attached to it. The propeller will not revolve whilst the torpedo is drifting with the current, but the instant it is stopped by the action of the current the wheel will be caused to revolve, and after a few revolutions it will unscrew the barrel from

PLATE XXIX

Fig 102

Fig 101

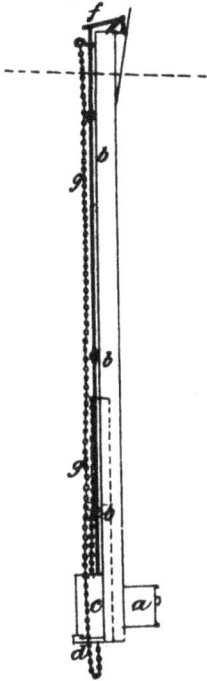

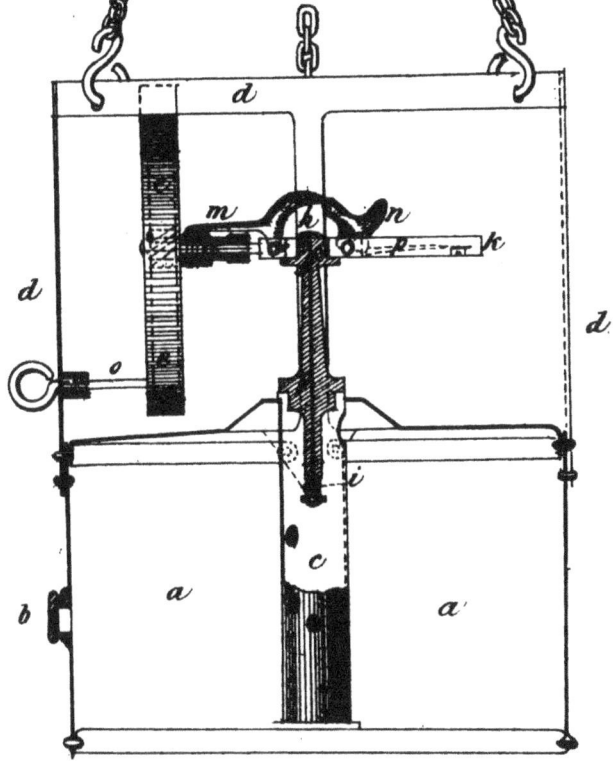

Fig 103

under the end of the lever k, and the latter, dropping the hammer n, will be forced by the spring p into contact with the thin steel plate h on the top of the fuze pillar, which blow is transmitted by means of the steel rod g to the percussion cap, and the torpedo exploded.

American Extempore Drifting Torpedo.—This form of drifting torpedo, which is readily made, was used in great numbers by the Confederates, and though not successful in sinking any Federal ships, caused their vessels considerable annoyance and delay.

At Fig. 103 is shown a sketch of this torpedo. It consists of a tin case containing about 70 lbs. of powder. A stiff wire a, b passes through a hole punctured in a strip of tin c, and a stuffing box d; the end a of the wire is covered with fulminate, and so arranged that the friction caused by its passage through the strip of tin c will ignite it; a number of wires lead from b to pieces of driftwood on the surface e, e, e, and the case is supported at the proper depth by a line attached to a section of log.

Towing Torpedoes.—By towing torpedoes are meant those submarine machines which are so shaped and arranged, that when towed from a ship or boat in motion they will diverge to a considerable extent, thus enabling the towing vessel to pass clear of the ship attacked, and yet near enough to allow of the torpedo being brought in contact with some part or other of her hull.

Towing torpedoes were for the first time employed on actual service during the late Russo-Turkish war, when a modified form of the well-known Harvey torpedo, designed by a German officer, was used by the Russians, but in no case was it successful.

In this class of submarine offensive machines may be placed the following :—

1.—Harvey's towing torpedo.
2.—Menzing's towing torpedo.
3.—The French towing torpedo.

Harvey's Torpedo.—This form of towing torpedo was invented conjointly by Captain John Harvey and Commander Frederick Harvey, R.N., and is intended to be used at sea both as a means of offence and defence.

At Fig. 104 is shown in elevation the small sized Harvey towing torpedo, in which all the latest improvements that have been devised are represented.

a is the case of the torpedo, formed of Muntz's metal, but not provided, as the original ones were, with an exterior case of wood ; by this alteration greater capacity combined with extreme lightness is obtained, which undoubtedly much enhances the value of the small size torpedo which is intended to be carried by and manœuvred from boats ; *b* is the principal or after lever, hinged on the top of torpedo at *c*, and rests, when ready for action, in a crutch formed in the top of the exploding bolt *d ; e* is the foremost lever, hinged at *f*, and kept in position on the after lever *b* by a groove formed in it and a lashing which passes through a slot in the principal lever, as at *g* ; *h* is the side lever, pivoted at *i*, and exerting a pressure on the firing bolt *d* by means of a lanyard which is passed through the bolt *k* and over the principal lever *b* ; *l* is the top lever, pivoted at *m*, and exerting a pressure on the bolt *d* by means of a lanyard which is passed through the bolt *n* and over the principal lever *b* ; this top lever *l* has been added to ensure the action of the torpedo, on its strik-ing sideways against a vessel ; *o* and *t* are handles, to the former of which the lashings of the levers *h* and *l* are secured ; *p* is the ring used for attaching the buoy rope ; *r, r* are two loading holes, made in the side of the torpedo case, by which a charge of gun-cotton may be quickly and efficiently stowed ; this also is a new feature in the small size torpedo ; *s* is the rudder formed for the purpose of controlling the direction of the torpedo when the tow line is suddenly slacked.

In regard to the large size torpedo, the construction of the case remains as in the original ones, the improvements being, the enlarge-ment of the loading and fuze holes, and the addition of the top lever *l*, as shown at Fig. 104.

The small size torpedo is capable of holding 47 lbs. of water, whilst the large size one will contain 76 lbs. of water, or about 33 lbs. and 58 lbs. of gun-cotton respectively.

The slings are made of best Italian hemp, and consist of a span of four legs, which are secured to lugs at the corners of the torpedo and connected to an iron thimble, which is shown at Fig. 105 ; this thimble is made suitable for either wire or hemp rope, and is so arranged that should the seizing become slack, the parts of the slings cannot become detached from the thimble.

The legs of the slings should be so fitted that when stretched alongside the torpedo they extend 1 foot beyond the stem for the

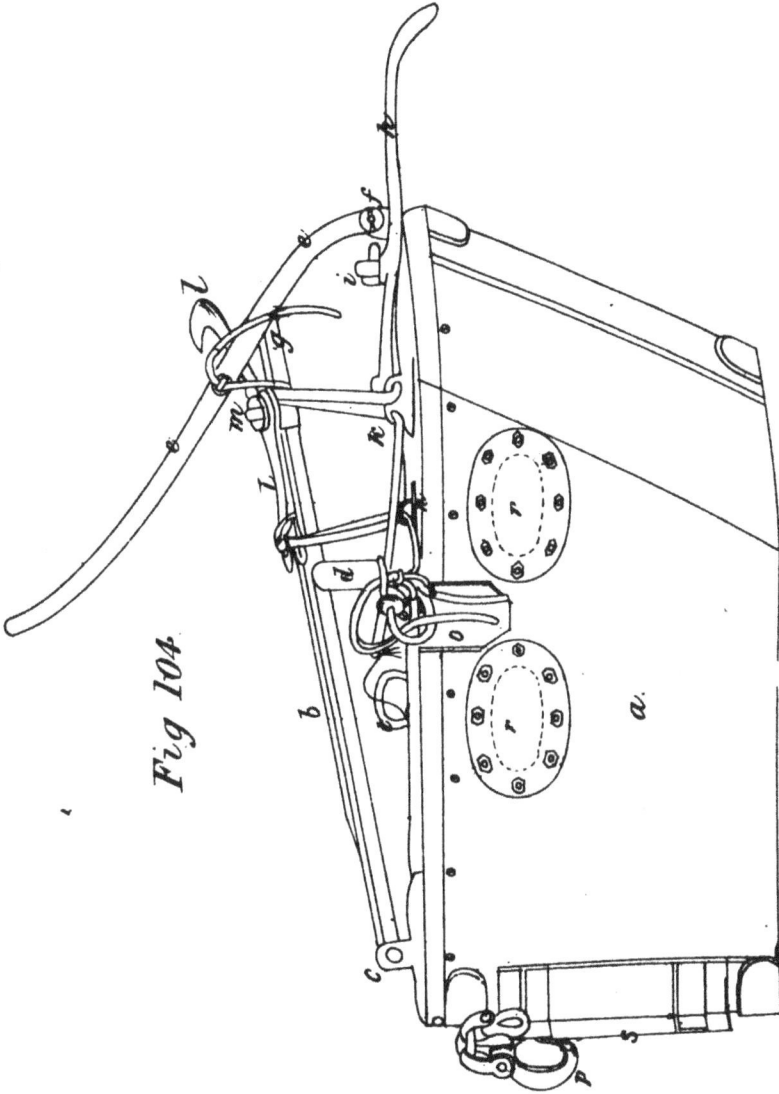

PLATE XXX

Fig 104.

large torpedo and 8 inches for the small one; the four legs should be so fitted that when an equal strain is brought on them, the thimble should be on a level with the upper lugs, and the upper fore span form an angle of 80° to 85° with the side of the torpedo; this is shown at Fig. 106. This arrangement gives the best divergence with the least strain on the tow rope, and is suitable when the torpedo is kept at short scope, as well as when a long length of tow line is out.

The mode of attaching the foremost and side levers is shown at Fig. 107. Before reeving the lanyards they should be well greased in the wake of the fair leads, but not where they are made fast. The lanyards should be made up like a reef point. Care should be taken that the short arm of the side lever *h* is brought close into the fair lead, and its lanyard should be set up sufficiently taut to give a slight spring in the principal lever *b* by the strain thus brought on it. This lever *b* has a steel fish on the top, in order to prevent it taking a permanent bend. If the side lever lanyard is properly set up, the bolt will spring down about $\frac{1}{8}$th of an inch when the safety key is withdrawn, owing to the spring in the lever, and the shrinking of the lanyard; this brings the muzzle $\frac{1}{8}$th of an inch nearer the pin without disturbing the side lever.

The bolt is so arranged that the torpedo can be fired by either of the following methods:—

1.—Mechanically.
2.—Electrically at will.
3.—Electrically on contact or at will.

Mechanically.—In this case the bottom of the inner cylinder, as at *a*, Fig. 108, is fitted with the ordinary mechanical chemical fuze, ignition being effected by the breaking of the glass vessel containing the sulphuric acid on being forced into contact with the needle *n*, by the action of the levers on the torpedo striking a vessel.

Electrically at Will.—For this purpose a platinum wire fuze is used, one terminal being connected to earth through the bolt, the other to a wire leading up through the core of the bolt, and connected by means of an ebonite joint with a single cored electrical cable leading from the torpedo vessel.

Electrically on Contact, or at Will.—In this case, a resistance coil is inserted in addition to the fuze, and is so arranged that on the bolt being forced down a short circuit is formed, cutting out the resistance

K

coil (about 20 ohms), and thus enabling the battery to fire the fuze, which, owing to the 20 ohms resistance in the circuit, it was previously unable to effect. Should the bolt so arranged be required to be fired at will, it is only necessary to put a more powerful battery in circuit, and so fire the fuze through the 20 ohms resistance.

Exploding Bolt.—The exploding bolt is fitted to act with a pressure of from 30 to 40 lbs. on its head for the large size torpedo, and from 15 to 20 lbs. for the small size one.

The bolts are all the same size, and differ only in the direction of the slot for the safety key *k*, being port or starboard bolts accordingly. The muzzle of the exploding bolt stands 1 inch off the pin when in the safety position, that is, when the safety key rests on the brass work of the priming case.

The safety key is secured in the slot of the exploding bolt, as shown at Fig. 108, by eight or nine parts of strong whitey-brown thread secured to the key, passed round the bolt, and securely knotted; the parts of the thread should come away with the key, in order that none of the parts may be worked down the tube by the exploding bolt.

In the event of the large torpedo being cut away in deep water after the withdrawal of the safety key, it will explode by pressure on the head of the bolt at about sixty fathoms depth; the small one at about thirty fathoms.

Buoys.—The buoys are of two sizes, and are made of solid cork (such cork only being used as will ensure great floating power after being immersed for a time); each buoy is built upon a galvanised iron tube running longitudinally through; on the ends of the tube are screwed wooden cones, which bind all together, and render the buoy indestructible.

Two buoys are used for each torpedo, the larger buoys for the large size torpedo, and the smaller buoys for the small size torpedo. The buoy rope is of hemp, about five or six fathoms in length and two inches in circumference, an eye being spliced in the end nearest the torpedo; to this eye is bent the tow rope, with a single or double sheet bend forming the knot by which the torpedo is towed; the other end of the buoy rope is passed through one of the rings in the stern end of the torpedo (according to whether working in deep or shallow water), then through the tube of the first buoy, and an overhand knot made in the rear; then through the next buoy, and a knot in the rear of that.   Recently, Captain Harvey has adopted a large and a small buoy for each torpedo, the large one being practically sufficient, the smaller one being added in the event of the other one becoming sodden.

Brakes.—The brakes are used for the purpose of controlling the tow ropes ; they can be fixed by screws into the deck at the most convenient place for command, and in a properly constructed torpedo vessel would be placed below the water line, to prevent exposure of the men working them.   They are so arranged as to admit of the tow rope being quickly veered, and at the same time are sufficiently powerful to bring the torpedo to the surface when required.   Success greatly depends on the skilful handling of these brakes, for in conjunction with the cork buoys they give the operator command of the depth at which the enemy is to be struck.   Unless a very high rate of speed is required, one handspike will control the tow rope ; the other strap can be thrown off the drum, and the handspike allowed to lie on the deck ready to be thrown into gear, if necessary.   The surface of the drum in contact with the strap should be powdered with rosin to increase the friction.   The tow rope should be so reeled up that in veering the reel may revolve towards the men at the handspike.   The spindle will contain several tow ropes, that, in the event of one torpedo being cut away, another can be immediately bent.

The brake for small torpedo requires only one drum and handspike.   It can be fitted to a steam launch by placing an extra thwart across near one of the others.

Care should be taken that the riding turns lie fairly over each other, to prevent a jamb when veering.

The brakes, both large and small, are so made as to ensure durability, they being considered a part of the ship's furniture.

Brake for safety key line is a small reel on the same principle. When going a slow speed, it may not be necessary, as the safety key line can be attended by hand ; but when going ten or eleven knots, it will be found of considerable advantage, both in keeping the bight of the safety key line from dragging astern, thereby lessening the divergence of the torpedo, and also in drawing the safety key when a strong stop is used.

Arrangements for Launching and Towing the Torpedoes.—A yard across either the main or mizen mast of a torpedo vessel, from 20 to 25 feet

above the water line, is a very convenient method for launching and
towing.   The leading block on the yard, through which the tow rope
is rove, may be fitted to a traveller on the yard with an inhaul and
outhaul, that the distance out from the ship's side may be regulated
as convenient.

In a large vessel, the leading block for tow rope can be fixed to
the end of the quarter boat's davits.   The brakes for commanding the
tow rope should be screwed firmly to the deck.   In a vessel properly
constructed for the service, they would be on the lower deck, the tow
rope having been led along the yard, and down each side of the mast.

A leading block for the tow rope is placed on the deck by span
or bolt a few feet in front of the brake.   The safety key reel, if
used, must be fixed in a convenient position on deck, that the man
attending it can see how to control it; in a properly constructed vessel
he would be in the pilot house.   The safety key line leads through a
small leading block on the ensign staff or some convenient point abaft
the lead of the tow rope, 15 to 20 feet above the water.   The leading
block on the yard may be fitted with a lizard, if thought necessary.
A sharp instrument should be kept by the brakes ready to sever the
tow rope.

In large men of war, arrangements are made for carrying a loaded
torpedo and two buoys in a convenient position on each side of the
vessel, in such a manner that the tow line can be bent, the exploding
bolt screwed in, the levers adjusted, and the torpedoes and buoys
dropped simultaneously when required.

Preparing the Torpedoes for Use.—The torpedoes, port and starboard,
loaded and ballasted, having been hoisted out of the torpedo room, are
placed on the deck on their own sides, with their heads forward under
the leading block, and the buoys placed abaft them and strung
together; the exploding bolts are now entered into the torpedoes, and
forced down until their safety keys rest on the brass work, taking care
that each safety key points in the direction of the eye through which
its lanyard has to pass; the levers are now secured by their lanyards,
as explained at pages 120 and 121.   The eye at the end of the buoy
rope is now rove through the large or small ring in the stern end of
the torpedo.   The tow rope having been previously rove through the
leading block on the deck and on the yard, is rove through the thimble
of the slings from forward aft, and bent, with a single or double sheet

bend, to the eye of the buoy rope.   The safety key line having been previously rove through the leading block on the ensign staff, and the lanyard on the safety key having been led through the eye of the handle, making a fair lead with the slit in the bolt, are bent together with a double sheet bend, and stopped to the eye of the handle by a split yarn of suitable strength, the yarn having been first secured to the line by a round turn outside the bend.

The line should also be stopped with another split yarn round all parts of the slings close up to the thimble, having first made an overhand knot in the line at a distance a few inches longer than that between the eye bolt and the thimble.

The crew having been stationed at their respective posts, the handles having been shipped on the tow reel, the tow line is then reeled up until the torpedo will launch clear, and swing out under the leading block on the yard.   Hold the torpedo by the handspikes, and take off the handles of the brake.   In swinging out, care should be taken that in starting from the deck the fore slings do not foul the fore top lever.   The stern of the torpedo can be steadied by keeping a slight strain on the buoy rope.   The safety key line must be kept clear, and not checked, or it might break the stop and draw out the key before intended.   The buoys must be placed in a proper position and hands stationed by them to launch them overboard the instant the torpedo takes the water.   It would be better to stop the screw, if circumstances would allow of it, when lowering the torpedo and buoys into the water, to prevent the chance of the buoys fouling the screw. The torpedo, on reaching the water, will *immediately* diverge clear of the ship ; the buoys being launched, as the strain comes on the buoy rope, they will be towed clear away from the screw, and full speed may be put on at once.   The men at the handspikes must veer steadily, occasionally checking the torpedo, that it may be kept near the surface, and not allowed to dive, which it will do if the tow rope is slacked up altogether, and then a sudden strain brought on it.

Eventually it will come to the surface, when the bow is pointed up by the strain on the tow rope ; greater the speed the more quickly will it be brought to the surface.   In shallow water this should be particularly attended to, as in diving it might strike the bottom and injure the levers, and, if the safety key has been withdrawn, explode ; moreover, it brings an undue strain on the tow rope.   The torpedo can now be gradually veered out to the distance required, the safety key line so attended that a sufficient strain is kept on it as not to allow of a long bight of line dragging astern of the torpedo ; at the same time having due regard to the strength of the yarn by which the line is stopped to the handle of the torpedo. The distance veered must depend upon the nature of attack. The tow line should be marked with knots every 10 fathoms : under some circumstances the torpedo would be close to the ship until passing the enemy; at other times veered to 40 fathoms it will be found most suitable.

The full divergence of 45° is obtained up to 50 fathoms ; beyond that the bight of the tow rope in the water drags the torpedo astern, unless the tow rope is triced much higher up, which has its disadvantage ; 40 to 50 fathoms of tow rope gives the best command of the torpedo, veering 2 or 3 fathoms of tow line suddenly will always sink the torpedo some feet below the surface. Should it become necessary to use the torpedoes with a stern board, they can be so used, but in this case the port torpedo is used on the starboard, bow and starboard on the port ; all other arrangements being exactly the same. In rough weather, advantage should be taken of the roll, and the torpedo allowed to swing out from the yard, and be let go by the run, checking the tow rope immediately the torpedo is in the water. It is not absolutely necessary to ease the vessel when launching ; the torpedo can be launched at full speed. In the event of its being found necessary to cut adrift the torpedo, in consequence of coming suddenly across a friendly vessel, the tow rope should be cut near the brake, and if the buoy rope has been rove through the large stern ring, the torpedo will sink and be lost, the buoy only remaining. If the buoy rope has been rove through the small stern ring, the torpedo will be suspended by the buoy rope ; and should the safety key not have been withdrawn, can be recovered with safety.

In the event of wishing to recover it when the buoy rope has been rove through the large ring, a toggle must be lashed on the tow rope abaft the leading block on the yard, when it can be recovered by the buoy rope ; as a general rule, however, it will be found best to expend the torpedo, and not attempt its recovery.

Recovering the Torpedo.—Should the safety key have been withdrawn, great caution is necessary. Tongs, shown at Fig. 109, for going round the upper part of the bolt, to take the place of the safety key, when

PLATE XXXI

Fig 105.

Fig 106

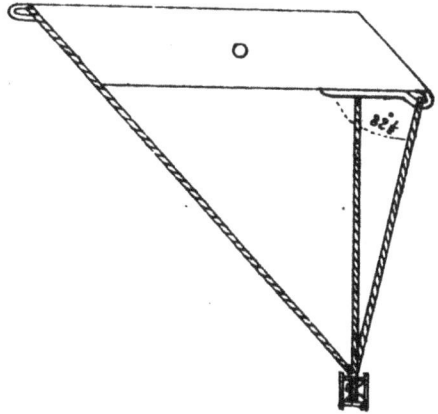

Fig 107

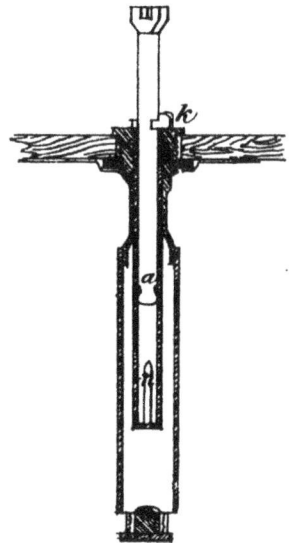

Fig 108

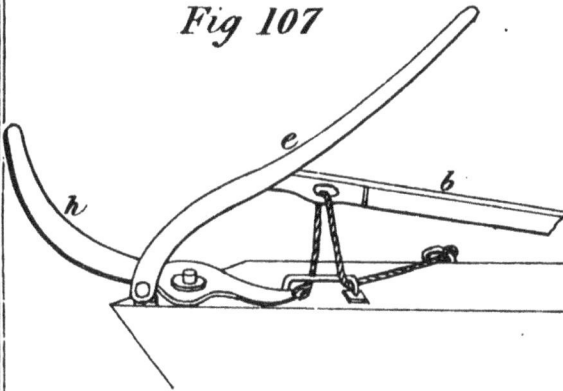

Fig 109.

PLATE XXXII

Fig 110.

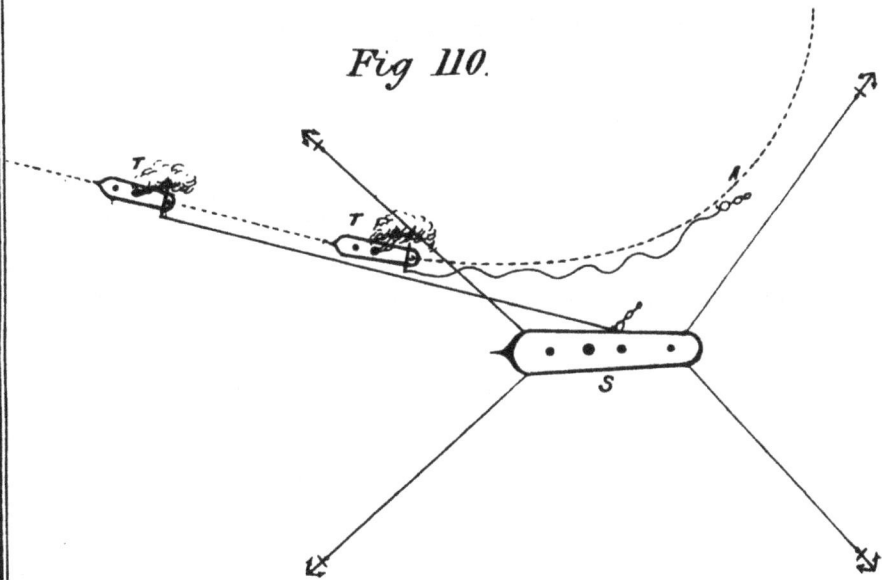

Fig 111

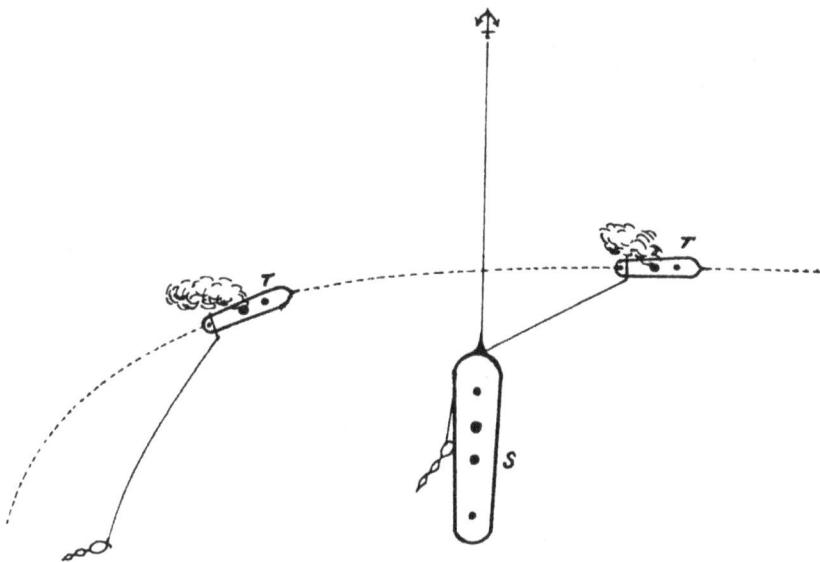

once clasped and secured round the bolt, render the torpedo safe to handle; this could only be done from a boat. With the safety key in, there is no danger in hoisting it inboard again by its own tow rope, and hoisting up the buoys at the same time with a grapnel.

Different Methods of Using the Torpedo.—There are two methods of employing the torpedo, either of which may be adopted, according to circumstances.

1.—When it is towed with a length of line varying from 25 to 60 fathoms, and dipped when in position to strike the attacked vessel.

2.—When it is kept suspended from the yard, &c., and dropped at the spot, where according to the first method it would have been dipped.

In the first method, it is not necessary to withdraw the safety key till just before dipping; in the second method the safety key line is belayed at about twenty fathoms, and the key withdrawn when the line is tautened by the ship going ahead.

Tactics.—Description of the various attacks that may be made with the Harvey torpedo against a ship at anchor or under way. In the following diagrams T is the torpedo vessel, S the ship attacked.

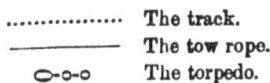

> .... The track.
> ———————— The tow rope.
> ○-o-o   The torpedo.

Attacking a Vessel moored Head and Stern.—In this case the torpedo vessel steers in for the bow or quarter of the vessel attacked, according to the direction of the current, and on the side approached launches the torpedo between the moorings, as at A; leaving the tow rope slack, the torpedo vessel proceeds ahead or astern against the current, and when at a sufficient distance off, the tow rope is held fast, which will cause the torpedo to diverge into contact with the vessel attacked, as shown by Fig. 110.

Attacking a Vessel at Anchor by Crossing her Bow.—In this case the torpedo is sufficiently diverged when near to the vessel with a good scope of tow rope out. After having crossed her bow, proceeding onwards, the tow rope will be brought obliquely across her cable, and the torpedo will swing into her, as shown at Fig. 111. It may be here remarked, that in all cases the depth of the explosion can be obtained by the sudden slacking of the tow rope; and the tow rope once under the keel, causes the torpedo to be hauled down near to it before exploding.

Attacking a Vessel at Anchor by coming up from Astern on either Side.—In this case the torpedo is launched when on the quarter of the vessel attacked, as at *A*, the tow rope left slack. After steaming ahead some distance, hold fast the tow rope, when, by continuing to steam on, the torpedo will diverge into contact with the bottom of the vessel attacked, as shown at Fig. 112. *When skilfully performed*, the total destruction of the enemy is certain, since the torpedo is springing from a depth to the surface, and will, in consequence, strike near her keel. The torpedo vessel can pass at her greatest speed, and, if thought necessary, near enough to clear away any of the ordinary obstructions, such as booms, nets, &c.

Passing Down between Two Lines of Vessels at Anchor.—In this case it would be impossible to fire at the torpedo vessel, for fear of injury to their friends. Two or more torpedo vessels following each other with preconcerted signals would cause great destruction. See Fig. 113.

Attacking a Vessel in Motion from Right Ahead.—In this case two torpedoes are launched, port and starboard, each diverging to its full extent; when passing the vessel attacked, one or the other of the tow-ropes is brought across the cut-water, and by the simultaneous motion of the two vessels in opposite directions, the torpedo is brought along-side of or under the bottom of the vessel attacked, as shown at Fig. 114. The torpedo vessel should keep the masts of her enemy in one until close to, when either torpedo will be used, according to the movement of the enemy. At the time of the tow rope taking the cut water, the brake is suddenly eased up; the tow rope will then pass under the bottom, when by checking the tow rope the torpedo will be hauled under the bottom.

To execute this attack, judgment, skill, and nerve of the highest order will be required, as the risk of being run down will be imminent.

The Attack from Astern.—In this case two torpedoes are launched, and diverged as in the previous case; it is assumed in this instance that the torpedo vessel can outspeed the vessel attacked, which will enable her to bring a torpedo under the run of the attacked vessel, as shown at Fig. 115.

If Chased by a Hostile Vessel, and unable to Face her.—In this case veer a torpedo astern, having first obtained a position a little on the

PLATE XXXIII

Fig 112

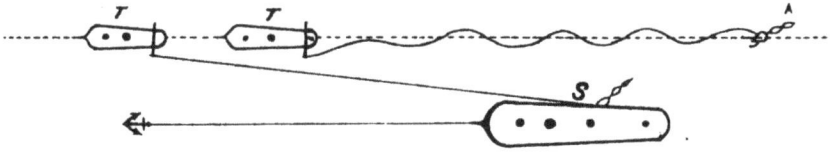

Fig 113.

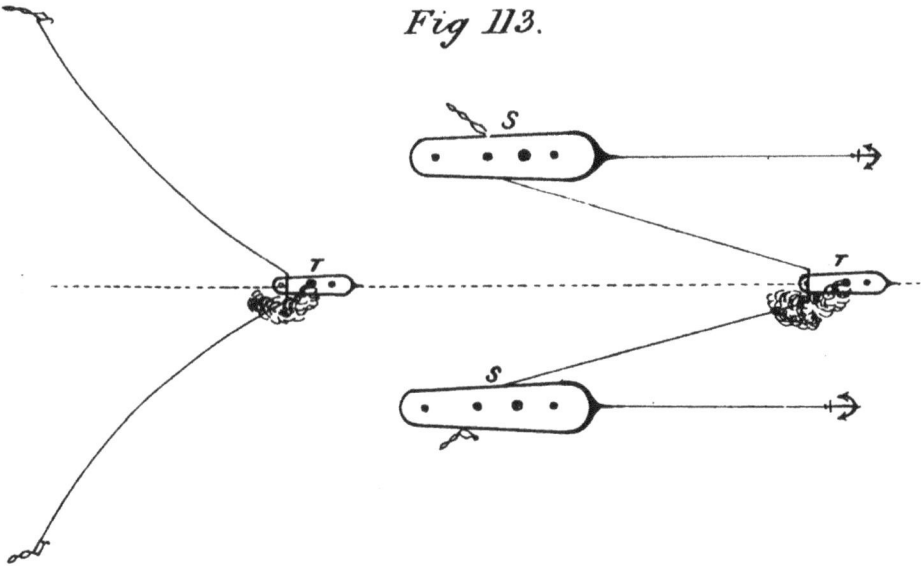

PLATE XXXIV

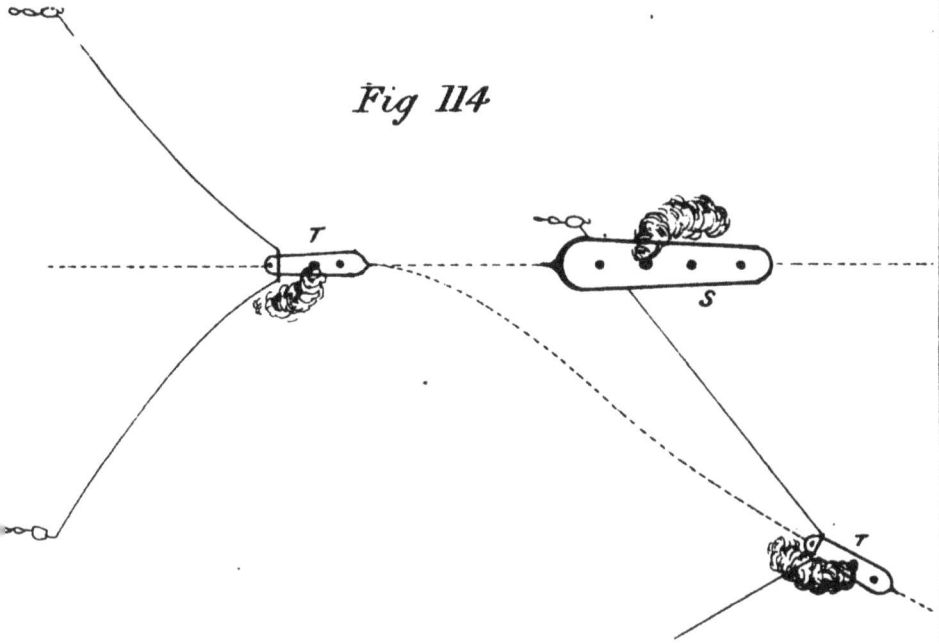

Fig 114

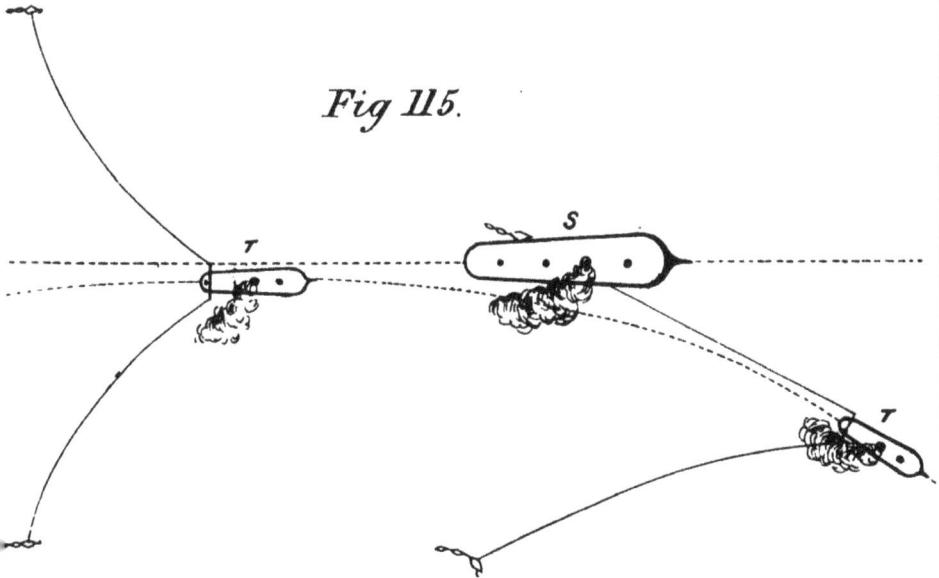

Fig 115.

bow of the chasing vessel. When it is known by the length of the tow rope out that the torpedo is about abreast of her bow, hold fast the tow rope, which will cause the torpedo to diverge, and be brought into contact, as shown at Fig. 116. As a last resort drop spanned torpedoes.

Torpedoes can be used with a stern board, if necessary. The port torpedo, in this case, will be launched on the starboard side, and the starboard on the port side.

It should be here remarked that, although great speed is essential in the torpedo vessel to come up with the enemy and choose an advantageous position, it is not advisable to tow the torpedoes, if it can be avoided, at a greater speed than 11 knots; because the strain brought upon the towing gear is excessive, and the torpedo would require a large addition of ballast to keep it sufficiently immersed to attain the full divergence.

There is, however, one style of attack in which the highest speed can be maintained, viz. by dropping the torpedo alongside in passing.

This mode of attack is one of the best, particularly under cover of darkness, against a ship at anchor.

The position of the torpedo is known, and the tow line is never in contact with the enemy during the operation; a skilled hand at the brakes is all that is required, the vessel keeping a straight course at the highest speed, passing as close as possible to the enemy, in order to clear away all obstructions. The tow rope must not be checked by the brake too suddenly.

Defensive Purposes.—The Harvey torpedo may be used as a means of defence by large ships against a torpedo vessel attacking with that species of submarine weapon, as the latter would be forced to pass outside the former vessel's torpedo, and thus decrease the chance of a successful dip. Again, in the case of an attack by the ram, these torpedoes afford some protection, as a deterrent.

Night time.—Though a dark night and tempestuous are favourable to a surprise, yet in the case of a Harvey torpedo attack it is essential that the weapon should be seen to dip it at the proper time, therefore daylight is necessary to this species of torpedo attack.

Value of the Harvey Torpedo.—The Harvey torpedo is undoubtedly of considerable value when *ably handled*, yet the skill and judgment required is very great, and can only be acquired by *constant* practice.

Description of the Menzing Towing Torpedo.—This modified form of the Harvey towing torpedo was designed by Captain Menzing, of the German navy, to remedy what is considered by the Germans as the chief defect of that weapon, viz. its liability to injure friendly vessels, and also to do away with the necessity of using two torpedoes, one for each side of a ship.

At Fig. 117 is shown a plan and elevation of this towing torpedo. *a* is the body of the torpedo, somewhat similar to the Harvey, but narrower at the stern, and bevelled on both sides towards the bow ; *b* is an iron frame placed in the bow, capable of being turned either to the right or left ; *c* is the hole for the introduction of the fuze, and *d* is the loading hole ; *e* is a rudder placed at the stern of the torpedo ; *f, f* are levers, by pressure against which the torpedo may be fired mechanically, or electrically at will ; these levers are connected to a block of wood fitted with stops to prevent them being pushed too far over ; *s* and *p* are two towing ropes, one on each side of the torpedo, which pass from its stern through the point of the frame *b*, and thence to the vessel, these are also connected to the rudder *e* in such a manner that on either of the ropes *s* and *p* being tautened the rudder *e* is turned in the opposite direction ; *w* is an electric cable, strong enough to bear the whole pressure of the torpedo when being towed right aft.

To diverge the torpedo on the starboard quarter of the ship, the line *s* must be slackened, and the whole towing strain brought on the rope *p*, causing the frame *b* to be pulled over to a knot *k* in the rope *p*, made at the proper position to ensure the torpedo towing at the correct angle from the course of the vessel, and at the same time causing the rudder *e* to be turned to starboard ; this is shown at Fig. 117 by the dotted lines.

To diverge the torpedo on the port quarter, the towing rope *p* would be slackened and the whole strain brought on the rope *s*, and an action opposite to that already described would be the result.

Two cork buoys are used, similar to those employed with the Harvey torpedo ; one being attached at a distance of 10 feet from the stern of the torpedo, and the other at such a distance astern that the torpedo would be placed at a distance below the surface to allow of safety to a friendly vessel.

The torpedo is manipulated in a similar manner to the Harvey, the circuit being closed at the moment of the first buoy disappearing, at

PLATE XXXV

Fig 116.

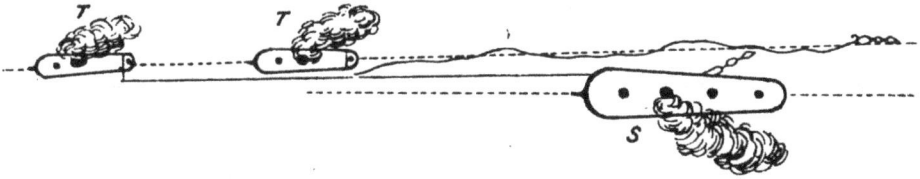

Fig 117

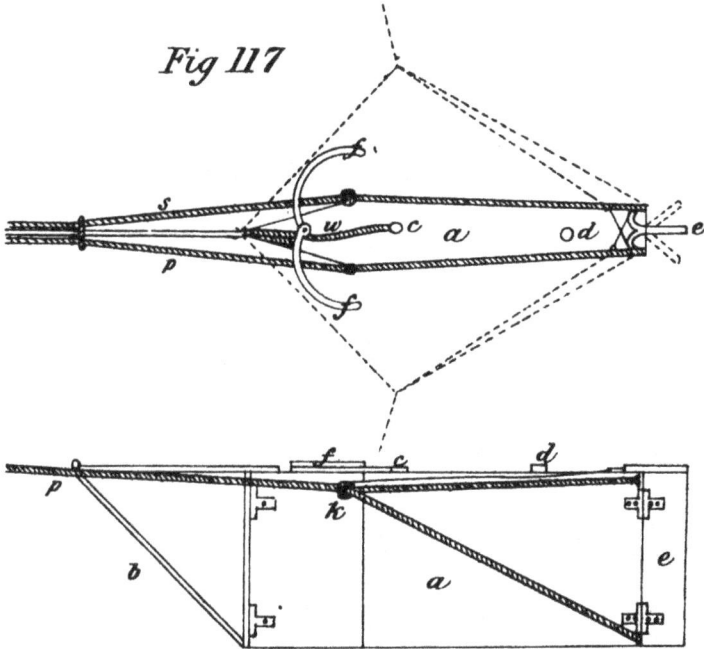

Fig 118

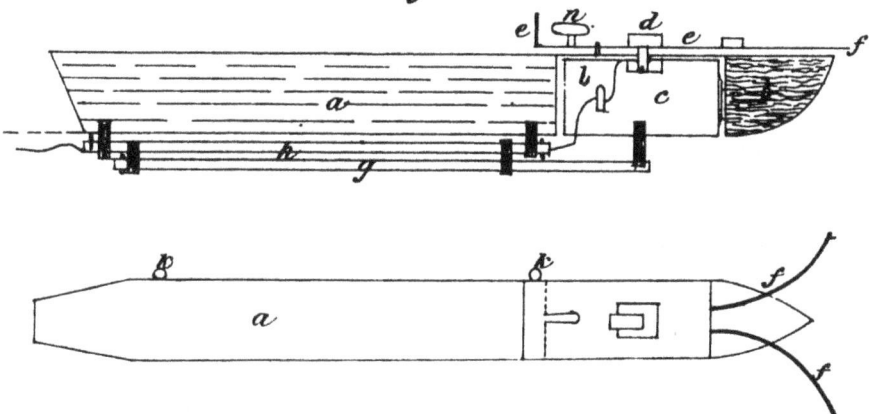

which time the torpedo would be about ten feet below the surface. The two buoys are together capable of supporting the torpedo, and thus by means of the second one it may be picked up, should it be necessary to cut the towing ropes.

Description of the French Towing Torpedo.—The towing torpedo used by the French is represented in section and plan at Fig. 118.

a is the body of the torpedo, formed of wood enclosed in a thin steel case; *b* is the head made of cork; *c* is the case containing the charge, which is generally 33 lbs. of dynamite, this case is supported by the bolt *d* resting on the plate *e*; *f, f* are whiskers, which are connected to the plate *e*; *g* and *h* are hollow tubes, one end of *g* being attached to the case *c*, and one end of *h* to the rear end of the body of the torpedo *a*, and they are so arranged that when the case *c* is released, its weight will draw out the tube *g*, which slides along the tube *h* to nearly the full extent of the latter; *k, k* are bolts, to which the towing sling is attached; *l* is the fuze, and *n* is a small gun used for firing the torpedo at will. The hole in the plate *e* through which the bolt *d* passes is larger than the latter, so that when the plate is moved backwards by pressure being applied to the whiskers the bolt is freed from support, and case *c* attached to it falls.

The modes of firing are as follows :—

1.—The automatic plan of firing is effected by the tube *h*, after it has fallen a certain distance, corresponding to a depth of 9 feet for the case *c*, drawing down by means of a line attached to it a plug contained in the body *a*, which completes the circuit of the firing battery.

2.—The plan of releasing the charge at will is effected by means of the small gun *n*, which is fired by electricity, and by its firing forces back the plate *e*, thus releasing the charge, which is then exploded, as previously explained.

Locomotive Torpedoes.—By " Locomotive " torpedoes are meant those that possess within themselves the power to move through the water, when once started in a given direction.

Of this species of submarine weapons, the following are the most efficient and are the ones most generally used :—

1.—The Whitehead fish torpedo.

2.—The Lay torpedo.

Invention and Adoption of the Fish Torpedo.—The idea developed by the fish torpedo is due to an Austrian marine artillery officer, who is now dead. In 1864, Mr. Robert Whitehead, then superintendent of iron works at Fiume, acting upon the suggestions of a Captain Lupuis of the Austrian army, commenced a series of experiments to ascertain the practical value of the above idea, the result being a fish torpedo, commonly called " The Whitehead," which though far inferior to the fish torpedo of the present day, was then considered to be a fearful and wonderful weapon.

The Austrians were the first to purchase this weapon, and two years later, in 1870, Mr. Whitehead came to England, and prosecuted numerous experiments with his fish torpedo under the supervision of several English officers, and on the 8th of October of the same year he succeeded in completely destroying an old hulk moored at the mouth of the Medway. The fairly successful results of these experiments induced the English government to purchase the secret and several of Mr. Whitehead's fish torpedoes, under the following conditions :—

1.—The right of manufacturing them in England.

2 —To be kept fully informed of all improvements, as soon as made.

3.—The right of using all such improvements.

And the total amount paid to Mr. R. Whitehead at that time was the sum of seventeen thousand five hundred pounds, which did not include the sum of two thousand five hundred pounds claimed for the expenses attendant on the Medway experiments. Since then a large number of Whitehead's fish torpedos have been purchased from time to time, especially during the Turco-Russian war, when some two hundred were ordered, also great numbers have been manufactured at Woolwich. The English fish torpedo, as far as can be ascertained, is a vastly superior weapon to the Whitehead fish torpedo, possessing as it does increased speed, and therefore far greater accuracy.

Besides Austria and England, nearly all the European governments have purchased the Whitehead secret and torpedoes, but in the case of some of them, the last two clauses of the English conditions of purchase were omitted.

The Turkish is the only government that has obtained the Whitehead secret and torpedoes without paying for it. This was managed as follows :—

" On the night of the 20th of December, 1877, the Russians made an attack with Whitehead torpedoes on an Ottoman squadron lying in

PLATE XXXVI

Fig 119.

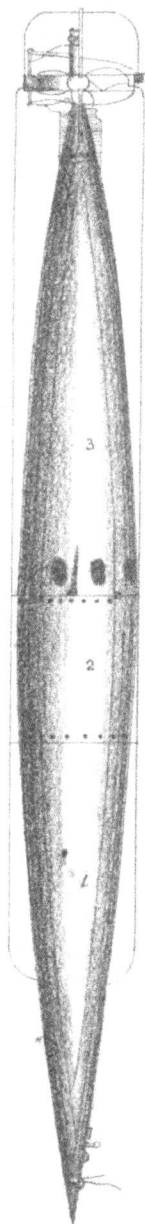

the harbour of Batoum, but owing to a want of practical knowledge of the manipulation of such weapons, no vessels were sunk or damaged, but two fish torpedoes, one in perfect condition, were found the next morning high and dry on the beach at that place."

The American government have up to the present time not sanctioned the purchase of the costly Whitehead torpedo, preferring their own locomotive torpedo, which will be fully described further on. On a government purchasing the fish torpedo, a certain number of their naval or military officers are sent to Fiume in Austria, where Mr. R. Whitehead's manufactories are situated, and where the necessary very exhaustive experiments with his torpedoes are carried out, and are there thoroughly instructed in the manipulation of these machines, and are also supplied with a double set of drawings of the various parts of the torpedo. These officers, and all others whom it may be necessary to initiate into the mysteries of the Whitehead secret, are bound on their honour not to divulge it.

Employment of Fish Torpedoes in War.—The fish torpedo has been employed on actual service on three known occasions only, in two of which it failed to fulfil its deadly mission.

On the 29th of May, 1877, a Whitehead fish torpedo was fired by H.M.S. *Shah* against the Peruvian ironclad *Huascar*, but failed to strike her, owing to the latter vessel altering her course at the moment of the torpedo being discharged. The next instance of the employment of the Whitehead torpedo was that one mentioned at page 132. The last and only successful attempt yet made occurred on the 26th of January, 1878, when the Russian steamer *Constantine* fired a Whitehead torpedo against a Turkish guard vessel off the harbour of Batoum, and completely destroyed her.

Description of Torpedo.—A general view of the Whitehead fish torpedo is shown at Fig. 119. It is divided into three parts, connected together by screws.

1.—The charge chamber.

2.—The adjustment chamber, in which is placed what is known as the secret.

3.—The air and engine chamber.

Vertical and horizontal steel fins are fitted for the purpose of maintaining the torpedo in an upright position whilst passing through the discharge tube, or frame ; the former fins run nearly the whole length of the weapon, while the latter are considerably shorter. The motive power of the torpedo is compressed air, forced by means of a powerful steam air compressing pump into a portion of the steel chamber (3) at a tension of upwards of 1000 pounds to the square inch, which is equivalent to about sixty atmospheres, and which by means of a set of small three cylinder Brotherhood engines, contained in the steel chamber (3), drives two screw propellers. These engines are capable of exerting a force of forty indicated horses, and yet only weigh about thirty-five pounds, from which it will be understood that to attain these results the workmanship and materials employed in their manufacture are of the very highest order and fineness.

The torpedo is made of various sizes, ranging from 14' long and 14" maximum diameter to 19' long and 16" maximum diameter.

Capabilities of the Fish Torpedo.—The capabilities of the fish torpedo are as follows :—

1.—If adjusted for a certain depth, from 5 to 15 feet, and pro-jected from above water, or if started from the surface, or if discharged from a submerged tube, it will rapidly attain that depth, and maintain it during the run.

2.—If fired in still water, it will make a straight run in the line of projection, provided that an allowance has been made for the deflection due to transverse currents.

3.—It can be adjusted to stop after having run any distance up to its extreme range, and after stopping to sink, float, or explode.

4.—Its range and speed vary considerably, according to the pattern of the torpedo.

Yards.	Whitehead Fish Torpedo.			Woolwich Fish Torpedo.
	14' long, 16" max. diam. one screw.	14' long, 16" max. diam. two screws.	14' long, 14" max. diam. two screws.	14·5' long, 14" max. diam. two screws.
200	..	..	20 knots.	25¼ knots.
250	9½ knots.	..	..	..
300	..	12¼ knots.	19¼ knots.	24¼ knots.
400	8 knots.	..	18 knots.	23 knots.
600	..	11 knots.	..	20 knots.
750	..	10¼ knots.	..	..
800	7 knots.	..	16¼ knots.	18 knots.
1000	..	9 knots.	..	15¼ knots.

Pressure of air in engines varies for distance and speed from 40 atmospheres to 14 atmospheres.

Placing the Charge.—The explosive is generally placed in what is termed the cartridge case, which case is similar in shape to the interior of the charge chamber (1), and is fixed thereto by means of wooden wedges.

Ignition.—The method of ignition is mechanical, and is arranged as follows :—Extending from the nose of the torpedo to the cartridge case is a tube terminating in a copper case, in which is placed the priming charge and detonating composition; within this tube is a steel rod some 2 feet long, fitted with a needle point at its inner end, and its outer end screwed into a frame ; this frame is capable of moving in and out, and is connected with a spiral spring which tends to force it, and consequently the steel rod, or striker, inwards. By compressing this spiral spring, the inner end of the frame is butted against a catch, by which it is prevented from acting. On this catch being released, no matter by what means, the spring is brought into action and forces the frame and steel striker inwards, the needle point of the latter coming into contact with the detonator fires the priming charge, and so explodes the torpedo. The foremost extremity of the torpedo, which is termed the nose piece, is so fitted that it is capable of being forced inwards, but in a position of rest its inner edge is just clear of the catch. On a pressure being brought on the nose piece in a direct line with the length of the torpedo, it will be forced inwards, the result being the releasing of the catch and explosion of the torpedo. In addition to the nose piece, horizontal and vertical levers, or whiskers, may also be used, a slight pressure on either of which will similarly effect the explosion of the torpedo ; also cutters for penetrating nets, &c., are fitted to the nose piece when desired.

Safety Wedge and Key.—For safety purposes a wedge is employed, which when in the safety position prevents the catch from acting ; this wedge is so arranged that it may be withdrawn by the action of the machinery after the torpedo has run a certain distance, and also may be replaced by similar means in the safety position on the completion of the run. As an additional precaution a safety key is used, which is inserted in the head of the torpedo through the spring of the frame.

Description of Adjustment Apparatus.—For adjusting the length of range for withdrawing and replacing the safety wedge, &c., the following apparatus is employed.

Two cog wheels, a large and a small one, are fixed on the upper part of the after end of the torpedo, just in front of the screw propellers : the small wheel is fitted with a certain number of teeth, thirty for instance, which gears into an endless screw attached to the propeller in such a manner that one revolution of the propeller moves the wheel one tooth, therefore thirty revolutions would turn the wheel one complete revolution. The big wheel is fitted with much larger teeth than the small one, and by means of a pin on the latter wheel is moved round one tooth for every complete revolution of the small wheel, and clamped in this new position by a spring catch, which is also worked by the pin on the small wheel. In front of these wheels is a stud which works fore and aft in a slot, and attached to a spring which tends to draw it to the after end of the slot. This stud is connected by means of a wire rod to the valve that admits the compressed air to the engines ; when the stud is in the fore part of the slot the valve is open, and when in the after part it is closed.

Adjusting Length of Range.—By means of a lever the spring of the stud is compressed, and the stud moved to the fore part of the slot; then the big wheel is moved round until a stud on its face is the required number of teeth above the lever. For every thirty revolutions of the propeller, and consequently one tooth of the big wheel, a certain known distance is traversed, which varies according to the pattern of the torpedo.

Adjusting Apparatus.—When the propeller has made the number of revolutions corresponding to the length of range required, and consequently has moved the big wheel the number of teeth it was set above the lever, the stud on the big wheel presses against the lever and so releases the spring in the slot, causing the slot stud to fly from the fore part to the after part of the slot, by which action the valve admitting the compressed air to the engines is closed, and consequently the engines cease to work.

Attached to the axle of the big wheel is a small brass arm, which is connected by means of a brass rod to the safety wedge, and is so arranged that after the required number of revolutions of the propeller, the safety wedge will be drawn out ; or it may be drawn out at the instant of the torpedo leaving the tube, carriage, &c. Also by means of an additional lever at the fore part of the torpedo, which is connected by means of a wire rod to the valve that admits the air to the engines, and by arranging the attachment of the safety wedge to the brass rod from the big wheel, so that on the wedge being withdrawn it is released from that brass rod, on the torpedo having completed its run, the action of closing the valve which admits the air to the engines causes the additional lever to force the wedge into the safety position.

Torpedo to Float at End of Run.—This is due to the difference of buoyancy at the end of a run from what it was at the commencement, owing to the compressed air being used in working the engines.

Torpedo to Sink at End of Run.—This is effected by means of the adjustment chamber (2), in the after end of which there is a spiral spring valve, which can be attached to the brass rod on the outside of the torpedo that works the valve which admits air to the engines, in such a way that on the valve being closed, and therefore the run of the torpedo completed, the spiral spring valve is opened, admitting water to the adjustment chamber (2) of sufficient amount to sink the torpedo.

To Explode the Torpedo at End of Run.—This is effected by connecting the vertical firing whisker to the rod which otherwise would be connected to the safety wedge lever, by which means, on the valve admitting air to the engines being closed, a force is transmitted to the vertical whisker instead of to the safety wedge lever, and consequently the torpedo is exploded.

Adjusting the Depth.—A small wheel, the face of which is marked in feet, is placed on the left side of the fore part of the adjustment chamber (2). To adjust for depth, by means of a key turn the wheel until the number corresponding to the depth of run required is opposite the pointer.

The torpedo is maintained at the desired depth by means of certain mechanical apparatus contained within the adjustment chamber (2), and which constitutes what is termed the secret of the fish torpedo. This chamber is connected by screws to the foremost and after chambers of the torpedo, in such a manner that by means of a number of small holes bored round the circumference, as shown at (2), Fig. 119, the faces of the chamber are exposed to the pressure of the water, which varies with the depth to which the torpedo descends. Within the adjustment chamber is an endless strong spiral spring, attached to the after face of the chamber, and so arranged that after being set to a certain tension, capable of resisting an equivalent pressure on the outside of the aforesaid face, any increase or decrease in this exterior

L

pressure will cause the spiral spring to work a rod by which the horizontal rudders of the torpedo are regulated, and thus the desired depth for which the spring is set is maintained. The course of the torpedo is represented by a series of curves, above and below the line, representing the depth it is set for, these curves gradually decreasing until at 100 yards' distance from where the torpedo was started the curves are so small that the path of the torpedo is almost identical to that of a straight line.

Within this adjustment chamber is also placed an automatic balance, which also assists to maintain the torpedo at the desired depth, by reason of its swinging forward on the torpedo descending, and swinging aft on its rising, which motion is used to regulate the horizontal rudders. The above is merely a general idea of the arrangement used in the Whitehead fish torpedo, to enable it to reach and maintain whatever depth it may be necessary to use it at from 5 to 15 feet.

Projecting the Torpedo.—The fish torpedo may be projected in various ways, viz. :—

1.—Through a submerged tube in the stem, or on the broadside.

2.—From a carriage above the surface.

3.—From the surface.

Discharging Torpedo through a Submerged Tube in the Stem.—In this case a tube is fitted to an orifice in the stem; this opening is as far below the water line as possible, and is closed by a watertight cap and a sluice valve; the inner end of the tube is fitted with a watertight door; the torpedo being prepared for action is placed inside the tube, the inner door closed, and the tube filled with water; then the watertight cap and sluice valve are opened, and the torpedo started by means of a piston which is worked by compressed air. This piston can be worked from deck, and so the torpedo fired at the proper instant. To prevent the torpedo from slipping out of the tube, a stop is placed in the fore end of it, which can be withdrawn at the same time as the compressed air is admitted behind the piston. The torpedo being clear of the tube, the sluice valve and watertight cap are closed, and the tube emptied of the water, the projecting piston being at the same time forced back.

On the Broadside.—In this case, the discharging tube works inside an iron casing, through a stuffing box at the inner end, and in a shield attached to the outer end of the tube. This shield, placed on the fore side of the orifice, is of such a length as to protect the torpedo from the pressure of the water passing the vessel. The mode of discharging the torpedo in this case is similar to that used when projecting it through the stem.

Comparison of the Stem and Broadside Methods of Projecting the Torpedo.—The former method of projecting the torpedo seems the most suitable to specially built torpedo vessels, but not so to large ironclads, on account of the difficulty of fitting a tube to the stem of such a ship, and also that in so doing the efficiency of the vessel as a ram would be impaired.

In regard to the accuracy of the firing of the above methods, both seem equally good, though in the case of firing on the broadside it would be necessary to prepare carefully calculated tables of deflection, any mistake in the using of which would be fatal to a successful torpedo shot.

Projecting a Torpedo from above Water.—In this case an iron carriage is used, which is fitted with a frame, in which the torpedo rests ; the outer end of this frame is provided with a lip, some few feet long, by which means the rear end of the torpedo is slightly canted up on leaving the frame, and any undue strain on the tail of the torpedo is prevented. The frame is mounted in the iron carriage in such a way that it can be elevated or depressed by means of a screw, as in the case of a gun mounted in an ordinary carriage. The torpedo is ejected from the frame by means of a piston as previously explained, a small reservoir of air being attached to the carriage, so that it can be used at any port.

Firing a Torpedo from the Surface.—The torpedo possesses sufficient buoyancy to float with a small portion of its upper surface above water ; such being the case, it is only necessary to set the various adjustments, point it in the required direction, and by hand turn back the lever on the upper part of the weapon (which opens a communication between the air chamber and the engines), when it will instantly dart off and very rapidly attain the depth it is set for.

Method of Firing a Fish Torpedo from a Boat.—To manipulate a fish torpedo from a boat, it may be carried in a light frame, which can be lowered or raised by means of a pair of davits. When required to discharge the torpedo, the frame containing it is lowered into the water, so as to bring the torpedo about two feet below the surface, the head being somewhat lower than the tail.

Thornycroft's Method of Firing Fish Torpedoes from a Boat.—Another method, which has been patented by Mr. J. I. Thornycroft, of the firm of J. I. Thornycroft and Co., steam launch builders, and which is fitted to the torpedo boats built by them for foreign governments, is shown in elevation and plan at Figs. 120 and 121.

The apparatus consists of two or more bent levers A securely and rigidly fixed on a shaft B, which works in bearings fixed on the deck of the vessel C from which the torpedo is to be discharged.   On the ends of the levers A furthest from the shaft B are pivoted other levers D, to which the cradle or case E for sustaining the torpedo is suspended.   The other ends of each of these levers are connected to the vessel by means of rods or tubes F, jointed at each end in such a way that when the shaft B is made to revolve in its bearings, the case containing the torpedo is guided over the side of the vessel and close to it, and is held in a position convenient for discharging the torpedo, as shown at Fig. 120.

The shaft B may be made to revolve by means of ropes G and pulleys H attached to the levers A, or by hydraulic or steam pressure, as may be found most convenient.

The torpedo case can be towed alongside the vessel if necessary without deranging the apparatus.   The torpedo case is carried in the angles of the bent levers, and is stowed away so that neither it nor the suspending levers project at all beyond the hull of the vessel ; also when lowered, the levers and suspending rods fold over one another so as to occupy very little space, and the torpedo is suspended close to the hull.

Also the torpedo during the operation of lowering as well as when in a firing position remains close to the side of the vessel, thereby obviating any risk or inconvenience from excessive leverage which would have a tendency to capsize the boat.

For especially built torpedo launches, the above mode of carrying and launching the fish torpedo is certainly the best yet devised.

Woolwich Fish Torpedo.—In the Woolwich torpedo, the engines exert a force of nearly 60 indicated horses, and work up to 1000 revolutions per minute ; the total weight of the torpedo fully charged (33 lbs. of gun-cotton) is about 500 lbs.

PLATE XXXVII

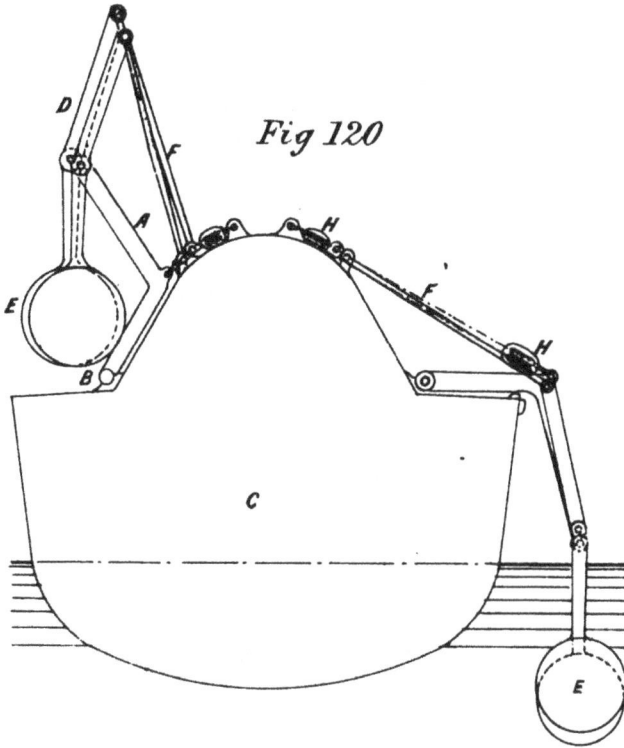

Fig 120

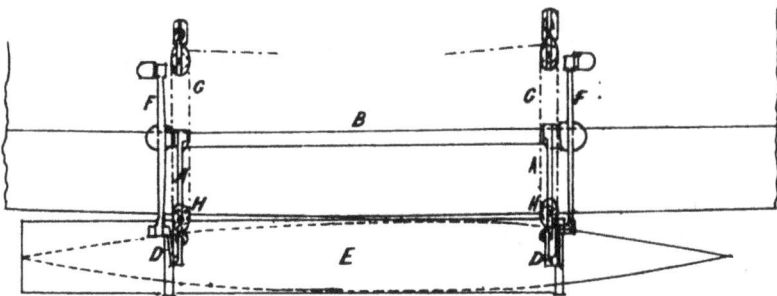

Fig 121.

The Whitehead fish torpedo costs about 380*l*., while the Woolwich one costs only 300*l*.

The Lay Torpedo Boat.—Priority of invention of this torpedo was on the 13th of June, 1873, awarded by the Commissioners of Patents to Mr. John Louis Lay, several other persons having claimed the invention, among whom was Colonel Von Scheliha, an officer of the Russian army.

This locomotive torpedo, or more properly called torpedo boat, has been for several years adopted by the American government, during which time it has undergone a series of exhaustive experiments, which has proved it to be a most valuable and efficient weapon of offence and defence. Lately the Russian government have adopted it, and intend using it extensively in the defence of their harbours, &c.

General Description of the Torpedo.—At Fig. 122 is shown a longitudinal section of a Lay torpedo boat constructed and provided with guiding and controlling apparatus, and with means for propelling it by ammoniacal gas. Fig. 123 is a horizontal section of the same; A is the hull or body of the boat, which has conical ends A^1, A^2, and is formed of thin plate iron, or steel, or other suitable material. The section in the end A^1 forms the magazine containing the charge of dynamite or other explosive material; A^3 is the section containing the gas reservoir or holder; the compartment A^4 contains the apparatus for holding and paying out the electric cable; the compartment A^5 in the end A^2 contains the motor engine, the steering apparatus, and other parts to be hereinafter described. All of these compartments or sections are separated from each other by means of air-tight bulkheads A^6. The torpedo boat may be propelled by means of a single screw, double screw, or two screws. In the latter method, which is shown at Figs. 122 and 123, the propellers B and C are made to revolve in opposite directions; the shaft D of the propeller B is hollow or tubular, and the shaft E of the screw C passes through the same; these screws are actuated by an engine shown at F. H, H are the horizontal rudders, or side wings, two forward and two aft; these wings are mounted on shafts or spindles passing transversely through the boat; these rudders may be set to occupy a horizontal position, or a more or less inclined position in the proper direction, to cause the submerging of the boat by the action of the water on the said rudders as the boat moves forward, and they are adjusted before starting. N, N are two guide rods, one aft and one forward, which project up from the boat to enable the operator to determine its position at any part of its run, and in the case of a night attack they are provided with lights; the said rods can be raised or lowered at the will of the operator. Q is the electric cable, which affords a medium of communication between the operator on shore, &c., and the torpedo boat, whereby it may be started, stopped, steered, fired, and has her position ascertained; this cable is carried in the boat in a coil arranged longitudinally in the air-tight chamber A^4 in the reel frame B, and is payed out as the torpedo progresses through a tube S, projecting aft under the boat and beyond the rudders and propellers, so that the said cable will not be fouled by the same; or it may be payed out through a hollow shaft in the centre of the boat. One end of this cable is connected to a keyboard at the station on shore or on board of the ship or other structure from which the torpedo boats are controlled. This keyboard is provided with a suitable battery or other means for generating the electric current, as hereinafter described.

The said cable is composed of several wires, each of which is insulated from the others. One of these wires is connected with the mechanism for starting and stopping the boat, one is connected with the steering apparatus, one serves for indicating to the operator at all times the exact position of the rudder, one is connected with mechanism for elevating and depressing the said guide rods, and one serves for firing the charge in the magazine.

The motive power for effecting the necessary movements of the mechanism or apparatus in performing the above operations is obtained from the aforesaid engines, which are provided with suitable valves arranged in combination with electro magnets, shunts, and the devices connected with the said wires of the cable, as hereinafter set forth.

This form of cable has since been replaced by one which consists of two wires only, the one for performing all of the necessary operations, exclusive of the firing or exploding of the magazine, and the other exclusively for this latter purpose. This improvement is effected by employing a series of relays or resistance coils, or a multiple, or compound relay in the boat. The advantages gained by this improved form of cable are :—

1.—Increased flexibility.

2.—A greater length of cable may be coiled in a given space.

3.—A thicker coat of insulating material may be used, thereby
    more perfectly insulating it.

4.—It is much cheaper.

Two rudders are generally used, one below and one above the boat,
as shown at U, Fig. 122. These rudders are operated and controlled
by means of a small auxiliary engine T, Fig. 122, which is started,
stopped, and reversed by the electric current conducted through the
cable Q in connection with magnets attached directly to a valve
forming part of the said engine. This valve is so actuated by the
magnets that when the current passes in one direction the engine T
will move the rudder to starboard, and when the current acts in the
opposite direction it will turn the rudder to port.

The mechanism for firing the charge in the magazine A^1 is clearly
shown in Fig. 124, and operates as follows:—Projecting from the
front extremity or stem of the boat is a rod or pin V, which extends
through a suitable packing box W into the said magazine or charge
chamber; when the boat strikes an object, the said rod is forced
inward into contact with the springs or points X, thereby closing an
electrical circuit and igniting a cartridge, shown at Y, in the magazine.

The charge in the magazine can also be fired at any moment by
the operator on shore closing a circuit on the keyboard and thereby
cutting out one of two resistance coils placed in the circuit to prevent
accidental or premature discharge—that is to say, there are two
resistance coils. The battery is not sufficiently powerful to fire
through both resistance coils at the same time. When the boat
strikes an object, the resistance coil in the magazine is cut out by the
driving inward of the rod V, as above described; the battery then
fires through the one on the keyboard. On the other hand, if the
operator desires to fire the torpedo boat before she touches the object
of attack, he manipulates the switch to cut out the coil in the keyboard, the charge then being fired through the coil in the magazine.
This arrangement of the two resistance coils is very effectual in
preventing accidents.

In some instances the magazine is made detachable from the hull
of the boat, so that on striking an object it will descend or drop down
in the water before exploding. This modification is shown at Figs.
125 and 126.

The magazine A^* is attached at its lower side to the boat by a chain or other suitable connection. At its upper edge it is held by a rod a^*, as shown in Fig. 125. This rod is fitted to slide in dovetailed bearings, as shown at b^*, and when this magazine is in its place on the boat the said rod is engaged with a catch or stop c^*, but when the said rod is driven against any object it is forced back and released from the said catch or stop, and the magazine then drops, as in Fig. 126, and is fired.

To effect the firing a ball d^* is used and placed in a tube containing two springs or plates e^* and arranged in an upwardly inclined position, as shown in Fig. 125, one of the said springs being connected with the cable and the other with a wire that passes through the cartridge to earth.

While the magazine is in the position shown in Fig. 125 the circuit is incomplete, but when the magazine drops the said ball falls into the position shown in Fig. 126; the circuit is then completed, and the magazine is fired.

The electrical or electro-magnetic apparatus for generating, directing, and controlling the currents, whereby the above-described operations are effected, may be of any suitable kind, the following being the form of apparatus usually employed.

A battery r, shown at Fig. 127, consists of any desired or requisite number of cells constructed and arranged in any suitable manner, and connected by proper conducting wires with the keyboard s. The latter is provided with a series of pole changers s^1, s^2, s^3, s^4, and switches s^5, s^6, and is shown in Fig. 128.

Each of these pole changers is arranged to effect and control one of the above-named operations, and is therefore connected with one of the aforesaid insulated wires forming the cable. For instance, the pole changer s^1 effects the starting and stopping of the propelling engine; s^2 controls the steering apparatus; s^3 is connected with the steering index; s^4 operates or adjusts the aforesaid guiding rods; and the switches s^5, s^6 control and effect the firing of the charge in the magazine.

The connections between these pole changers and switches, and the apparatus they operate or control on board the boat, are as follows —that is to say, the said propelling engines have a throttle valve, which controls the admission of the gas from its generator or reservoir to the cylinders of the said engine, and in combination with this

LAY'S LOCOMOTIVE TORPEDO.

PLATE XXXVIII

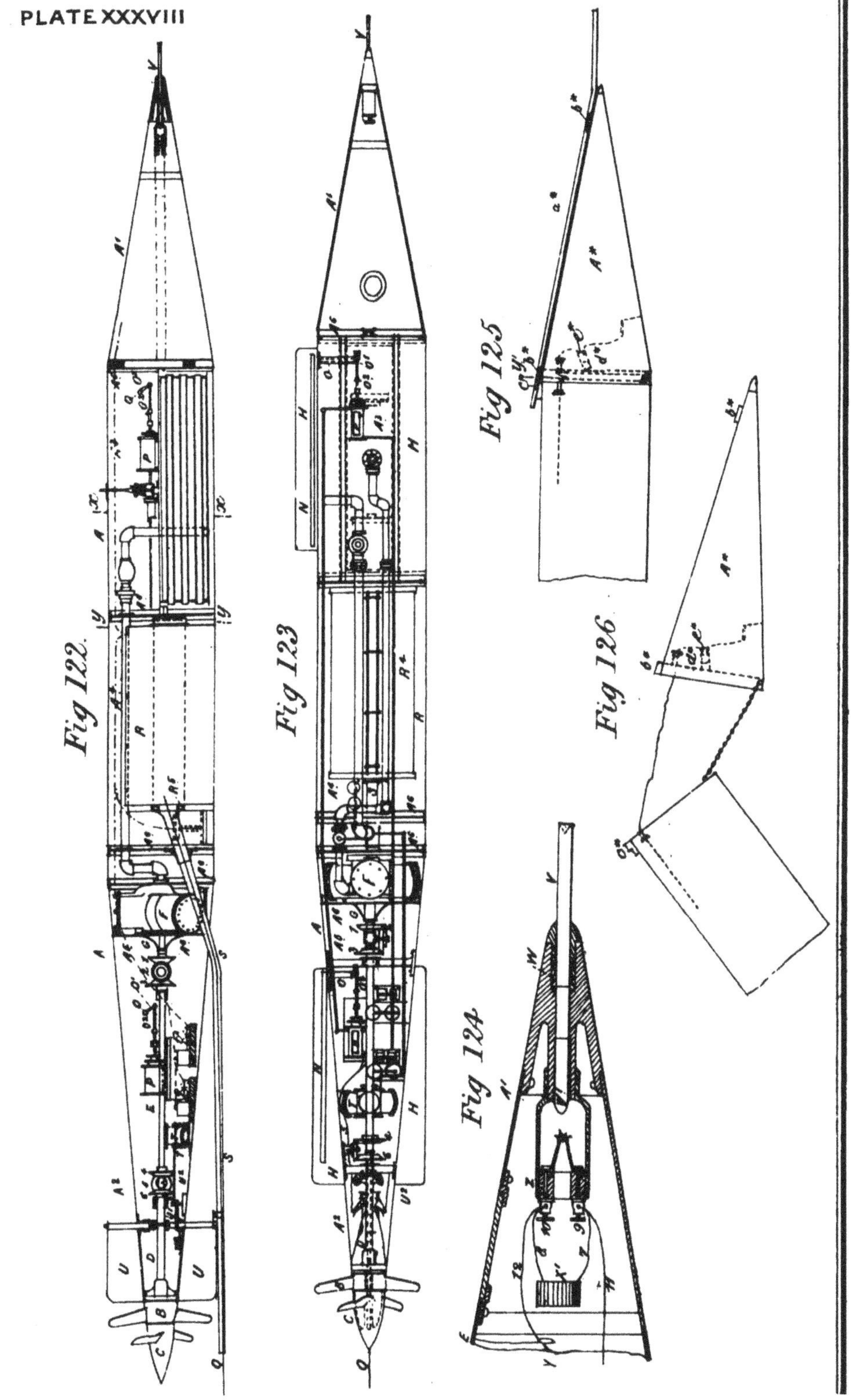
Fig 122.
Fig 123
Fig 124
Fig 125
Fig 126

PLATE XXXIX

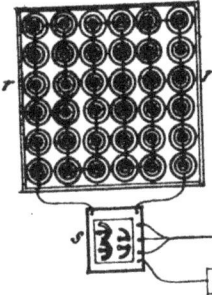

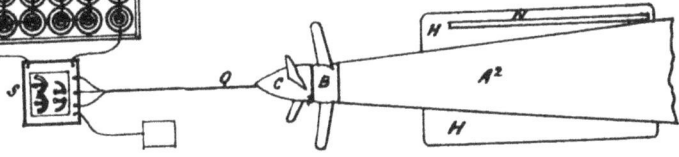

Fig 127

Fig 128

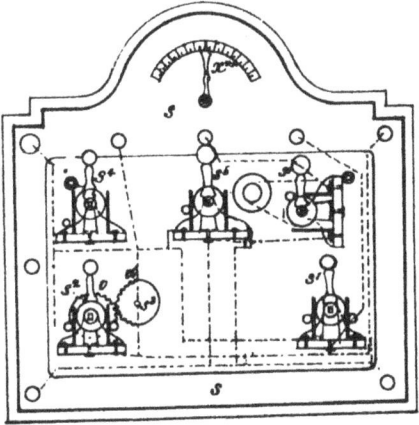

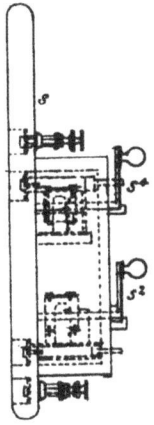

Fig 129

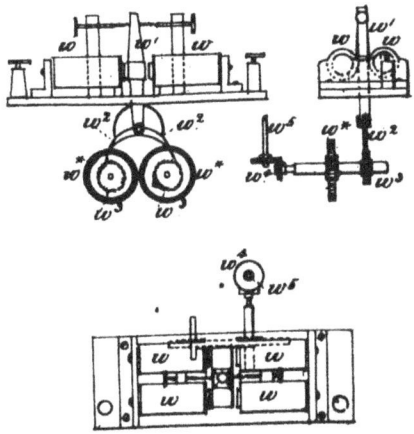

valve in the boat there is a shunt and set of electro magnets. The armature of the latter is connected with a lever, which is pivoted, so that the action of the electric current in one direction through these magnets will pull one end of the said lever down, and the action of the current in the other direction will pull its other end down—that is to say, by reversing the current through these magnets the movement of the said lever is reversed; and this lever, connected by suitable means with the slide of the said throttle valve, will open or close the same, and thereby start or stop the engine as required.

For operating and controlling the above-described steering apparatus, and indicating the position of the rudder to the operator on shore, the following devices are employed, in combination with the pole changers s^2, s^3 on the keyboard:—The pole changers are geared together by insulated toothed wheels, which are fixed on the spindles or axes of the said pole changers, so that the latter work accurately together and maintain the same relative positions to each other. The pole changer s^2 is connected by one of the said insulated cable wires with a shunt on board the boat, which shunt is connected with a set of magnets arranged in combination with the valve of the engine that drives the steering apparatus, and which valve is reversed or opened and closed by the reversal of the currents through the said magnets, as above described, and the said engine moves the rudder to port or starboard at the will of the operator. In order that the operator may know the exact position of the rudder at any moment, a series of pins or projections fixed on an arc or other portion of the rudder stock, and arranged in combination with an insulated spring projecting into the path of the said series of pins, are employed. This spring is connected by one of the cable wires with the pole changer s^3 on the keyboard, which is geared with and moves in unison with the pole changer s^2, so that the electric current that controls the steering engine, and the current that returns the indication of the rudder's position, will both be reversed simultaneously. A separate battery is connected with the index on the said keyboard, whereby a constant current is maintained between this index and the indicating apparatus on the boat.

The current passing from the said spring to the shore is made to indicate the position of the rudder by the index on the keyboard by the contrivance shown in Fig. 129. This contrivance consists of a

set of magnets w, which have a vibrating armature w^1 pivoted to
oscillate between them.   One end of the armature lever is provided
with insulated spring pawls w^2, which take into ratchet wheels w^3.
On the same shafts on which these ratchet wheels are fixed are wheels
w^* formed with insulated teeth and geared with each other.   The shaft
of one of these wheels is geared by bevel pinions w^4 with a vertical
shaft w^5, to which is attached the index needle or finger x^{**}, Fig. 128.
Therefore it will be obvious that this index finger is placed in connection with the aforesaid spring and series of pins attached to the
rudder yoke on board the boat.

Now it will be obvious that when the rudder is turned in either
direction these pins will come successively in contact with the said
spring, and at each contact and separation the circuit will be made
and broken, and an impulse will be transmitted through the cable,
whereby a corresponding movement will be transmitted to the said
index finger or pointer x^{**} on the keyboard.

The pole changer s^4 is connected with another of the insulated
wires of the cable, which on board the boat is connected with a shunt
and set of magnets arranged in combination with the aforesaid
cylinders that operate the said guiding rods, so that by sending the
current in one direction the said rods will be raised, and by sending
the current in the opposite direction the said rods will be lowered.

The switch s^5 is connected with another of the said insulated
wires of the cable, which forms the circuit, including the aforesaid
two resistance coils.

By adjusting this switch the operator completes the circuit through
the two resistance coils, and then, but not till then, the charge can
be exploded, either by the operator, or by the action of the firing pin
or rod when the same is driven in and cuts out the other resistance
coils as above described.   The resistance coil X^1, Fig. 124, is connected to the binding screws 9, 10 by the wires 7 and 8.   These
binding screws are in metallic connection with the two springs X, but
otherwise they are carefully insulated.   One pole of the fuze Y is
connected to the binding screw 10, the other put to earth through the
body of the boat, as at E; the main wire 11 is connected to the
binding screw 9.   Now when the operator cuts out the resistance coil
at the firing station, which is done by moving the switch s^6, the
electric current is sufficiently powerful to ignite the fuze Y through

the resistance coil X^1, so that at any moment the torpedo may be exploded by the operator on shore, or by the contact between the torpedo and the attacked vessel the rod V will be driven in, and, coming in contact with the springs X, will bridge over the space that originally existed between them and so cut out the resistance coil X^1, and the torpedo will be exploded automatically.

Capabilities of the Lay Torpedo Boat.—The capabilities of the Lay torpedo boat are as follows:—

1.—It may be launched from the shore, a vessel, or a structure, and be kept under observation, and accurately guided or directed to the ship or other object to be attacked; and it may be exploded at any desired moment, or it may be caused to return to the original point of departure without being fired.

2.—It may be totally and instantaneously submerged to prevent its destruction or capture by the enemy, and it may be raised to the surface, as soon as the danger has passed, in a condition fit for immediate action.

3.—It may be used as a tug or towing boat to take out a number of torpedoes, which may be sunk and exploded when desired.

4.—It may be used in connection with certain apparatus to clear away obstructions found to prevent the entrance of ships into harbours, and it may also be used to clear harbours of mines, &c.

Launching the Lay Torpedo Boat.—For facilitating the launching and controlling of the Lay torpedo boats, a structure or submarine fort is used. This structure may be square, or oblong, and may be made to carry any number of the torpedo boats. The body is constructed of plate or sheet iron of suitable strength and stiffened with angle iron, or otherwise, and divided longitudinally or transversely into water-tight compartments, into which the water is admitted to sink the said structure. At the top or upper side, cylinders or tubes are placed, each of which is capable of containing and launching one of the torpedo boats. At the forward end of each tube is a door, or cover secured to a rod or shaft fitted to turn in suitable bearings; this rod or shaft is provided with an arm which is connected to the piston rod of an engine worked by gas contained in a reservoir, or by other suitable means. The slide or other valve which controls the admission of the gas, &c., to this engine is arranged in connection with electro magnets, connected by a suitable cable with a keyboard on shore, or wherever the operator's station may be. By sending an electric current through this cable in one direction through the electro magnets, the door is closed; and by sending such a current in the opposite direction it is opened. The cables carried in the torpedo boats, and through which the mechanism on board each torpedo boat is operated and controlled, are also in this case connected with the keyboard, which must be provided with a number of sets of pole changers and switches, or equivalent devices, corresponding with the number of boats to be controlled by means of the said keyboard.

This apparatus will form a very convenient adjunct to fortifications or stations liable to be attacked by sea. The said fort may be prepared for use by placing torpedo boats in the said tubes, and may be kept floating until the enemy's ships have arrived closely enough to permit the determination of the point where the said fort can be most advantageously located for operating against the said ships. The fort is then towed to this point, or taken as near as possible thereto on rails, and towed the remainder of the distance. It is then submerged, and will be ready for immediate operation. The said fort is provided with suitable valves for the admission of water to sink the same, and with means for forcing in air through the pipe P^* to expel the water when the fort is to be raised.

When it is desired to launch either of the said torpedo boats, the door of its tube or cylinder is first opened by sending a current through the cable that controls the door, as above described. Then the current is sent through the boat's cable to start her propelling engines. The said boat will then emerge from the cylinder or tube and will rise to the surface, or as near the surface as may be desired, and may then be directed and controlled by the operator at the keyboard, as previously described. And one after another of the said torpedo boats may be thus launched and exploded, without giving to the enemy any clue to the point or position from which they are being sent.

Launching the Torpedo from a Ship.—The method of launching the Lay torpedo boat from an ironclad or other large ship is shown at Fig. 130. The tubes or cylinders S in which the torpedo boats A are held

PLATE XL

Fig 130

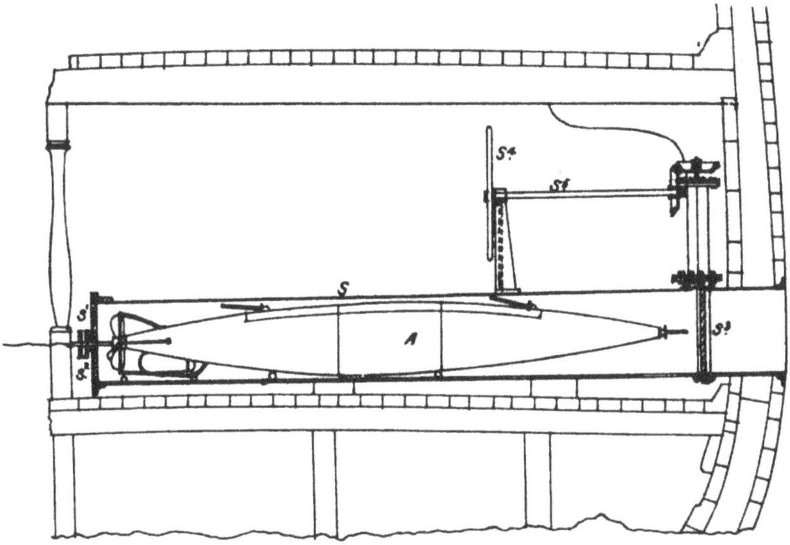

Fig 131

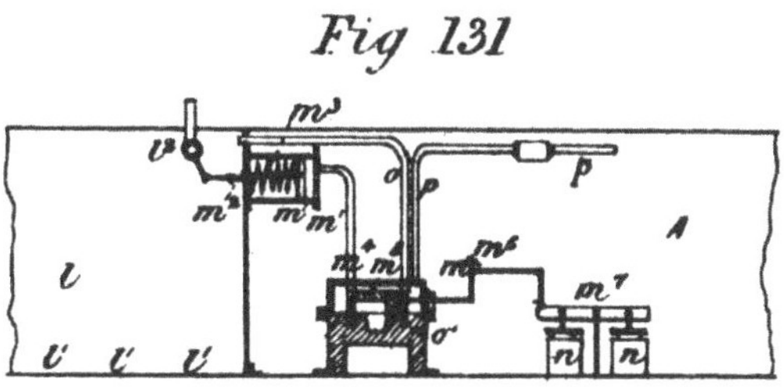

are, in the apparatus shown at Fig. 130, closed at their inner ends by plates, or covers S^1, which are provided with suitable water-tight and insulating packing boxes S^2 for the passage of the electric cables of the said torpedo boats, each cable being connected with the keyboard, which is placed in any convenient part of the ship, and at their outer ends the said tubes are furnished with strong and well-fitted slide valves, or sluice gates S^3, which are opened by screws, connected by gearing with a hand wheel, and shaft S^4, S^5, for the admission and exit of the said torpedo boats. Also these cylinders are provided with packing pieces at their sides, arranged to be pressed by screws or otherwise up to the sides of the torpedo boats in these cylinders, and thereby hold them firmly and immovably in rough weather.

The Method of Sinking and Raising a Lay Torpedo Boat.—The apparatus by which this is effected is shown at Fig. 131, which is a longitudinal section of a portion of a torpedo boat. The hull A of the torpedo boat is provided with a water chamber l, which has holes or apertures l^1 in the bottom of the same, and is also provided with an air cock at l^2. In connection with this chamber is arranged a small cylinder m, provided with a piston m^1, whose rod m^2 is attached to the lever of the said cock. A spiral spring m^3 is provided to resist the inward movement of the said piston. The said small cylinder m is connected by a pipe m^4 with a valve chest, in which is arranged a slide valve m^5. The said slide valve is connected by a rod or rods to the lever or levers m^6, whose fulcrum is at m^*, and the said levers are connected by the links or rods m^7 with the armatures of electro magnets n, which are included in the circuit of the cable, whereby the boat is controlled from the keyboard at the station; o is a pipe extending from the said valve chest to the aforesaid water chamber l; p is a feed pipe by which gas is conducted from the reservoir or generator to the valve chamber.

When it is desired to sink the torpedo boat an electric current is sent in one direction through the said magnets, and thereby operates the slide valve to admit gas to the cylinder m in front of the piston m^1, which is thus forced inward and opens the air cock l^2. The opening of this cock permits the escape of the air from the water chamber l, and consequently the entrance of water through the apertures l^1, and the boat then immediately sinks.

When it is desired to raise the boat a current is sent in the opposite direction through the said electro magnets, thereby operating the said valve and piston in such a manner as to close the cock l^2 and open the port o^1 and the pipe o, thereby allowing the gas to pass from the valve chamber into the compartment l; this gas by its pressure expels the water from the said compartment, and the boat then having its normal buoyancy restored immediately rises to the surface.

The Lay Torpedo Boat used as a Tug to take out a Number of Small Torpedoes.—This arrangement is shown at Figs. 132 and 133. The small vessels or torpedoes are designed to be first sunk and then exploded, chiefly for clearing harbour or the like of mines or other obstructions. These results are accomplished by means of the following devices and arrangements, that is to say, each of the small vessels or torpedoes F is provided with apparatus which is included in an electrical circuit formed by a suitable insulated cable G, extending throughout the train of small vessels or torpedoes F. One vessel of this train, preferably the rear one, is connected with the station by an electrical cable H, which is payed out from a coil or coils, or a reel or reels, in the said vessel as the same travels through the water. This cable H connects with the cable G, which is connected with the towing boat A, and passes through the series of boats F to the said cable H. One wire of the said cable is arranged in combination with sealed or covered apertures in the bottom of a compartment or compartments of these small vessels F, as shown at I, the covers of these apertures being so formed as to be ruptured or destroyed by the explosion of a cartridge or cartridges placed in the said compartment or compartments. When a current of electricity is sent through the aforesaid wire of the cable it will explode the said cartridges and open the apertures, thereby admitting water into the said compartments so that the vessel F will sink.

The cable G that passes through the train of torpedoes or vessels F is so arranged that when a current passes through the other wire of the said cable it will fire cartridges placed in the charge chambers or magazines of the said small vessels, as shown at J. The part of the cable or towing line G, which connects the towing boat A with the train of small boats or torpedoes F, is attached to a hook or other device, which can be disengaged by sending a current through the cable K, connecting the boat A with the shore or other station. It will be understood that when being used for this purpose the said boat A is not or need not be charged with explosive material.

PLATE XLI

Fig 132

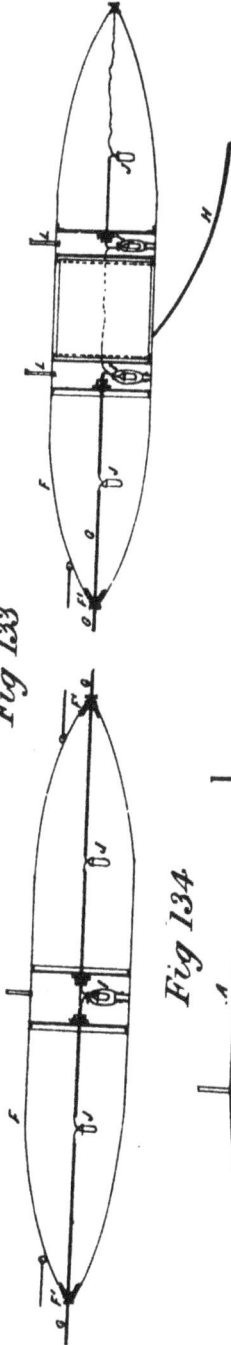

Fig 133

Fig 134

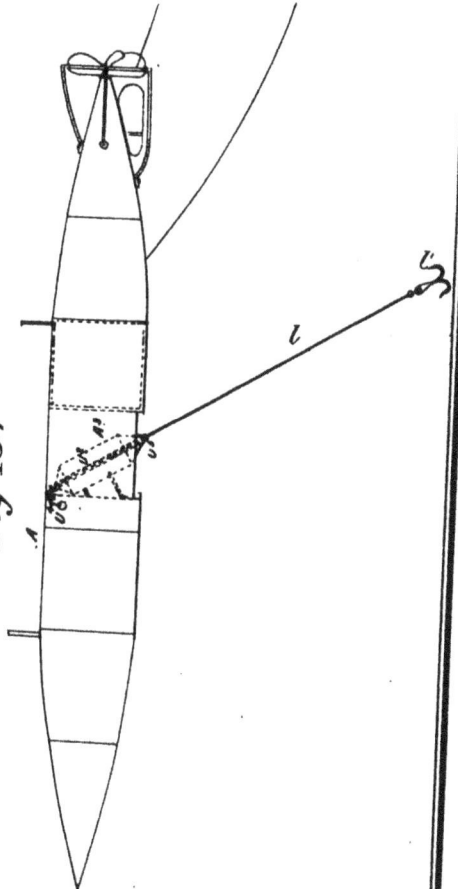

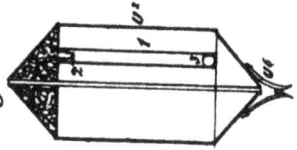

Fig 135

The aforesaid towing boat A takes the train of torpedoes F to any required position. It is then disengaged from the train, leaving the said small vessels or torpedoes F floating in such position. Then by sending a current first through one wire of the cable H the boats F are first sunk by the explosion of the cartridges and opening of the apertures, as above described. They may then be discharged immediately by sending a current through the other wire of said cable H and firing the cartridges in their magazines, or they may be left submerged to form mines which may be exploded at any desired moment.

The said small vessels or torpedoes may be provided with vertical rods to indicate their position to the operator at the station; these rods are shown at L, and they should be made hollow to allow the air in the water compartments or chambers to escape to permit the water to enter the same when the vessels F are to be sunk; or other suitable provision may be made for the escape of the air from these compartments.

The said vessels F are preferably made cylindrical with conical ends, and are provided with suitable insulating and water-tight packing boxes, as shown at F^1 for the cable G to pass through at the stem and stern of each vessel.

The Lay Torpedo in Clearing Obstructions.—For this purpose the torpedo boat is provided with an apparatus, shown at Figs. 134 and 135, in combination with the electric cable, whereby the said boat is controlled and guided, and there is arranged in the boat A a compartment A^3, from which extends down into the water a line or rod U, provided at its outer end with a hook or claw U^1, properly formed to take hold of any chain or bar with which it may come in contact. In the said compartment A^3, and upon the upper end of the said line or rod U, is placed a small case or cylinder U^2 containing a charge of dynamite or other explosive material and a cartridge or fulminating cap, or a bottle of sulphuric acid, surrounded with a certain quantity of chlorate of potash and sugar. This case or cylinder U^2 is shown detached and drawn to an enlarged scale at Fig. 135, and it will be seen that the said case is provided with a tube 1 containing a cartridge, or a phial filled with explosive substance at 2, and a ball or weight at 3. The said case is fitted to slide upon the said line or rod U, and when placed at the upper end thereof and not held or retained will slide to the lower end of the same. In the said compartment A^3 is arranged at U^4 an electro-magnetic apparatus, included in the circuit of the said cable, and connected with a bolt or catch which in its normal position holds the said explosive case and prevents its running down on the grappling line or rod U. This explosive case is also provided at its lower end with a grappling hook U^5.

When the grappling hook U^1, on the lower or outer end of the line or rod U, engages with any obstruction the boat will be stopped, and this stoppage will be indicated on the keyboard. The operator by this indication is apprised of the stoppage of the boat by an obstruction, and by sending a current through the cable by means of a switch provided for this purpose on the keyboard he can immediately release the explosive case U^2, which runs down the line or rod U, and engages by its grappling hook U^5 with the hook U^1. The line or rod U is then disengaged from the boat A, and the explosive case U^2 turns or falls over. As it turns over the ball or weight 3 contained in the tube 1 drops on the said phial 2, fractures it, and thereby allows the acid to mix with the explosive or fulminating charge and explode the case U^2. This explosion will rupture or destroy the obstructing chain or bar, so that the ironclad ships or other vessels can pass freely and safely into the harbour or beyond the point where it was intended to stop them.

Used to clear away Mines and Electric Cables.—For this purpose there is an implement V provided, Fig. 136, somewhat of an anchor form, but with four or any desired number of arms V^2 extending outward at a suitable angle from its shank V^1. In the neck of each of these arms are fitted two small plain or toothed discs V^3, which are so arranged as to present their teeth to any object lying in the angle or corner formed by and between the arms V^2 and shank V^1 of the said implement, as shown at W.

In using this implement it may be attached to a line or cable coiled in the torpedo boat, which, in this case, is used without being charged with explosive material, and is sent in advance of any ship that has to enter or pass through the suspected water. This line must be arranged in combination with a detaching apparatus controlled by electro-magnetic apparatus included in the circuit of the cable which connects the torpedo boat with the keyboard at the operating station.

By sending a current from the station the operator releases the said implement or its line from the detaching hook or holding device. The said implement then sinks to the bottom ; then the said boat returns

PLATE XLII

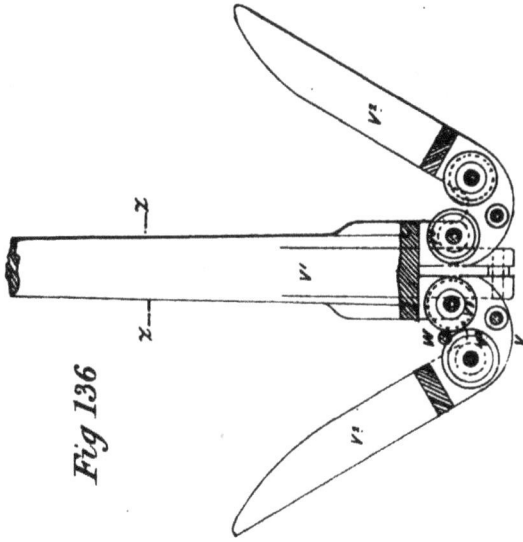

Fig 136

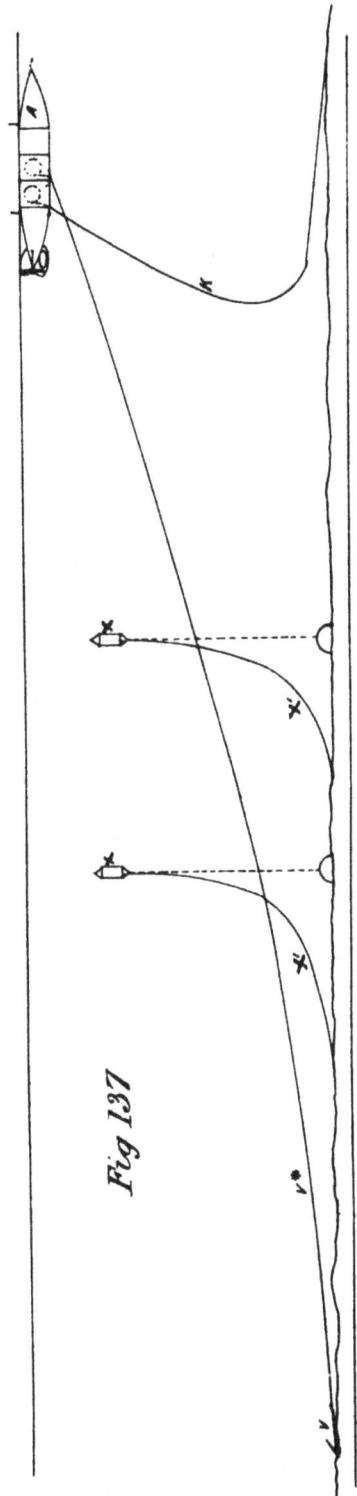

Fig 137

to the ship, paying out the said line as she so returns. The end of this line is then taken by a steam tug or other vessel, and the said grappling implement is thereby dragged along through the water over which the ships are to advance, thus breaking any wires or cables that may be in its course. This operation is shown at Fig. 137, in which A is the towing boat, K the controlling cable, V the said implement, V^* the line attached to the implement V, X X submerged mines, and X^1 X^1 are the mine cables.

In some instances it may not be practicable to reach the enemy's ship or other object of attack directly from the station to which the torpedo boat is connected, and from which it is controlled. In this case a small boat, &c., is used in addition, which should be so arranged as to present to the enemy's view as slight a surface as possible. This mode of attack is shown at Fig. 138, where A is the torpedo boat, and N is the small auxiliary boat. This boat N is provided with a keyboard and battery like that described at page 144, and the electric cable L, carried on and payed out from the torpedo boat A, is connected with the keyboard. The boat N is also attached to and towed by the torpedo boat A by the tow line O; and the torpedo boat is steered and guided by means of the said keyboard in the boat N. The auxiliary boat is designed to contain two men, who lie down, one at the bow, the other in any convenient position abaft him; the latter has control of the keyboard, while the former by the aid of a telescope keeps the torpedo boat in view, and transmits his orders to the man at the keyboard. On arriving at such a distance from the enemy as to render an attack practicable, the tow line O is disengaged, and the torpedo boat A, guided and controlled, and fired from the boat N. The torpedo boat being exploded, the auxiliary boat can be rowed back to the station or ship to which it belongs. By this means the range of action of the torpedo boat is greatly extended, and with comparatively slight danger to those employed in making the attack.

A more recent form of the Lay torpedo boat is shown at Figs. 139, 140, and 141, where Fig. 139 is a plan or top view of such a boat, Fig. 140 is a side elevation of the same, and Fig. 141 is a midship section on the line x x. A is the hull of the boat, a is the main or central portion of the said hull, b, b are side or auxiliary portions of the same. These parts a and b may be oval or circular in transverse section; they are constructed of thin steel or other suitable sheet metal,

M

and secured together by riveting or bolting. The side or auxiliary portion *b* form the reservoirs or chambers for the gas; they also serve to contain the propelling engines. *c* is the magazine, *d* the chamber or compartment for containing the coiled cable, *e* is the compartment containing the electrical steering and other apparatus, *f* is the firing rod or pin, *g* is the water ballast chamber, *h* is the cable, *i* the paying-out tube, *j, j* are the screws or propellers which rotate in opposite directions, and *k, k* are the sight or guiding rods.

The parts of the apparatus or mechanism whereby the various operations of the torpedo boat are effected are connected to the cable and controlled by electric currents transmitted from the station through the cable, as previously described. The Lay torpedo boat weighs about 1 ton, its length is 23 feet, and speed 12 knots per hour.

Spar or Outrigger Torpedo.—By a spar or outrigger torpedo is meant a torpedo which is carried at the end of a pole or spar projecting from a boat or vessel, and which may be fired either by contact or at will.

This system of submarine offence has up to the present time been the only one that has successfully stood the crucial test of actual warfare.

During the civil war in America the spar torpedo attack was resorted to by the Confederates and Federals, principally by the former, the result being the loss of two large men of war and severe injury to several other ships composing the Federal fleet, and the loss of one vessel of war belonging to the Southerners.

The spar torpedo was also used on several occasions by the Russians in their attacks on the Turkish ships in the war of 1877–8, but in only one attempt was it the means of sinking a Turkish vessel.

Description of McEvoy's Duplex Spar Torpedo.—At Fig. 142 is shown a sketch of Captain McEvoy's improved patent duplex spar torpedo, which is the form most generally used at the present time, and which seems to fulfil all the requirements of such a submarine weapon, viz. :—

1.—Handiness, at the same time capable of containing a charge of gun-cotton sufficient in contact to destroy the most powerful vessel afloat.

2.—Certainty of action.

3.—Capable of being fired either on contact or at will.

4.—Mode of attaching the spar simple and very secure.

LAY'S LOCOMOTIVE TORPEDO.

PLATE XLIII

Fig 138.

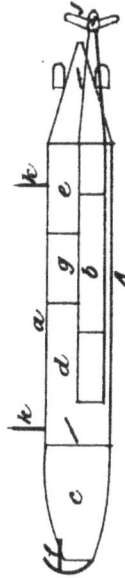

Fig 140

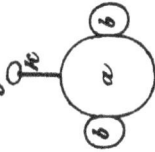

Fig 141

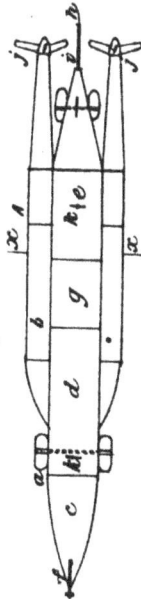

Fig 139

In Fig. 142, a is the case, capable of containing some 33 lbs. of gun-cotton ; b is the tube through which the three wires w, w^1, and w^2 are led ; c is the socket in which the wooden or steel spar is introduced and secured. d is the striker, which is attached to a brass contact plate within the head of the case a in such a manner that any pressure either on the head or side of the striker d will force the aforesaid plate in contact with the two studs to which the battery wires are attached ; e is a cradle affixed to the striker d to ensure its action on contact being made by the torpedo with the attacked vessel ; the explosive is inserted at f, the socket c being made to screw on and off.

When a hollow steel spar is used, the battery wires are sometimes led through the interior of the torpedo and the spar, by which means they are well protected; the only objection to this method of leading the wires being the probability of injury to them, should the spar be broken on contact, or by a shot.

McEvoy's Arrangement of Torpedo Wires.—At Fig. 143 is shown the arrangement of wires as devised by Captain McEvoy, whereby the spar torpedo may be exploded at will or on contact. c and z are the poles of the firing battery, to which are attached respectively the wires d and d^2; f is the fuze, which is placed in the centre of the charge, and to the poles of which the wire d^2 is attached, the other end of this wire being connected with the stud s; to the stud s^1 is attached the other end of the wire d, and at the point c in the same wire is inserted a contact breaker ; another wire d^1 is connected to the wires d and d^2 at the points r and r^2 respectively, and at the point k in this same wire is inserted a firing key, which latter is shown in section at Fig. 144, from which the mode of connecting the two ends of the wires and of using the key will be at once apparent.   The contact breaker is somewhat similar to the firing key, but there is no spring in it, contact being made or broken by screwing the two parts together or apart. The object of the contact breaker is to prevent the torpedo being exploded by contact, and so to place the control of the weapon entirely in the hands of the operator.   As will be seen from Fig. 143, if contact is broken at c, it is impossible to fire the torpedo unless the firing key k be pressed in ; but should contact be made at c, then either by means of the firing key k, or by the torpedo striking the hostile vessel, its ignition will be effected.

The foregoing method of arranging the spar torpedo wires is certainly very neat and effective, and is at the present time in extensive use. As yet it has not been adopted by the English government, they still preferring to fire the spar torpedo at will alone.

The different methods of manipulating the spar torpedo from boats will be described in the following chapter.

General Remarks on Offensive Torpedoes.—The torpedoes that have been described in this chapter are the only ones that at the present time can be considered as having been proved to be practically useful, and which in future wars may be employed against ships with some chance of success.

The spar, the Whitehead fish, and the Harvey towing torpedo have each been subjected to the test of actual service, the former weapon being the only one that has under those conditions been successfully used. Taking this fact into consideration, also the high pitch of excellence that has been attained in the construction of steam torpedo boats, and also the results of the numerous exhaustive experiments that have been from time to time carried out in England, America, and Europe, with various modifications of the locomotive, towing, and spar torpedoes, there can be no two opinions as to which of the numerous species of offensive submarine weapons is the most practicable and effective, and that is the spar or outrigger torpedo.

To manipulate successfully locomotive and towing torpedoes in an attack against hostile vessels, the operators must be not only unusually fearless and self-possessed, but also must possess a thorough practical knowledge of the complicated method of working and manœuvring those weapons—in fact, they must be specialists; whilst in the case of the spar torpedo, which may be fired by contact, it is only necessary to employ men capable of handling a boat well, and possessed of dash and pluck, to ensure an attack by such means being generally successful. Of course under some circumstances, such as in a general action, when the locomotive and towing torpedoes are manipulated from specially constructed torpedo vessels, they will prove of great value, and the fish torpedo fired from a boat, in close proximity to the attacked vessel, in smooth water, and unmolested, would sink a vessel which under the same circumstances, owing to her being protected by booms, might prove impregnable to a spar torpedo attack; but such favourable conditions will not often occur in war time.

PLATE XLIV

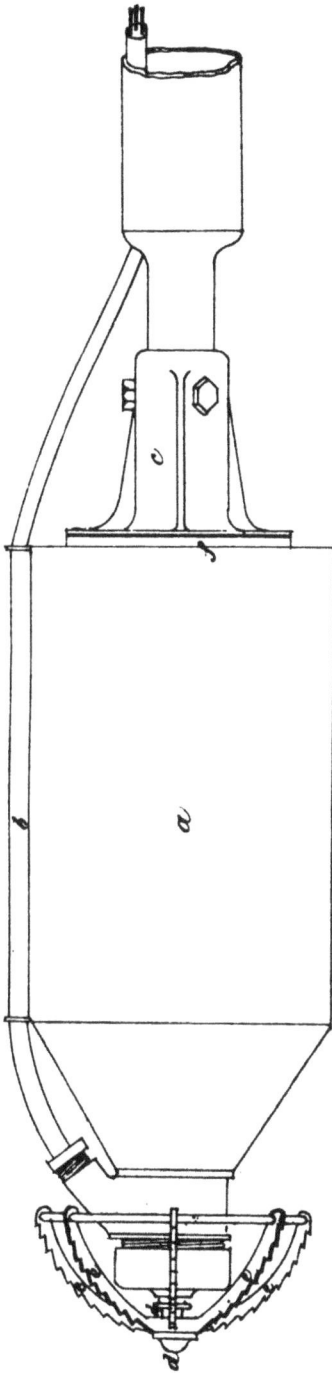

Fig 142.

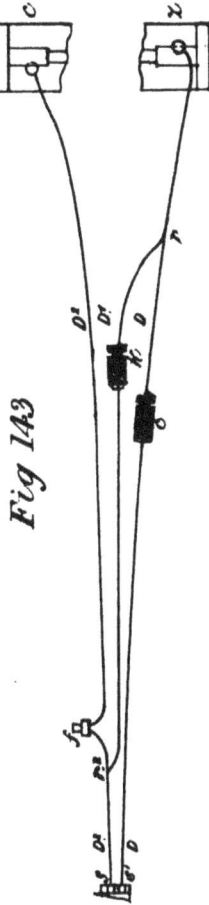

Fig 143.

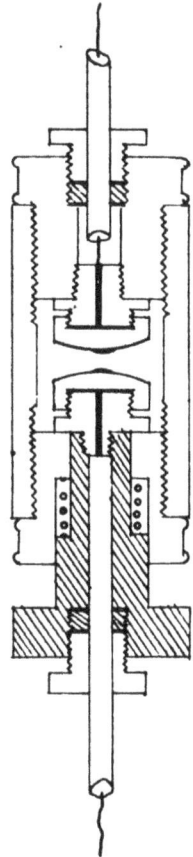

Fig 144.

As an offensive submarine weapon of defence, the Lay torpedo boat should prove of real value; and also manœuvred from specially constructed vessels, it seems capable of being used in a variety of ways. As yet little is known of this weapon, all the experiments carried out with it having been confined to America; but now that Russia has adopted it, and one or two have also been secured by the Peruvians, its practical value will become more generally known.

CHAPTER VI.

TORPEDO VESSELS, BOATS, AND SUBMARINE BOATS.

EMPLOYMENT of Torpedo Ships.—Torpedo ships, that is to say, sea-going vessels, very fast, handy and impregnable, specially designed to carry and operate offensive submarine weapons, such as locomotive, towing, and the spar torpedoes, especially the former, are now considered as a necessary and valuable adjunct to a fleet, their special work being to give the coup de grâce to disabled ironclads in a general action; they will also be used to attack the ships of a blockading force, and against rival torpedo vessels. As a general rule these torpedo ships will be armed with the ram and torpedoes only, heavy guns being dispensed with, though the Nordenfelt and other machine guns will be considered necessary.

The German Torpedo Vessel Uhlan.—This torpedo vessel was built in Germany by the Stettin Engine Company, and launched in 1876.

She is armed with a contact torpedo charged with dynamite carried on a 10-foot ram, lying deeply under the water line. To protect the vessel from the effects of the discharge of the torpedo, she is built with two complete parts, sliding one within the other, and having a considerable extent of intermediate space between them. This space is filled with a tough and elastic material (cork and marine glue), which even in the case of the bows being carried away, would afford a second line of resistance. The *Uhlan* carries an engine of one thousand indicated horse power. The steam is supplied by Belleville's tubular generator. These engines occupy by far the greater space of the vessel, only a very small portion being left for her crew and coal. This great power of the engines is necessitated by the fact that she has to be driven at a very high speed, at the same time she has a very great draught, also the greatest facility of steering has to be attained; hence the proportion of width to length, 25 to 70 feet. In order to save the crew at the worst, a raft is constructed, which is also filled with a mixture of cork and marine glue, and is placed near the helm. The mode of operating with the *Uhlan* is as follows :—

The dynamite torpedo is affixed to the point of the ram by the aid of divers.   The rudder is then fixed, and the crew opening a wide port on the vessel's side, jump on the aforesaid raft.   The steamer then rushes forward, and explodes its torpedo in contact with the hostile vessel.   The crew hold on to the torpedo ship, and in case she is not injured board her again and repeat the manœuvre, if necessary.*

This is a novel form of torpedo boat, but does not seem to be a very practicable method of torpedo attack.

Admiral Porter's Torpedo Ship Alarm.—The *Alarm* torpedo ship was built from plans designed by Admiral David D. Porter, U. S. N. Her total length, which includes a ram 32 feet long, is 172 feet ; her beam is 27 feet 6 inches, and her draught of water is 11 feet.   She is built of iron on the bracket plate system, that is to say, she has a double hull, one shell being constructed inside the other.   Her double bottom is divided into a number of water-tight compartments.   The whole interior of the vessel is also built in compartments, which may be hermetically closed, so that in case of both the shells being ruptured, it would still be impossible to fill the entire ship with water.   She is steered by the same apparatus which propels her, viz. the Fowler wheel, which is illustrated at Fig. 145.

This wheel turns on a vertical shaft, and its paddles are feathered by an eccentric cam in such a manner that at one part of their revolution they have a pushing and drawing action on the water, while at another part they present only their edges.   In fact it is simply a feathering paddle wheel, turned horizontally instead of vertically.   By suitably turning the cam wheel, which is done from the helm, the feathering of the paddles is caused to occur at different points ; and in this way the vessel may be turned, or rather her stern twisted around, as if on a pivot.   At the same time, by suitably adjusting the paddles, the ship goes ahead, or astern, the engine meanwhile running in the same direction.

By the apparatus above described it is considered that the *Alarm* is afforded not only a means of speed, but of being handled with the

---

* Extract from ' European Ships of War,' &c., by J. W. King, U.S.N., page 312.

utmost readiness, which latter is absolutely essential in such a vessel, as she must always meet her antagonist bows on.

The steering is accomplished from the wheel house located aft on the deck, or below deck, as all the appliances in the wheel house for steering, &c., are duplicated below. By means of a hand lever beneath the wheel, steam is admitted to a small auxiliary engine which works the cam that adjusts the paddles. Then by turning the horizontal hand wheel in either direction, the helmsman controls the movement of the cam, as desired. Just above the wheel is a dial with a pointer, which enables him to note the position of the paddles, and so adjust them as ordered. Inside the wheel house there are also devices for communicating with the men working the bow gun, and with those managing the torpedoes.

Her Armament—Engines.—At Fig. 146 is shown the spar and mode of working it. It consists of a long hollow iron cylinder lying on its supports between decks. Its outboard end rests in a kind of trough, and to this extremity the torpedo is fixed. The spar is controlled by means of tackles and a steam winch. The side spars are 18 feet, and the bow spar 32 feet in length. If the hostile vessel is defended by torpedo guards, by means of a mechanical contrivance the torpedo signals the fact, and is not exploded until the vessel has forced the obstructions. The engines of the *Alarm* are compound, with four cylinders, the condenser being placed between them. There are four cylindrical tubular boilers with an aggregate heating surface of 4,600 square feet. Her speed is about 16 knots. Her upper deck is only 3 feet above the water. She is fitted with an electric light, and also with machine guns on her broadside.*

This is undoubtedly a most formidable vessel, both as a ram and a torpedo ship, and if capable of performing all that is expected of her, will prove a valuable addition to the United States Navy.

Captain Ericsson's Torpedo Vessel "Destroyer."—This torpedo vessel was devised and built by Captain John Ericsson. The *Destroyer* is 130 feet long, 11 feet deep, and 12 feet beam, extreme; both ends of her hull are precisely alike, and terminate with very fine wedges. The rudder is attached to a vertical wrought iron post welded to a prolongation of the keel, just abaft the propeller, as shown at Fig. 147.

* Extract from *Engineering*, under date April 13, 1877.

PLATE XLV

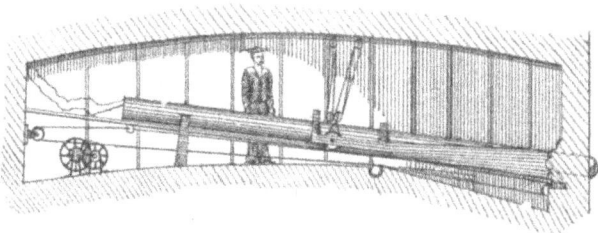

Fig 146

Fig 145

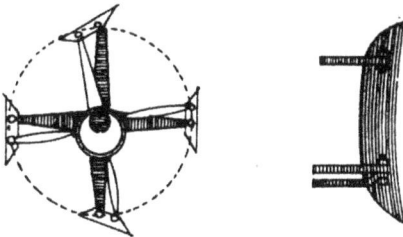

The tillers consist of thin plates of iron riveted on opposite sides of the rudder, a few inches from its bottom. These tillers are operated by straight rods connected to the pistons of horizontal hydraulic cylinders of 5 inches diameter, which are attached to the sides of the keel. The steering gear by the above arrangement is placed 10 feet below the water line, while the top of the rudder is 6 feet below the same, and thus perfect security is afforded to this most important feature of a torpedo vessel. The intention of the designer in constructing this vessel is to render her so far impregnable, that in attacking bow on she can defy the opponent's fire, at the same time offering absolute protection to her commander and steersman, and also protecting the base of her funnel. The leading feature of the construction of the hull of the *Destroyer* is its being provided with an intermediate curved deck, which extends from stem to stern, and which is composed of plate iron strongly ribbed, and perfectly water-tight. This intermediate deck supports a heavy solid armour plate, fixed transversely to the line of keel, and 32 feet from the bow, inclined at an angle of 45°, and supported on its after side by a wood backing 4 feet 6 inches in thickness. Behind this formidable shield the steering wheel is manipulated, a wire rope extending from its barrel to a four-way cock placed near the stern, by means of which water pressure is admitted alternately to the hydraulic cylinders, previously mentioned, the motion of whose pistons actuate the rudder. The lower division of the vessel is ventilated by powerful blowers, and contains the machinery ; it also affords a safe retreat for the crew during the attack. The upper division is filled with blocks of cork, excepting a small part near the bow, occupied by the aforesaid armour plate and wood backing.

The deck house is 70 feet long, and composed of plate iron, riveted water-tight to the upper part of the hull. As there are no openings in the sides of this deck house, the vessel may be run with her upper deck under water.

Armament of the " Destroyer."—The *Destroyer* is to be armed with torpedoes somewhat similar to the projectile torpedo, drawings of which were submitted by Captain Ericsson, the inventor, to Emperor Napoleon III. in 1854. The present weapon is composed of a solid block of light wood, the explosive charge being contained in a metallic vessel inserted at its forward end. Instead of being circular, as was the case with the original torpedo, its transverse section is square, with parallel top and bottom and vertical sides, forming very sharp wedges at both ends, cased with steel plates. The extreme length of the *Destroyer* torpedo is 23 feet. Ignition is effected by means of a percussion fuze placed in the head of the weapon.

Operating the Torpedo.—The method of operating the torpedo is that of inserting it into a horizontal tube near the bottom of the vessel, provided with valves for keeping out the sea during the process of insertion, as shown at Fig. 148. When near the hostile vessel, this valve is opened, and the torpedo expelled by a piston actuated by steam power, the expulsion being effected without recourse to gunpowder or other explosive agent. The area of the actuating piston of the *Destroyer* is 314 square inches, while the sectional area of the projectile is only 196 square inches; this difference in size of the two areas is a special and important feature of the invention, as will be understood from the following: the tension of the acting medium in the *Destroyer* exceeds 200 lbs. per square inch, therefore the torpedo will be pushed out by a force of $\dfrac{314 \times 200}{196}$ 320 lbs. per square inch, and as the distance passed by the piston while impelling the torpedo is 30 feet, an energy of nearly 2,000,000 foot-pounds will be imparted to the projectile.

When making an attack, it is intended that the vessel should at the instant of firing her torpedo reverse her engines, this retrograde motion being greatly assisted by the recoil, which must attend the discharge of a body weighing some 1,400 lbs. impelled by the aforesaid enormous force, and moving through a distance of 30 feet before reaching the water.[*]

Certainly this new system of submarine attack seems feasible, but it has yet to prove, in common with all other new inventions, whether its theoretical capabilities are also practical ones. At Fig. 149 is shown a general view of this novel torpedo vessel under weigh.

Torpedo Boats.—In offensive torpedo warfare, whether using the spar, locomotive, or towing torpedo, especially in the case of the former class of submarine weapons, to ensure a successful attack it is absolutely essential to operate those weapons from steam boats, which

---

[*] Extract from letter of Captain Ericsson that appeared in *Engineer*, under date Nov. 8, 1878.

are capable of fulfilling as near as possible the conditions herein enumerated :—

1.—They should be capable of steaming at least 18 knots per hour.

2.—Their engines should be noiseless, and easily managed.

3.—They should be extremely handy.

4.—No smoke should enable their approach to be detected, or glare from their fires.

5.—That it should be possible to raise steam in them in a few minutes.

6.—They should be built in water-tight compartments, and covered fore and aft to prevent being swamped.

7.—The crews should be protected as far as practicable from rifle fire.

In addition to the foregoing, for the purpose of rendering these craft capable of defending themselves against the attack of guard boats, and also of being employed as such, and on river expeditions, &c., they should be built sufficiently strong to enable them to carry a small gun either in the bows or stern ; this would apply more especially to those torpedo boats which are part of a ship's stores.

During the last four years a very large number of torpedo boats have been built, which more or less fulfil the aforesaid conditions, nearly the whole of which have been constructed by the two English firms, viz. Messrs. Thornycroft and Co. and Messrs. Yarrow and Co., and to the latter firm is due the honour of constructing the fastest vessel as yet in the world.

Up to the present time, a specially built torpedo boat has on only one occasion been used on active service, viz. at the attack on a Turkish monitor on the 20th of June, 1877, which is detailed at length in the following chapter. This boat was one of Messrs. Thornycroft and Co.'s launches, and from all accounts she behaved wonderfully well under the most untoward circumstances.

Thornycroft Torpedo Launches.—Messrs. Thornycroft and Co., of Chiswick, London, have during the last six years built a large number of torpedo launches for the English government and for several of the principal European governments.

Norwegian Launch.—The first torpedo boat ever built by this firm was the one shown at Fig. 150, for the Norwegian government.

This boat was 57 feet in length by 7 feet 6 inches beam, drew 3 feet of water, and the stipulated speed was 16 English statute miles, or nearly 14 knots per hour; which speed was not to be ascertained by a mere measured mile trial, but was to be 16 miles through the water in a run of one hour's duration.

The hull of the vessel was constructed entirely of steel plates and angle bars, and, as may be seen from the diagram, was divided into six water-tight compartments, A, B, C, D, E, F.

The compartments marked A and F in the stem and stern were for stores; those marked B and E were fitted with seats for the crew, and were provided with movable steel covers, so that on going into action, or during rough weather, they might be completely covered.

The compartments C and D are for the steersman and the machinery respectively, and were covered completely by steel plating $\frac{3}{16}$ of an inch in thickness—a thickness sufficient to withstand Snider or Martini-Henry bullets, fired from a distance of twenty paces.

The compartment D was furnished with a hood, having slits $\frac{1}{4}$ of an inch wide, all round, through which the steersman could see with sufficient distinctness to direct his course easily. Motion was communicated from the wheel to the tiller by means of steel wire ropes, which it was originally intended should be encased in wrought iron tubes.

The possibility however of these tubes being bent by a shot, and so jamming the wire ropes, led to this arrangement being abandoned, and the ropes were simply run through eyes at intervals along the side.

The armament consisted of a cylindro-conical shaped torpedo towed from the top of the funnel, round which a ring was fitted with two pulleys for the towing rope, the strain being taken off by means of two stays attached forward.

The length of this torpedo was 13 feet and the diameter 9 inches, and with a speed of 11 knots it has diverged to about 40 degrees from the direction of the boat's motion when running in smooth water.

The torpedo is worked by means of a small winch and brake fixed on the after part of the engine room skylight; davits are provided for dropping the torpedo overboard.

The engines were compound, of the usual inverted double cylinder direct acting type, capable of developing about 90 indicated horse power, and were fitted with a surface condenser, so that the vessel could run in salt water, without danger of injuring her boiler.

A small tank contained a supply of fresh water, to make good deficiencies arising through leakage, and from steam escaping at the safety valves, &c.

The circulating, air, and feed pumps were driven by a separate engine.

The boiler was of the locomotive type, the shell being made of Bessemer steel; the fire box and its stays of copper, and the tubes of solid drawn brass.

On the official trial, which took place on the Thames on the 17th of October, 1873, the number of revolutions done in the hour was found to be 27,177, and the number required to do a mile in still water was 1578. The distance run in the hour was then, $\dfrac{27,177}{1578} = 17.22$, or very nearly $17\frac{1}{4}$ miles.

The steam pressure during the trial averaged 85 lbs. per square inch, and the vacuum $25\frac{1}{2}$ inches.

Swedish and Danish Boats.—Boats of the same size and similar in all particulars to the foregoing one—excepting the engines, which are improved by driving the air pump, feed pump, and circulating pumps off the main engines, and abolishing the auxiliary engine, which performed these duties in the case of the Norwegian boat—were made for the Swedish and Danish governments. The result was an increase of speed to 17·27 miles in the case of the Swedish boat, and to 18·06 miles, or $15\frac{3}{4}$ knots, in the case of the Danish boat.

There is no information regarding the armament of the Swedish boat, but the Danish boat was armed with two spindle-shaped torpedoes 12 feet long and $11\frac{1}{2}$ inches diameter, somewhat like the Whitehead torpedo. They were placed on deck longitudinally near the funnel, so as to facilitate launching, and were arranged to be towed from an upright pole 8 feet high, placed about 6 feet from the stem.

A small winch was fixed on either side aft, to pay out the towing line, and to bring back the torpedo. By these arrangements the torpedo could be projected at a large angle from the direction of the boat's motion, and at considerable velocity. The speed of the boat when towing one of these torpedoes is about 10 knots.

Austrian and French Boats.—The next size of torpedo vessel is that supplied to the Austrian and French governments, which is shown at Fig. 151. The dimensions are:—length, 67 feet; beam, 8 feet 6 inches; draught of water, 4 feet 3 inches. The guaranteed speed in the case of the Austrian boat was 15 knots in a run of one hour's duration, and in the case of the French boats 18 knots, in a run of two hours' duration. These boats were built of somewhat thicker plating than the 57 feet type, and the armour was extended.

They were divided into six water-tight compartments, and they differed from the Scandinavian boats in having the spaces forward and aft of the machinery permanently decked, instead of being covered with movable steel covers only.

The machinery was somewhat similar to that in the Scandinavian boats, excepting that the engines were capable of developing 200 indicated horse power, and that the air was supplied to the furnace by being forced into an air-tight stoke hole, instead of being forced directly under the fire grate.

The armament of these vessels consisted of two torpedoes attached to the end of wooden poles, $4\frac{1}{2}$ inches diameter and about 43 feet long, connected to the battery by insulated wires, and arranged to be fired either by coming in contact with the enemy's vessel or at any distance from it, at the will of the operator.

The torpedoes themselves were simply copper cases, of sufficient size, in the case of the Austrian boat, to contain 11,000 cubic centimetres of explosive, and in the case of the French boats, to contain 25 kilogrammes of dynamite.

The mode of arranging the wires is similar to that explained at page 155. The method of manipulating the torpedo poles consists of two tubes riveted together at right angles, so as to form something like the letter T. The torpedo pole is put through the horizontal tube, which is free to move round the centre of the vertical tube, and the vertical tube is free to move through a quarter circle at right angles to the centre line of the vessel.

In attacking in front, the vertical tube is laid over till it is parallel to the water surface, and the horizontal tube is allowed to incline sufficiently far to allow of the end of the pole, when run out, to be depressed from 8 to 10 feet below the water-line. It is held in this position by a pair of blocks attached to the top of a short mast.

In attacking on the broadside, the vertical tube is laid over till it assumes a position such as to allow of the pole, when swung round, to touch an enemy's vessel at about 8 or 10 feet below the water line.

The speed trials of the Austrian boat took place on the 11th of September, 1875, when she did 24,700 revolutions on her hour's run on the Thames, and the number of revolutions required to do a knot in still water was found to be 1357. This gives the distance run in the hour as 18·202 knots, or 3·202 knots over the contract speed. The steam pressure averaged 105 lbs. per square inch, and the vacuum 25½ inches during the run.

In the case of the French boats, the total number of revolutions done in the two hours' run in the roadstead off Cherbourg was 49,818, and the number required to do a knot in still water was found to be 1382, so that the distance run in the two hours was 36·05 knots, or just over the contract speed. During the two hours, the average steam pressure was 108 lbs. per square inch, and the vacuum 25 inches.

The Austrian boat was sent to her destination on board a steamer, but the French boats, under the command of an experienced captain, steamed by themselves from Chiswick to Cherbourg, not crossing at the nearest points, and running along the shore, but going boldly from Dover direct to Cherbourg.

Shortly after the arrival of the French boats in Cherbourg, they were altered so as to attack in front only, as the French authorities found that these small vessels were better adapted for resisting the effects of an explosion at the bow than at any other part.

The arrangement adopted is shown at Fig. 152, and consisted of a steel pole about 40 feet in length, having one end about 6 inches diameter, and solid, and the other about 1½ inches diameter, and hollow; this pole was mounted at its solid end on small pulleys, which ran upon two ropes stretched fore and aft of the vessel; the other end, to which the torpedo was attached, was led over a pulley fixed on the bow. Ropes passing over pulleys to a windlass in the after compartment were attached to the inboard end, and by turning the windlass the pole was drawn backwards or forwards as required.

It will be observed that as the pole is drawn forward, the inboard end being constrained to move in a line parallel to the deck, the outer end is depressed in the water, and is so adjusted that when the pole is run out to its full extremity, the torpedo is depressed to about 8½ feet below the water level.

Dutch and Italian Boats.—The third size of boat built by this firm for the Dutch and Italian governments are 76 feet long and 10 feet beam, and are guaranteed to do a speed of 18 knots. These boats are similar in design to the Austrian and French boats previously described, but differ from them in having engines of 250 indicated horse power, and in having more free board forward, so as to make them better sea boats.

The Dutch type are armed with the outrigger torpedo, as fitted to the French boats, and the Italian type with the Whitehead fish torpedo.

The " Lightning " Type of Boat.—Now comes the *Lightning* type of vessel, which is shown at Fig. 153. This vessel, built for the English government, is 84 feet long over all, 10 feet 10 inches beam, and draws about 5 feet of water. The machinery on board the *Lightning* is similar in design to that already described, and is capable of indicating 350 horse power. The hull of the *Lightning* is made of heavier plating than usually employed, and her lines are fuller, as she is intended for use in a tolerably rough sea if necessary; and in order that she may be able to remain at sea for some time, cabin accommodation on a scale larger than in any of the other boats is provided for the officers and crew. The steering gear is arranged so that the vessel may be steered from the deck, or from the conning tower, and the usual telegraph gear is fitted to communicate from the deck, or from the conning tower, to the engine room.

The top of the conning tower is supported on three screws, so arranged that it may be raised or lowered, and the space for sight adjusted according to the range of vision required, or the risk to be run from the enemy's missiles.

The *Lightning* is armed with fish torpedoes, which are discharged from her deck forward by means of a discharging apparatus.

The torpedoes are charged with air, by means of one of Mr. Brotherhood's air-compressing pumps.

The *Lightning* on her preliminary runs attained a speed on the measured mile of 19·4 knots per hour, a speed which will be somewhat reduced when she has her torpedoes, &c., on board, but which will then be over 18 knots per hour.

Several torpedo boats have been built and are in process of construction by this firm for the English government.

PLATE XLVII

Fig 150

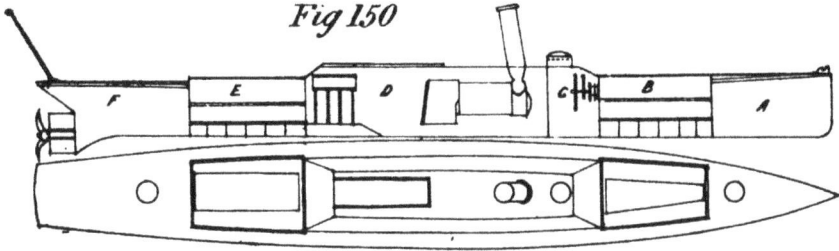

Fig 151

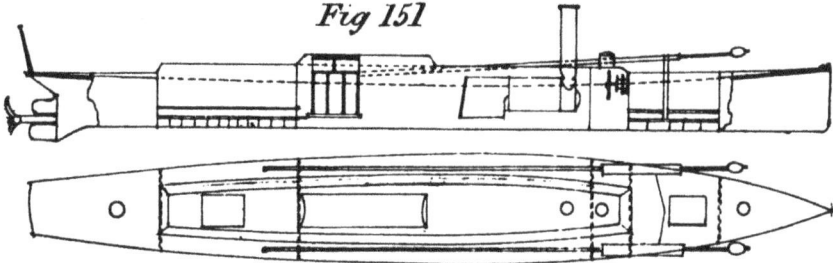

Fig 152

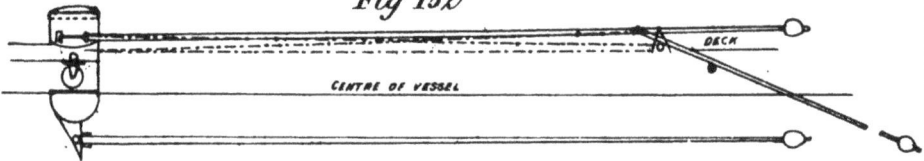

Fig 153

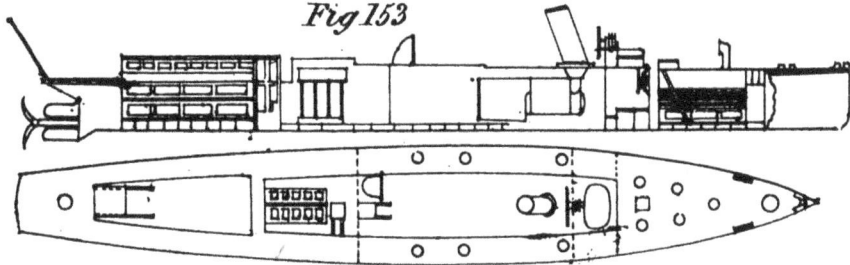

French Boats.—The next size of boats is the 87 feet type, as shown at Fig. 154. Of this type of torpedo launch several have been built and are now under construction for the French government.

These vessels are 10 feet 6 inches beam; draught of water about 5 feet. They are built of heavier plating than the *Lightning*, and are guaranteed to maintain a speed of 18 knots. The propellers in these boats are placed in front of the rudder, so as to give increased readiness in steering. In order to prevent oxidation as far as possible, the plates and frames below the water line are galvanised. A spark-catching apparatus is fitted to the base of the funnel, so as to prevent the position of the boat being betrayed to the enemy at night.

The armament of these vessels consist of an outrigger arrangement similar to that described at page 167. They are also well adapted for the Whitehead torpedo. They are also provided with a strong buffer in the bows for deadening the shock, in the event of their coming into contact with an enemy's vessel at too high a rate of speed.

" Second Class " Boats and Mode of Manipulating the Fish Torpedoes from them.—Another type of Thornycroft torpedo boats, several of which have been built for continental governments, and which is termed " Second class," is shown at Fig. 155. These boats are 60 feet long, 7 feet 6 inches beam, and draw some 3 feet of water; their guaranteed speed being 16 knots per hour. The mode of carrying the Whitehead fish torpedo, and manipulating it from such a boat by means of Mr. J. I. Thornycroft's invention, which has been fully described at page 140, is shown at Figs. 155 and 156, where Fig. 155 represents both torpedoes housed, and Fig. 156 one torpedo in the firing position, the other one being housed.

Four of this type of Thornycroft torpedo boats were attached to H.M.S. *Hecla* during her recent cruise in the Mediterranean, and have been very favourably reported on as follows :—They do not suffer from the blows of the sea, nor from the strains incident upon hoisting in and out; nor yet when they are suspended ready for lowering, in which latter position they have frequently remained for twenty-four hours; that under careful management they are perfectly safe in a heavy sea, and they possess good manœuvring powers.

The Thornycroft torpedo frames were found to perform well the services for which they are intended. When proceeding at ordinary

N

speed they are nearly noiseless, and cannot be seen on a dark night at a distance of 100 yards.

The Thornycroft Propeller.—All the torpedo boats built by this firm are fitted with the propeller invented by Mr. Thornycroft, and which bears his name. It is a modification of what is known as the Dundonald propeller, the principal difference being that in the Dundonald propeller the blades are inclined backward in straight lines, while in the Thornycroft propeller they are curved.

Experiment at Cherbourg.—The following account of an experiment which took place at Cherbourg in March 1877, whereby to test the efficiency of a Thornycroft torpedo boat in exploding a spar torpedo under the bottom of a vessel proceeding ahead at the time, is taken from the *Times*, under date the 13th of March, 1877.

"Admiral Jaurez, who commands the squadron, ordered a disabled ship, the *Bayonnaise*, during a rather rough sea, to be towed out by a steamer belonging to the navy. A second lieutenant, M. Lemoinne, was sent for, and informed that he had been selected to make the experiment of launching the Thornycroft against the *Bayonnaise* while both were in full sail. He accepted the mission without hesitation, picked out two engine men and a pilot, and went down with them into the interior of the Thornycroft, of which only a small part was above water; this visible portion being painted of a greyish colour, so as to be easily confused with the sea. The torpedo was placed so as to project from the bow of the vessel, at the extremity of which were two lateen sailyards about three metres in length. The towing steamer then took up its position in front of the squadron, and the Thornycroft also assumed the position assigned for it; an interval of three or four marine miles separating the torpedo boat and the *Bayonnaise*. On a signal being given, both were set in motion, the steamer advancing in a straight line, and the Thornycroft obliquely, so as to take the *Bayonnaise* in flank. The steam tug went at 14 knots an hour, going at full speed in order to escape the Thornycroft. The latter went at 19 knots an hour, a rate not attained by any vessel in the squadron. The chase lasted about an hour, the squadron keeping in the rear, so as to witness the operations. At the end of that time the distance between the Thornycroft and the *Bayonnaise* had sensibly diminished, and at a given moment the former, in order to come up with the latter at the requisite distance, had to slacken

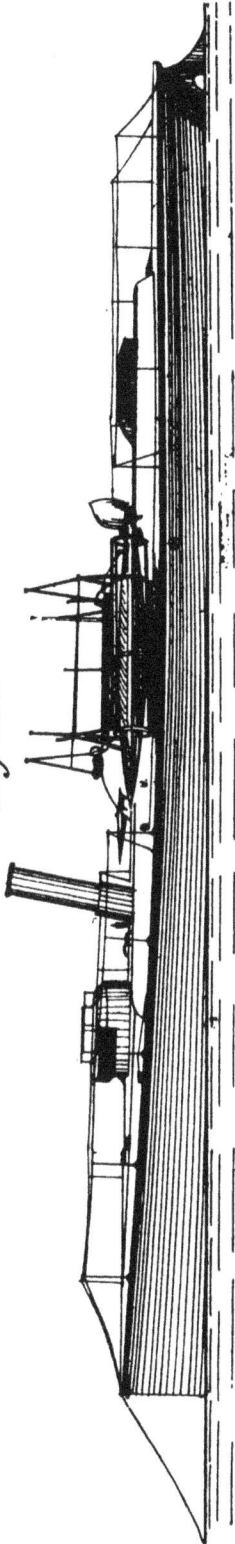

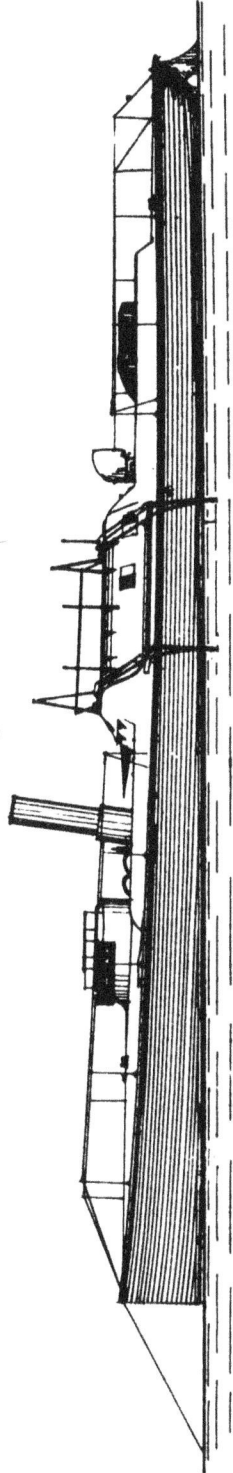

PLATE XLVIII

Fig 154

Fig 155

Fig 156

speed to 8 knots an hour. The whole squadron watched this last phase of the struggle with breathless interest, and people asked themselves whether the shock of the torpedo would not infallibly destroy the little vessel which bore it. It was feared that the lives of the second lieutenant, Lemoinne, and his three companions were absolutely sacrificed. However, the two vessels got visibly nearer. All at once the Thornycroft put on a last spurt, and struck the *Bayonnaise* with its whole force on the starboard bow. The sea was terribly agitated, a deafening report was heard, and the *Bayonnaise*, with a rent as big as a house, sank with wonderful rapidity. As for the Thornycroft, rebounding by the shock about fifteen metres off, even before the explosion occurred, it went round and round for a few moments, and quietly resumed the direction of the squadron. No trace remained of the *Bayonnaise;* it was literally swallowed up by the sea."

The experiment was a most complete success, the torpedo boat not being in the least degree injured.

The Power of Flotation of a Thornycroft Boat after being pierced by a Rifle Shot.—On the 5th of July, 1877, Messrs. Thornycroft and Co. made an experiment with one of their torpedo boats to ascertain under what conditions flotation is still retained after the boat has been pierced by a rifle shot.

The torpedo boat experimented on was similar to the one which has been described at page 169. A Martini-Henry was fired through her side, about a foot under water in the stoke hole. Whilst at anchor the water entered in sufficient quantity to fill an ordinary size bucket in twenty-five seconds, but when she was driven ahead less water entered, and on the speed of 10 knots being reached, little or no water entered. The hole was a little more than three quarters of an inch in diameter.

The engagement on the Danube between the torpedo boat *Schootka* and some Turkish vessels, in which the former vessel was pierced by bullets, but yet did not sink, led to the above experiment being carried out.

Efficiency of Thornycroft's Engines.—As a practical proof of the efficiency of the engines supplied by Messrs. Thornycroft and Co. to their torpedo boats, a similar engine has been used for over two years to work the various machines in connection with their works at Chiswick.

Torpedo Boats built by Messrs. Yarrow and Co.—Messrs. Yarrow and Co., of the Isle of Dogs, London, are also very well-known torpedo boat builders, and have during the last four years constructed a considerable number of such vessels for the English and different continental governments, and, as has been before stated, they are the constructors of the fastest vessel in the world.

Dutch Torpedo Launch.—In 1875 this firm built a torpedo launch for the Dutch government, specially designed for ocean purposes. It was 66 feet long, 10 feet beam, and 5½ feet deep. She was driven by a pair of inverted direct acting engines. The boiler was of the locomotive type, with a working pressure of 140 lbs. per square inch, and capable of exerting a force of some 200 indicated horses.

Russian Torpedo Boat.—This firm also constructed for the Russian government two torpedo steamers 85 feet in length. The guaranteed speed of these vessels being 20 knots per hour. In 1878 the Russian government ordered one hundred exactly similar boats to be constructed, mostly at St. Petersburg, thus proving the high estimation held by that government of Messrs. Yarrow and Co.'s torpedo boats.

Description of a Yarrow Torpedo Launch.—Figs. 157, 158, and 159 show an elevation, section, and plan of a torpedo boat, Yarrow type, a large number of which have been built for the Russian and other continental governments.

The length of this boat is 75 feet, its beam 10 feet, and draught of water 3 feet. She is built of steel of the best quality, no other metal possessing the requisite strength and stiffness for scantling, and plates of such lightness. It is divided into eight compartments by seven transverse bulkheads, the forward and after compartments being used for stores, the two central ones enclosing the machinery, while the steersman and operator are placed in the compartment immediately abaft the engines.

The steersman's head projects above the deck, and is protected by a rifle proof steel truncated cone, the top part of which is movable like the visor of a helmet. The hull is decked over from end to end with a curved shield, the midship plating of which is capable of resisting rifle shots, even at close quarters; its curved form being well adapted for giving the maximum strength to the structure, and quickly frees itself from any large body of water.

The propelling machinery consists of a pair of inverted compound

PLATE XLIX

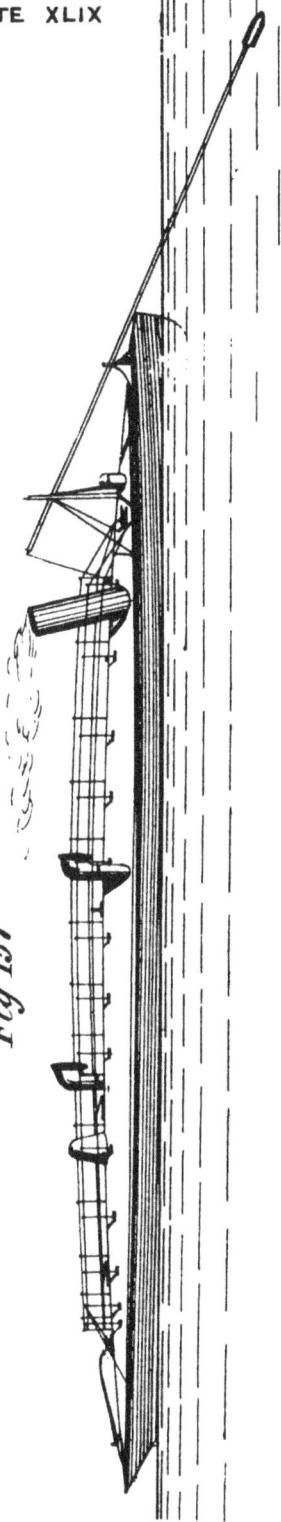

Fig 157

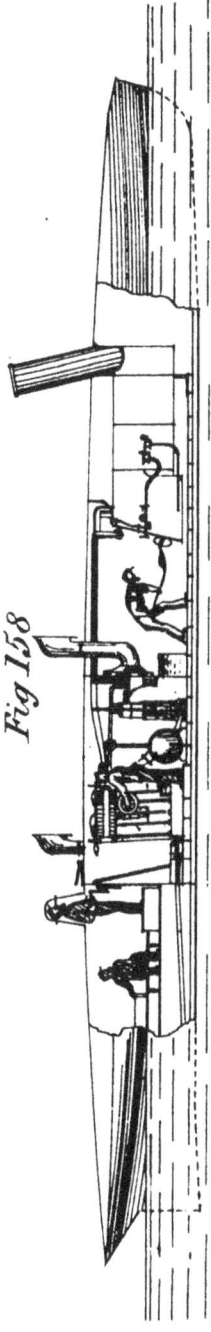

Fig 158

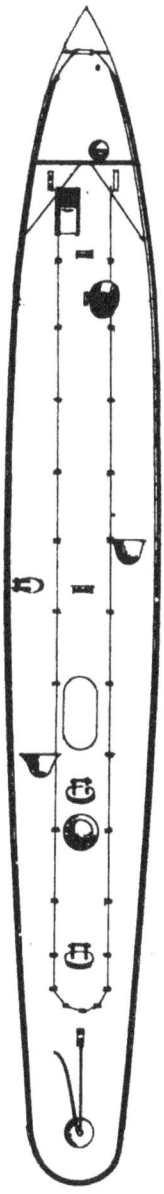

Fig 159

condensing engines.   The revolutions per minute at full speed are about 470, and the indicated horse power about 280.   The propeller is of steel.   The funnel is fixed at one side of the centre line, to be out of the way of the bow torpedo pole and gear.

This type of torpedo boat attains a speed of from 17½ to 18½ knots per hour.

The armament of some of these boats consists of three spar torpedoes, a bow, and two quarter ones.   The bow pole, which is strong and heavy, is hauled out and in by means of a small auxiliary engine.

Boats similar to these, but of larger dimensions, viz. 84 feet long and 11 feet beam, have also been constructed by this firm.   Speed from 19 to 20 knots per hour.

English Torpedo Boats.—The following account of two torpedo boats which had been originally built by this firm for the Russian government, but, owing to the proclamation issued by the English government at this time prohibiting torpedo boats leaving England, were seized by the Customs authorities when on the point of completion, and were ultimately purchased by the English government, is an extract from the *Times* under date the 4th of July, 1878.

" These vessels are each 85 feet long with 11 feet beam, and draw, when fully equipped for service, an average of 3 feet of water.   They are strongly constructed of steel, and are fitted with compound surface condensing engines capable of indicating 420 horse power.   The high pressure steam cylinder of these engines is 12½ inches in diameter, and the low pressure 21½ inches, both having a 12 inch stroke.   These boats are at present known by their builders' numbers, one being No. 419 and the other No. 420.   The former is propelled by a three-bladed screw, 5 feet 6 inches diameter and 5 feet pitch ; and the latter by a two-bladed screw of similar proportions.   Messrs. Yarrow adopt supplementary engines for driving the air pump, circulating pump, and feed pumps ; they consider this plan preferable to that of working these pumps direct off the main engine, as is sometimes done.   One advantage in having separate pumping engines is that, whether the vessel is in motion or stationary, a powerful means is available for pumping her out, should the necessity arise.   It is estimated by her builders that if the air pump and circulating pump were both utilised for this purpose, the water could be pumped out as fast as it could enter either of these vessels through one hundred holes made in the skin by Martini-Henry rifle bullets.   If this is the case, these craft may be deemed safe from sinking so long as their machinery is working efficiently.   The boiler is of the locomotive type, placed in the forward part of each vessel, and has a closed stoke hole.   In connection with the boiler a very important improvement has been introduced by Messrs. Yarrow.   This consists in a means of rendering the closed stoke hole safe for the men in the event of the collapse of a boiler tube—a contingency which cannot be absolutely guarded against.   Its efficiency was proved beyond all question upon a previous trial of one of these boats.   This was No. 419, which was tried on the 24th of May last under the supervision of the Admiralty officials.   Upon that occasion an accidental rupture of one of the boiler tubes occurred nearly at the close of the runs over the measured mile, which so far had been very successful.   When the boiler tube gave way the steam rushed out of the foremost hatchway from the compartment in which the smoke box end of the boiler is situated, and soon after from the two funnels.   The men in the stoke hole, however, being shut off from the boiler, were uninjured, and remained at their post several minutes after the first outburst of steam. The accident, although an untoward event, was considered by the Admiralty officials as affording a highly satisfactory proof of the efficiency of Mr. Yarrow's invention.

" The engines are placed amidships, and each vessel has spacious cabin accommodation aft, as it is intended that they may be used either as despatch or torpedo boats.   For the latter purpose the cabin framings above deck are removed and replaced by steel plating.   They are steered from the cabin, there being a look-out for the steersman just above deck level.   The deck is clear of all obstructions, the two funnels being placed one on either side.   They are fitted with balanced rudders and steer well, answering their helms very quickly."

The trials of these two torpedo boats are taken from the *Engineer* under date the 19th of July, 1878.   At that time these boats completely eclipsed in speed everything that had hitherto been done.   At Fig. 160 is shown in elevation this type of torpedo launch.

" The trials were personally conducted by Mr. Yarrow, under the superintendence of the authorities from Whitehall, and consisted in a two hours' run without stopping, during which time the boats were tested at the measured mile at Long Reach.   Each boat was run six times over the mile, three runs with the tide and three runs against it.

The boats and machinery are similar in every respect, excepting that No. 419 is fitted with a three-bladed propeller, and No. 420 a two-bladed one, their diameters and pitch being the same in both cases. The weights on board were accurately weighed, and amounted to 6 tons in each boat, including coals, water, crew, and ballast.

" *Trial of No.* 419.

	Min. Sec.	Knots per hour.
1st run down occupied	2 36	23·076
1st run up „	3 20	18·000
2nd run down „	2 35	23·226
2nd run up „	3 16	18·367
3rd run down „	2 32	23·684
3rd run up „	3 14	18·557

Mean of the six runs, 20·818 knots per hour.
Mean steam pressure, 115 lbs. per square inch.
Vacuum, 23½ inches.
Mean revolutions of main engines per minute, 456.

" *Trial of No.* 420.

	Min. Sec.	Knots per hour.
1st run down occupied	2 33½	23·452
1st run up „	3 25½	17·518
2nd run down „	2 32½	23·606
2nd run up „	3 21	17·910
3rd run down „	2 32	23·684
3rd run up „	3 24	17·647

Mean of the six runs, 20·636 knots per hour.
Mean steam pressure, 115 lbs. per square inch.
Vacuum, 24 inches.
Mean revolutions per minute, 466.

" The highest speeds were obtained by No. 419, during the third runs up and down, the mean of which give 21·12 knots, which is equal to 24⅓ statute miles per hour, during which time the engines were making 470 revolutions per minute. At the close of the runs, the bearings were found to be in first-class condition, and there was not the least sign of anything getting warm during any part of the trials."

Spanish Torpedo Boat.—The following description of a torpedo boat built by this firm for the Spanish government, enumerating all the improvements that have of late been effected in the construction of such vessels by members of this firm, is taken from the *Engineering* under date the 21st of February, 1879.

" The alterations have a twofold character, and have reference to the arrangements for discharging the products of combustion from the furnaces and to those for steering the vessel.   In brief, the boat is funnelless and is fitted with two rudders, one at each end.   The main object in dispensing with the funnel is to enable the torpedo boat to approach as closely as possible to an enemy without being seen, a secondary, although still an important, consideration, being the absence of any obstruction to the steersman's view, such as a funnel on deck. The outlets for the smoke in the present instance are two ports, one on either side of the vessel, and placed about 15 feet in from the bow. Each of these smoke ports is fitted with a damper, and the smoke can be turned through either or both of the passages as desired.   The control of these dampers is given to the steersman, who, on approaching an enemy, can direct the products of combustion through the port on the unexposed side of the vessel.   The emission of smoke by day and of the glare and sparks by night are thus to a very large extent hidden from view, thus enabling the torpedo boat to approach very closely to the point of attack without being observed.   The outlets are fitted with valves which are kept open by the blast, but which close on being struck by a passing wave.   Should the vessel have to be out when a heavy sea is running the ports are closed, and a spare funnel is rigged up on deck, on one side.   Although the smoke ports are placed forward in this boat, it is intended to place them aft in the next that Messrs. Yarrow build, as. that arrangement will obviate the incon- venience at present experienced by those on deck from the heated gases of the furnace being carried along it at times by the wind, when on a certain course.

"The steering powers of the boat have next had attention from Messrs. Yarrow, and they have sought to remedy the defective steering common to these large quick-speed torpedo craft.   To do this they have fitted the vessel under notice with two balanced rudders, one of which is placed forward about 10 feet from the bow, and the other in its usual position at the stern with the screw abaft it.   Both rudders are con- nected with the same steering gear, and are operated simultaneously by one steersman.   The forward rudder can be raised out of the water into a casing inside the boat if desired by means of a screw cut on the upper part of its spindle.   By the same means, by unscrewing the collar on the spindle, the rudder can be released and dropped into the water should the necessity arise for so doing, by reason of its becoming fouled or damaged.   In trials which have been made with this double-

PLATE L

Fig 160

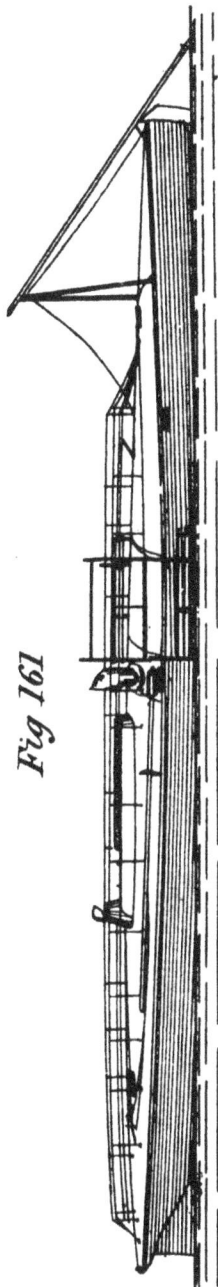

Fig 161

Fig 162

steering system, it has been found that when steaming at high speeds the forward rudder has a much greater control over the motion of the boat than the stern one. The reason assigned for this is that at high speeds the forward part of the boat is lifted out of the water, and consequently offers a diminished side resistance to any turning motion brought to bear upon it.

" The boat in which these improvements have been introduced is 86 feet long by 11 feet beam and 5 feet 6 inches deep. She is fitted with compound engines having 22 inch and 12½ inch cylinders, with a 12 inch stroke, and making 520 revolutions per minute when running at full speed. She is propelled by a three-bladed screw 5 feet 6 inches in diameter and 5 feet pitch. Put through some evolutions with the view of testing her steering powers, the double rudder arrangement was found to answer exceedingly well, and she turned a circle of a diameter equal to about three times her own length in 1 minute 15 seconds. She turned equally well either going ahead or astern, and in fact her steering capabilities were satisfactorily demonstrated. The new arrangement for carrying off the smoke also answered very well, with the exception that the heated gases occasionally swept the deck, which objectionable result will be avoided in future boats."

These boats are to be armed with spar torpedoes, and with the Whitehead fish torpedo, the cradles and fittings for which are shown at Fig. 161.

The Fastest Vessel in the World.—Another type of torpedo boat, of which one of the same dimensions has been built by this firm for the English government, is shown at Fig. 162. This vessel is as yet the fastest vessel in the world. The trials with this boat were made in March of this year, and were as follows :—

Runs.	Time, Min. sec.		Knots per hour.				Knots per hour.
First. . . .	2	37	=	22·93	} Mean of first pair	=	21·35
Second . . .	3	2	=	19·78			
Third . . .	2	33	=	23·53	} Mean of second pair	=	22·05
Fourth. . .	2	55	=	20·57			
Fifth . . .	2	30	=	24·00	} Mean of third pair	=	22·23
Sixth . . .	2	56	=	20·45			

giving as a mean 21·93 knots per hour, or 25¼ statute miles. The boat was fully equipped for active service, i.e. with a load of 6¾ tons on board It was found during the trial that at speeds of 17 and 19 knots the vibration of the boat was considerable, but when running over 20 knots it was hardly perceptible; the excessive vibration taking place when the revolutions of the engines became a multiple of the natural vibration of the boat.

Torpedo boats are at the present time being built by this firm for the English, French, Spanish, Austrian, and Italian governments.

Russian Torpedo Boats, built by Mr. S. Schibau, Prussia.—Mr. S. Schibau, of Elbing, Eastern Prussia, in 1878 constructed ten torpedo boats for the Russian government, similar to the one shown at Fig 163.

These boats are each 66 feet long, and 11 feet 3 inches beam. They are built of steel plates about an eighth of an inch thick. Their engines consist of three cylinder compounds, with surface condensers; and they run at 380 revolutions per minute, at full speed, driving a screw 4 feet in diameter. They have been variously armed, some with the spar, some with the Whitehead fish, and some with the Harvey towing torpedo. Their speed is about 18 knots per hour.

Messrs. Herreshoff's Torpedo.—Messrs. Herreshoff, of Rhode Island, U.S.A., have also constructed several torpedo boats. One of these, built for the English government, is shown in section at Fig. 164. This boat is 59 feet 6 inches long, 7 feet 6 inches beam, and 5 feet 6 inches deep; she draws about 1 foot 3 inches of water.

"The vessel is constructed with five water-tight bulkheads, and her hull is of composite construction below the water line, having a steel framing covered with wood planking. The upper part of the hull is wholly of steel, the plates being $\frac{1}{16}$ inch thick, the top sides sloping inwards and the upper work forming a protective superstructure for the crew and machinery. She is propelled by a screw which is placed beneath the vessel in a central position, and which is driven by a direct acting condensing engine placed in the forward part of the boat. The diameters of the steam cylinders are $10\frac{1}{2}$ inches and 6 inches respectively, with 10 inch stroke, and they are of 100 horse power estimated. There is an independent feed pump and air pump. The stoke hold is enclosed and is supplied with air by a Sturtevant blower, which is driven by an independent engine of $2\frac{1}{2}$ horse power. The propeller is a two-bladed screw 38 inches in diameter and 5 feet pitch, the screw shaft being 23 feet in length. The vessel is steered by means of a balanced rudder placed a short distance from the stern and under the ship, the helmsman being located in a stern cabin with a protected look-out raised just above the

PLATE LI

Fig 163

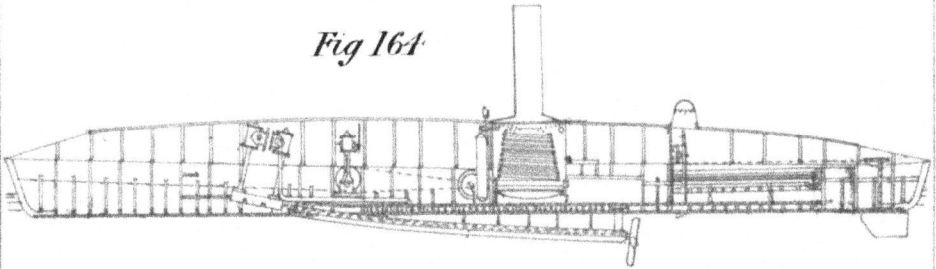

Fig 164

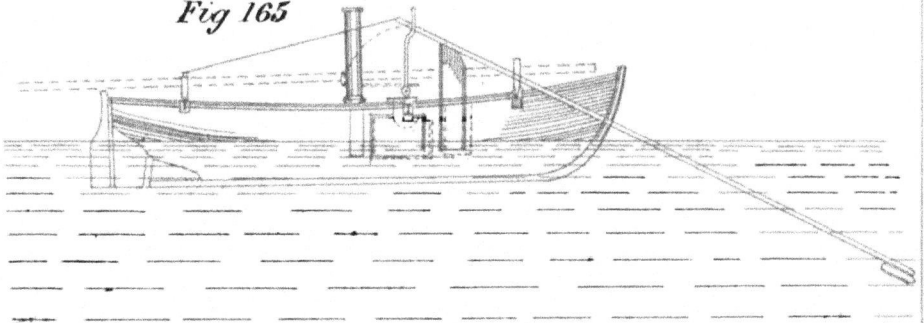

Fig 165

deck. The hull and machinery together weigh 6 tons, but with the working crew of four men and fuel, stores, and two torpedoes on board, boat weighs about 7½ tons.

"Steam is supplied by a Herreshoff coil boiler, which constitutes another novelty in this boat. This boiler consists of a circular combustion chamber, which in the present instance is 4 feet in diameter internally, and within which is a coil of about 300 feet of 2 inch pipe coiled to nearly the diameter of the chamber. This coil is continued at the top so as to form a kind of dome under the cover of the combustion chamber. By the side of the boiler is a separator, into which the steam passes before it goes to the engine. The water from the feed pump is admitted at the top of the coil, and during its course to the bottom the greater portion of it becomes converted into steam. Having passed through the entire length of the coil, the steam and water are discharged together into the separator in such a manner that the water is entirely separated from the steam, and can be blown off as required. The steam is taken from the top of the separator, and returns through a short coil placed inside the combustion chamber, where it becomes superheated, and is led thence to the engines. It is claimed for this boiler that it cannot explode destructively, inasmuch as there is but a very small quantity of water in it at any time, and that it is distributed along the entire length of the coil. A rupture at any point would only be attended by a moderate blowing off of steam. The rapid circulation of the water is found to prevent the deposit of salts, the surplus water not converted into steam carrying with it all impurities. A good working pressure can be obtained within a few minutes of lighting the fire, and the boiler can be blown off in a few seconds. The large combustion chamber enables the full economy of the fuel to be realised."*

This vessel is guaranteed for a speed of 16 knots per hour. She can be propelled ahead or astern with equal speed, and can be brought to a dead stop when going full speed within a distance equal to her own length. Her turning powers are equally good. Her armament will probably be the fish torpedo.

Ordinary Torpedo Boat.—The most efficient and simple method of fitting and working a spar torpedo from an ordinary steam launch or

* Extract from the *Engineering* of the 10th of January, 1879.

pinnace is shown at Fig. 165. This method will be readily understood from the figure; the dotted lines show the position of the spar and upright, when rigged in. The speed of this type of torpedo boat ranges from 6 to 9 knots. Occasions would no doubt occur in time of war when a torpedo attack by such boats would be a feasible matter, and therefore everything should be done to render these boats fit for that special service.

Defects.—The most important defects of such craft are :—

1.—The noise created by their engines, thus rendering an undetected approach to a hostile vessel impracticable.

2.—Their liability to be swamped by the explosion of the torpedo.

Of course there are many minor defects, but above are the principal ones, both of which might, to a considerable extent, be modified.

Torpedo Boat Attacks.—It is impossible to attempt more than a very general idea of how to conduct a torpedo boat attack, as so much depends upon the circumstances, ever changing, under which each particular attack would have to operate.

The spar and the fish torpedo are the submarine weapons that can best be manipulated from boats, the towing torpedo requiring a more roomy craft than the torpedo boat generally is to operate it from with any chance of success.

Methods of Protecting Ships from Boat Torpedo Attacks.—The principal methods that exist at the present time of protecting a ship from a boat torpedo attack are as follows :—

1.—Booms by themselves, or supporting nets hung vertically, surrounding the ship at a distance of 10 or 15 feet from the side of the vessel.

2.—A crinoline of wire, or chain, fixed by stays to the vessel's side, but capable of being lifted out of the water if required.

3.—The above methods supplemented by guard boats, and a cordon of boats.

4.—A cordon of boats, that is, boats connected at certain distances by means of hawsers, or chain cables, and at a distance of some 200 or 300 yards from the vessel, supplemented by guard boats, but without other protection.

5.—Electric lights and torpedo guns. These latter are small guns capable of penetrating the side of a torpedo boat and of being depressed at a very small angle.

As it is against these defences that torpedo boats would have to contend, therefore they have been described previous to explaining the mode of conducting a torpedo boat attack.

The first two methods of defence are of course quite impracticable when the attacked vessel is one of a blockading squadron, and it is against such vessels that a torpedo boat attack will generally be used and oftenest be successful.

In the case of a vessel forced to anchor in a harbour which is accessible to the torpedo boats of the enemy, by the application of either of the first two methods, supplemented by guard boats and electric lights, she would undoubtedly be almost impregnable against a torpedo boat attack, even were the boats armed with the fish torpedo, though she would of course not be in that state of readiness which is essential to a man-of-war's efficiency. As a general rule, no man-of-war should anchor unless absolutely necessary in the vicinity of an enemy's ports, and then should retain the power of moving in any direction in the quickest space of time possible, using the electric light and guard boats as a means of protection.

An attack by boats armed with the spar torpedo must always partake of the nature of a forlorn hope, this especially applying to the boats themselves, the crews of which, provided they are supplied with good life belts, would seem to run a far greater risk of a wetting and a prison than of being shot.

Not less than four torpedo boats should compose the attacking force. The crews of the boats, consisting of only those actually required, should fully understand " *that the hostile vessel is to be torpedoed,*" i.e. they are not to give up the attack on the vessel opening fire, nor in the case of one or more of the torpedo boats being sunk, but to remember that one boat is sufficient to effectually carry out the object of the attack, viz. the sinking of the ship.

In making the attack, one boat should be directed on each bow, and one on each quarter, the final rush being as combined as possible. There must not be the *slightest hesitation,* and each boat must make *direct* for her point of attack.

The cause of the Russians failing so often in their torpedo boat attacks during the war of '77 may be traced to the absence of anything like a system, and to their giving up the attack directly they supposed themselves discovered.

When using the towing torpedo, two boats only could be used, and they should make the attack, either coming down from ahead, one on each side of the vessel, or coming up from the stern, one on each side of the vessel, or by the boats crossing the bow and stern of the vessel in different directions.

In the case of the fish torpedo the attack must be conducted in a different manner, the object in this case being to get within a certain distance only of the vessel undetected, and from thence send the missile on its deadly course. The distance should not be more than 500 yards; the closer up to 200 yards the better. In connection with such an attack, the torpedo boats might be supported by guard boats, whose particular duty it would be to engage the enemy's guard boats and so leave the torpedo boats free to do their particular work.

It has been suggested to use the electric light from the bows of torpedo boats, but this would do away with one of the chief characteristics of such boats, viz. their invisible and unknown approach, on which the whole success of the attack in a great measure depends.

Fosberry's Patent Torpedo Boat Protective.—To enable torpedo vessels and boats to remain afloat after being struck by shot from mitrailleuses, rifles, and other arms usually employed against such craft, and at the same time to retain their structural lightness, Colonel G. V. Fosberry, of the English army, has designed the following method, which is based upon the discovery that when india-rubber or the like is placed and secured on a metal plate, and is penetrated or punctured by a rifle bullet or similar projectile, which also passes through the metal plate, the hole or orifice so formed in the india-rubber will, after the projectile has passed through it and the metal plate, immediately be closed by the elasticity of the surrounding portions, so that no water can follow the projectile through the said hole or orifice. India-rubber or other elastic material, or a combination of such materials, in the form of sheets, belts, or coats, is placed upon or around those portions of the hull of the boat which are to be protected. Vulcanised or mineralised india-rubber is the material usually employed by Colonel Fosberry. Between the metal plates and the india-rubber covering an intermediate substance, generally kamptulicon, is interposed, which is cemented or riveted to the said metal plates, and to which the india-rubber is attached. This intermediate substance, which is the feature of the invention, must be of such a nature that it may be caused to adhere closely and tightly to all parts of the metal, and also to the india-rubber covering, while the same are unperforated, but when the said india-rubber covering and the metal plate under the same are perforated by a bullet, the portion of the said intermediate substance adjacent to the perforation must be detached from the elastic covering and metal plate, and leave the former free to act like a valve, and close up over the hole so that no water may enter; and this intermediate substance, as applied by the inventor in the immediate vicinity of the perforation, will by the effect of the shot be so broken up and detached from the india-rubber covering as to allow the same to recover its original position independently of the new shape or position of the injured and deformed metal plate.

Should the india-rubber be placed upon the metal plates and be so attached to the said plates as to adhere and conform to them in or after their deformation, a hole made in the india-rubber would remain open ; on the other hand, should the india-rubber without any intermediate substance be attached to the metal plate in such a manner that it will recover its position after perforation, water would penetrate between the metal and the india-rubber, and by the pressure of this water the india-rubber would be liable to be detached from a large area of the metal plate, and so become ineffective or even dangerous to the boat. Moreover, if the india-rubber is fixed directly upon the metal plates, in the case of a shot passing completely through the boat, that is to say, passing into the boat at one side and out at the other side, a large portion of the india-rubber adjacent to the hole made by the shot in leaving the boat will be torn or destroyed, but this will not be the case in boats constructed according to Colonel Fosberry's patent.

The French government have recently applied this invention to one of their torpedo boats with very successful results, thereby proving that it is not merely a theoretical idea.

Submarine Boats.—Submarine boats, if they could be constructed to fulfil the conditions hereinafter enumerated which are essential to a perfect boat of that nature, would for many reasons be a very important point solved in connection with torpedo operations, and therefore it is most extraordinary that a practicable submarine boat has not yet been designed and built.

Bushnell's Submarine Boat.—The first submarine vessel built for torpedo purposes was designed and constructed by David Bushnell in 1775. This vessel, operated by a Sergeant Esra Lee, was employed in an attempt in 1776 or thereabouts on the *Eagle*, an English man-of-war, which proved unsuccessful, owing to the sergeant not being thoroughly versed in the management of his curious craft. She was soon afterwards sunk in the Hudson river, but was subsequently recovered by the inventor, though never used again. This vessel was capable of holding one person, and air sufficient to support him thirty minutes without receiving fresh air, and is fully described in 'Barnes's Submarine Warfare.'

Qualifications essential to a Submarine Boat.—A submarine boat should possess the following qualifications :—

1.—It should be of sufficient displacement to carry the machinery necessary for propulsion, and the men and materials for performing the various operations.

2.—It should be of such a form that it may be easily propelled and steered.

3.—It should have sufficient interior space for the crew to work in.

4.—It should be capable of carrying sufficient pure air to support its crew for a specified time, or of having the means of purifying the air within the boat, and exhausting the foul air.

5.—It should be able to rise and sink at will to the required depth, either when stationary or in motion.

6.—It should be so fitted that the crew possess the means of leaving the boat without requiring external assistance.

7.—It should carry a light sufficient to steer by, and to carry on the various operations.

8.—It should possess sufficient strength to prevent any chance of its collapsing at the greatest depth to which it may be required to manipulate it.

The results of former experiments with such boats prove that manual power, which was the original mode of propulsion, is not the motive power best adapted to such a boat ; compressed air, gas as used in the Lay torpedo boat, and steam, are all of them far preferable to the original method, but which of these modern ones is the most practicable has yet to be decided.

The most difficult point to be overcome in connection with a submarine boat is that of steering it correctly when beneath the surface of the water.

Confederate Submarine Boat.—The Confederate submarine torpedo boat that sunk the Federal vessel of war *Housatonic* on the 17th of February, 1864, was built of boiler iron, 35' long, 3' beam (extreme), 5' high in the centre. She carried a crew of nine men. She was propelled by means of a screw propeller worked by eight of the crew, her greatest speed being four knots an hour in smooth water. She carried a sufficient quantity of air to enable the crew to remain submerged for the space of two to three hours. Two fins were fitted on the outside for rising and falling at will, when in motion. There were two manholes provided, fitted with bull's-eyes. This boat was intended to pass under a vessel's bottom, towing a torpedo after her, which was arranged to explode on contact. She was the means of drowning fourteen men before she made her last attempt, when nine others were added to the above list. In her successful attack on the *Housatonic*, she was armed with the bow spar torpedo, and was sunk, owing to her running into the hole formed by the explosion of her torpedo. About three years after the American civil war was over, this submarine boat was recovered. Divers went down, and found her lying alongside the hull of the *Housatonic*, with the remains of the nine men in her.

French Submarine Boat "Plongeur."—The boat termed the *Plongeur* was designed by Admiral Bougois and M. Brune, and was exhibited at the Paris Exhibition of 1867. She was 26' long, 9' deep, and fitted with centre and bilge keels. She carried two small tanks containing compressed air, and four large tanks were placed at the bottom of the boat for the purpose of sinking her, these latter tanks communicating with the water outside and the air tanks. She also was fitted with a compass for steering by, a water gauge to show the depth of submersion, and an air gauge to show the pressure of air in the boat. Rectangular valves were placed at the bottom of the boat for entrance or exit therefrom, for the use of divers, and to affix torpedoes to a ship's bottom. On the top a circular opening for entrance and exit was arranged, also an iron cupola fitted with bull's-eyes. She was also fitted with an apparatus for spraying water through the air in the interior of the boat on its becoming foul, and escape valves for releasing any foul air were placed at the top of the boat. The water tanks were filled by means of pumps, and emptied by means of the compressed air. She was propelled by a three-bladed screw worked by four men. Her rate of progression was about four knots per hour. The anchors consisted of two 15 inch shot, fitted with wire rope cables, working through watertight stuffing boxes.

This vessel has been subjected to some experiments, but with what results is not generally known.

One of the most important uses to which a submarine boat would be put in connection with torpedo operations would be " to discover the exact position and number of an enemy's submarine mines, and if necessary destroy them," the former being an operation in the present day quite impossible to perform, and the latter one rarely to be depended on.

CHAPTER VII.

TORPEDO OPERATIONS.

A REVIEW, however brief, of the numerous torpedo operations that have of late years been carried out in actual war, must prove not only of great interest, but of material aid to those who may be desirous of studying this branch of naval warfare, for the experience so gained ought alone to be the basis on which a system of submarine offence and defence should be constructed.

No new torpedo invention should be adopted, however theoretically perfect it may be, until it has been subjected to a very severe practical test, under conditions as nearly analogous to those that would occur on active service as it would be possible to obtain. The vast importance of a carefully planned and executed system of submarine *defence* is an established fact, and it only remains to discover what are the best weapons for, and most practicable mode of manipulating a system of submarine offence, to establish torpedo warfare in all its branches as a necessary function of naval warfare.

It would be a mere waste of time to dwell on the Anglo-French and American wars of the beginning of this century (1797–1812); though during that period various attempts were made by Fulton and others to destroy hostile vessels by means of submarine infernal machines, inasmuch as they all partook more or less of the nature of experiments, and were all failures, but come at once to the Crimean war (1854–1856), when what may be termed a systematic employment of torpedoes for harbour defence was first employed.

CRIMEAN WAR (1854–56).

Defence of Sebastopol Harbour, &c.—The Russians employed a large quantity of submarine mines, both electrical and mechanical, principally the latter, in their defence of the harbours of Sebastopol, Sveaborg, and Cronstadt.

According to General Delafield, U.S.A., the arrangement of the mechanical mines was entirely new, the conception and idea of an eminent Russian chemist, Professor Jacobi.

Electrical Mines.—No mention is made by the General of the employment of electrical mines, but the fact of a hulk being captured by the Allies at Yenikale, with a number of torpedoes on board, and all the arrangements necessary to explode them by electricity, such as Voltaic piles, electric fuzes, several miles of conducting wire, &c., is sufficient proof of this type of submarine mine being extensively used by the Russians in their harbour defences.

Many of their mechanical mines were picked up by the Allies, several of which were found to have their safety caps on. Owing to this neglect, and the smallness of the charge of the torpedoes (only some 25 lbs. of gunpowder), it is not to be wondered at that no serious injury was done to any ships of the allied squadron.

Deterred most probably by the failures of Bushnell, Fulton, and others in previous years with the submarine and other torpedo boat attacks, nothing of this description was attempted by either side.

Russian Mechanical Mines.—The Russian mechanical mines consisted of barrels of powder fitted with fuzes, so arranged that a blow would smash a glass tube containing sulphuric acid, causing the acid to mix with some chlorate of potash, resulting in combustion and the explosion of the mine.

Austro-Italian War (1859).

Defence of Venice by Von Ebner.—During this brief struggle, defensive torpedo operations were carried out under the direction of Colonel Von Ebner, of the Imperial Austrian Engineers.

The harbour of Venice was protected by a most elaborate system of submarine mines, devised by the above-named officer. Though the importance of his system was proved by the fact of no attempt being made on Venice, yet no opportunity was afforded of *practically* testing its efficiency.

American Civil War (1861–65).

Cause of the Present Importance of the Torpedo.—The prominent position the torpedo now holds as a most important and legitimate function of naval warfare is owing without doubt to the successful and extensive employment of them on the part of the Confederates during this long and bloody struggle.

Reasons which induced the Confederates to employ Torpedoes.—The numerous harbours and navigable rivers in the possession of the Southerners, the few ships of war at their disposal, the overwhelming fleet of the Northerners, and the introduction for the first time of ironclads in naval warfare, are the principal causes which forced the Confederates to resort to torpedoes as a means of offence and defence.

Though a few rude and extempore submarine mechanical mines were met with by the Federals during the earliest part of the war, it was not until many months after the commencement of hostilities that the Confederates, finding themselves quite unable to cope with their rivals on the sea, set to work in earnest to organise a system of submarine warfare on a grand scale.

Torpedo Corps formed, &c.—Loss of " Cairo."—By October, 1862, a secret service torpedo corps, with headquarters at Richmond, was in full swing, and the principal harbours and rivers of the Confederates were systematically protected by means of electrical and mechanical mines, also a scheme of offence by drifting and spar torpedoes was in preparation, and in December of the same year they experienced the first-fruits of their labour by the total destruction of the Federal war steamer *Cairo*.

The following brief review of the numerous torpedo operations carried out by both sides, and the effect their use had on the war, will be sufficient to enable the general reader to gain some idea of the vast importance of this submarine weapon in future warfare.

Fuller and more detailed accounts will be found in Commander S. Barnes's, U.S.N., Colonel Von Scheliha's, and Captain H. Steward's torpedo works.

Every Species of Torpedo used—Frame Torpedoes at Charleston, &c. —Federal Ship Disasters—Small Effect of Electrical Mines—Loss of the " Commodore Jones," &c.—Every species of submarine mine seems to have been used by the Southerners for their harbour and river defence, the most effectual of which were the barrel, frame, and Singer's torpedoes. These were all mechanical, fired by means of sensitive concussion fuzes.   At Charleston and elsewhere the frame torpedo, which also acted as an obstruction, was largely used, and where this species of mine was known to be laid, the Northerners never attempted to force a passage.   Out of some thirty or forty Federal ships sunk or injured by torpedoes, by far the larger proportion of such disasters was effected by means of the barrel and Singer's mines.   Though electrical mines were very extensively used on the St. James River and at Charleston, &c., yet only one Federal steamer, the *Commodore Jones*, was sunk, and only one other, the *Commodore Barney*, was injured.

Case of the " New Ironsides."—The Federal ship *New Ironsides*, at the attack on Charleston in 1863, was anchored for one hour and a half exactly over a 5000 lbs. electrical mine, which despite all the efforts of the Confederates could not be exploded.   The reason of this was owing to the deterioration of the primer, due to too constant testing.

Welden Railway.—A notable instance of the effect of torpedoes on the war was the saving of the Welden line of communication in December, 1864.   The Welden Railway was the principal artery of communication to Richmond for the Confederates.   To intercept this, by destroying the railway bridges, a fleet of nine Federal gunboats was sent up the Roanoke river; when nearly arrived at their destination, and though every precaution in the shape of bow projecting spars, creeping, &c., was taken, seven of the vessels were either sunk or severely injured by submarine mines.   Thus the expedition ended in a most disastrous failure.

General Butler's Attack on Richmond.—Again, in April, 1864, General Butler's attack on Richmond utterly failed, owing to the Federal fleet being unable to co-operate with him, the destruction of the *Commodore Jones* completely checking any further advance of Admiral Lee's ships, thus allowing the Confederates to employ the garrisons of their river batteries in their land line of entrenchments.

More than One Line of Torpedoes required.—The capture of the Spanish fort at Mobile in April, 1865, by a Federal fleet under Admiral Lee, proves the necessity of employing more than one line of torpedoes, where the safety of a position depends almost entirely on those means of defence, as this one did.   Here, though several Federal vessels were either sunk or severely damaged, yet the fort was captured.

Boat Torpedo Attacks.—In regard to boat torpedo attacks, the Confederates were only successful in two out of many attempts made by them to sink Federal vessels.

The " Housatonic" and " Minnesota."—These successes were the complete destruction of the *Housatonic* by a submarine boat, fitted with a spar torpedo, and serious injury caused to the *Minnesota* by the explosion of a contact spar torpedo, carried by an ordinary gig, commonly termed "David's."   In the former instance the attacking boat was sunk,* in the latter instance she was uninjured.

Destruction of the " Albemarle."—On the part of the Federals, Lieutenant Cushing with a steam launch fitted with a Wood and Lay torpedo, succeeded in sinking the Confederate ram *Albemarle.*   The boat in this instance was swamped by the column of water thrown up on the explosion of the torpedo, she having been driven full speed at the *Albemarle.*

Ship Spar Torpedoes.—On both sides, spar torpedoes fitted to the bows of ships, and also on rafts slung over the bows, were somewhat extensively used, but on no occasion were they the means of injuring or sinking any vessels.

To increase the difficulties of the Northerners in searching for submarine mines, the Southerners laid down a great number of dummy torpedoes, also erected false torpedo stations, and laid false wires.

It must always be borne in mind, in connection with the torpedo operations above detailed, that the apparatus were very crude, and the operators at the commencement inexperienced.

Paraguayan War (1864–68).

Torpedoes employed by the Paraguayans.—During their protracted struggle with the Brazilians, the Paraguayans employed submarine mines for the protection of their river forts, &c.

Loss of the " Rio Janeiro "—Brazilian Fleet entrapped.— On the 2nd of September, 1866, the Brazilian ironclad *Rio Janeiro*, after being well-battered by the guns of the Curupaity fort, was sunk by a torpedo.

---

* See page 185.

Later on, near the same place, a whole fleet of Brazilian war ships were entrapped by the Paraguayans, between two rows of submarine mines, but owing to faulty arrangements they escaped unharmed.

Austrian War (1866).

Venice, Pola, &c., protected by Torpedoes.—During this war, torpedoes for the defence of Venice, Pola, &c., were extensively used by the Austrians, under the direction of Baron von Ebner, but as in '59 no opportunity was afforded of proving their practical worth, though morally they were of great value, the Austrian harbours so defended being considered impregnable by the enemy, and therefore no attempt was made to force them.

Franco-German War (1870–71).

Little or nothing in the matter of torpedo operations was attempted by the Germans, and on the part of the French nothing whatever.

Germans employed Submarine Mines.—Electrical and mechanical mines were placed in several of the German harbours, the former containing about 200 lbs. of dualine, the latter some 80 lbs. of gunpowder. The only attempt to destroy French ships by means of offensive torpedoes was made by the German vessel the *Grille*, off Rügen, which resulted in failure.

In laying down and in picking up after the war was over their mechanical mines, several exploded, killing some ten to fifteen men.

Boats necessary.—Towards the end of the war, the Germans were constructing special torpedo boats, believing that such were necessary for the complete defence of harbours. This war added another proof of the moral worth of submarine mines, the French fleet not daring to approach German waters *supposed* to be defended by such means.

Russo-Turkish War (1877–78).

Superiority of Turkey to Russia in the matter of Ships.—On the Danube, in the Black Sea, and Mediterranean, where the principal naval portion of the war was carried out, Turkey was possessed of a fleet of ships infinitely superior to Russia, both in point of numbers and strength, and therefore, to enable her to hold her own against this vast superiority of the Turks, the Russians resorted to an extensive employment of torpedoes, for both offensive and defensive purposes.

Russian Torpedoes.—For many years previous to the outbreak of hostilities in April, 1877, the Russians had been studying the subject of torpedo warfare in all its branches, a certain number of their naval and military officers and men having every year passed through a regular course of torpedo study, at a school specially formed for such a purpose; they had also laid in large stores of submarine mines, spar torpedoes, and were in possession of the Whitehead and towing torpedoes, and also several electric lights, and a few months after war was declared they obtained a fast Thornycroft torpedo boat.

Turkish Torpedoes.—On the other hand, the Turks were only in possession of a number of those huge, unwieldy 500 lbs. buoyant mines, and one electric light; circuit closers, contact mines, boats (steam or otherwise) fitted for use with torpedo, or offensive torpedoes, being conspicuous by their absence.

Thus it will be seen that in the matter of submarine offence and defence, the Russians were as superior to the Turks as the latter were to the former in the matter of ships.

Turkish Defensive Torpedo Operations.—The defensive torpedo operations carried out by the Ottoman naval officers and men were as follows :—

The harbour of Batoum in the Black Sea was protected by a few 500 lbs. buoyant mines, arranged to be fired by observation.

The mouth of the Bosphorus and the Dardanelles were similarly defended. For this work great praise is due to those who executed the work, for the very strong current and great depth met with in those waters would render such a service a work of great difficulty, even when properly constructed mooring boats, and men trained to such, were employed, both of which in this particular instance were absent.

Soulina, one of the mouths of the Danube, and Suda Bay (Candia) were also protected by similar means.

Russian Defensive Torpedo Operations.—The Russian defensive torpedo operations were very extensive, their principal harbours in the Baltic, as well as those in the Black Sea, were carefully defended by electro-contact mines of the latest type; so also they protected their numerous bridges across the Danube, double and sometimes treble rows of such mines being moored on either side, and in addition they also placed several mines in the Danube, on the chance of destroying the Turkish Danube flotilla.

Destruction of Turkish Gunboat "Suna" by a Russian Submarine Mine.—The only instance that occurred during this war of a vessel being sunk by a stationary submarine mine was that of the Turkish gunboat *Suna*, at Soulina, in October, 1877, on the occasion of the unsuccessful attack on that place made by the combined Russian and Roumanian flotilla.

About 6 A.M. on the morning of the attack, a "loftcha" containing two of the enemy's electro-contact mines, fitted for laying down, was captured by the Turks, from which it was evident that the Russians had been employed during the night in torpedoing the reach immediately above the Turkish defences. However, not heeding this very practical warning, the Pacha in command of the Soulina squadron ordered the *Kartal* (a paddle-wheel tug vessel) and the *Suna* (an old wooden gunboat) to reconnoitre up the river; they accordingly started, the *Kartal* leading the way. At 8.5 A.M., about fifteen minutes after the two vessels had left their moorings, an explosion was heard, and almost at the same instant the unfortunate gunboat *Suna* was observed to go down head foremost, her masts only remaining above water. The *Kartal*, which at the time of the catastrophe was some distance in advance, at once turned back to the assistance of her consort, and managed to save a number of the gunboat's crew, this work having to be performed under a galling fire from the allied flotilla. Owing to this day being the "Feast of Bairam," the unfortunate gunboat was dressed with masthead flags, thus four Turkish ensigns fell into the hands of the enemy, the Pacha refusing permission for any attempt to be made to save them. The reason that the *Kartal* escaped the fate of her consort was due to her only drawing some 5 feet of water, while the *Suna* drew at least 8 feet.

The gunboat struck the mine that sunk her on her port bow, the effect of the explosion being to completely smash in that side of her bow, dismount her foremost guns, and carry away her foremast just above the deck (the mast remained standing, though inclined forward); the second lieutenant of the *Suna*, who was at the time of the explosion standing on her fore bridge, was thrown off and killed, and some twelve of the crew were killed and wounded. To complete the destruction of the *Suna*, another torpedo was exploded under her port quarter by the Russians. The torpedo that was used on this occasion is detailed at page 68.

Offensive Torpedo Operations.—The numerous boat torpedo attacks made by the Russians against the Turkish fleet will now be considered. The following accounts have been carefully compiled from two sources, viz. an article written by Captain Chardonneau, which appeared in the 'Revue Maritime et Coloniale,' 1878, and which has been recently translated for the Journal of the Royal United Service Institution by Lieutenant J. Meryon, R.N., and notes taken by the author during his service with the Imperial Ottoman Navy (1877-78).

1ST AFFAIR.

The Batoum Attack.—The first torpedo boat attack occurred on the night of the 12th-13th of May at Batoum.*

On the night of the attack there were lying in the harbour several vessels of the Ottoman fleet, including ironclads, transports, despatch-boats, &c. These vessels were totally unprotected by guard boats, booms, electric lights, &c., and only the usual number of sentries were posted, the Turks at that time not quite believing in such boat attacks, thus offering peculiar advantages for a torpedo attack.

Four torpedo boats formed the attacking force, viz. the *Tchesme*, *Sinope*, *Navarino*, and the *Soukoum Kalé*.

These boats were carried by a ship of the Maritime Company of Odessa, named *Grand Duke Constantine*. She was an iron screw steamer, able to steam about 10 knots per hour, and fitted to hoist up the above-mentioned torpedo boats. She was armed with four 4-pounders, and torpedoes.

Early in the evening of the 12th the *Constantine* left Poti, and proceeded off the harbour of Batoum, her captain (Lieutenant de Vaisseau Makaroff) deeming it advisable to lay to seven miles from the harbour, the supposition that the Turks had placed submarine mines off the entrance being the cause of his so doing.

About 11 P.M. the four torpedo boats started to the attack,

---

* A Turkish port, situated on the east coast of the Black Sea, capable of holding several large ships when anchored head and stern, but otherwise only a few.

Makaroff being in command of one of them. They were all painted sea green, and possessed a high speed. The night being dark, and having been despatched some distance off, they reached the entrance in somewhat straggling order. The *Tchesme*, commanded by Lieutenant Zatzarennyi, and armed with a towing torpedo, was the first to enter the harbour, and, without waiting for her consorts, dashed at the Ottoman fleet, and succeeded in getting close to a large Turkish paddle-wheel transport, and her commander dipping his torpedo, struck the ship under her quarter; but that little something which so often causes a failure in this mode of warfare occurred, and no explosion followed the pressing down of the firing key, much to the chagrin and disgust of Zatzarennyi. As might be supposed, by this time an alarm had been raised, and guns, rifles, &c., were fired in and from every direction, causing the torpedo boats to beat a precipitate and hasty retreat. Fortunately the Turks were not possessed of any steamboats, nor were any of their ships ready to dash out, or the defeat would have been a far more disastrous one than was the case. Neither of the boats were damaged, nor any of the crews injured.

The failure of this first attempt was due in a great measure to the mode of attack, no system or unanimity of action on the part of the four commanders being observable; and also to the somewhat half-hearted support given to the *Tchesme*, for had her three consorts only dashed at the Turkish ships as boldly, one at least of the Ottoman fleet would have been sunk, the only defence resorted to being their guns and small arms.

The moral effect of torpedoes was displayed here, causing the *Constantine* to lay too far off the entrance to the harbour, thus decreasing the chance of her boats making a successful attack.

The Russian version finishes up by saying, "although this first endeavour was unsuccessful, the authors of it were received at Sebastopol with enthusiasm."

2ND AFFAIR.

The Matchin Attack.—The second attempt was made on the 25th–26th of May on two Turkish monitors, the *Fettu Islam* and the *Duba Saife,* and a small river steamer, the *Kilidj Ali,* lying at anchor off Matchin.*   .

---

* A town situated on the south bank of the Danube, about eight miles from Brailoff.

Four Russian torpedo boats were sent to the attack, viz. the *Czarowitch*, Lieutenant Doubasoff; the *Xénie*, Lieutenant Chestakoff; the *Djiquite*, Midshipman Persine; and the *Czarevna*, Midshipman Bali. The total number of officers and men carried by these boats on this occasion was forty-six.

The night of the attack was rainy, but not completely dark, since the moon was above the horizon during nearly the whole of the expedition.

The force left Brailoff at one o'clock on the morning of the 26th, and advanced in two columns up the river, finding great difficulty in stemming the strong current.

A boat from the *Duba Saife*, rowing guard some 500 yards in advance of the squadron, observed the approach of the Russian boats, but allowed them to pass on their voyage of destruction without attempting to stop them, or alarm the vessels. On reaching within 150 yards of the *Duba Saife*, Dubasoff in the *Czarowitch* was challenged, and failing to give the correct answer was immediately fired at; but, nothing daunted by the hail of shot and bullets, he dashed on, and succeeded in exploding one of his spar torpedoes on the port side of the *Duba Saife*, just under her quarter, a column of water and *débris* being thrown up to a height of 120 feet, which partly filled his boat, but notwithstanding managed to get safely away. The monitor not sinking as soon as expected, Chestakoff in the *Xénie* dashed in, and completed the work of destruction, the unfortunate ship sinking in a very few minutes after this last explosion. The *Djiquite* was struck in the stern, and had to be run ashore for repairs, but eventually all four boats reached Brailoff in safety. The Russians allowed to neither killed nor wounded, which, when the time they were exposed to the fire of the three Turkish ships (about twenty minutes), the number of men (forty-six) engaged, and their very close quarters, seems miraculous.

The *Duba Saife*, thus lost to the Turks, carried two 12 cm. Krupp guns, and a crew of some sixty officers and men, few of whom were saved. Lieutenants Dubasoff and Chestakoff were decorated with the 4th Class of the Cross of Saint George, and three seamen received the insignia of the Order of Military Merit.

This attack was conducted in a most gallant manner, and far more systematically than the Batoum affair. If instead of holding one of the boats in reserve, which was part of Dubasoff's plan, and the remaining three attacking one vessel, the force had divided itself into two parties, and had made a simultaneous attack on both the monitors, the probability is that the *Fettu Islam* would have shared the fate of her consort.

The officer of the Turkish guard boat was tried by court-martial, but what his ultimate fate was is not generally known. He certainly deserved nothing less than death.

3RD AFFAIR.

The Soulina Attack.—The third attempt took place on the 9th–10th of June, 1877, on a Turkish squadron lying at anchor off Soulina.* This squadron consisted of the three ironclads *Feteh Bulend, Moocardemikhair,* and *Idglalieh,* and a tug, *Kartal.*

The Russian attacking force consisted of six torpedo boats, viz. the No. 1, Lieutenant Poutschin; the No. 2, Lieutenant Rojdestvenski; the *Tchesme,* Lieutenant Zatzarennyi; the *Sinope,* the *Navarino,* and the *Soukoum Kalé.* The No. 2 was a specially constructed torpedo boat, 68 feet long, and very fast. All were armed with spar torpedoes, with the exception of the *Tchesme,* which carried a towing torpedo. The boats were convoyed from Odessa by the *Constantine,* some being carried, and some being towed; another steamer, the *Vladimir,* supported her. The Turkish squadron were anchored in quarter line, about one mile from the harbour; the *Kartal,* under weigh, being used as an advance guard, and a few boats rowing guard close to the ships being *the only means of protection* adopted by the Turks. Passive obstructions, such as booms, nets, crinolines, &c., were not thought of, much less used.

On arriving about five miles from Soulina, the boats were formed into two groups, the first consisting of the No. 1, the No. 2, and the *Tchesmé,* and despatched on their way. The working of their engines was scarcely heard, and all lights were carefully hidden by tarpaulins.

The first casualty that happened was the disabling of the *Tchesme,* by the electric wire of her towing torpedo fouling the screw, this obliging her to return to the *Constantine.* Aided by good fortune, and by the darkness of the night, the No. 1 and the No. 2

---

* One of the principal mouths of the Danube.

succeeded in getting close to (30 yards) one of the Turkish vessels, the *Idglalieh*, before being discovered, when they were at once hailed, and, not answering, a tremendous fire of big guns and rifles was directed on them from the *Idglalieh*, which was promptly followed by that of the whole squadron, though from the other ships nothing of the boats could be seen.

According to the Russians, the No. 2 succeeded in exploding her torpedo close to, if not in contact with, a Turkish vessel, but from eye-witnesses on board the squadron only one explosion was heard, viz. that of Lieutenant Poutschin's torpedo. Any way, no damage whatever was experienced by the Ottoman squadron. The No. 1 came down on the *Idglalieh's* starboard bow, fouled her cable, and swung alongside, exploding one of her torpedoes in so doing, but with no other result than a wetting to those of the ironclad's crew, who were on the fore-castle. Alongside Poustchin remained for some minutes, but at last managed to get clear, and then was either sunk by the *Idglalieh's* fire, or, as he avers, on finding his screw foul, he sunk his boat, rather than let her fall into the hands of the Turks. Poutschin and four of his crew were picked up, after being some hours in the water, by the squadron's boats.

The No. 2 seems to have suffered severely, her funnel being bent, the axle of the steering wheel damaged, sixteen rivets were started, and the iron keel plate had dropped some 18 inches, and finally the lower part of her rudder broken, and one of the blades of her screw bent aft; part of this damage was no doubt the effect of the explosion of her torpedo, which was probably not in position, but unless she ran over some loose stones of the Soulina breakwater, the damage to her keel and rudder cannot be accounted for.

The second group of boats had followed up the first, but on hearing the noise of the explosions and roar of the guns and rifles they returned to the *Constantine*.

That ship, on observing the firing, endeavoured to close the land, but she grounded, and remained until daylight in a difficult position, but at last got afloat, and returned to Odessa with five out of her six torpedo boats.

Lieutenant Rojdestvenski, the Commander of the No. 2, received the 4th Class of the Cross of Saint George, and three seamen the insignia of the Order of Military Merit.

On the part of the No. 1 and No. 2, this was a most gallant affair, though unsuccessful, but as regards the remainder of the boats the less said the better.

Had the Turkish squadron slipped the instant the alarm was given, and steamed full speed in the direction of Odessa, the *Constantine* and her convoy might have been cut off. Both the *Moorcademikhair* and *Feteh Bulend* were 13 knot ships, and therefore considerably faster than the enemy. But, as usual, the Turks were far too dilatory to take advantage of the occasion.

4th Affair.

The Rustchuk Attack.—The fourth torpedo attack was made on the afternoon of the 20th of June, 1877, on a Turkish monitor off Rustchuk.

The only Russian torpedo boat sent to the attack on this occasion was a Thornycroft named the *Choutka*, commanded by Lieutenant Skrydloff, and accompanied by a celebrated Russian artist, Verechtck-aguine by name. The instant the torpedo boat was observed, so well directed and steady a fire was kept up by the monitor that both the lieutenant and the artist were badly wounded, and the electric wires of the torpedo severed, thus obliging the *Choutka* to beat a retreat. According to the Russian account, the monitor was struck by the boat's torpedo spar, but the above seems the more likely version. This was certainly a most audacious attack, and had the Turks only succeeded in hitting the *Choutka* with her big gun, it would have ended fatally for the Russians ; as it was, the boat was struck by several bullets, but none of the crew were wounded.

5th Affair.

The Aluta Attack.—The fifth attack was made on the 30th of June, 1877, on a Turkish monitor off the mouth of the Aluta, in the river Danube. This attempt, like the last, took place in broad daylight. Four Russian boats were sent forward, but in spite of the captain of the Turkish vessel doing all he could to run the boats down, none of them succeeded in getting sufficiently near the vessel to enable a torpedo to be placed in contact. The captain of the monitor took the precaution to rig his lower booms out, and so managed to keep the enemy's boats at a respectful distance, they imagining that mines were fixed to the ends of the booms.   After two hours of this dodging about, the Russians, finding the case hopeless, abandoned the attack.

The Russian account states—1st, that the captain of the monitor was an Englishman; 2nd, that the vessel was protected by nets and torpedoes lashed to the extremities of her booms—both of which statements are radically wrong.

The torpedo boats forming the attack were the *Choutka*, Midshipman Niloff, and the *Mina*, Sub-Lieutenant Arens, both armed with the spar torpedo.

Unless indeed the Russians acted up to the old proverb which says " Discretion is the best part of valour," it is difficult to understand how four small easily handled boats could have been for one hour endeavouring to strike a ship (which ship was at the same time being manœuvred with a view of running them down) without either effecting their object or being sunk or damaged in the attempt.

The Russians, though unsuccessful, behaved gallantly. Midshipman Niloff was severely wounded, but no mention is made as to the number of the crew that were killed and wounded, or of the damage received by the boats.   Niloff received the 4th Class of the Cross of St. George, and Arens the Order of Military Merit.

The Turkish captain, Ali Bey, behaved most pluckily and skilfully. The only wonder is that both the boats were not sunk by the monitor's fire.

6TH AFFAIR.

The Soukoum Kaleh Attack.—The sixth attempt was made on the 23rd–24th of August, 1877, on a Turkish ironclad, the *Assari Shefket*, at the time lying at anchor off Soukoum Kaleh.* Four torpedo boats composed the attacking force, viz. the *Sinope*, Lieutenant Pisarefski; the *Torpedoist*, Midshipman Nelson Hirst; the *Navarino*, Lieutenant Vichnevetski; and the *Tchesme*, Lieutenant Zatzarennyi, the latter officer being in command.   These boats had been brought to the entrance of the harbour by the *Constantine*, and were despatched on their mission of destruction about half past ten.

An eclipse of the moon occurred on this night, and, taking advantage of this fact, the four Russian torpedo boats dashed into the harbour at full speed and made for the Turkish vessel.

* A place taken from the Russians in the early part of the war, situated on the east coast of the Black Sea.

Fortunately for the safety of his ship and lives of his crew, the captain of the Turkish ironclad had several boats rowing guard round his ship, and otherwise everything on board in readiness for immediate action. On the attacking flotilla nearing the guard boats, blue lights were burnt, rifles fired, &c., and the alarm given to those on the look-out in the *Assari Shefket*. The moment the enemy were within range, such a well-directed and heavy fire was poured on them that the attack was completely foiled. One of the Russian torpedoes was exploded, but failed to do more than throw a quantity of water up. The next morning a pole with torpedo fixed on it was found by the Turks, and on the strength of this and the numerous fragments of wood similarly found, one if not more of the enemy's boats it was supposed must have been sunk, or much knocked about.

This was a much better planned and executed attack, but was unsuccessful owing to the extreme vigilance of the Turks.

This attempt will always be remembered by the Turks, on account of the general order that appeared in the papers on the part of the Russians, in which " the brilliant exploit and successful destruction of the Turkish ironclad *Assari Shefket* " was set forth at great length; she at the time that this appeared being quietly at anchor off the dockyard at Stamboul, not having received any damage whatever.

7TH AFFAIR.

The Second Batoum Attack.—The seventh attempt was made on the night of the 27th–28th of December, 1877, on several Turkish men-of-war anchored in the harbour of Batoum (the scene of the first Russian torpedo attempt and failure). Four boats composed the attacking force, viz. the *Tchesme*, Lieutenant Zatzarennyi, in command, armed with a Whitehead fish torpedo, containing 32 kilog. of gun-cotton, fitted to fire from a tube under the boat's keel; the *Sinope*, Lieutenant Stchelinski, armed with a similarly charged fish torpedo, fitted to fire from a raft, which was towed by the boat, and two other boats, armed with spar and towing torpedoes.

The means employed at Batoum for the safeguard of the Ottoman fleet there against such an attack was that of guard boats and a barrier formed of logs of wood, with planks secured to them, so arranged by means of weights that the planks remained perpendicular to the surface of the water when in position.

Owing to the extreme darkness of the night, the Russians managed to evade the guard boats, and when, as they imagined, some 60 to 65 yards from a Turkish ironclad, the *Tchesme* and *Sinope's* Whitehead fish torpedoes were started on their deadly mission; but, owing most probably to the want of practice of manipulating these somewhat delicate instruments, also to the darkness, and the slight swell there was on at the time, both missed their mark, and were landed high and dry on the beach astern of the ship.

One of these weapons was perfect, the other minus her fore compartment, this having been knocked off by the torpedo colliding with some hard object. No explosion was heard or seen by the Turks.

This was the second time that the fish torpedo had been employed on actual service, and, as in the previous instance, failed.

The guard boats and barrier of the Turks seem to have been of little avail.

8TH AFFAIR.

The Final Attack.—The eighth and last attempt was made on the night of the 25th–26th of January, 1878.

This was originally intended to be an attack on the Turkish fleet at Batoum, but on entering that harbour the two Russian torpedo boats, the *Tchesme*, Lieutenant Zatzarennyi, and the *Sinope*, Lieutenant Stchelinski, were met by a Turkish revenue steamer, against which the boats discharged their Whitehead torpedoes, resulting in her complete destruction, at the same time arousing the squadron, and causing the boats to beat a retreat.

Though the vessel destroyed was not a frigate, yet the expedition was successful in so far as proving that it is possible to project Whitehead fish torpedoes from boats at a distance of 70 to 90 yards from an enemy's ship, on a dark night, and strike her with them.

This concludes the whole of the offensive torpedo operations that were carried out during the war, of which two out of eight attempts were successful, which is without doubt a fair percentage.

There seems every probability that the present struggle between Chili and Peru, in the Pacific, will afford torpedoists further experience of the various offensive torpedoes, when subjected to the test of active service.

CHAPTER VIII.

ON EXPLOSIVES.

EXPLOSION may be defined as the sudden or extremely rapid conversion of a solid or liquid body of small bulk into gas or vapour, occupying very many times the volume of the original substance, and which in addition is highly expanded by the heat generated during the action.

This sudden or very rapid expansion of volume is attended by an exhibition of force which is more or less violent, according to the constitution of the original body and the circumstances of the explosion.

Any substance capable of undergoing such a change on the application of heat or other disturbing cause is called an "explosive."

Explosive Force.—Explosive *force* is *directly* proportional to the heat of combustion and the volume of gas, and *inversely* to the specific heat of the mixed products.

Explosive *effect* is *directly* proportional to the volume of gas produced and the temperature of the explosion, and *inversely* as the time required for the change to take place.

Explosive Effect and Force compared.—Explosive effect depends upon the rapidity with which the conversion is effected, while the same amount of explosive force may act suddenly or gradually.

As before stated, explosions are more or less violent according to the *circumstances* under which they take place. These may be considered as follows :—

1.—The physical state of the explosive substance.
2.—The external conditions under which the explosive body is fired.
3.—The mode of firing.

The Physical State of the Explosive Substance.—Numerous instances may be cited to show the influence the physical condition of an explosive body has upon its explosion.

Thus, gunpowder may, by merely varying the size, shape, and density of the grain, be made to ignite rapidly but burn comparatively slowly, or be made to ignite more slowly, but once inflamed to burn very rapidly.

Again, gun-cotton in a loose, uncompressed state, will, if ignited, only flash off; if it is spun into threads or woven into webs, its rate of combustion may be so much reduced that it can be used in gunnery or for a quick fuze; while if powerfully compressed and damp it burns slowly. Wet gun-cotton requires a primer of dry gun-cotton and a fulminate fuze to explode; dry, it may be exploded by a fulminate fuze, &c.

Then nitro-glycerine, when exploded by 15 grains of fulminate of mercury, and at a temperature above 40° F., is very violently detonated; below 40° F. it freezes and cannot be similarly exploded.

To obtain the full effect of all explosives, confinement is absolutely necessary.

The more rapid the explosion the less confinement required, approaching in the case of some explosives to so small an amount that it need not, for practical purposes, be considered.

Thus a charge of nitro-glycerine or gun-cotton, when detonated in the open air, will destroy wrought iron rails, large blocks of stones, balks of timber, &c.

In the case of the former body, the confinement of the atmosphere is sufficient.

In the latter, the mechanical cohesion due to compression is sufficient restraint.

Abel states that if the film of atmosphere surrounding the nitro-glycerine, not exceeding $\frac{1}{1000}$ inch in thickness, be removed, the explosive effect is much lessened.

A large charge of gunpowder fired in the ordinary way under water requires a strong case to retain the gases until the action has become general, or, owing to its slow rate of burning, the case would be broken before the whole of the charge had been ignited, and part of the charge drowned.

This is often to be noticed when firing fine-grained powder in heavy guns.

Igniting the charge at several points diminishes the confinement needed.

Mode of Firing.—The application of heat, directly or indirectly, is the principal means of causing an explosion.

The flame from a percussion cap or primer, or a platinum wire heated to incandescence by an electric current, will *directly* ignite a charge. Friction, concussion, &c., will *indirectly* ignite a charge due to the conversion of mechanical energy into heat.

It would appear that when one explosive body is used as a means of firing another, the resultant explosion is due to the blow suddenly formed by the gas of the firing charge acting percussively upon the mass to be exploded. If such were the case, then the most powerful explosive would be the best agent for causing an explosion. But it is not so.

For example, nitro-glycerine, which is far more powerful than fulminate of mercury, requires more than 1000 grains to explode gun-cotton, while only 15 grains of the latter is needful for the same work, &c.

A small quantity of an explosive substance which is sensitive to friction or percussion is often used to ignite the original charge.

Detonation.—The instantaneous explosion of the whole mass of a body is defined as "detonation."

The essential difference between an explosion and a detonation is the comparative suddenness of the transformation of the solid or liquid explosive substance into gas and vapour.

Some explosive bodies, such as the fulminates, &c., always detonate, while the detonation of others depends on the mode of firing.

Nitro-glycerine always explodes violently, but when fired with an initiatory charge of fulminate of mercury it is much more powerful than when fired with gunpowder.

Compressed gun-cotton in the air-dry state can be detonated by 2 grains of fulminate of mercury embedded in the material, but when it contains 3 per cent. of water over and above the 2 per cent. which exists normally in the air-dry substance, 15 grains of the fulminate will not always do so.

Theory of Detonation.—The theory of detonation is not yet thoroughly understood. That it is not alone due to the heat caused by the impact of the mechanical energy of the particles of gas, set free from the initiatory charge on the principal mass, is proved by the fact of its being possible to detonate wet gun-cotton.

Professor Bloxam terms detonation to be "sympathetic" explosion.

Experiments carried on in England by Professor Abel, and in

France by MM. Champion and Pellet, tend to show that it is due to the vibratory action of the detonating agent.

Thus a glass may withstand a strong blow, though a particular note or vibration will smash it.

All explosive compounds and mixtures, including gunpowder, are susceptible of violent explosion through the agency of a detonation.

Roux and Sarrau.—Roux and Sarrau divide explosions into two orders :—

1st order.—Detonations.

2nd order.—Simple explosions.

Simple explosions are produced by direct inflammation, or by a small charge of gunpowder.

Detonations are obtained from nitro-glycerine, gun-cotton, &c., by exploding with fulminate of mercury.

They state that fulminate of mercury does not detonate gunpowder; but if the exploding charge is a small amount of nitro-glycerine, itself detonated by fulminate of mercury, then an explosion of the first order is obtained.

The relative effects were approximately measured by determining the quantities necessary to rupture small cast iron shells of supposed equal strength.

Results of their Experiments.—The following are some of the results :—

	Explosive Effect.	
	2nd Order.	1st Order.
Gunpowder	1·00	4·34
Gun-cotton	3·00	6·46
Nitro-glycerine . . .	4·80	10·13

According to the above table, nitro-glycerine is more than ten times, and gun-cotton more than six times, as powerful as gunpowder fired in the ordinary way (2nd order).

The want of reciprocity between two detonating agents is shown in a remarkable degree by the following experiments, carried out by Professor Abel :—

1.—The detonation of ¼ ounce of gun-cotton (the smallest quantity that can be thus applied) induced the simultaneous detonation of nitro-glycerine, enclosed in a vessel of sheet tin, and placed at a distance of 1 inch from the gun-cotton.

2.—The detonation of ½ ounce of gun-cotton produces the same effect with an intervening spaces of 3 inches between the substances.

3.—The detonation of 2 ounces of nitro-glycerine in *close contact* with compressed gun-cotton failed to accomplish the detonation of the latter, which was simply dispersed in a fine state of division, in all the instances but one, in a large number of experiments.

Explosive agents are divided into explosive mixtures and compounds.

In the former the ingredients are mechanically mixed, and can be separated by mechanical means.

In the latter the ingredients are chemically combined, and can only be separated by chemical change.

Torpedo Explosive Agents.—The explosive agents that are practically the most important, as far as their employment as torpedo charges are concerned, are as follows :—

Explosive Mixtures.—A.—Explosive mixtures.

1.—Gunpowder.

2.—Ammonium picrate, or picric powder. } Nitrate class.

Explosive Compounds.—B.—Explosive compounds.

1.—Nitro-glycerine.

2.—Dynamite (No. 1).

3.—Gun-cotton.

4.—Fulminate of mercury.

A.—Explosive Mixtures.

Gunpowder.—This explosive mixture is composed of seventy-five parts of nitre (saltpetre), fifteen parts of charcoal, and ten parts of sulphur.

On being ignited, the oxygen which is feebly held by the nitrogen combines with the carbon, forming carbonic oxide gas, whilst the sulphur unites with the potassium of the nitre, the whole combination being accompanied by a great evolution of heat and expansion of gas, and the nitrogen is set free.

Properties, &c.—A spark, friction between hard bodies, or a temperature of 572° F., are any of them sufficient to cause an explosion of gunpowder.

Slight moisture, due to damp air, &c., produces caking and deterioration.

Wetting causes permanent destruction.

Frost does not injure it.

It can be fired by ordinary methods.

It can be transported and handled with safety and great ease.

It is not a suitable explosive agent for torpedoes, on account of its liability to be injured by damp, as well as its not being sufficiently violent, though for the sake of convenience, &c., it is often employed for such work.

The effect produced by the explosion of a charge of gunpowder, ignited by the ordinary method, is that of an uplifting rather than a shattering effect.

This evil may be greatly remedied, when gunpowder is used as the charge of a torpedo, by firing it with a detonator, by which means its fullest explosive effect is developed.

Picric Powder.—The picrates are salts of picric acid.

Picric acid is formed by the action of nitric acid on carbolic acid.

The picrate employed by Professor Abel is prepared from picric acid and ammonium. This preparation, or salt mixed with nitre (saltpetre), forms Abel's picric powder.

Properties, &c.—It is prepared for use in a similar manner to gunpowder, and it can be handled in the same way.

It is less violent than dynamite or gun-cotton, though much more so than gunpowder.

It is difficult to explode it by blows or friction.

If flame be applied to it, the part touched burns, but the combustion does not become general.

This explosive agent will probably be used for spar torpedoes, when gun-cotton or dynamite are not employed.

B.—Explosive Compounds.

Nitro-glycerine.—Nitro-glycerine is formed by the action of nitric acid upon glycerine at a low temperature.

The manufacture of this compound consists, first, in the slow mixture of the glycerine with the acid, at a low temperature; secondly, in washing the nitro-glycerine from the excess of acid with water.

The nitric acid before use is mixed with a certain proportion of strong sulphuric acid, so that the water formed during the reaction may be taken up, and thus any dilution of the nitric acid is prevented.

Nitro-glycerine is composed of carbon, hydrogen, nitrogen, and oxygen, as indicated by the equation $C_3 H_5 N_3 O_9$.

Properties, &c.—At ordinary temperatures nitro-glycerine is an oily liquid, having a specific gravity of 1·6.   Freshly made it is creamy white and opaque, but clears and becomes colourless on standing for a certain time, depending on the temperature.

It does not mix with, nor is it affected by, water.   It has a sweet, aromatic taste, and produces a violent headache if placed upon the tongue.

The opaque, freshly made nitro-glycerine does not freeze until the temperature is lowered to 3°—5° below zero, F., but, when cleared, it freezes at 39°—40° F.   Nitro-glycerine freezes to a white crystalline mass, and in this state it can be thawed by placing the vessel containing it in water, at a temperature not over 100° F.

If flame is applied to freely exposed nitro-glycerine, it burns slowly without explosion.

Nitro-glycerine in a state of decomposition becomes very sensitive, exploding violently when struck, even when unconfined.

Pure nitro-glycerine does not spontaneously decompose at any ordinary temperature, but if it contains any free acid, then decomposition may happen.   When pure, it is not sensitive to friction, or moderate percussion.   If struck with a hammer, only the particle receiving the blow explodes, the remainder being scattered.

The firing point of nitro-glycerine is about 356° F., though it begins to decompose at a lower temperature.

The mode of firing nitro-glycerine usually employed is that of a fulminate of mercury detonating fuse.

Nitro-glycerine in the frozen state cannot be fired even by large charges of fulminate.

In one instance, 1600 lbs. of liquid nitro-glycerine exploded in a magazine containing 600 lbs. of the same substance in a frozen state, but failed to fire the latter, only breaking it up and scattering it in every direction.

Dynamite.—This explosive compound is merely a preparation in which nitro-glycerine is itself presented for use, its explosive properties being those of the nitro-glycerine contained in it, as the absorbent is an inert body.

Dynamite is formed of seventy-five parts of nitro-glycerine absorbed by twenty-five parts of a porous siliceous earth or " kieselguhr."

The best substitute for " kieselguhr" is ashes of bog-head coal.

Dynamite is a loose, soft, readily moulded substance, of a buff colour.

The preparation of dynamite is very simple.

The nitro-glycerine is mixed by means of wooden spatulas with the fine white powder (kieselguhr) in a leaden vessel.

It freezes at 39°—40° F., and when solidly frozen cannot be exploded, but if in a pulverised state it can be exploded, though with diminished violence.

It can be easily thawed, by placing the vessel containing it in hot water.

Friction or moderate percussion does not explode it.

Its firing point is 356° F.

If flame be applied to it, it burns with a strong flame.

It is fired by means of fulminate of mercury, and its explosive force is about seven times that of gunpowder.

For ground and buoyant mines, where actual contact between the hostile vessel and the torpedo will be rarely achieved, this being next to nitro-glycerine the most violent of all known explosive agents, and being cheaply and readily procured, is the very best explosive for such torpedoes.

That it is not generally adopted is owing to its containing a large proportion of that seemingly dangerous substance, nitro-glycerine, which makes the handling of dynamite a somewhat hazardous operation.

According to Professer Abel, there are now as many as fifteen dynamite factories in different parts of the world (including a very extensive one in Scotland) working under the supervision of Mr. Nobel, the originator of the nitro-glycerine industry ; and six or seven other establishments exist where dynamite or preparations of very similar character are also manufactured.

The total production of dynamite in 1867 was only eleven tons, while in 1878 it amounted to 6140 tons.

This explosive compound is most extensively used for general blasting purposes all over the world, and for this purpose, owing to its cheapness and the convenience in manipulating it, is far superior to compressed gun-cotton.

Gun-cotton is formed by the action of concentrated nitric acid on cotton, its composition being indicated by the formula $C\ H_7\ (NO_2)_3\ O_5$.

Professor Abel's process for manufacturing pulped and compressed gun-cotton is as follows :—

Cotton waste is the form of cotton used ; it is picked and cleaned, thoroughly dried at 160° F., and then allowed to cool.

The strongest nitric and sulphuric acids are employed, mixed in the proportion of one part of the former to three of the latter by weight.   These are mixed in large quantities, and stored in cast-iron tanks.

The cotton in 1-lb. charges is immersed in the acid mixture, which is contained in a trough surrounded by cold water.   After being subjected to the action of the acid for a short space of time, the cotton is taken up, placed upon a perforated shelf, and as much as possible of the acid squeezed out of it.   It is then put into jars, covered with fresh acid, and the jars placed in fresh water, remaining there for twenty-four hours.

To remove the acid, the gun-cotton from the jars is thrown into a centrifugal strainer, by which nearly all the acid is expelled.   It is then diffused quickly in small quantities through a large volume of water, and again passed through a centrifugal machine.

The next process is that of thoroughly washing the gun-cotton, for the purpose of removing the traces of the acid still adhering to it.   By pulping, which operation is performed in pulping engines or beaters, the washing is expeditious and thorough.

A *beater* is an oblong tub in which is placed a revolving wheel carrying strips of steel on its circumference.   From the bottom under the wheel project similar steel strips.

The action of this machine is as follows :—

By the rotation of the wheel, the gun-cotton which is suspended in water circulates around the tub, and is drawn between the two sets of steel projections, by which it is reduced to a state of *pulp*.

The bottom of the tub is movable, and thus the space through which the gun-cotton must pass may be contracted, as the operation proceeds.

The pulping being complete, the contents are run into *poachers* for the final washing.

A *poacher* is a large oblong wooden tub.* On one side at the middle is placed a wooden paddle-wheel, which extends half way across the tub.

In the poacher the pulped gun-cotton is stirred for a long time with a large quantity of water. The revolution of the paddle-wheel keeps up a constant circulation, and care is taken that no deposit occurs in any part of the tub.

Having converted the cotton into gun-cotton, reduced it to a state of pulp, and thoroughly washed it, the next process is to separate the water from the pulp, and compress it into cakes or discs.

This is accomplished by means of two presses, the first of which has 36 hollow cylinders, in which perforated plungers work upwards.

These plungers having been drawn down, the cylinders are filled with the water-laden pulp, and their tops covered with a weight; the plungers are then forced up by hydraulic power, compressing the pulp, and forcing the water to escape through their perforations.

The second one is used to more solidly compress the cylindrical masses of gun-cotton formed by the action of the first press, a pressure of 6 tons to the inch being in this case applied.

About 6 per cent. of moisture still remains in the discs, which can be readily removed by drying.

Properties.—Cotton converted into gun-cotton is little changed in appearance, though the latter is harsher to the touch than the former.

If a flame be applied to dry loose gun-cotton, it flashes up, without explosion; if compressed it burns rapidly, but quietly.

Moist compressed gun-cotton under the same circumstances burns away slowly.

Gun-cotton containing 12 to 14 per cent. of water is ignited with much difficulty on applying a highly heated body. As it leaves the hydraulic press upon being converted from the pulped state to masses, it contains about 15 per cent. of water; in this condition it may be thrown on to a fire or held in a flame without exhibiting any tendency to burn; the masses may be perforated by means of a red-hot iron, or with a drilling tool, and they may with perfect safety be cut into slices by means of saws revolving with great rapidity. If placed upon a fire and allowed to remain there, a feeble and transparent flame flickers over the surface of the wet gun-cotton from time to time as the exterior becomes sufficiently dry to inflame; in this way a piece of compressed gun-cotton will burn away very gradually indeed.

To test the safety of wet gun-cotton, the following two experiments among many have been made:—

Quantities of wet gun-cotton, 20 cwt. each, packed in one instance in a large, strong wooden case, and in the other in a number of strong packing cases, were placed in small magazines, very substantially built of concrete and brickwork. Large fires were kindled around the packages in each building, the doors being just left ajar. The entire contents of both buildings had burned away, without anything approaching explosive action, in less than two hours.

This comparatively great safety of wet gun-cotton, coupled with the fact that its detonation in that state may be readily accomplished through the agency of a small quantity of dry gun-cotton, termed a "primer," which, by means of a fulminating fuze, or detonator, is made to act as the initiative detonating agent, gives it important advantages over other violent explosive agents, when used for purposes which involve the employment of a considerable quantity of the material, on account of the safety attending its storage and necessary manipulation.

From experiments conducted by engineer officers in Austria, it was found that if boxes containing dry compressed gun-cotton are fired into from small arms, even at a short range, the gun-cotton is generally inflamed, but never exploded, the sharpness of the blow essential to effect an explosion, which the bullet might otherwise give, being diminished by its penetration through the side of the box before reaching the explosive. Wet gun-cotton, containing even as little as 15 per cent. of water, is never inflamed on these conditions.

Dynamite, on the other hand, is invariably detonated when struck by a bullet on passing through the side of the box.

Gun-cotton is insoluble in and unaffected by water.

The firing point of gun-cotton is about 360° F.

The temperature of explosion of gun-cotton is about 8700° F., being more than double that of gunpowder. Gun-cotton is not sensitive to friction or percussion.

If not perfectly converted or thoroughly washed, gun-cotton is liable to spontaneous decomposition, which under favourable conditions may result in explosion.

Compressed gun-cotton is free from such danger, as it may be kept and used saturated with water. It is stored in the wet state, care being taken that it is not exposed to a temperature that will freeze the water in the cakes, as if this occurs they are liable to be disintegrated by the expansion of the water in freezing.

Gun-cotton is the agent most extensively used for all kinds of military engineering and submarine operations in Great Britain, it being especially manufactured by the English government for that express purpose; but in other countries it is not so manufactured, and therefore, as it is little used for other than military purposes, it is not to any extent privately manufactured, as is the case with other explosives, such as dynamite, dualine, lithofracteur, &c., and thus, in case of war, would be somewhat difficult to obtain out of England.

Compared with dynamite, it is not so violent, and occupies more space, weight for weight, and also requires a more complicated means of detonating it. On the other hand, gun-cotton is infinitely safer to store and manipulate, and is not so subject to detonation by concussion (not being so sensitive) as dynamite.

Fulminate of Mercury.—Fulminate of mercury is formed by the action of mercuric nitrate and nitric acid upon alcohol. The mode of preparation is as follows :—

Dissolve one part of mercury in twelve parts of nitric acid, and pour this solution into twelve parts of alcohol.

Pour this mixture into a vessel which is placed in hot water until it darkens and becomes turbid and begins to evolve dense white fumes, then remove it from the water. The reaction goes on, with strong effervescence and copious evolution of dense white ethereal vapours. If red fumes appear, cold alcohol should be added to check the violence of the action.

The operation should be performed at a distance from a fire or flame, and in a strong draught, so that the vapours may be carried off.

When the liquid clears, and the dense white fumes are no longer given off, further action is stopped by filling up with cold water. The fulminate settles to the bottom of the vessel as a grey crystalline precipitate. The liquid is then poured off, and the fulminate washed several times by decantation or upon a filter.

Dry fulminate of mercury explodes violently when heated to 367° F., when forcibly struck by the electric spark, &c.

When wet it is inexplosive, and therefore it is always kept wet, being dried in small amounts when required for use.

Fulminate of mercury is applied in many ways, either pure or mixed with other substances, as in percussion caps, percussion powder, primers, detonators, &c.

For the purpose of detonating nitro-glycerine or its preparations, 15 grains of the fulminate are sufficient, but to detonate gun-cotton 25 grains are necessary. The fulminate in detonating fuzes should be enclosed in a copper case or cap, and must never be loose. The fulminate should be wet when charging the detonators, as it is very dangerous to handle when dry.

Great care is requisite in handling this explosive compound.

In addition to the foregoing explosive compounds and mixtures, the following explosive agents have also been employed for the purposes of submarine operations, though only to a small extent.

Dualin.—Dualin is a nitro-glycerine preparation formed by mixing sawdust and saltpetre with that substance.

This preparation, inferior to dynamite, was employed by the Germans as the explosive agent for their submarine mines during the Franco-German war (1870–71).

Lithofracteur.—Lithofracteur is also a preparation of nitro-glycerine. It is composed of the following materials :—Nitro-glycerine, kieselguhr, coal, soda, saltpetre, and sulphur.

This explosive agent, also inferior to dynamite, is used, though not very extensively, by the French for their submarine mines.

Horsley's Powder.—Horsley's powder is a chlorate mixture formed of potassium, chlorate, and galls. This explosive mixture was formerly used by Captain Harvey for his towing torpedo, but has recently been discarded for compressed gun-cotton.

Abel's Detonation Experiments.—The following are the results of experiments carried out by Professor Abel, C.B., F.R.S., on the subject of detonation :—

1.—A fuze containing rather more than 1 ounce of gunpowder, strongly confined, exploded in contact with a mass of compressed gun-cotton, *only inflames it*, although the explosion of the fuze is apparently a sharp one.

2.—45 grains of fulminate of mercury, exploded unconfined on the surface of a piece of compressed gun-cotton, only inflames or disperses it.

3.—A fuze containing 9 grains of fulminate of mercury, strongly confined, exploded in contact with compressed gun-cotton, or dynamite, detonates it with certainty.

4.—An equal quantity of fulminate of mercury, similarly confined, does not detonate *uncompressed* gun-cotton in which it is imbedded, but merely disperses and inflames it.

5.—150 grains of compressed gun-cotton, detonated in proximity to dynamite, *detonates the latter*.

6.—3 ounces of dynamite, and very much larger quantities, detonated in contact with compressed gun-cotton, only disperses it.

7.—A wrought-iron rail can be destroyed by detonating 8 ounces of compressed gun-cotton placed unconfined on the rail.

8.—A piece of wet gun-cotton, quite uninflammable, removed from a fire, and detonated upon a block of granite, using a small primer of dry gun-cotton, shatters the block.

9.—A submerged charge of wet gun-cotton, open on all sides to the water, and merely confined around the dry initiative, or primer, by means of a net, can be exploded.

Explosive Agents in Torpedoes.—The explosive agents that at the present time are most generally used in torpedoes are gunpowder, gun-cotton in the wet compressed state, and dynamite, and these may be compared as to their properties and their explosive effects.

Gunpowder.—Gunpowder is a familiar material, in general use for all military purposes. It can be handled and transported with safety and ease, and it can be fired by ordinary methods. But for submarine purposes it has the disadvantage of being very easily injured by water, so that it is absolutely necessary to enclose it in water-tight cases.

Gun-cotton.—Gun-cotton is free from liability to accidents, and in this matter, and the safety of its manufacture, it compares favourably with gunpowder.

It is peculiarly adapted to submarine work, being unaffected by water. And as it may be kept in water, ready for use, it can be safely carried on board ship in large quantities. It is far more violent in its action when detonated than gunpowder. The chief objection to its use is, that being applied only·for special purposes, it is not readily obtained. Also it requires a peculiar and somewhat complicated mode of firing it.

Dynamite.—Dynamite is more easily manufactured than the two foregoing explosives. The fact of it containing nitro-glycerine, which has a bad reputation, has militated against its use as a torpedo explosive agent, though for blasting purposes it is most extensively used. Though not directly affected by water, its firing is hindered when diffused through water. Another disadvantage is its high freezing point. Like gun-cotton, it requires special means to fire it, though much simpler, and also is much more powerful than gunpowder. The explosive effect of dynamite or gun-cotton is a rending or a shattering one, while that of gunpowder is an uplifting or heaving one.

Again, it is necessary when using gunpowder that the object be in the line of least resistance, but with dynamite or gun-cotton the effect is nearly equal in every direction, therefore for submarine operations, either dynamite or gun-cotton is the explosive agent that should be invariably used.

Size of Torpedo Charges.—For permanent mines, a charge of 700 lbs. to 1000 lbs. of gun-cotton is quite sufficient, though too large a charge cannot be employed, except as regards the matter of convenience.

For buoyant mines, 500 lbs. to 700 lbs. of gun-cotton is an ample charge, and for contact mines, 200 lbs. to 300 lbs. of gun-cotton is sufficient. In spar torpedoes, where lightness is a consideration, gun-cotton charges of 30 lbs. to 50 lbs. will be found ample, and similarly in the case of the towing or locomotive torpedoes. Of course, with regard to such a submarine weapon as the Lay torpedo boat, any size charge may be carried, according to the wish of the builder.

Torpedo Explosions illustrated.—At Fig. 166 is represented a sketch of a torpedo explosion, from a photograph taken at the moment the column of water was at its greatest elevation. The torpedo contained 432 lbs. of gun-cotton, and was exploded under 27 feet of water.

The height of the column thrown up measured 81 feet, and the diameter at the base 132 feet.

At Fig. 165 is shown a sketch of two submarine mine explosions from an instantaneous photograph; the schooner which is shown in

PLATE LII

Fig 166

PLATE LIII

Fig 167

the sketch happened to be passing at the moment of explosion, thus affording a comparison as to the size of the columns of water thrown up.

The column on the left was due to the explosion of a submarine mine containing 100 lbs. gunpowder at a depth of 10 feet below the surface. That on the right was the result of an explosion of a similar mine, but at a depth of 41 feet below the surface. Its extreme height was 400 feet.

CHAPTER IX.

TORPEDO EXPERIMENTS.

THE following are some of the more important torpedo experiments that have been carried out in England and Europe, to investigate the subject of submarine explosions as applied to ships and to mines, &c., these experiments extending over a space of thirteen years.

Experiment at Chatham, England, 1865.—This experiment was carried out to ascertain the effect of gunpowder torpedoes on the bottom of a wooden ship.

Target:—H.M.S. *Terpsichore,* a wooden sloop of war.

Torpedo:—150 lbs. of fine-grained powder. Two were used. They were placed on the ground, about 13′ below the ship's keel, and 2′ horizontally clear of her side.

Effect of explosion:—A hole of about 4′ radius was made, about 19′ nearly vertical from the charge; the *Terpsichore* sinking a few minutes after the explosion.

Experiment in Austria.—The object of this experiment was to ascertain the effect of a very large charge of gun-cotton exploded at some distance from the side of a wooden vessel.

Target:—A wooden sloop.

Torpedo:—400 lbs. of gun-cotton, placed 10′ below the surface of the water, and 24′ horizontally from the bottom of the vessel.

Effect of explosion:—Complete destruction of the vessel.

Experiments at Carlscrona, Sweden, 1868.—These experiments were made to investigate the effect of submarine contact mines, charged with dynamite, against a strong wooden vessel, as well as against a double-bottomed iron vessel. They were carried out under the supervision of Lieut.-Colonel Zethations, of the Royal Swedish Navy.

Target:—The hull of a 60 gun frigate, which had been built in 1844; it had been cut down to the battery deck, and the copper removed. Her timbers and planking were quite sound; timbers of oak about 13" square, and 1" apart; planking of Swedish pine, 5½"; bottom strengthened inside with wrought-iron diagonal bands, 6" by 1¼"; inside planking running half way up to the battery deck of oak; 6" thick. This completes the wooden target.

On the port side a quadrangular opening was made, and fitted with a construction representing a strong double iron bottom, firmly fastened to an oaken frame that had been put on inside, on the four sides of the opening, and with through-going bolts, 1" in diameter, to the timbers.

Torpedoes:—No. 1.—13 lbs. dynamite, enclosed in $\frac{1}{13}$" iron case. It was placed on the starboard side, amidships, 7' below the water line, and 2' 2" from the bottom of the ship.

No. 2.—16 lbs. dynamite, enclosed in a glass vessel. It was placed on the starboard side, 7¾' below the water line, 3' from the bottom of the ship, and 40' from her stern.

No. 3.—16 lbs. dynamite, enclosed in $\frac{1}{13}$" iron case. It was placed on the port side, 5¾' below the water line, 2' from the bottom of the ship, and 30' from her stern.

No. 4.—10 lbs. dynamite, in a case as above. It was placed on the port side, 6½' below the water line, 2⅙' from the bottom of the ship, and 70' from her stern.

No. 5.—13 lbs. dynamite, in case as above. It was placed 7⅓' below the water line, 2⅙' from the centre of the *iron* bottom.

These five torpedoes were fired at the same moment.

Effect of explosion:—The hull of the ship was lifted about a foot, and sunk in 1½ minutes.

No. 1 Mine.—Timbers broken and thrown inside, into the hold, on a space of about 15' × 8'; three more timbers on one side of this hole broken; inside oak planking rent off on a length of 14'; two iron bands torn up and bent, one of them broken in two places; outside planking torn off on a space of 21' × 12'; several planks still higher up broken.

No. 2 Mine.—Timbers blown away on a space of about 8' square; inside planking torn off on a length of 20'; two iron bands broken, and torn up and bent; and outside planking rent off on a space of 19' × 12'.

No. 3 Mine.—Timbers blown away on a space of 10½' × 12' at one end, and 6' at the other; inside planking off for a length of 14; one iron band torn up, and one broken; outside planking off on a space of 18' × 25' × 15'.

No. 4 Mine.—Timbers blown away on a space 4' × 16'; on the sides of this hole, ten timbers were broken; two iron bands torn up, and one broken; inside planking off for a length of 20'; outside planking off for a space of 20' × 23' × 10', and 13 feet.

No. 5 Mine.—The gas sphere of this mine had hit the middle of the outside plates on one of the angle-iron ribs. This rib was torn from the timbers and bent up, nearly 2' in the middle, but not broken. There was an oval hole in the outside plates 4' × 3' between two ribs, which ribs, with the plates on edge riveted to them, were bulged out about 5 inches. The inner plate, one large piece was blown up in a vertical position, after having cut all the bolts and rivets, sixty of 1", and thirty of $\frac{3}{4}$", save those that fastened the lower side to the oaken frame and timbers. On a length of 30' and height of 20', the bottom, on all sides of the iron construction, had been bent inwards; the greatest bend was about 5"; three deck beams above had been broken.

By the joint effect of all the mines, almost all the iron deck beam knees had been rent from the side, and there was an opening between deck and hull on both sides for a length of about 130 feet.

Experiment at Kiel.—Target:—A large gun-boat, greatly strengthened internally by solid balks of timber.

Torpedo:—200 lbs. gunpowder. It was placed nearly under her keel, at a distance of 15 feet.

Effect of explosion :—Complete destruction of the vessel.

Experiment in England, 1874.—Target:—A rectangular iron case 20' long, 10' high, and 8' wide, divided into six compartments by means of one longitudinal bulkhead midway between the front and rear faces of the target, and two athwartship bulkheads equidistant from the ends of the target. Thickness of front and rear faces $\frac{11}{16}$", of longitudinal bulkhead $\frac{1}{4}$", of athwartship bulkheads $\frac{3}{8}$".

Torpedo:—100 lbs. of gunpowder, enclosed in a spar torpedo case and fired by two detonators. It was exploded in contact with the target, $7\frac{1}{2}$' below the surface of the water, and 7' from top of target.

Effect of explosion on the target :—" Front of centre compartment destroyed and top blown off. Plate representing inner skin destroyed. Back of centre compartment (rear face of the target) much bulged, and penetrated; the hole measured 36' × 15". Large portions of the target were thrown to a height of 150 to 200 feet, and from 80 to 100 yards' distance."

The effect of explosion on a ship's pinnace, which had been placed 16 feet from and at right angles to the front face of the target, with steam up, and canopy and shield in position, was that a large quantity of water was thrown back in the boat, putting the fires out, and filling the boat up to her thwarts, but otherwise the boat was uninjured.

Experiments at Copenhagen, Denmark, in 1874.—The object of these experiments was to ascertain if a ship's armoured side would be seriously injured by a torpedo exploded in contact with it.

1st Experiment.

Target :—1″ thick, and 2′ × 2′, supported in a horizontal position on a substructure consisting of 8″ timber resting on two pieces of 6″ timber under two sides, and completely supported by earth up to lower edge of substructure.

Torpedo :—33 lbs. of dynamite, enclosed in a square wooden case 2¼″ high, and 5·5″ × 5·5″; it was placed on the middle of the earth with 8″ of earth tamping; this tamping representing the resistance of a thin stratum of water.

Effect of explosion :—The plate was broken into four pieces, and substructure crushed.

2nd Experiment.

Target :—2″ thick, and 2′ × 2½′, supported in a horizontal position on a substructure as above, but resting on four piles of 6″ × 6″ timber.

Torpedo :—8·9 lbs. of dynamite, enclosed in a wooden case 4″ high, and 5″ × 10″. It was laid with one edge on the plate, the other edge 3″ above the plate; same tamping as above.

Effect of explosion :—The plate broken into three pieces, and substructure crushed.

3rd Experiment.

Target :—5″ thick, and 3′ 8″ × 4′ 7″, supported in a horizontal position on a substructure as above, but eight piles of 6″ × 6″ timber used. Plate bolted to the structure with eights.

Torpedo :—44·4 lbs. of dynamite, enclosed in a wooden case, of same thickness as the Harvey torpedo, and $4'' \times 13'' \times 21''$; it was placed with surface against the plate, one edge $2''$ and the other $5\frac{1}{2}''$ from the plate; tamping as before.

Effect of explosion :—Plate bulged $3\frac{1}{4}''$ in the middle; substructure completely crushed.

4th Experiment.

Target :—$5''$ thick, and $3' 8'' \times 4' 7''$; this was the same plate as used in the previous experiment, laid with bulge uppermost on two beams under the short sides.

Torpedo :—44·4 lbs. of dynamite, enclosed in a cylindrical tin box $7\frac{1}{2}'' \times 2'$; it was placed on top of plate $11''$ from one side and with ends $9\frac{1}{2}''$ from edge of plate; tamping as before.

Effect of explosion :—A corner of the plate broken off.

5th Experiment.

Target :—Same plate placed vertically in the earth.

Torpedo :—44·4 lbs. of dynamite, enclosed in a cylindrical tin box $8·5'' \times 18''$; it was placed on timber, so as to rest against the face and centre of the plate; tamping as usual.

Effect of explosion :—Plate broken into four pieces, two of which were large; pieces hurled over parapet, one fell at a distance of 400 feet.

Experiments at Carlscrona, Sweden, in 1874–75.—These experiments were carried out by the Swedish torpedo authorities, to ascertain the effect of different sized charges of dynamite and gunpowder, enclosed in divers cases, and exploded at various distances from a target which represented in all respects, with the exception of the armour, a section of the side of H.M.S. *Hercules* before the boiler room, she being at that time one of the most powerful vessels afloat.

Target :—$32'$ in length, and fitted into the side of an old line of battle ship. Similar in shape to a wing tank, and comprised a double bottom in four water-tight compartments, a wing passage in two water-tight compartments, and two large water-tight compartments in rear of all. It extended from $2'$ above the water line to within about $5'$ of the vessel's keel. The thickness of the plates forming the target were :— outer bottom, lower portion $\frac{13}{16}''$; part where torpedo took effect, $\frac{3}{4}''$.

Inner bottom, and wing passage bulkhead $\frac{1}{2}$". Vertical and longitudinal frames, both solid and bracket, $\frac{7}{16}$". The longitudinal frames were bracket frames, with the exception of the second, which was solid and water-tight, with its outer edge about 8' below the water line. The vertical frames, of which there were seven, were placed 4' apart, the central one being solid and water-tight, the others being bracket frames. The ship was moored in 42 feet of water; the charges were detonated, one fuze being used in all but No. 3 experiment, when five fuzes were employed.

1ST EXPERIMENT.

Torpedo :—33 lbs. of dynamite, enclosed in cylindrical steel case, no air space; height 10·75", diameter 10·75", and thickness $\frac{1}{34}$". It was placed 25·5' from the target, opposite No. 7 frame, and 9·25' below the surface of the water.

Effect of explosion :—Ship appeared to be lifted bodily. A rivet in the midship longitudinal bulkhead of fore compartment was loosened. The torpedo was fired from the ship, and the shock felt was not very great.

2ND EXPERIMENT.

Torpedo :—47·2 lbs. of dynamite, in cylindrical steel case, no air space; height 12", diameter 12", and thickness $\frac{1}{34}$". It was placed 25·5' from No. 5 frame, 9·25' below the surface of the water.

Effect of explosion :—Ship appeared to be lifted bodily. A leak was started in the outer bottom opposite to charge, caused by the loosening of five rivets.

3RD EXPERIMENT.

Torpedo :—112 lbs. of gunpowder, rifle small grain, enclosed in cylindrical steel case placed inside an iron case, with an air space all round ; steel case, $9\frac{1}{2}" \times 22\frac{1}{2}" \times \frac{1}{34}"$; iron case $33" \times 25" \times \frac{1}{4}"$. It was placed 12' from No. 5 frame, 9·25' below the surface.

Effect of explosion :—Centre of ship lifted bodily, as if her back was broken ; ship then rolled heavily to port. On board fire engines and troughs displaced several feet : shores and struts started, showing that the shock was considerable. The outer bottom on each side of the centre dividing plate indented to a depth of 1 to 1½ inches; numerous rivets started, and some sheared. The leak was considerable, owing to the number of rivets that were started. The strength of the plates was not considered to be materially affected by the indentations; the rivets, 239 in number, were replaced; and the target prepared for the next experiment.

4th Experiment.

Torpedo:—33 lbs. of dynamite, enclosed as in first experiment. It was placed 15' from No. 7 frame, 9·25' below the surface of the water.

Effect of explosion:—Ship rolled slightly to port. A bolt securing the midship transverse bulkhead to beam was sheared. No damage done to the target.

5th Experiment.

Torpedo:—66 lbs. of dynamite, enclosed in steel cylindrical case, no air space, $13·5'' \times 13'' \times \frac{1}{3·2}''$. It was placed 21' from No. 3 frame, 9·25' below the surface of the water.

Effect of explosion:—A rivet in outer bottom, above water line at fore end of target, was sheared. A few rivets in outer bottom opposite charge, and two in after compartment, were started, but no leak was perceptible. Several shores slightly displaced.

6th Experiment.

Torpedo:—33 lbs. of dynamite, enclosed as in first experiment. It was placed 12·75' from No. 7 frame, 9·25' below the surface of the water.

Effect of explosion:—Ship not lifted as much as was the case in No. 3 experiment; but explosion much sharper. On board, fire engines were capsized, and vertical shores displaced. Outer bottom opposite charge indented to a depth of about ½ an inch, other parts less bulged, and many rivets started.

7th Experiment.

Torpedo:—33 lbs. of dynamite, enclosed as in first experiment. It was placed 4' from No. 4 frame, 9·25' below the surface of the water.

Effect of explosion:—Effect very great; ship hurled suddenly to starboard. On going on board two minutes after the explosion, the fore compartment was found full, the after compartment became full ten minutes later. Shores and struts were considerably displaced, and there was evidence that the ship had sustained a severe shock. Outer bottom injured over an area 14′ × 16′, the plates being split in all directions; one piece, 5′ square, was torn completely off, and an irregular hole was formed in the outer skin 14′ × 12′. In the inner bottom below the wing passage bulkhead a piece 6′ × 9′ was blown completely out; the wing passage bulkhead was torn from the longitudinal frame and split from top to bottom. The inner skin above the upper longitudinal frame was torn from the latter, and forced in and upwards, but was not otherwise damaged. The vertical bracket frames Nos. 3 and 4, the latter opposite the torpedo, were destroyed, but the solid frame No. 5 was almost uninjured. The outer bottom, where it was not torn off, was forced in 7′, or 4′ beyond where the *inner* bottom had been.

8TH EXPERIMENT.

Torpedo :—660 lbs. of gunpowder, enclosed in a buoyant cylindrical ¼ iron case. It was placed 32·3′ from No. 4 frame, 29·25″ below the surface of the water.

Effect of explosion:—The ship and target had been thoroughly repaired, and were in good condition when this experiment was made; the ship was in this case moored in 65 feet of water. No effect was produced on the target by the explosion.

9TH EXPERIMENT.

Torpedo :—19 lbs. of dynamite, enclosed in a cylindrical steel case with arched ends. It was placed 10·5′ from No. 3 frame, 9·25′ below the surface of the water.

Effect of explosion :—Effect produced apparently equal to that by No. 3 charge of 112 lbs. of gunpowder at 12′; indentation being from ½ to 1¼ inches in the outer skin opposite the torpedo.

10TH EXPERIMENT.

Torpedo :—19 lbs. of dynamite, enclosed in a case similar to that used in the 9th experiment. It was placed 3·3′ from No. 7 frame, 9·25′ below the surface of the water.

Effect of explosion :—Hole produced in outer skin, 6·5′ × 2′ to 5′; inner skin only bulged and slightly cracked in two places. Above the longitudinal frame, a bulge was made in the outer skin 8′ × 7′, with the above-mentioned hole ; below the longitudinal frame the indentation was 14′ × 5′ and 2·1″ deep, with two horizontal cracks 10′ × 13′, and several inches broad.

11th Experiment.

Torpedo :—112 lbs. of gunpowder, enclosed in a cylindrical case of $\frac{3}{64}$″ steel, placed in a $\frac{3}{16}$″ steel case, with 223 lbs. of buoyancy. Ignition effected by a glass igniting bottle. It was placed 5·75′ from No. 5 frame, 9·25′ below the surface of the water.

Effect of explosion :—There was but little upcast of water outside the ship, but a great upcast through the ship. She immediately lurched to starboard, and on boarding her five minutes after, the target was found full of water.

The effect on the target was as follows, above the 2nd longitudinal frame, where strengthened by the wing passage bulkhead :—Outer bottom blown away from the 4th to the 6th frames for a length of 8 feet and a height of 4½ feet, and bent in 6½ feet. Inner bottom bent in and broken through between the 4th and 5th frames, with an irregular hole 8′ square, and between the 5th and 6th frames, a similar sized hole. Wing passage bulkhead was bent in 2″ to 3″, and riven for a length of 29′; in the water-tight middle bulkhead athwartships the rivets in two vertical joints were completely torn away.

Between the 2nd and 3rd longitudinal frames, and below the wing passage bulkhead, both the inner and outer bottoms were completely blown away for a length of 12 feet and a height of 4 feet. The vertical and horizontal frames between the two bottoms had kept their position unchanged, and excepting that the bracket plate by frame No. 6 was bent, cracked, and torn away, the damage they had sustained was limited to some comparatively slight bending. The open hole formed in the target measured 76 square feet in outer bottom, and 60 square feet in inner bottom.

Comparing the effect of this torpedo with the 7th, 33 lbs. of dynamite ; with the latter charge the breach was made at the cost of the bottom plates as well as the vertical and longitudinal frames, which were completely torn asunder and strained ; with the gunpowder charge, only the bottom plates were broken through, whilst the plates whose directions were nearly parallel to the lines of explosive effect were but little affected.

Experiments at Portsmouth, England, 1874–75.—The object of these experiments was to ascertain the effect of 500 lbs. gun-cotton torpedoes exploded at various distances from a target representing the double bottom of H.M.S. *Hercules.*

They were carried out in Stokes Bay, under the supervision of officers belonging to the torpedo department of the Royal Engineers, and a torpedo committee, composed of naval and military officers.

The *Oberon,* the vessel chosen for these experiments, was fitted with a double bottom, representing as nearly as possible that of the *Hercules* without the armour; also with a surface condenser, and its connections; a donkey Kingston feed-valve; and athwartship water-tight bulk-heads, which divided the ship into seven water-tight compartments. The outer skin was composed of $\frac{3}{16}''$ and $\frac{1}{8}''$ iron plates. In her starboard side at different points were fixed forty-four crusher gauges, and over each side were suspended six shots, each fitted with a crusher gauge.

Displacement of the *Oberon* about 1100 tons.

The ship was anchored head and stern. Her mean draught of water during the experiments was 11 feet.

1st Experiment.

Torpedo :—500 lbs. of gun-cotton, in discs saturated with water, and enclosed in an iron cylindrical case, $34'' \times 30'' \times \frac{1}{4}''$, with arched ends; the primer consisted of two dry discs, and two detonators. It was placed 101′ horizontal from the target, and opposite the condenser on the starboard side; 47′ below the surface of the water, on the ground.

Effect of explosion :—No damage was done to the hull, or condenser, but light articles, such as bunker plates, gratings, tank lids, &c., were displaced.

2nd Experiment.

Torpedo :—As in first experiment. It was placed on the ground, 80′ horizontal and opposite the condenser on the starboard side, 48′ below the surface of the water.

Effect of explosion :—No damage was done to the hull, or condenser, but the bunker plates, gratings, &c., were displaced to a greater extent than in the previous experiment.

3RD EXPERIMENT.

Torpedo :—As before. It was placed on the ground, 60' horizontal, and opposite the condenser on the starboard side ; 47' below the surface of the water.

Effect of explosion:—No damage was done to the hull. Flanges of the condenser inlet pipe were cracked, and several of the joint bolts were broken. The condenser had been thrown up bodily, and had torn away its holding down bolts; but it was not as well secured as it would have been had it formed part of the machinery of a ship.

4TH EXPERIMENT.

Torpedo:—As before. It was placed on the ground, 50' horizontal, and opposite the condenser on the starboard side ; 48' below the surface of the water.

Effect of explosion :—Outer bottom on starboard indented over a length of about 100', being forced in between the frames; maximum indentation, $\frac{3}{4}''$. Many bracket frames were disturbed, and outer angle iron of water-tight longitudinal was started for a length of 30', and made to leak slightly. The shell of the condenser was cracked in two places, 3' and 5' in length. Bolts securing condenser, and flanges of pipes and valves, were all more or less damaged. Condenser was rendered unserviceable.

5TH EXPERIMENT.

Torpedo:—Same charge as before, but the primer consisted of four dry discs, and two detonators. It was placed 28·5' horizontal, opposite No. 9 frame, on the starboard side, 36' from the stern ; 48' below the surface of the water, and 22' from the ground.

Effect of explosion :—Bow observed to be lifted several feet. Several angle irons and bracket frames were cracked, and numerous rivets in outer bottom were broken off. The outer bottom on the starboard side was indented between the frames, and brackets were disturbed over a space of 100 feet ; inner bottom uninjured.

6TH EXPERIMENT.

Torpedo :—As in previous experiment. It was placed on the ground, 28·5′ horizontal, opposite No. 36 frame on the starboard side, and 30 feet from the stern ; 49·5′ below the surface of the water.

Effect of explosion :—Several plates in the outer bottom were cracked, and outer bottom made to leak in several places, owing to the fractures in the plates, rivets being started, and seams being opened. Considerably more damage was effected than in previous experiment, but inner bottom still remained uninjured.

7TH EXPERIMENT.

Torpedo :—As in the 5th experiment. It was placed on the ground, immediately under the edge of the outer bottom, 39¾′ from the target, and opposite No. 18 frame, 70′ from the stern ; 50′ below the surface of the water.

Effect of explosion :—Outer and inner bottom broken entirely asunder at No. 19 frame on the starboard side, and between Nos. 16 and 17 on the portside. A fracture was caused in the outer bottom extending from the shelf plate to upper edge of strake next the keel on the starboard side, and from the shelf plate to upper edge of flat keel plate on the port side. A fracture was also caused in the inner skin extending from the topside to the outer edge of the garboard strake on the starboard side, and from the topside to upper edge of garboard strake on the port side ; this including a fracture of the keel at No. 17. The vertical keel, the longitudinals, as well as numerous bracket plates and angle irons, were broken, and about 2000 rivets in the outer bottom were rendered defective.

The outer bottom was indented over a considerable length, the indentation being greatest between the frames, and the maximum being 8 inches. The inner bottom was not indented or damaged, with the exception of the fractures before mentioned.

Experiments at Pola, Austria, 1875.—These experiments were carried out to determine the effect of very heavy charges of dynamite on an iron pontoon fitted with a double bottom, similar to that of H.M.S. *Hercules.*

Target :—An iron pontoon 60′ long and 40′ beam, with circular ends and fitted with a double bottom, also a condenser and two Kingston valves.

1st EXPERIMENT.

Torpedo:—617 lbs. of dynamite. It was 62′ horizontally from the keel, 53′ actual distance from the side, and opposite amidships, 40·5′ below the surface of the water, and 20′ from the ground.

Pontoon:—Draught of water 19′, and moored in 62′ of water.

Effect of explosion:—The pontoon moved away bodily a distance of 13 feet; a few rivets in the outer bottom were started, and the outer skin was slightly indented between the frames; the maximum indentation being 1·5″. No other damage was sustained by the hull. Several of the screws securing the flanges of the Kingston valves were slightly loosened.

2nd EXPERIMENT.

Torpedo:—585 lbs. of dynamite. It was placed 60′ horizontally from the keel, 48′ actual distance from the side, and opposite amidships; 36′ below the surface of the water, and 42′ from the ground.

Pontoon:—Draught of water 19·5′, and moored in 74′ of water.

Effect of explosion:—The pontoon, which had been more rigidly moored than in the previous experiment, was moved bodily away a distance of 4 feet. Many rivets were loosened, and a few connecting the angle irons were sheared; also the outer skin was slightly indented. No damage was done to the condenser or Kingston valves.

Experiment in the Sea of Marmora, 1875.—This experiment was carried out by Turkish officers attached to their naval school at Halki, an island in the Sea of Marmora, about eight miles from Stamboul. It consisted in destroying a Turkish schooner by the explosion of an 100-lb. gun-cotton mine in contact with her, moored in 58 feet of water, and 10 feet beneath the surface.

Experiment at Carlscrona, Sweden, 1876.—This experiment was a continuation of those previously carried out in 1874-75, and which have been detailed at page 224, &c.

Target:—The same as had been used for the previous experiments (1874-75), and which had been thoroughly repaired.

EXPERIMENT.

Torpedo:—660 lbs. of gunpowder, enclosed in a buoyant cylindrical $\frac{1}{4}″$ steel case with domed ends, and contained in an inner $\frac{1}{16}″$ steel case. It was ignited by two Von Ebner fuzes placed in a charge of ¼ lb. of gunpowder and enclosed in a glass bottle. It was placed 5′ horizontally from the water line, 23·75′ actual distance from target, and opposite No. 5 (middle) frame of target, 29′ below the surface of the water.

Effect of explosion :—The ship was moored in 54′ of water. She was lifted by the explosion, rolled over to port, and then settled to starboard, sundry large pieces of timber being thrown up in the air. The outer bottom of the target was broken through above the second longitudinal frame, from the fourth to the seventh frames laterally, and from the top of the target to the second longitudinal frame vertically, the hole made measuring about 9′ high by 12′ wide, or about 100 square feet in area. The inner bottom was also broken through between the top of the target and second longitudinal frame, and between the fourth and seventh vertical frames, the hole made being about 75 square feet in area. The bracket frames within the damaged area were but little damaged. The wing passage bulkhead was broken through opposite to Nos. 5 and 7 frames, the holes made being respectively 18 and 17 square feet in area. Through these holes the force of the explosion had made its way to the horizontal iron deck, forming the top of the target, which was completely broken through a little abaft No. 5 frame, the hole made measuring about 100 square feet in area. A piece of this iron deck, weighing, with the iron fastenings attached to it, about 1650 lbs., was thrown 16′ against the upper deck beams. The target below the second longitudinal frame was comparatively but little injured. The outer bottom was indented and cracked in one or two places, but the inner bottom was uninjured. In addition to the damage to the target, the ship herself sustained serious injury, eleven of the lower deck beams, with their knees being broken (six being broken completely across). The main keel immediately under the target was also opened at the scarf, and the back of the ship was apparently broken. The hull had given out laterally to such an extent as to prevent the ship being taken into dock.

Experiments at Portsmouth, England, 1876.—The object of the following experiments was to determine the effect of comparatively small charges of gunpowder and gun-cotton exploded in actual contact with an ironclad, as would be the case in a torpedo attack either with locomotive towing or spar torpedoes.

Target:—the same as used in the experiments of 1874–5, which have been detailed at page 229, &c., viz., the *Oberon* fitted to represent H.M.S. *Hercules* without the armour. Her mean draught was 11', and she was moored in 26½' of water. The *Oberon* had been placed in a thorough state of repair.

1st Experiment.

Torpedo:—60 lbs. of gun-cotton in slabs, saturated with water. Total weight of charge 75 lbs. It was enclosed in a $\frac{1}{4}''$ iron case with cast iron ends. It was placed at 15' actual distance from the nearest side of the case to the target, and opposite No. 4 frame on the port side, 10' below the surface of the water.

Effect of the explosion:—The effect upon the vessel was unappreciable. This charge represented the large Whitehead fish torpedo, and its position corresponded to that of this torpedo when striking a net at a small angle with the keel.

2nd Experiment.

Torpedo:—The Harvey towing torpedo, charged with 66 lbs. of gunpowder, primed with gunpowder, and fired by means of an electric fuze. It was placed at 3' actual distance from the target, measuring from the centre of the torpedo, and opposite No. 4 solid frame on the starboard side, the vertical axis of the torpedo being at right angles to the vessel's side, 9¼' below the surface of the water.

Effect of explosion:—This and the two following torpedoes were fired simultaneously. The outer bottom was blown in from the upper edge of the flat keel plate to the underside of the water-tight longitudinal, and fore and aft from No. 2 to No. 6 frames; an area 16' × 8⅝'. Flat keel plates were broken between No. 2 and No. 4 frames, and the 4th strake of the bottom plating was broken, and the frames for that space blown in. Two holes were blown through the inner bottom, measuring respectively 2' × 2' and 7' × 1', making the total area of the inner bottom destroyed, 11 square feet.

3rd Experiment.

Torpedo:—33 lbs. of granulated gun-cotton, saturated with water; total weight of charge being about 41 lbs. It was enclosed in a

¼" iron case, 12½" × 12" × 12½", the primer being 2½ lbs. of slab gun-cotton, included in the 33 lbs. It was placed at 4' actual distance from the target, measuring from the centre of the case, and opposite No. 30½ solid frame on the starboard side ; 9¼' below the surface of the water.

Effect of explosion :—Outer bottom blown in from upper edge of the lower longitudinal to the lower edge of the upper longitudinal between Nos. 28 and 32 frames; an area of 18 × 11 feet. The butts of the flat keel were started and the plating broken across No. 30½ frame from the flat keel plate to the upper deck. Shelf plate at Nos. 30½ and 32½ frames was broken. Nos. 29, 30, and 31 frames were blown in from first to third longitudinal; lower longitudinal from No. 28 to 31 also blown in. Two holes were blown through the inner bottom, measuring respectively 6 .× 1·5' and 5' × ·25', making the total area of inner bottom destroyed 10 square feet. A steam launch with steam up and outrigger torpedo gear in place, one pole being rigged out, was placed with the stem of the boat 22' horizontally from the torpedo. She was uninjured and shipped very little water.

4th Experiment.

Torpedo :—31 lbs. 14 oz. of gun-cotton in slabs, saturated with water, total weight about 40 lbs. It was enclosed in a ¼" iron case 12½" × 12½" × 6" ; primer being 20 oz. of gun-cotton, included in the 31 lbs. 14 oz. It was placed at 4' actual distance from the target measuring from the centre of the case, and opposite No. 30½ solid frame on the port side ; 9¼' below the surface of the water.

Effect of explosion :—Outer bottom and frames injured in a similar manner to that described in the third experiment. Outer angle irons of the 1st, 2nd, and 3rd longitudinals were started in the wake of the broken place. A hole was blown through the inner bottom, measuring 9·5' × 1', or about 10 square feet in area. The bolts of the outer bottom plate of stern post much open, and at Nos. 16 and 17 on the port side the upper two strakes were buckled and the shelf plate started.

A steam launch, arranged in the same manner as in the fourth experiment, was uninjured, and shipped but little water.

Experiments with Countermine.—The following experiments have been carried out in England and other countries to ascertain some reliable data for countermining operations.

1st Experiment.

Experiments in the Medway, England, 1870.—Countermine :—432 lbs. of compressed gun-cotton, enclosed in a $\frac{3}{16}$" iron case. It was moored at a depth of 37' below the surface of the water.

Submarine mines :—A series of similar cases containing coal dust, &c., were moored at distances of 50' to 100' from the countermine, and 37 feet below the surface.

Effect of explosion :—The submarine mine at 80' distance was completely destroyed ; the dome of its circuit closer was dented in.

2nd Experiment.

Countermine :—As before, but moored 27' below the surface.

Submarine mines :—As before, but moored at distances of 70' to 120' from the countermine, and 27' below the surface.

Effect of explosion :—The submarine mine case at 120' distance was dented, but remained water-tight ; the copper guard of fuze piece collapsed, and the earth connection of the fuzes was ruptured ; the dome of its circuit closer was dented.

3rd Experiment.

Countermine :—As before, but moored 47' below the surface.

Submarine mines :—As before, but moored at distances of 70' to 200' from the countermine.

Effect of explosion :—The submarine mine case at 200' distance was dented, but it did not leak.

1st Experiment.

Experiments at Stokes Bay, England, 1873.—Countermine :—500 lbs. of gun-cotton, enclosed in a $\frac{3}{16}$" iron case. It was placed on the ground, in 47' of water.

Submarine mines :—Six ground mines, $\frac{1}{4}$" thick cases, fitted with circuit, 10' below the surface, at distances of 100' to 200' from the countermine.

Effect of explosion :—Submarine mines at 100' and 120' distance were destroyed, and their circuit closers thrown out of adjustment ;

submarine mines at 140' and 170' distance were much bulged, and leaked, and their circuit closer spindles were bent; submarine mine at 200' distance was uninjured, but its circuit closer was thrown out of adjustment.

2ND EXPERIMENT.

Countermine:—100 lbs. of gun-cotton enclosed in case, thickness No. 12 B. W. G. It was moored 10' below the surface, in 35' of water.

Submarine mines:—Five similar mines placed at same depth, at distances of 50' to 150' from the countermine.

Effect of explosion:—The submarine mine at 50' distance showed continued or dead earth, two screws broken, and its case dented; the other mines were uninjured.

1ST EXPERIMENT.

Experiments at Carlscrona, Sweden, 1874.—Countermines:—226 lbs. of dynamite, enclosed in a case $17\frac{1}{2}'' \times 20'' \times \frac{1}{8}''$. It was moored $9\frac{3}{4}'$ below the surface, the depth of water being 41 feet.

Submarine mines:—(a) cast iron ground 600 lb. mines, dome shaped, $48\frac{3}{4}'' \times 21\frac{1}{2}'' \times 2''$; ($b$) cylindrical cases, wrought iron, empty, $11\frac{1}{2}'' \times 11\frac{1}{2}'' \times \frac{1}{8}''$; ($c$) cylindrical cases, wrought iron, charged, $11\frac{1}{2}'' \times 11\frac{1}{2}'' \times \frac{1}{8}''$; ($d$) cylindrical cases, wrought iron, $30\frac{1}{4}'' \times 30\frac{1}{4}'' \times \frac{1}{4}''$; ($e$) spherical cases, wrought iron, $32\frac{1}{2}'' \times \frac{1}{8}''$; ($f$) spherical cases, tinned steel, $12'' \times \frac{1}{8}''$.

Effect of explosion:—(b) mine, at 34' distance, was destroyed, and one at 92' distance was slightly bulged; (c) mine, 58' distance, mouthpiece injured and case leaky; (d) mine, 244' distance, a rivet started.

2ND EXPERIMENT.

Countermine:—As before, but moored at $29\frac{1}{4}'$ below the surface; depth of water, 41 feet.

Submarine mines:—As before.

Effect of explosion:—(a) mine, at 146' distance, split in two; (b) mine, 34' distance, destroyed; at 49' distance, fractured; at 68' distance, indented but not fractured; (c) mine, 58' distance, case much bulged, and leaky; (d) mine, at 244' distance, rivets started, case half full of water; at 195' distance, sunk, several rivets started; (e) mine, at 195' distance, bolt loosened; (f) mine, at 68' distance, not injured.

3rd Experiment.

Countermine :—453 lbs. of dynamite, enclosed in a case, $24\frac{1}{2}''$ ×
$28\frac{1}{4}'' \times \frac{1}{4}''$. It was moored $9\frac{3}{4}'$ below the surface; depth of water as
before.

Submarine mines :—As before.

Effect of explosion :—(b) mine, at 49′ distance, sunk and not recovered; at 58′ distance, very much indented; (c) mine, at 58′ distance,
case much indented and leaky; (f) mine, at $48\frac{1}{2}'$ distance, uninjured.

4th Experiment.

Countermine :—As before, but moored $29\frac{1}{4}$ below the surface.

Effect of explosion :—(a) mine, at 195′ distance, completely stove in;
(c) mine, at 58′ distance, case indented but charge dry; (e) mine, at 175′
distance, slightly leaky; (f) mine, at $48\frac{1}{2}'$ distance, upper half indented
in three places. It was also discovered during the above experiments
that submarine mines charged with dynamite can be caused to explode
by the detonation of a charge of the same explosive, at distances from
it considerably beyond those at which the cases themselves are
damaged by a similar charge. To prevent the foregoing, it is necessary
to pack the dynamite very carefully, using at the same time special
precautions.

CHAPTER X.

THE ELECTRIC LIGHT—TORPEDO GUNS—DIVING.

ELECTRIC lights combined with fast steam launches as guard boats and specially constructed torpedo guns, such as the Nordenfelt and Hotchkiss machine guns, are at the present time the only *truly practicable* means afforded to a man-of-war of defending herself against the attack of torpedo boats, whether these latter are armed with the spar, fish, or towing torpedo; the torpedo gun sinking the boats after the electric light and guard boats have detected their approach and position.

As has been before stated, nets, shields, booms, &c., placed around a vessel of war, must, however slightly constructed, affect to a considerable degree her efficiency, by decreasing her power of moving quickly in any desired direction, which is essential to the utility of such a vessel in time of war; and thus on electric lights, guard boats, and torpedo guns must the safety of ships in future wars really depend, when attacked by torpedo boats.

The Electric Light.—The phenomenon of the *Voltaic arc* was first discovered by Sir Humphry, then Mr., Davy at the beginning of the present century. The following is an account of the matter as given by him in his " Elements of Chemical Philosophy " :—

" The most powerful combination that exists, in which number of alternations is combined with extent of surface, is that constructed by the subscription of a few zealous cultivators and patrons of science in the laboratory of the Royal Institution. It consists of 200 instruments, connected together in regular order, each composed of ten double plates arranged in cells of porcelain, and containing in each plate thirty-two square inches; so that the whole number of double plates is 2,000, and the whole surface 128,000 square inches. This battery, when the cells were filled with sixty parts of water, mixed with one part of nitric acid, and one part of sulphuric acid, afforded a series of brilliant and impressive effects. When pieces of charcoal about an inch long and one-sixth of an inch in diameter were brought near each other (within the thirtieth or fortieth part of an inch), a bright spark was produced, and more than half the volume of the charcoal became ignited to whiteness, and by withdrawing the points from each other, a constant discharge took place through the heated air, in a space equal at least to four inches; producing a most brilliant ascending arch of light, broad, and conical in form in the middle. When any substance was introduced into this arch, it instantly became ignited. Platina melted as readily in it as wax in the flame of a common candle ; quartz, the sapphire, magnesia, lime, all entered into fusion ; fragments of diamond, and points of charcoal and plumbago, rapidly disappeared, and seemed to evaporate in it, even when the connection was made in a receiver exhausted by the air pump ; but there was no evidence of their having previously undergone fusion."

The philosopher also showed that, when the Voltaic or electric arc is produced in the exhausted receiver of an air pump, the phenomena are as brilliant in character, and the charcoal points can be more widely separated, thus proving that the electric light is quite independent of the oxygen of the air for its support.

Owing to the crude nature of the Voltaic batteries of that day, and also to the great expense of maintaining a large battery of that nature, nothing practical resulted from Davy's discovery of the electric or Voltaic arc. Professor Faraday, the great physicist, by his discovery of the principle of magneto-electricity, has enabled the electric light to be brought into practical use. As early as 1833 Pixii applied the principle practically in the construction of a magneto-electric machine with revolving magnets ; he was followed by Laxton, Clark, Nollet, Holmes, and others, who made machines with fixed magnets. In 1854 Dr. Werner Siemens, of Berlin, introduced the "Siemens' Armature," which, from its compact form, permitted a very high velocity of rotation in an intense magnetic field, giving powerful alternating currents, which, when required, were commutated into one direction.

The latest improvement has been that from the magneto-electric to the dynamo-electric machine. It is due to both Dr. Siemens and Sir C. Wheatstone. Induced currents are directed through the coils of the electro-magnets which produce them, increasing their magnetic intensity, which in its turn strengthens the induced currents, and so on, accumulating by mutual action until a limit is reached.

Siemens' Electric Light.—The following is a description of Messrs. Siemens Brothers' dynamo-electric light apparatus, which, for use on board ship against boat torpedo attacks, &c., is equal, if not superior, to any similar apparatus yet produced, and which is extensively used in the German and other European navies. This apparatus was one of many others experimented on by Dr. Tyndal and Mr. Douglas, M.I.C.E., for the Trinity House.

Dr. Tyndal says : " I entirely concur in the recommendation of Mr. Douglas, that the Seimens machine recently tried at the South Foreland be adopted for the Lizard. From the first I regarded the performance of this handy little instrument as wonderful. It is simple in principle, and so moderate in cost that a reserve of power can always be maintained without much outlay. By coupling two such machines together, a great augmentation of the light is moreover obtainable."

Principle.—When a closed electrical circuit is moved in the neighbourhood of a magnetic pole, so as to cut the lines of magnetic force, a current is generated in the circuit, the direction of which depends upon whether the magnetic pole is N or S; it also depends on the direction of motion of the circuit, and according to the law of Lenz, the current generated is always such as to oppose the motion of the closed circuit.

All magneto-electric and dynamo-electric machines are based on the principle stated above, and are subject to many modifications.

The name *dynamo*-electric machine is given to it, because the electric current is not induced by a *permanent magnet*, but is accumulated by the mutual action of electro-magnets and a revolving wire cylinder or armature. It is found that, as the dynamic force required to drive the machine increases, so also does the electric current ; it is therefore called a dynamo-electric machine.

Description.—In the machine here described, of which Fig. 164 is an elevation, Fig. 173 a part elevation, and Fig. 165 a longitudinal section, the electric current is produced by the rotation of an insulated conductor of copper wire or armature coiled in several lengths, 8, 12, 16, &c., up to 28, and in several layers, longitudinally, upon a cylinder with a stationary iron core $n\,n'\,s\,s'$, so that the whole surface of the armature is covered with longitudinal wires and closed at both ends, as in Fig. 165. This revolving armature is enclosed to the extent of two-thirds of its cylindrical surface by curved soft iron bars NN_1, SS_1.

The curved bars are the prolongations of the cores of the electro-magnets $EEEE$. They are held firmly together by screws to the

Fig. 164.

sides or bottom of the cast iron frame of the machine, making it compact and strong.

The coils of the electro-magnet form with the wires of the revolving armature one continuous electric circuit, and, when the armature is caused to rotate, an electric current (which at first is very feeble) is induced by the remanent magnetism in the soft iron bars and directed through the collecting brushes into the electro-magnet coils, thus strengthening the magnetism of the iron bars,* which again induce a still more powerful current in the revolving armature.

---

* In wrought iron there is always some residual magnetism; there is therefore no necessity to start the magnetism with a permanent magnet.

The electric current thus becomes stronger and stronger, and the armature therefore revolves in a magnetic field of the highest intensity, the limit of which is governed by the limit of saturation of the soft iron.

At each revolution the maximum magnetic effect upon each convolution of the armature is produced just after it passes through the middle of both magnetic fields, which are in a vertical plane passing through the axis of the machine (i. e. $N_1 S_1$ in Fig. 173). The minimum effect is produced when in a plane at right angles to it, i. e. horizontal.

According to the law of Lenz already referred to, when a circuit starts from a neutral position on one side of an axis towards the pole of a magnet, it has a direct current induced in it, and the other part

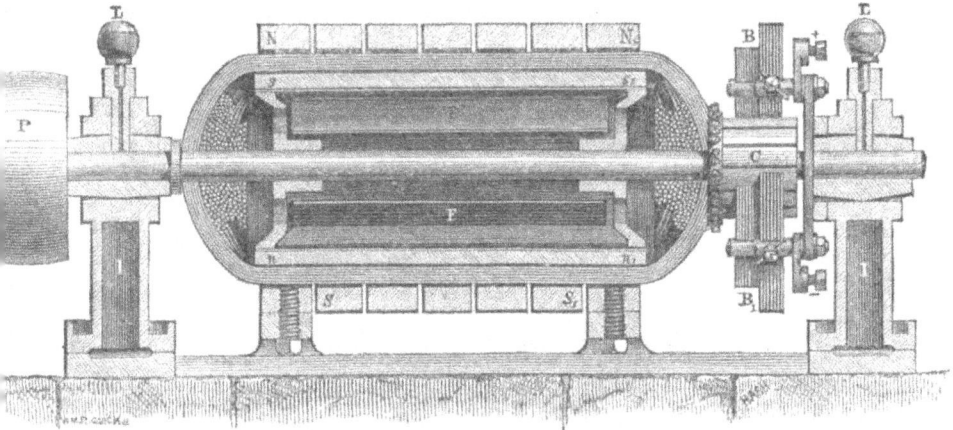

Fig. 165.

of the circuit which approaches the opposite pole of the magnet has an inverse current induced in it; these two induced currents are, however, in the same direction as regards circuit. A similar current will also be induced in all the convolutions of wire in succession as they approach the poles of the magnets.

These currents, almost as soon as they are induced, are collected by terminal rollers or brushes B, usually the latter, placed in contact with the commutator in the position which gives the strongest current. The position giving the strongest current gives also the least spark, so that when there are no sparks at the commutator the best lighting effect is produced. Fig. 166 shows position of brushes when the armature revolves in the direction indicated by the arrow.

The circumference of the revolving armature is divided into an even number of equal parts, each opposite pair being filled with convolutions of insulated wire wound parallel to the axis of the armature.

The ends of these wires are brought to a commutator and connected to the segments either by screws or by soldering.

The brushes collect the electric currents as they are induced, which is nearly constant and continuous.

The collecting brushes are combs of copper wire placed tangentially to the cylindrical commutator, and press lightly upon it with an elastic pressure.

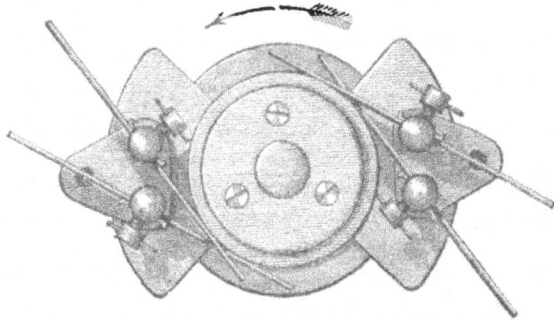

Fig. 166.

Power and Light produced.—An increase of the armature speed produces a corresponding increase in the current produced, but not in the same proportion. The current increases more rapidly than the speed, and could be made to reach any intensity but for considerations explained below. With increase of current there is also increase of heat.

The speed for continuous work must not be taken too high, because the heat developed at high velocities might destroy the insulation of the coils of the electro-magnet. The speed given for this machine produces no such injurious heating effect.

The strength of the current is also influenced by the resistance of the electric lamp and its leading wires. With an electric lamp in a circuit of proper resistance the armature should revolve at the rate given in the following Table. The heating will then reach its maximum, which is very moderate, in about three hours after which there will be no further change.

TABLE.

Size.	Number of revolutions of armature.	Intensity of light in standard candles.	HP (actual) to drive.
Medium	800 to 850	4,000 to 6,000	3½ to 4

The intensity of the unassisted light is given in standard candles. The standard here used is a stearine candle consuming 10 grammes per hour.

Regulation.—From the fact that a closed circuit rotating in a magnetic field experiences resistance to its motion which a broken circuit does not, motive power to any extent is only required when the circuit is closed. An interruption of the current is therefore equivalent to removing the load from the motor, which for mechanical reasons may be injurious to it and for electrical reasons to the dynamo machine.

The sudden interruption of the circuit of the large machine produces an electric tension so dangerously high as to strain or destroy the insulation of the machine. When contact is again made after such interruption, the increase of speed resulting from the interruption causes a momentary current of great intensity, accompanied by sparks at the commutator.

In order that the light may be quite steady the speed should be as uniform as possible. As too high an increase of speed may result in temporary extinction of the light, it ought never to be permitted. The motor should therefore be provided with a good and sensitive governor, that will keep the speed perfectly uniform however the steam and load may vary. A large and heavy fly-wheel is also very useful in keeping the speed nearly uniform during change of load.

Although the circuit, when the machine is in full action, should never be suddenly interrupted, interruption arising from the extinction of the light is *not* dangerous, because it is always preceded by a decrease in the strength of the current. When it is desired to divert the current into another circuit it is advisable to stop the machine. Although in practice with small machines this is rarely done, with large machines it is necessary.

Self-acting Shunt.—For great security, especially with the two machines coupled together, where the electric current is strong and the light equivalent to about 14,000 candles, it is advisable to insert in the circuit a self-acting shunt.

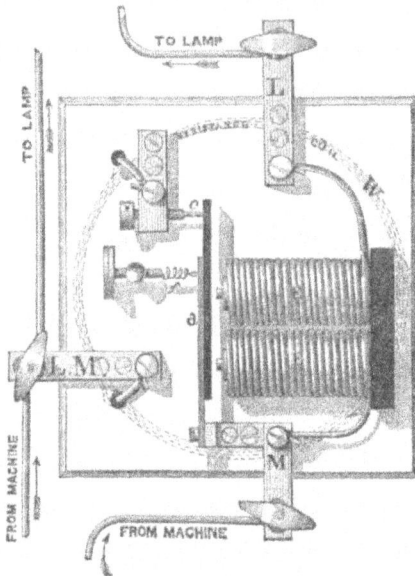

Fig. 167.

This is placed between the lamp and machine and connected to both leading wires. Its principle is as follows :—

The terminal M, Fig. 167, is joined by a short connecting wire to one terminal of the machine. The terminal L M is connected to the remaining terminal of the machine and also to one of the lamp terminals.

The terminal L is connected to the other terminal of the lamp.

The shunt contains a small electro-magnet E mounted upon a square wooden slab or baseboard with its armature a, a contact c, and, below the slab, a resistance coil W, which is equal to the resistance of the electric arc of the light, about 1 S. u.*

As long as the lamp is burning well, the current circulates in the coils of the electro-magnet, and the armature a being strongly attracted, there is no contact at c. The resistance coil W is therefore not in electrical circuit. When the light is extinguished the current in the coils of the electro-magnet ceases, and the armature is withdrawn by the spring f making contact at c. This offers to the electric current a path through W of equal resistance to that of the lamp, and the current is subjected to scarcely any change, so that the motor has practically no cause to alter its rate.

When the carbon points of the lamp again touch, the electric current returns to them, breaking contact at c, re-establishing the former conditions.

Direction of Rotation.—The armature may revolve in either direction. If it becomes necessary to drive it in the opposite direction to that for which the machine has been made, it is only necessary to reverse

* Siemens' unit.

the brushes, placing their points in the direction of motion, and to change two of the wire connections, which operations can be effected in a few minutes. Fig. 166 shows the position of brushes for one direction of rotation and Fig. 168 that for the other.

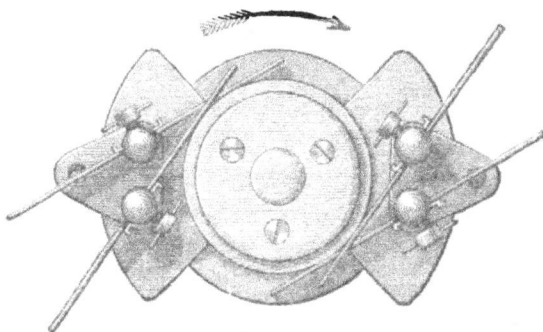

Fig. 168.

Conducting or Leading Wires.—The leading wires are usually of copper of high electrical conductivity. They must be insulated from one another the whole of their length and not placed too close together. As their resistance affects the intensity of the light very much, the section must be carefully proportioned to the distance of the lamp from the machine.

The best practical result is obtained when their resistance together with that of the lamp is equal to the total internal resistance of the dynamo machine. Wires of various sizes are therefore required.

Decrease in strength of the current caused by a leading wire of too high resistance can be overcome by a higher velocity, which is obtained only by increased motive power, but if the wire is much too small, it will become heated. The proper remedy is to increase the sectional area of the leading wire.

Bright sparks should never be allowed to appear at the commutator and brushes, as sparks result from a rapid burning of the metallic parts. They can easily be avoided by properly inclining the two arms which carry the brushes.

The position of the brushes yielding the least spark at the commutator is that giving the highest intensity of light in the electric arc.

The commutator should, while in motion, be freely oiled, to prevent the brushes wearing away too rapidly. The sticky oil should from time to time be removed by washing with paraffine oil or benzoline.

Wear and Tear.—The chances of stoppage so common to the old forms of electric light apparatus have in this form been reduced to a minimum, and now do not exceed those that arise with machines generally. The Trinity House Report states that the Siemens' machine worked well for a month without any necessity for stopping. The brushes are the only parts which wear away, and they are very easily replaced.

In thick weather they should be connected in what is called parallel circuit (or parallel arc, or for "quantity"), because it has been found that when they are so arranged the intensity of the electric light produced exceeds by some twenty per cent. the intensity of the sum of the two when worked separately. Thus the two machines, giving respectively a candle power of 4,446 and 6,563 when worked separately (total 11,009), have given when coupled up in parallel circuit a light equivalent to 13,179 candles; just as in telegraphy it has been found that the rate of sending can be increased from 20 to 25 per cent. when the apparatus is coupled up in parallel arc. For this reason it is usual to employ two machines of medium size instead of one machine of large size. The intense light so produced is also much more uniform than from one large machine.

Automatic Electric Lamp.—Automatic electric lamps have been constructed with spring clockwork to cause the carbons to approach one another to a certain point, when, by means of an electro-magnet, the clockwork is checked, and the carbon points are allowed to burn away to such a distance that, by the decrease of current, the clockwork is released and the carbons caused to approach again. With such lamps the clockwork has been a source of trouble, and it is liable to get out of order.

Siemens' Patent Electric Lamp.—The lamp here described is actuated without clockwork; it also automatically separates the carbons after they have approached too closely or touch, and, by this combined action of approaching and separating, the carbon points are kept at a proper distance apart, and a steady light is obtained.

The working parts are represented in the diagram Fig. 169, and at Fig. 170 is shown the size employed on board ship.

E is the horse-shoe magnet with the armature A placed in front of its poles a short distance from them. A regulating screw b with the spiral spring f is attached to the lever A', forcing it against the stop d, and withdrawing the armature from the poles of the electro-magnet.

When a current traverses the coils of the latter of sufficient strength to attract the armature and overcome the tension of the spring f, contact is made at c, which diverts the current from those coils. The consequent release of the armature breaks contact at c, the armature is again attracted, and this action is repeated, producing a vibrating motion of the lever and armature, which continues as long as there is sufficient current to overcome the tension of the spring.

The spring pawl s at the upper end of the lever A', and oscillating with it, actuates a ratchet-wheel u, which is in gear with a train of wheels and the carbon holders; it thus opposes their tendency to approach by pushing them apart, tooth by tooth, until the current is so much weakened by the increased length of electric arc that the armature and lever cease to oscillate enough to move the teeth of the ratchet-wheel, and it rests near the stop d.

. While in this position the spring pawl is released from the ratchet-wheel and the preponderating weight of the

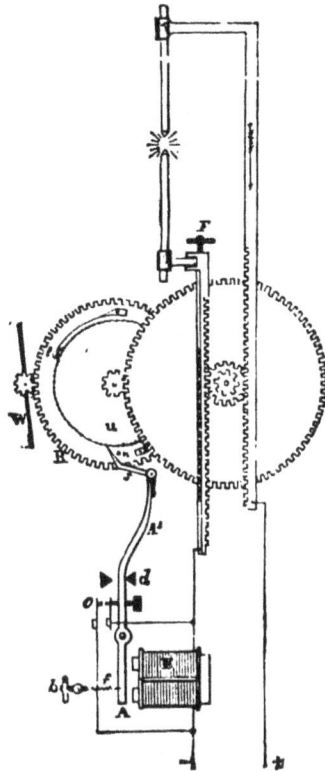

Fig. 169.

upper carbon holder causes the carbon points to approach again. Increase of current follows decrease of resistance, the armature again oscillates, and this cycle of action is continuously repeated.

When in action the movements of the carbons are scarcely perceptible, but when, by any external cause, the carbons are separated so as to extinguish the light, they immediately run together until they touch, when they ignite and separate to a proper working distance by means of the electro-magnet above described.

The only operation requiring attention in the use of this lamp is the adjustment of the tension of the spring f. When this tension is once regulated to the current at disposal, the lamp will continue to give a steady light as long as the current remains uniform.

S

The relative rate of consumption of the two carbon points differs. The positive carbon burns away rather more than twice as quickly as the negative carbon.

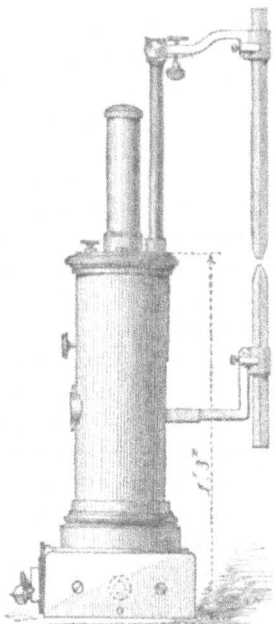

Fig. 170.

The duration of the light depends mainly on the lengths and sizes of the carbons.

Provision is made in this lamp that the rack which supports the negative carbon may be made to gear either into the teeth of the same pinion as that of the positive carbon, or into one of about half the size. By these means the light, when once focussed in a reflector, will remain in focus as long as the carbons last, whether permanent or reversed currents are employed.

Besides its twofold application, the lamp is very compact, is simple in construction, and therefore not likely to get out of order, and it is capable of being regulated with great precision.

There is no spring to be wound up. The contact need not be cleaned, as the sparks are scarcely perceptible.

By removing two screws in the outside casing, all the chief working parts can be easily removed and inspected.

Carbons are made from the hard carbon deposited in the interior of gas retorts, also from graphite. Various sizes, both square and round in section, of from 5 to 20 mm. in diameter, are used in the electric lamp according to the intensity of the electric current. Those commonly employed are from 10 to 12 mm. in diameter.

The carbons supplied with the Siemens patent lamp are coated with a thin film of copper. This enhances the cost somewhat, but it greatly improves the result, as the carbons burn longer, and do not split, when so coated.

By coating them the resistance is diminished, except at the points, so that all the heat is concentrated in the electric arc, and a brighter light is the result.

When two dynamo machines are coupled together (see page 248), to give a very powerful current, the sizes up to 20 mm. are required.

The consumption varies a little, but the average is from 3 to 4 inches per hour.

Concentration of Light.—Two kinds of concentrating apparatus are supplied in combination with the automatic lamp, both of which are capable of giving a powerful parallel beam, which will reach to an enormous distance, and are well adapted for naval purposes. The one

Fig. 171.

kind consists of a parabolic reflector of stout metal, its concave surface being silvered and burnished. The apparatus is mounted with a ball-and-socket joint upon a wooden stand, as shown in Fig. 171.

The other kind is the Fresnel catadioptric lens or holophote, Fig. 172, which may be substituted for the reflector, and gives a more powerful beam than one given by reflection. The lens is surrounded by a metal case or lantern, in which is placed the electric lamp upon a slide for focussing. Behind the carbon points a hemispherical reflector is placed, to catch all the back rays, and reflect them back through the lamp focus. The entire lantern is capable of revolving on horizontal rollers, and swings upon pivots. Two handles are placed at the back to manipulate it.

As the electric arc is much too bright to be looked into with the naked eye, both concentrating apparatus are supplied with a lens, called a focus or flame observer, by means of which an image of the burning carbons is thrown upon small screens at the back, so that the

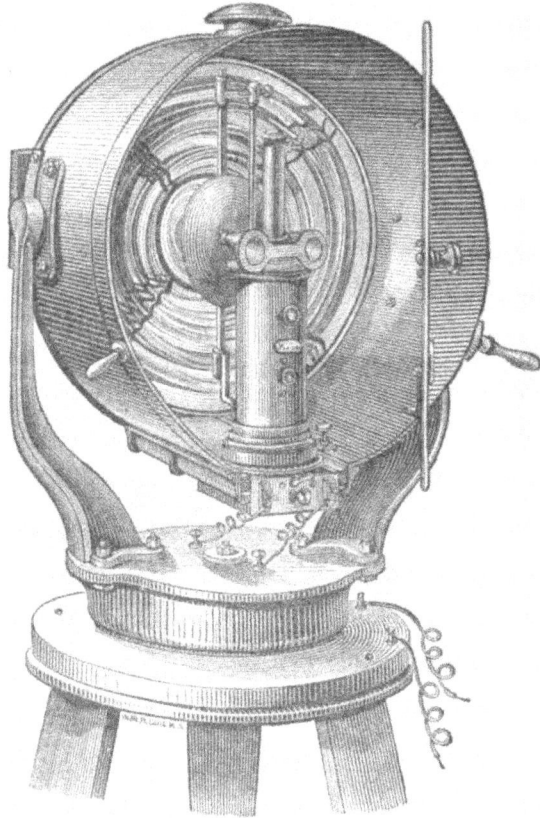

Fig. 172.

lamp can be easily adjusted without fatigue to the eye. The **focus** observer is shown on the lamp in holophote, Fig. 172.

Precautions.—Before starting the apparatus, the electric **lamp** terminals and those of the dynamo machine must be *connected up* by means of the leading wires provided with each set of apparatus. The terminals are marked C and Z respectively, and they should be connected, C of machine to C of the lamp, and Z of the machine to Z of the lamp, in order that the electric current may be sent in the proper direction through the carbons of the lamp. Should it, however, be found that the top carbon (which should consume twice as fast as that of the bottom one) does not consume so fast as the bottom one, it may be assumed that the dynamo machine has reversed its poles, and the leading wires will consequently require changing across. This reversal of poles, though possible, is of *very rare* occurrence.

The dynamo-electric machine should not be driven without its proper leading wires to lamp and lamp being connected up, or at least an external resistance equivalent to that of the lamp (which is approximately one Siemens' unit) must be inserted. In other words,

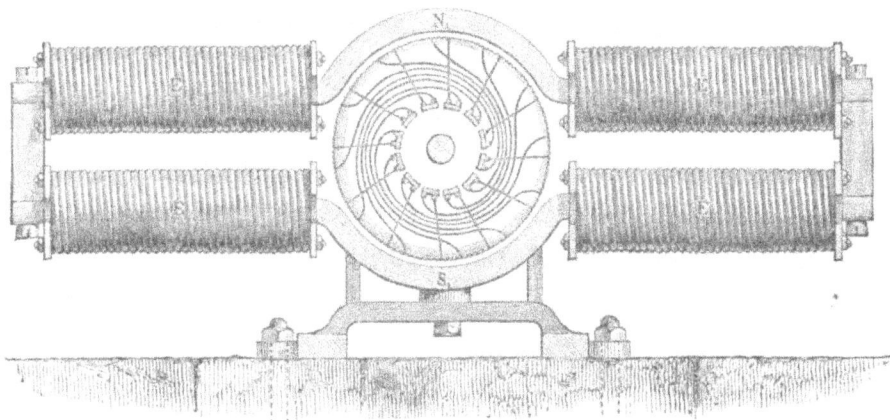

Fig. 173.

the machine must not be driven when a wire of small resistance connects the two terminals C and Z. This is expressed more briefly by saying the machine must not be *short-circuited*. If it is short-circuited when in motion the electric current becomes so powerful that it will leap from segment to segment of the commutator, where very bright and large sparks will be seen, and if continued would destroy the insulation, thus weakening the current generated.

The leading wires should never be disconnected suddenly while the machine is revolving at its full speed, as such a sudden interruption will produce an intense spark, which will burn the ends of the wire where the contact is suddenly broken. When it becomes necessary to disconnect the wires, the belt should be pushed on to the loose pulley by means of the striking gear, or the steam engine should be stopped.

It may be here stated that all connections should be cleaned bright and screwed tightly, to ensure perfect metallic contacts being made.

Coupling two Machines.—At Fig. 174 is shown a diagram of how to make the connections when coupling two machines in parallel circuit. *MM′, m, m′*, represent the ends of the wires of the electro-magnets; *BB′* are the branches; *C* and *Z* are the terminals of each machine respectively.

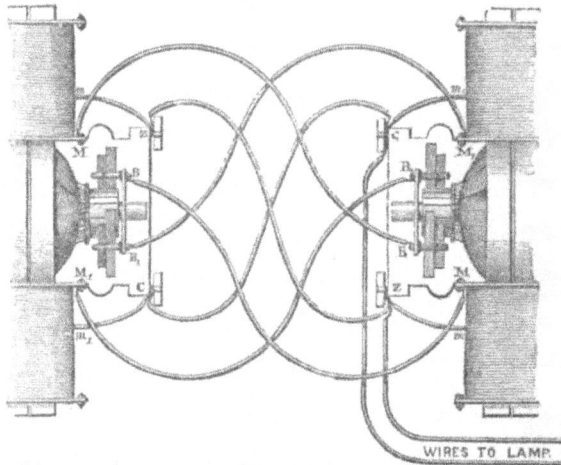

Fig. 174.

The three ways in which the various wire connections of these machines are joined up, and which are enough for all ordinary purposes, are given below in paragraphs (*a*), (*b*), and (*c*).

(*a*) When the machine is working *singly* and revolving in the direction indicated in Fig. 166, the following connections are made :—

$$M \text{ is connected with } B,$$
$$M' \quad\quad ,, \quad\quad B',$$
$$m \quad\quad ,, \quad\quad Z,$$
$$m' \quad\quad ,, \quad\quad C,$$

and the leading wires of the lamp are connected with *C* and with *Z* as explained.

(*b*) When working *singly* and revolving in the direction indicated in Fig. 168 :—

M is connected to B',
M'　　　" 　　　B,
m 　　　" 　　　Z,
m' 　　　" 　　　C.

Thus the only change necessary when the machine is to be driven in the opposite direction to that for which it is made, is to disconnect at B the wire from M to B and at B' the wire from M' to B', and to cross them. The machine will then be connected as above (b).

(c) When working *two* machines in parallel circuit, as in Fig. 174, they must be connected as follows (that on the left of the page being called the first machine, and that on the right the second machine):—

C of first to C of the second.
Z 　　" 　　Z 　　　"
M 　　" 　　B 　　　"
B 　　" 　　M 　　　"
M' 　　" 　　B' 　　　"
B' 　　" 　　M' 　　　"

and then connect C and Z of the second machine with the leading wires of the lamp.

The connections m to Z and m' to C in each machine are the same as in cases (a) and (b). They do not require to be altered, and may therefore be left out of consideration in all three cases (a), (b), and (c). The whole of the connections here indicated can be quickly made by means of a cross-bar commutator or switch, which is supplied with the machines in cases where such changes are likely to be required frequently. This is usually attached to a wall, leading wires being taken to it from the dynamo machines separately, and others from the switch being led to the electric lamps.

The leading wires from machine to lamp should, whenever possible, be kept *separate*, to prevent them rubbing together and making contact. A distance of two inches is quite sufficient to prevent accidents of any kind.

When the leading wires are erected in places where they are likely to rub and chafe against hard substances, it is advisable to enclose each wire separately in india-rubber tubing at all the points where they are likely to be rubbed. This becomes very important on board ship, where everything is in motion, and special care is in consequence required.

Some dynamo machines are coupled direct to the crank shaft of the steam engines; they require the same kind of attention as others, that is to say, they should be driven at a uniform speed, should be well oiled as well as the steam-engine, and they should be kept clean and free from sharp grit.

Application.—The electric light used in the case of a *direct* attack by torpedo boats, without the assistance of guard boats, will not prove of much assistance, on account of the very small space covered by the beam of light, and therefore if the direction of attack is not exactly known, the beam of light must be kept continually sweeping round the horizon on the chance of picking out the attacking boats, and thus, while flashing in one direction, they may be approaching in another, and effect their deadly mission.

Every man-of-war should be fitted with at least three electric lights, whereby the above-mentioned want of space covered would be to a considerable degree obviated.

If a powerful beam of light be thrown in a particular direction, and there kept stationary, all boats or vessels crossing its path at a distance not exceeding 1600 yards from the ship using the electric light, would become distinctly visible to observers placed behind the light; these vessels remaining visible as long as they continue in such a position that the beam of light acts as a background to them. Under very favourable circumstances, the distance at which the above effect may be observed is much increased.

The parabolic reflector extends only about an arc of 33° at 540 yards' distance from the light.

One defect of this form of reflector is, that it is rapidly dimmed by spray, rain, and by the particles given off by the carbons.

The catadioptric lens, or holophote, gives a far more powerful but a more concentrated beam than the parabolic reflector. By means of such a beam of light, a torpedo boat may be discerned at about one mile distance. By adding divergent lens to the holophote, a less powerful and less concentrated beam of light will be thrown out; in this case about 20° of surrounding water would be well illuminated at about 900 yards' distance, while without the divergent lens there would be only about 5° so illuminated but far more brilliantly.

The distance at which objects can be detected by the electric light depends on their size and *colour*, more particularly on the latter.

The observer should as a rule be well removed from the light.

In the case of an electric light being thrown on the observer, the vessel, &c., using it would to that observer be invisible, the light only being seen; also when directed on any particular object, surrounding objects would be thrown into shade.

The electric light will be found very useful for signal purposes by fitting a plane mirror in front of the catadioptric lens; so arranged that it be turned to any desired angle to the axis of the beam of light. By altering the angle of the mirror, the reflected beam of light can be swept from the horizon on one side, through the zenith, to the horizon on the other side. The time of passing the zenith being equivalent to the long and short flashes of the usual night signal code.

In addition to using the electric light to detect the approach of torpedo boats, it may be used by the boats themselves to prevent the attacked vessel from discerning them.

In turret ships, electric lights may be so arranged that the instant an object is brought into the field of the beam of light, the turret guns will be bearing on it.

One great disadvantage of electric lights is the impossibility of protecting them from the enemy's fire, and this is a defect that cannot be eradicated, though it may be lessened, by manipulating them from the tops of a ship.

Torpedo Guns.—Hitherto by torpedo guns has been meant small guns mounted on carriages so constructed that a shot may be fired into the water only a few feet from the ship's side, or mitrailleuses, Gatlings, &c. Here the term is applied only to machine guns, which are constructed to fire either volleys, or, extremely rapidly, single shot, each shot of which would be capable of *penetrating* and *sinking* torpedo boats, such as Messrs. Yarrow and Thornycroft are daily launching from their yards. Of such weapons there are at present only two, viz., the "Nordenfelt" and "Hotchkiss" gun. The former has, after very exhaustive experiments, been adopted by the English, Austrian, Swedish, and other naval authorities, while the latter has been adopted by the French government.

Nordenfelt Torpedo Gun.—This gun, as it at present is constructed, consists of four barrels of 1 inch calibre.

The barrels are fixed in a horizontal plane, and are not moved during the firing; and the movement of the lever, the loading, the firing, and the extracting are all performed in the same plane, so that the *elevation* of the gun is not disturbed by the firing.

The gun is fed by means of hoppers, each of which contains ten rounds per barrel, *i. e.*, forty shots.

The continuous supply of cartridges, as well as the firing and extracting, are all performed by one motion of the lever, thus enabling the gunner to use his left hand to lay the gun.

A volley of four shots can be fired at the same moment, or one shot can be fired separately. Eight shots can be fired in $1\frac{1}{4}$ seconds; twenty, thirty, or forty shots can be fired at a rapidity of two hundred shots per minute without difficulty.

The recoil being taken up by the whole framework of the gun does not in the least disturb the aim.

The entire mechanism of the gun can be opened up without undoing a single screw, in less than 20 seconds.

All the four spiral firing springs can be taken out, without opening the rest of the mechanism, in $1\frac{1}{2}$ seconds.

All the parts of the mechanism are made interchangeable, so that reserved parts can at any time be substituted. The gun can be placed on half cock, so that the strikers do not act; and for further security the lever can be locked. The carrier block, without which the gun cannot be fired, is loose, and can be taken away, in case it becomes necessary to abandon a gun, which is thus made useless to the enemy.

The bullets are solid steel, weighing about $\frac{1}{2}$ lb. At 1760 yards at right angles this gun will penetrate a $\frac{3}{16}$ inch steel plate, which represents the thickness of the plates of a torpedo boat.

At 200 yards at right angles it will penetrate one $\frac{3}{16}$ inch steel plate placed in front of a $\frac{1}{2}$ inch steel plate with a space of 3 feet between them, this target representing the plates and boiler of a torpedo boat.

At the same distance, at 30° angle against the line of fire, it will penetrate a $\frac{1}{2}''$, $\frac{1}{4}''$, or $\frac{3}{16}''$ steel plate.

The holes in some instances are from 6 to 11 inches in length, and $2\frac{1}{2}$ inches in height. Angle of depression 20°, of elevation 30°, and of direction 360°.

Weight of the gun $3\frac{3}{4}$ cwt., and weight of carriage $2\frac{1}{2}$ cwt.

Hotchkiss Torpedo Gun.—This gun consists of a group of five barrels, revolving on a central shaft, a breech block, containing the firing mechanism, a feeding hopper, and the necessary hand crank for training and firing. The gun is mounted on trunnions attached to a vertical column, which rests in a suitable socket bolted to the ship's side; by this means a universal motion is obtained.

The essential difference between this and the Nordenfelt gun is, that the *barrels* and mechanism are put into rotatory motion.

Another point of difference is that single shots only can be fired, and not a volley, as in the Nordenfelt gun.

With the Hotchkiss gun, only some thirty shots can be fired in one minute at an advancing torpedo boat. The weight of the Hotchkiss steel shot is about 1 lb., but owing to the low velocity of the gun, its penetrative power is little more than that of the Nordenfelt $\frac{1}{2}$ lb. bullet.

The object to be gained in firing at an attacking torpedo boat is to sink her, and not merely to kill or disable her crew, for supposing the attack to be made with a contact spar torpedo, and the boat to have reached within 300 yards' distance from the ship, then, even if all the crew (probably two or three men) were disabled or killed, the boat would, if not sunk, still carry out its work of destruction; therefore the projectiles to be used under such circumstances should be only those capable of penetrating a torpedo boat's plates, *i. e.*, solid steel shot, not shells.

Diving.—In laying down and in picking up submarine mines, divers will be found extremely useful; also in clearing a passage in a river, &c., of an enemy's torpedoes in time of war. During the late Turco-Russian war, the harbour of Soukoum Kaleh taken by the Turks was *popularly* supposed to have been cleared of its mines by native divers (Lazees), but as the torpedoes so captured were never seen at Stamboul, it must have been a stretch of imagination; probably such would have been done, had there been any mines in the harbour to clear away.

The following is a general description of Messrs. Siebe and Gorman's improved diving apparatus.

The apparatus consists of

    1. An air-pump.
    2. The diving dress.

3. The breast-plate.
4. The helmet.
5. The boots.
6. The crinoline.

Air-pump.—This improved air-pump consists of two double action cylinders, each cylinder capable of supplying about 135 cubic inches per revolution. The advantage of this air-pump is, that it can supply air to two divers, working independently and at different levels, each diver being in direct connection with one of the cylinders. The air-pipes are in lengths of 45 feet and 30 feet, made of vulcanised india-rubber with a galvanised iron wire imbedded; this protects from corrosion, and allows the air to pass through the pipes with less friction.

Diving Dress.—The diving dress is made of solid sheet india-rubber, covered on both sides with tanned twill; it has a double collar, the inner one to pull up round the neck, and the outer one of vulcanised india-rubber to go over the breast-plate and form a water-tight joint. The cuffs are also of vulcanised india-rubber, and fit tightly round the wrist, making, when secured by the vulcanised india-rubber rings, a water-tight joint, at the same time leaving the diver's hand free.

Breast-plate.—The breast-plate is made of tinned copper, and has a valve in front, by which the diver can regulate the pressure of air inside his dress and helmet. The outer edge of the breast-plate is of brass, and is secured by screws to the outer collar of the dress.

Helmet.—The helmet is made of tinned copper, and has a segment bayonet screw at the neck, corresponding to that of the breast-plate, which enables the helmet to be removed from the breast-plate by one-eighth of a turn. It has three strong plate glasses in brass frames, protected by guards; two oval at sides, and a round one on the front; the front one can be unscrewed, to enable the diver to give and take orders. At the side is an outlet valve, which, by inserting a finger, the diver can close, and so rise to the surface. The valve allows the foul air to escape, and prevents the entrance of the water. An elbow tube is securely fitted on the helmet, to which is fixed an inlet valve, to which the air-pipe is attached. The inlet valve is made that the air can enter, but in case of a break in the air-pipe it cannot escape.

The front and back weights are of lead, heart-shaped, and weigh about 40 lbs. each.

Boots.—The boots are made of stout leather, with leaden soles, and are secured over the instep by a couple of buckles and straps. Each boot should weigh at least 20lbs.

Crinoline.—The crinoline or shackle is used for deep water; it is placed round the body and tied in the front of the stomach: being supported by braces, it affords protection to the stomach, and enables the diver to breathe more freely.

Ladder.—An iron ladder should be provided with stays to bear against the side of the boat from which the diving is carried on, to which may be attached (if working in deep water) an ordinary rope ladder, with ash rounds, and weighted at the end. Some divers have the ladder only 20 feet long, to the last round a rope with a weight attached, which rests on the ground; by that means they descend.

Directions for using the Apparatus.—The ladder having been fixed, the position of the pump should be decided on, and it should be securely lashed by means of the ropes attached to the handles down to a stage, into which the *screw-eyes* should be fastened if necessary; the pump should be placed out of the way of the divers, the men attending on them, and all the men employed. The best position for the pump is facing the head of the ladder, and about six feet from it.

While the diver is dressing, the pump should be prepared for use, the winch handles should be taken out of the pump case, the nipples protecting the crank axles removed, the nuts being replaced on their screws. The nuts for the ends of the crank axles are taken off, the fly-wheel placed on the shaft, and the winch handles put on, and secured by the nuts, which are screwed home with the spanner. The pump is always worked in its case.

The flaps covering the pressure gauges and that at the back of the pump case should be opened, the screw on the overflowing nozzle of the cistern removed, and the cistern filled with water; the caps of the air delivery pipes should be removed, the necessary lengths of air-pipe should be put together carefully with washers in place, and all the screws must be worked home by means of the *two* double-ended spanners. The air-pipes should be tested by holding the palm of the hand to the end of the pipe, till the pressure shown on the pressure gauge is considerably above that corresponding to the depth the diver is to descend.

Dressing the Diver—Crinoline only for Deep Water.—The diver having taken off his own clothes, puts on a guernsey, a pair of drawers, very carefully adjusted outside the guernsey, and securely fastened by the tape round the waist, to prevent them from slipping down, and then a pair of inside stockings. If the water be cold, the diver may put on two or more of each of the above articles. He then puts on the crinoline and woollen cap, drawing the latter well over his ears; some divers find relief from putting cotton saturated with oil in their ears.

The *shoulder pad* is then put on, and tied under the diver's arms. He then gets into the diving-dress, which in cold weather should be slightly warmed, drawing it well up to his waist; he next puts his arms into the sleeves, an assistant opening the cuffs by means of the cuff expanders, or by inserting the first and second fingers of both hands, taking care to keep his fingers straight. The diver, by pushing, forces his hand through the cuff. He puts on a pair of outside stockings and a canvas overall to preserve the dress from injury.

The diver then sits down, and the inner collar of the dress is drawn well up and tied round the neck with a piece of spun yarn, and the breast-plate put on, great care being taken that the india-rubber of the outer collar is not torn in putting it over the projecting screws of the breast-plate. The four pieces of the breast-plate band, which with the thumbscrews had been previously placed for safety in one of the boots, are then put over the outer collar, and secured to the projecting screws by means of the thumbscrews; the centre screw of each plate should be tightened first. It will generally be sufficient if the thumbscrews be screwed up hand-tight, the spanner being only used when necessary. The canvas overall is now adjusted and the boots are put on.

The rings are passed over the cuffs, and the sleeves of the overall are drawn down to cover them. If gloves are to be used, the rings will be put on over them, as well as the cuffs. The helmet (without the front bull's-eye) is then put on; before doing so, the attendant should blow through the outlet valve of the helmet; he can do so by placing his head in the interior, and placing his mouth to the hole where the air escapes. Blow strongly ; if in proper working order, the valve will vibrate. A loop of the life line is placed round the diver's waist, the line brought up in front of the man's body, and secured with a piece of small rope passing round his neck, or to the stud on the helmet. The waist-belt is buckled on with the knife on the left side, the end of the air-pipe being passed from the front, through the ring on the belt on the man's left, and up to the inlet valve on the helmet, to which it is secured ; the upper part of the pipe is then made fast by a lashing to the stud on the left of the helmet. The diver then steps on the ladder, and two men are told off to *man the pump.*

The weights are then put on, the front weight first, the clips being placed over the studs on the breast-plate. The back weights are then put on, and the clip lashings over the hooks on the helmet, and the two are secured to the diver's body by means of the lashing from the back weight, which is passed round the waist, through the thimble beneath the front weight, and tied to the other end of the lashing at the back weight.

When the signalman is sure that all is right, and that the diver understands all the signals, he gives the word *Pump*, and screws the centre bull's-eye into the helmet securely ; this done, he takes hold of the life line and "pats" the top of the helmet, which is the signal for the diver to descend.

Signals employed.—The signalman is the responsible person, and must be very vigilant all the time the diver is down ; occasionally he will give one pull on the life line, and the diver should return the signal by one pull signifying "all right ;" if the signal be not returned, the diver must be hauled up, but if the diver wishes to work without being interrupted by signal, he gives one pull on the line, independently, for "All right ; let me alone." If the signalman feels any irregular jerks, such as might be occasioned by the diver falling into a hole, he should signal to know if he is all right, and if he does not receive any reply, he should haul him up immediately. If the diver from any cause is unable to ascend the ladder, and wishes to be pulled up, he gives four sharp pulls on the life line. If while being hauled up the diver gives one pull, it signifies "All right ; don't haul me any more." The diver should be hauled up slowly and steadily. If the signalman wishes the diver to come to the surface, he gives four sharp pulls on the line, on which the diver should answer " All right," return to the foot of the ladder, and signal to be hauled up.

One pull on the air-pipe signifies that the diver wants more air. *Two* pulls on the life line and *two* pulls on the air-pipe in rapid succession, signify that the diver is foul and cannot release himself, and requires the help of another diver; on receiving such a signal, no attempt should be made to haul the diver to the surface.

The above signals are to be invariably used; but other signals may be arranged as is most convenient for any particular work, as a great variety can be made with the life line and air-pipe. The diver can communicate with the surface by means of a slate.

Further information on this subject, especially with regard to the foregoing diving apparatus, will be found in Messrs. Siebe and Gorman's " Manual for Divers."

CHAPTER XI.

THEORY of Electricity.—The theory most readily understood, and which most satisfactorily explains the various electrical phenomena, is as follows:—

" That every substance and every atom of the world is pervaded by a peculiar, subtle, imponderable fluid which is termed *Electricity*, but which is not known to exist, or remains in a state of *electrical equilibrium*, until evoked by certain causes."

The effect of causing a disturbance of this equilibrium is to increase the normal, or natural, electricity in some particles, and to equally decrease it in other particles, i.e. what one loses the other gains. An excess of natural electricity is denoted by the term *positive*, or mathematical symbol (+), while a deficiency is denoted by the term *negative*, or symbol (—).

Like electricities repel each other.

That is to say, two bodies charged with an excess of, or positive, electricity, being brought together repel each other, neither wishing to increase the excess that has been evoked in them.

Similarly in the case of two bodies charged with a deficiency of, or negative, electricity, neither wish to add to the deficiency already there.

In both these cases there can be no tendency to electrical equilibrium, which is the principle at work. In the former case, there being already too much, more will but increase the disturbance.

In the latter case, further deficiency will but add to the irregularity.

Unlike electricities attract each other.

That is to say, if two bodies, one charged with positive, or having an excess of electricity, the other charged with negative, or having a deficiency of electricity, be brought together, they will attract each other; both being desirous of altering their existing state, the

T

one by decreasing its excess, and the other by decreasing its deficiency of electricity.

In this case, there will be a tendency to equilibrium, caused by attraction. The earth is supposed to be a vast reservoir of electricity, from which a quantity can be drawn to fill up a deficiency, and which is always ready to receive an excess from other bodies. Every body in nature has its own natural quantity of electricity, and when an object is negatively electrified, or has a deficiency in its normal quantity, there is a tendency to receive a supply from any convenient source. Such an object would receive electricity from the earth if means were afforded; and a body *positively* electrified, would tend to part with its excess in the same manner. Where such facilities for establishing electrical equilibrium are afforded, the result is the passage of a *current* of electricity.

Conductors.—Sensible effects can be produced by electricity at great distances from the source, provided there be a medium of communication, that is, good *conductors* to transfer it. When a glass rod is rubbed with a piece of silk, it becomes charged with an excess of, or positive, electricity, and at the same time the silk becomes charged with negative electricity.

The glass rod will retain the positive electricity upon it for some time, unless touched with the wet hand, a wet cloth, a metal, &c., when it will instantly cease to be electrified. The electricity is then said to have been conducted away, and the bodies which allow it to run off the glass are called *conductors* of electricity. Metals, water, the human body, charcoal, damp wood, and many other bodies are conductors.

Those bodies which conduct electricity hardly at all, such as the air, silk, glass, sealing wax, gutta percha, india rubber, &c., are termed *nonconductors* or *insulators*.

Strictly speaking, all substances *conduct* electricity in some degree, and a *nonconductor* is merely a *bad* conductor.

In the following table the bodies are arranged in their order of conductivity, i.e. each substance conducts better than that which precedes it; the first-named body is the best insulator, and the last-named one is the best conductor.

Dry air.	Shellac.
Ebonite.	India rubber.
Paraffin.	Gutta percha.

Resin.	Saline solutions.
Sulphur.	Acids.
Sealing wax.	Charcoal, or Coke.
Glass.	Mercury.
Silk.	Lead.
Wool.	Tin.
Dry paper.	Iron.
Porcelain.	Platinum.
Dry wood.	Zinc.
Stone.	Gold.
Pure water.	Copper.
Rarefied air.	Silver.
Sea water.	

Though two substances are near one another in the above list, they do not necessarily approach one another in their power of conducting. For instance, taking the conducting power of pure silver as represented by the number 100, then

Pure Copper will be equal to 99·9,

Gold will be equal to 78·0,

while Zinc will be only equal to 29·0,

and pure water, which is half-way down the list, will offer 6,754 millions more resistance than silver to the passage of the electric current.

The metals being the best known conductors, are usually employed as the means of transferring the electric current from one place to another.

Electric Circuit.—The conditions attending this operation are different from those of any other known method of transmission.

A complete *circuit* must always be formed by the electric current, i.e. it cannot start from one place *A*, travel to another place *B*, and cease there, but the current must be completed before it can be said to have reached *B*. There cannot be a current of electricity without a means of recombination, which recombination must be at the *source*, or place of original disturbance.

This "place of disturbance" or *source* must be considered as having two sides, i.e. at some spot the normal or natural electrical equilibrium is disturbed, and electricity is separated into too much (positive) on one side, and too little (negative) on the other side. If then no means of recombination be afforded, the electricities remain separated, and no current exists; but if a *conductor* be made to connect the two sides, electricity is set in motion, and a current established. Originally to form a circuit between two stations *A* and *B*, a conducting wire and a return wire were necessary, but in 1837 Steinway discovered that the earth itself answered all the purposes of a return wire, in fact under favourable conditions much better. Thus, to form a circuit between *A* and *B*, a conducting wire is required, and a buried metal plate at *A* and *B*, the earth by these means taking the place of the return wire.

The aforesaid metal plates are technically termed *earth plates*. The greater the size of the earth plates (up to certain limits), the deeper they are buried, and the better the conducting power of the soil surrounding them, the better conductors the plates become, or the less resistance the earth portion of the circuit offers. If either plate be not in communication with the earth, or else be separated from the wire, the circuit is not complete, or, as it is termed, " it is broken," and no current will flow, the signal not made, torpedo not fired, &c.

" *Short*" *Circuit*.—Due to the fact that recombination, or a tendency to equilibrium, is always at work when electricity has been evoked, the conducting path along which the electric current flows must be covered with a nonconducting substance, or, as it termed, " insulated," or else the current would not perform its duty, but escape to earth, and so form what is termed a " short circuit."

A current of electricity always chooses the *easiest path* to effect recombination, or electrical equilibrium.

Insulators, &c.—On land, telegraph wires are as a rule laid above the ground, and therefore require supporting at every few yards; this is done by means of posts, and as these are formed of substances which are conductors of electricity, the wires require to be insulated from them. The insulators generally employed for such purposes are cup-shaped pieces of porcelain, or pottery, fixed to the head of the telegraph posts. By means of these insulators, the current of electricity is prevented from escaping to the earth by the post conductors.

A certain amount of leakage, or loss of electricity, must occur at each of these posts, as there is no such thing as a perfect insulator. When the wires are laid on the ground or under ground, or under water, they are insulated by covering them with gutta percha, india rubber, &c., and any loss of current is thus prevented.

Methods of generating Electricity.—For the purposes of torpedo warfare there are two methods of evoking electricity, viz.—

1.—By *chemical action.*

2.—By *friction.*

By Chemical Action.—*Chemical action* is the chief source of free electricity, the representative of which is the galvanic, or Voltaic, battery.

The electricity so generated is also termed dynamical electricity, due to there being a constant electric current, so long as the poles of the battery producing it are kept closed ; the electricity being thus in a *dynamic* or moving state.

By chemical action is signified that which occurs when two or more substances so act upon one another as to produce a third substance differing altogether from the original ones in its properties, or when one substance is brought under such conditions that it forms two or more bodies differing from the original ones in their properties.

Definition and Properties of a Voltaic Cell.—The *Voltaic* cell consists of an insulating jar, containing a liquid, in which are placed two plates or pieces of dissimilar metals ; the liquid must be composed of two or more chemical elements, one of which at least tends to combine with one or other of the metals, or *with both in different degrees.*

By a Voltaic *battery* is meant a number of cells above one ; this term, however, is often applied to a single cell when working by itself.

A "*simple* Voltaic cell," "element," or "couple," consists of two metals placed in a conducting liquid. If two metals—for instance, zinc and copper—are placed in water slightly acidulated, without touching each other, no effect is apparent ; but if they be made to touch, bubbles of hydrogen gas are formed over the copper plate, and continue forming these until the plates are separated. After being in contact for some time, the copper plate will be found unaltered in weight, but the zinc plate will have lost weight, and the portion so lost will be found in the liquid in the form of sulphate of zinc. The same effects are also produced by connecting the two plates by means of some conducting substance, instead of placing them in contact.

Zinc is invariably employed as one of the metal plates, on account of the ease with which it dissolves in dilute acids; and the greatest results are obtained when the second metal plate is not acted upon at all by the liquid, for then the whole effect due to the oxidation of the zinc plate is obtained ; but when the second plate is also chemically acted upon, then only the effect due to the difference between the two chemical actions is obtained, for, as will be explained further on, they each act in directly opposite directions.

Voltaic Current.—The Voltaic current makes its appearance under the general laws of electrical action.

When a body charged with an *excess* of, or *positive*, electricity, is connected with the earth, electricity is transferred *from* the charged body to the earth; and similarly when a body is charged with a *deficiency* of, or *negative*, electricity, is connected with the earth, electricity is transferred *from* the earth to the body.

Generally whenever two conductors in different electrical conditions are put in contact, electricity will flow from one to the other. That which determines the direction of the transfer is the relative *potential* of the two conductors. Electricity always flows from a body at *higher potential* to one at *lower potential*, when the two are in contact, or connected by a conductor. When no transfer of electricity takes place under these conditions, the bodies are said to be at the *same potential*, which may be either *high* or *low*. The *potential* of the earth is assumed to be *zero*.

Definition of Potential.—" The *potential of a body or point, is the difference between the potential of the body or point, and the potential of the earth.*"

Difference of potential for electricity is analogous to difference of level for water. Now, since, when a metal is placed in a vessel containing a liquid, electricity is produced, the liquid becomes of a different potential to the metal, each being electrified in an opposite way; and therefore, as above stated, there being a *difference* of potentials, electricity will tend to flow from one to the other.

This is evidence of a *force* being in action, for there can be no motion without some force to produce it.

Electro-motive Force.—*Electro-motive force* is the name given to a peculiar force to which is due the property of producing a difference of potentials. When it is said that zinc and water produce a definite electro-motive force, what is meant is, that by their contact a certain definite difference of potentials is produced.

The *electro-motive force* of a Voltaic element may be termed its *working* power, in the same way as the pressure of steam is the working power of a steam engine, though this is not to be considered as the real source of power, which, as will be seen, is uncertain. Due to the difference of potential of the metal and the liquid, a current of electricity will flow from one to the other, causing the chemical decomposition of the liquid, and the reaction may be taken as the origin of the power employed.

But while the expenditure of energy (which is necessary to produce a *force*) is accounted for by taking the chemical action as the source of power, the preceding cause of this chemical action, viz. the flowing of the current of electricity due to the difference of potential of the metal and the liquid, must also have first involved the expenditure of energy; thus the real source of power is very uncertain.

Electrolytes.—As before stated, a Voltaic cell consists of two plates of dissimilar metals, which must be immersed in a liquid composed of two or more chemical elements, one of which at least will combine with one or other of the metals, or both in a different degree. Those liquids which are thus decomposed by the passage of a current of electricity are termed *electrolytes*.

The elements, then, forming the electrolyte may have chemical affinity for both metals, though in a greater degree for one than the other.

"Oxygen" is the most important element of an electrolyte, and to the *affinity for oxygen of the metals* is the magnitude of the result and effect.

Terms Electro-positive and Electro-negative.—All metals have a definite relation to each other as to the potential which any one may have when brought into contact with another. Thus, when zinc is brought into contact with copper, the former has a potential positive to the latter, i.e. a current of electricity will tend to flow from the zinc to the copper. The metals may be so placed in a list that each one would be positive to any of those that follow it; it is then said to be electro-positive to them, and they are electro-negative to it. As those metals which are electro-positive to others have a greater affinity for oxygen, and those that are electro-negative to others a less affinity for this element, the terms electro-positive and electro-negative signify, in effect, greater or less affinity for this element. Conversely, oxygen will combine more readily with the former than with the latter.

The following list shows the commoner metals arranged in electro-chemical order.

+ Zinc.
Lead.

Tin.
Iron.
Antimony.
Copper.
Silver.
—Gold.

Take the case of a Voltaic cell composed of zinc and copper plates immersed in water.

The passage of electricity through the water will decompose it into its elements hydrogen and oxygen, the latter having an affinity for both the plates, but considerably more so for the zinc plate.

Then, an electro-motive force will be generated at each metal, and these forces will act in opposition to each other, but the greater strength of the one will overcome the weaker, and the real power of the electric current will be the difference between the two.

Definition of "Elements."—The battery plates are termed the positive and negative *elements.* A Voltaic battery has two *poles*—a positive and a negative—which are the terminations of the plates.

Direction of Current.—The course of the current in a Voltaic cell is as follows :—*Within* it leaves the electro-positive plate (or element), and flows to the electro-negative plate, but *outside* the cell (or as it were on its return path) it flows from the positive *pole* to the negative *pole.* The current always leaves the battery by the positive *pole*, and thus the copper is the negative *element*, but the positive *pole*, because the current leaves the battery by it ; and the zinc is the positive *element* because the current begins there, *within* the cell, and the negative *pole* because it ends there, *outside.*

The positive pole is the terminal of the negative plate, and *vice versâ.* There is but one current from a battery, viz. a positive one ; what is called a negative current is merely the positive current passing in the reverse direction from the same pole, that is, the positive pole.

Single and Double Fluid Batteries.—Galvanic batteries may be divided into single fluid and double fluid batteries. The simplest form of galvanic cell practically in use is a single fluid cell, consisting of a zinc and a copper element, immersed in water slightly acidulated by the addition of a little sulphuric acid. In a battery of several cells, the zinc and copper plates are generally soldered together in pairs, and placed in a long stoneware or glass trough, divided into separate cells by means of partitions. By filling the cells with sand, this battery is made more portable, the plates being thus supported, and the liquid prevented from splashing about during transit.

In this form it is called the *common sand battery.*

Action in a Single Fluid Cell.—The following process goes on in the single fluid cell when the circuit is closed—that is, when the battery is set to work.

The water (composed of hydrogen and oxygen) is decomposed by the passage of the electric current, and oxide of zinc is formed. The oxygen of the water having greater affinity for the zinc, leaves the hydrogen. The zinc during the process is being consumed, as coal is consumed when it burns, while combining with the oxygen of the air. This oxide of zinc combines with the sulphuric acid, and forms sulphate of zinc; this salt is found to accumulate in solution in the liquid of the cell. At the same time the hydrogen of the water goes to the negative or copper plate, and gathers over it in bubbles.

The process will be better seen by the accompanying plan of the chemical decomposition and recombinations.

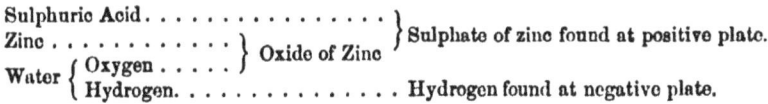

Sulphuric Acid. . . . . ⎱
Zinc . . . . ⎱ Oxide of Zinc ⎰ Sulphate of zinc found at positive plate.
Water ⎰ Oxygen . . . . . ⎱
⎰ ⎱ Hydrogen. . . . . Hydrogen found at negative plate.

No *single fluid* cell can give a constant electro-motive force because of the *polarisation* of the plates.

Definition of the term Polarisation.—The word *polarisation* means that the plates become coated with the products of the decomposition of the *electrolyte,* producing a diminution of current. In the above described battery, the hydrogen gathers on the surface of the copper plate, and an *electro-motive force* is set up which counteracts the electro-motive force producing the current—the copper plate is said to be *polarised.* By the bubbles of hydrogen collecting on the face of the negative plate, the *surface* in contact with the liquid is gradually decreased; thus the plate becomes practically smaller, and a single fluid cell which at starting gave a good current soon shows that it is really weakened. The consequence is that the zinc is consumed extravagantly as well as the acid, and the cell working with poor results. Also the *resistance* of the cell is increased, due to the sulphuric acid, which is added to the water to increase its conductivity, being gradually used up, by combining with the oxide (see plan) and forming sulphate of zinc. Liquids are very bad conductors of electricity; the greater part of the ordinary internal resistance of a battery arises from this cause. The common sand battery is the worst of all batteries as regards constancy of electro-motive force, the *polarisation* being greater in this battery than any other because the gas cannot readily escape. The common copper and zinc cell is the next in order of demerit. The *Smee* single fluid cell, in which the negative plate is a platinum instead of a copper one, is better than the copper zinc cell, because the free hydrogen does not stick to the rough surface of the platinum plate so much as to the copper.

Double Fluid Batteries.—All the defects of the single fluid battery, which are as follows—

1. Diminution of electro-motive force,
2. Inconstancy,
3. Increase of internal resistance,

are remedied in the *double fluid* battery, of which the *Daniell's cell* was the first invented, and is a good example. Of this kind of cell many forms are in use, but the principle is the same throughout. There is a positive and negative element, and the cell is divided into two receptacles for the two fluids. In the most constant form of Daniell cell, the zinc is plunged into a semi-saturated solution of sulphate of zinc, the copper in a saturated solution of sulphate of copper, and these two solutions are separated either by a porous barrier, or by taking advantage of the different specific gravities of the two solutions. By a *saturated* solution is meant a liquid which has dissolved as much of the substance as it possibly can.

The Chemical Action of a Daniell Cell.—The chemical action of this form of Daniell cell is as follows:—

The zinc electrode combines with oxygen; the oxide thus formed combines with sulphuric acid and forms sulphate of zinc. Oxide of copper is separate from the sulphate; and the copper in this oxide is separated from the oxygen. The oxygen of the water is separated at the zinc electrode from the hydrogen, and at the other electrode this hydrogen recombines with the oxygen from the oxide of copper. This alternate decomposition and recombination of the elements of water can neither increase nor decrease the E. M. F. of the cell, the actions being equal and opposite. The result of the series of actions above described is that the sulphuric acid and oxygen of the sulphate of zinc are transmitted to the zinc, combine with it, and form fresh sulphate of zinc; the sulphuric acid and oxygen of the sulphate of copper are transmitted to the zinc set free by the above process, and reconvert it into sulphate of zinc; the copper of the sulphate of copper is transmitted to the copper electrode, and remains adhering to it. The whole result is therefore the substitution of a certain quantity of sulphate of zinc for an equivalent quantity of sulphate of copper, together with a deposition of copper on the copper or negative electrode.* The following is a plan of the process :—

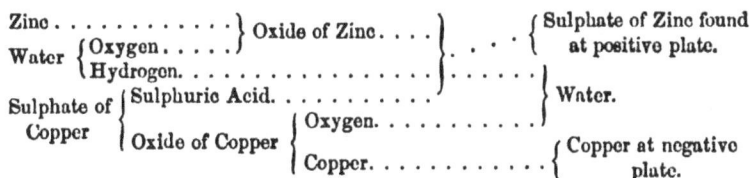

```
Zinc . . . . . . . . . . . }  Oxide of Zinc. . . . }           { Sulphate of Zinc found
Water  { Oxygen. . . . . }                         } . . . {     at positive plate.
        { Hydrogen. . . . . . . . . . . . . . . . }. . . . . . }
Sulphate of { Sulphuric Acid. . . . . . . . . . }           } Water.
   Copper   {                           { Oxygen. . . . . . . . . . }
            { Oxide of Copper {                           { Copper at negative
                              { Copper. . . . . . . . . . {     plate.
```

Description of the " Callaud " and " Marié-Davy " Batteries.—The Voltaic batteries in general use for the different purposes of torpedo warfare have been fully described in Chapter IV., and therefore it will be only necessary here to explain the construction of the " Callaud " and " Marié-Davy " batteries, these being much used abroad in connection with telegraphy.

The *Callaud* cell, named from the inventor, is a modification of the Daniell cell, and is also called a *gravity* battery, the liquids being simply prevented from mixing by the law of gravity forbidding the heavier of the two from rising through the lighter. It consists of a thin plate of copper, which is laid on the bottom of a good *insulating* jar having an *insulated* wire leading up the side, and on this plate are placed crystals of sulphate of copper. A solution of sulphate of zinc is then poured in, and on the top is fitted a zinc plate, which forms the positive element. The vessel must not be shaken, or the sulphate of copper when dissolving will mix with the solution above it.

The *Marié-Davy* cell consists of a carbon electrode in a paste of proto-sulphate of mercury and water contained in a porous pot, and a zinc electrode in dilute sulphuric acid, or in sulphate of zinc.

---

* Jenkins' ' Electricity.'

The Circuit.—In connection with the manipulation of batteries, there is one important item to consider, viz. the *resistance* in the *circuit*, which may be divided into *external* and *internal*.

Resistances.—The *external* resistance in practice is that which exists in the conducting line, and the various instruments connected with it.

The *internal* resistance is that which exists in the battery itself. All known conductors oppose a sensible *resistance* to the passage of an electric current, and the strength of the current, or in other words, the quantity of electricity passing per second from one point to another, when a constant difference of potentials is maintained between them, depends on the *resistance* of the wire on the conductor joining them. A bad conductor does not let the electricity pass so rapidly as a good conductor, that is, it offers more *resistance*.

Resistance in a wire of constant section and material is *directly* proportional to the *length,* and *inversely* proportional to the *area of the cross section.*

The electrical resistance of a conductor must not be considered as analogous to mechanical resistance, such as the friction which water experiences in passing through a pipe, for this frictional resistance *is not* constant when different quantities of water are being forced through the pipe, whereas electrical resistance *is* constant whatever quantity of electricity be forced through the conductor.

Application of Ohm's Law.—Ohm's law, which governs the strength of the current, is expressed by the equation

$$C = \frac{E}{R} \text{ or } R = \frac{E}{C} \text{ or } E = CR.$$

Where C is the strength of the current;

E is the E.M.F. or difference of potentials;

and R is the resistance of the circuit.

In words, *Ohm's law* means that the strength of the current is *directly* proportional to the E.M.F., and *inversely* proportional to the resistance of the circuit.

As before stated, the resistance of the circuit consists of an *external* and an *internal* resistance, therefore when these resistances are separately considered, the equation $C = \frac{E}{R}$ must be converted into

$C = \frac{E}{x + r}$, where x is the external, and r the internal, resistance.

The resistance of the battery or the *internal resistance* depends on the size of the plates and the distance between them, that is, it is *directly* proportional to the distance, and *inversely* proportional to the size.

The *electro-motive* force of a battery is dependent generally on the number of cells joined in *series*, and not on the *size* of the plates. The cells of a battery may be joined in two ways, as follows :—

1. In series : that is, by connecting the negative element of one cell to the positive element of another, and so on.

2. In multiple arc : that is, by connecting negative to negative, and positive to positive; which is the same as increasing the size of the cells.

If the conductor between the battery poles be such that the *external* resistance x may be practically left out, then $C = \dfrac{E}{r}$, and no change in the strength of the current will be effected by adding any number of cells in series, as r will increase equally with E, and therefore C will remain the same; but if under the same conditions the cells be joined in *multiple arc*, then r will decrease as E increases, and therefore C will be increased.

Thus with a short circuit of small external resistance, the strength of the current will be increased by increasing the size of the plates, or by joining the cells in multiple arc, but not in series.

If the conductor between the poles of the battery be such that the external resistance x becomes very great, then $C = \dfrac{E}{x + r}$, where x is very great compared to r. By joining the cells in multiple arc r is decreased, but E and x remain the same, and therefore C is not materially altered, as x is very great compared to r. By connecting the cell in series, r is increased, and so is E, but as r is still very small compared to x, the strength of the current C is increased.

Thus with a long circuit of great *external* resistance, the strength of the current will be increased by joining the cells in series, but not in multiple arc.

When the external resistance x is neither very large nor very small in comparison with the battery or internal resistance r, then the strength of the current C will be increased by adding the cells in series, and also in multiple arc. By the former process the E.M.F. E

is increased more than the resistance of the circuit R or $(x + r)$, and by the latter process, the E.M.F. E is unaltered, whilst the circuit resistance $(x + r)$ is decreased. All the above may be practically demonstrated by the employment of suitable *galvanometers*.

Frictional Electricity.—*Frictional* electricity is produced by the friction of two insulators. There is *no difference whatever in kind* between " Voltaic " and " frictional " electricity.

Comparison with Voltaic Electricity.—The electricity generated by friction possesses a great electro-motive force, producing on even a small conductor a large charge, whereas the electricity generated by the galvanic cell possesses a very small electro-motive force, and produces only a small charge on a small conductor. But when the conductor is large, the electricity produced by the galvanic cell will almost instantaneously charge the conductor to the maximum potential it can produce, the galvanic cell developing an immense quantity of electricity by the chemical reaction; whereas the quantity developed by friction between two insulators is so small, that if it be diffused over a large conductor the potential of the conductor will be very little increased.

The late Professor Faraday has proved that one cell of a Voltaic pile possesses the same quantity of electricity as an ordinary sized frictional machine after being wound round 800,000 times, thus showing the contrast between the qualities of frictional and Voltaic electricity.

The electricity of the frictional machine and that of the galvanic battery may be made to produce the same effect, there being no difference in kind between them. Frictional electricity can be made to pass in a current, but it is comparatively feeble. Again, Voltaic electricity can be made to produce a spark, but under ordinary circumstances it scarcely amounts to anything.

Description of a Frictional Electric Machine.—A frictional electrical machine consists of a vulcanite or glass disc or cylinder, which is made to revolve between cushions or rubbers of leather or silk. By the friction the (silk) rubbers become negatively, and the glass disc or cylinder positively, electrified. The revolving disc immediately after contact with the fixed rubbers passes close by a series of brass points, which are connected with a *condenser*. These points collect the positive electricity of the glass, the rubbers being put to earth. The positive electricity which the glass loses is supplied through the rubber; a stream of negative electricity flows from the rubbers to the earth during the charging of the conductor or condenser ; in other words, the positive electricity flows from the earth to the rubber, whence it crosses to the glass disc and so to the condenser.

Definition of a " Condenser."—A *condenser* is an arrangement for accumulating a large quantity of electricity on a comparatively small surface.

The " Leyden Jar."—The *Leyden jar*, which is the original type of the condenser, or accumulator, consists of a glass jar coated inside and out, up to within a few inches of the mouth, with tinfoil pasted on, but having no connection with each other.   The mouth is usually closed by means of a wooden stopper, through which a brass rod passes, to the head of which is affixed a brass knob, &c., the rod and knob being metallically connected with the *inner* coating by means of a chain.

The " Leyden jar " may be charged either by connecting the *outer* coating to earth (the rubbers of the machine being also to earth), and the *inner* coating to the conductor of the machine ; or else by connecting the outer coating to the rubbers, and the inner coating to the conductor, a complete circuit being necessary to charge the jar as highly as the frictional electrical machine will admit of.

The *conductor* of the machine being charged, also forms a kind of Leyden jar, the conductor in this case being the inner coating, the air, the *dielectric*, and the nearest surrounding conductors, such as the walls of the room, &c., being the outer coating.

Meaning of " Dielectric."—By *dielectric* is meant a nonconducting medium, which in the case of the " Leyden jar " is the glass.

Frictional Electricity very little used for Torpedo Purposes.—Frictional electricity is now seldom used in connection with torpedo warfare, as on account of its very great power, or electro-motive force, a very perfectly insulated cable must be employed, which is somewhat difficult to obtain ; it is also necessary to employ a condenser, which requires a certain time to charge.   For these and other reasons, frictional electricity has been abandoned for the far more practical Voltaic electricity.

Magnetism.—A *magnet* is a piece of steel, which has the peculiar property, among others, of attracting iron to its ends.

Certain kinds of iron ore, termed the *loadstone,* have the same properties. The word "*magnet*" is taken from the country Magnesia, where the loadstone was first discovered.

Magnetism in a body is considered to be a peculiar condition caused by electrical action. Both electricity and magnetism have the power of communicating their properties to other bodies without being in contact with them, i.e. *inducing* the power, which on the bodies being placed far apart becomes insensible.

The "Poles" of a Magnet.—Every magnet has two *poles*, called the *north* and *south* poles. A magnetic steel needle if pivoted on an upright point, or suspended from its centre, will fix itself, pointing north and south; in England the end of the needle pointing to the north is termed the north pole, but in France it is termed the south pole. The reason of this difference is owing to the fact that the north pole of one magnet attracts the south pole of another, and therefore, as the earth is considered as one vast magnet, the end of the magnetic needle attracted to the north pole of earth magnet should be the south pole of the magnet; thus the French south pole in a magnet is the English north pole, and *vice versâ*.

Permanent Magnets.—A piece of steel when magnetised is termed a *permanent* magnet, because it retains its magnetism for a considerable length of time; but soft iron cannot be permanently magnetised.

A piece of soft iron rendered magnetic by induction retains a portion of its magnetism for some time after it has been removed from the magnetic field, by reason of what is called its *coercive force*. This remnant of magnetisation is called *residual magnetism*.

Effect of an Electrical Current on a Magnetic Needle.—A magnetic bar or needle pivoted on its centre will point north and south, but if an electric current is caused to flow along a wire parallel to and either over or under the magnetic needle, the latter will be turned from its position, and remain so as long as the current continues; on the current ceasing the needle will resume its original position.

The magnetic needle can be turned either to the east or the west, according to the direction and course of the electrical current. Thus :—

        Current from S. to N. *over* deflects to W.
        Current from N. to S. *under* deflects to W.
        Current from N. to S. *over* deflects to E.
        Current from S. to N. *under* deflects to E.

The Galvanometer, the " Mirror," and " Thomson's Reflector " all depend on this principle for their usefulness.   These instruments have been fully described in Chapter IV.

The Electro-Magnet.—If a piece of insulated wire be coiled round a rod of soft iron, and a current of electricity be made to pass through the coil, the iron core becomes magnetic as long as the current passes ; when the current ceases the magnetism disappears.

During the passage of the electric current, the iron core possesses all the properties of a magnet.   Therefore if a piece of iron were placed near its poles it would be attracted and released from attraction as often as the current passed or ceased ; and supposing such a piece of iron to be retained by a spring, &c., a series of movements, attraction, and drawing back would be effected.

A piece of iron so arranged is termed an *armature,* and the instrument is called an *electro-magnet.*

The coil of wire must be carefully insulated, or else the electric current will pass through the iron core to earth instead of performing its proper work.

An electro-magnet is much more powerful than a steel magnet of equal dimensions, and depends on the strength of the current by which the magnetism is induced, and the number of turns of wire round the core.   The north and south poles of an electro-magnet are determined by the direction in which the current flows through the wire.

At the *south* pole the current passes *with* the hands of a watch, and at the *north* pole *against* the hands of a watch.

Definition of the " Ohm."—The " ohm " is the standard used for electrical resistance ; it is obtained by observing what effect is produced by a current of electricity on a certain conductor in a certain time.

The ohm is a small coil of German silver wire representing the resistance overcome by a current in a certain time.

APPENDIX.

———◦◦———

McEvoy's Single Main System.—Hitherto in connection with a system of electrical submarine mines, it has been necessary to employ either a single cable between each submarine mine and the torpedo station, or a single cable, termed a "multiple cable," containing a limited number of insulated wires, leading from the station, and branching off from a junction box to each mine, by which considerable cost and complication is incurred. To remedy the above serious defects of such a system, and also to simplify the arrangement of electrical tests, Captain McEvoy has devised and patented the following apparatus; at the firing, or torpedo station, the end of the single main cable, that is, the single core cable leading to the junction box, is connected to a make and break contact apparatus, by which, by the movement of a dial or pointer around a fixed centre, a battery can be successively put in connection with the wire, and disconnected from it, in a somewhat similar manner to Wheatstone's step by step dial telegraphs. In the junction box at the opposite end of the single core main cable is an electro-magnetic apparatus for working a dial or pointer in exact unison with the aforesaid dial or pointer at the torpedo station. This junction box dial or pointer serves as a contact maker to put the wire of the main cable successively in contact with the branch wires leading to the several torpedoes, as it is caused to turn with a step by step motion by the sending of a succession of currents from the firing station.

As the contact maker completes the circuit between the main cable and one of the branch wires, the current passes from the cable through the wire, and through the fuze of that particular torpedo to "earth"; but when any one or other of the torpedoes is to be exploded, the circuit between the main cable and the torpedo wire being completed, it is only necessary to send a current through the main cable of sufficient strength to ignite the fuze, and so explode the mine.

The strength of the current used for giving the aforesaid step by step motion to the junction box dial or pointer is not sufficient to cause the ignition of the fuzes in the torpedoes.

Again, if it be desired that the torpedoes should be so arranged that when any of them are struck by a passing vessel, the fact of its having been struck should be instantly signalled to the firing station. The dial apparatus in the junction box is arranged so that at one point of its revolution, termed the "zero point," all the torpedo branch wires are in circuit with the main cable, and that then a constant current is passing from the firing station through all the circuit closers, and out through resistance coils to "earth." In this case, if one of the circuit closers be struck, and therefore short circuit formed, the current passes direct to earth without going through the aforesaid resistance, and the fact of its having done so is at once indicated by a galvanometer at the firing point, by the movement of which a bell is rung at the station. The operator can then explode such torpedo at once by merely switching in the firing battery.

At the same time the passage of the strong firing current may fuze a connection in the junction apparatus, by which the exploded torpedo is detached, i.e. the direct "earth" connection of such a torpedo is cut off, and the remaining submarine mines are left in proper working order; this effect may also be arrived at by other means.

General Description of Apparatus.—The following is a general description of this exceedingly clever and useful invention :—

At Fig. 176 is shown a diagram view of the apparatus.

A is the instrument at the firing point on the shore or vessel; B is the cable wire led to a submerged box situated near the spot where the several torpedoes are grouped; C is the instrument enclosed in the submerged box; D, D are insulated wires led away from the box to the several torpedoes, there being a separate wire for each torpedo.

Each of the wires D is coupled to one or other of a series of metallic contact pieces E ranged in a circle round the axis of a metallic pointer F, which can be turned with a step by step motion and successively brought into electrical contact with the several contact pieces E. The axis of the pointer is in electrical communication with the wire of the cable. The wire from the cable is first led to the coils of an electro magnet G, and thence passes to the axis of the pointer. H is a magnetic armature in front of the electro magnet G ; when a positive current of sufficient strength is sent through the cable the armature is rocked in one direction, and when a negative current is sent, it is rocked in the opposite direction. From the armature motion is transmitted to a pawl which works into the teeth of a ratchet wheel on the axis of the pointer F, so that by sending a succession of reversed currents of sufficient strength through the cable, the pointer F is turned with a step by step motion and is successively brought into electrical contact with the several contact pieces E.

In the instrument at the firing point a is a handle, by the turning of which a step by step motion is given to the pointer of a dial b and a simultaneous movement to the pointer F of the instrument C in the submerged box. When the handle a has made a half turn it couples one pole of the battery to the cable and the other to the earth connection, and when it has made a complete turn the connections are reversed. The pointer of the dial

PLATE LIV.

Fig. 168.

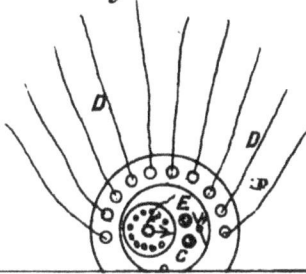

ERRATA.

2.12 (5ᵗʰ line) CH₇ ... 20 - C₆ - ... 5

Page 284, (Middle of page) " Fig. 176 " should be " Fig. 168."

Page 285 (4th line from bottom) " e " should be " d."

7 ... 4 " ?

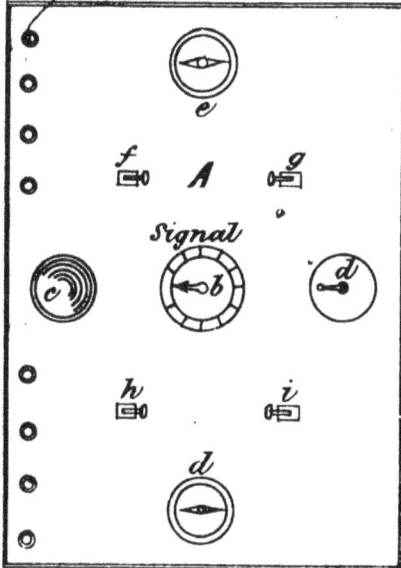

b then moves forward from one division of the dial to the next, and simultaneously the pointer F is turned in unison with it. The operator at the firing point can therefore always see which of the torpedoes is in electrical connection with the wire of the cable, and he can test each torpedo in succession by moving a handle, say at h, to cause the current passing back from the torpedo to pass through a galvanometer at e, and by the movement of the needle of the galvanometer it can be seen whether the resistance of the circuit through this torpedo is in its normal and proper working state.

When the pointer of the dial b is brought to zero, or as it is marked in the drawing to "signal," then the pointer F of the apparatus C is in electrical communication with a contact point which is coupled to all of the branch wires D, and usually the apparatus is left in this condition, the handle a being then locked and prevented from turning by a bolt actuated by a handle at G.

The current from the battery at the firing point then passes to earth through the resistances in all of the torpedoes. If now any one or other of the torpedoes is struck by a passing vessel and the wire from its fuze put directly to earth, so that the current passes freely to earth instead of having first to pass through the resistance, the fact of the current passing freely to earth is notified at the firing point by the movement of the needle of a galvanometer d; the movement of the needle of this galvanometer effects an electrical connection by which a small battery is caused to sound a bell at c. The operator at the firing point can then if he pleases at once fire the torpedo that has been struck by moving a handle at f and coupling up to the wire of the cable a battery of greater strength; the strong firing current will pass to earth through the fuze of the torpedo that has been struck, and will ignite this fuze, but will not affect the fuzes of the other torpedoes, as to pass through these fuzes it has also to pass through resistances which impede its passage and reduce its strength, so that the portion of the current which passes to earth through them is not of sufficient strength to ignite the fuzes.

When the fuze of any one or other of the torpedoes is exploded by the passing of a strong firing current through it, the wire leading from the box C to this torpedo is simultaneously cut off from electrical connection with the contact pin E to which it was previously connected, and this pin is put to earth through a resistance either somewhat greater or less than the resistances in the torpedoes, so that the firing of one or more of the torpedoes does not interfere with the power of being able to turn the pointer F of the apparatus C in unison with the pointer of the dial b.

Afterwards the operator at the firing point can ascertain which of the torpedoes has been fired by passing the pointer of the dial b to each of the divisions of the dial in succession, and ascertaining by the galvanometer e the resistance of the circuit through each of the torpedoes, so that he at once ascertains which torpedo has been put to earth through the greater or less resistance.

The cutting off of the wire D from its contact E when a strong current is passed through it may be effected by the wire being coiled around an iron core forming an electro magnet, which when a strong current is passed through the wire is of sufficient strength to shift the position of a contact apparatus and then effect the required alterations in the connections, but which is not of sufficient strength to effect any change when the weaker currents used for the signalling and testing operations are passed through the wire.

It will be evident that with the above described apparatus any one or other of the torpedoes can if desired be exploded by the operator at the firing point whenever he desires to do so. To effect this he would by turning the handle a bring the pointer of the dial b opposite to the division of this dial; that would indicate that the cable had been brought into electrical communication with the torpedo required to be exploded, and then when it is ascertained by previously adjusted sight points that the vessel is above the torpedo, he can fire the torpedo by passing a strong firing current to the cable.

In this way the apparatus can be used for firing any one or other of a group of sunken torpedoes, or if the torpedoes are buoyant ones, they need not be fitted with apparatus for putting the wire from their fuze directly to earth whenever the torpedo is struck by a passing vessel. The same arrangement of apparatus can also be used for firing any one or other of a number of mines or torpedoes on land and for separately testing the firing mechanism of each mine whenever desired.

Captain McEvoy's single main system will shortly undergo a series of experiments under the supervision of the English torpedo authorities at Chatham, which will most probably result in its adoption by the English government, and also by the principal continental powers.

TABLE*

SHOWING THE VALUE OF THE FRACTIONS A AND B FOR EVERY HALF DEGREE.

Arc.	A $\frac{150+a}{150-a}$	B $\frac{150-a}{150+a}$	Arc.	A $\frac{150+a}{150-a}$	B $\frac{150-a}{150+a}$	Arc.	A $\frac{150+a}{150-a}$	B $\frac{150-a}{150+a}$
a			a			a		
145	59·00	0·017	124·5	10·76	0·093	104	5·52	0·182
144·5	53·54	0·019	124	10·54	0·095	103·5	5·45	0·183
144	49·00	0·020	123·5	10·32	0·097	103	5·38	0·186
143·5	45·15	0·022	123	10·11	0·099	102·5	5·31	0·188
143	41·86	0·024	122·5	9·91	0·101	102	5·25	0·190
142·5	39·00	0·026	122	9·72	0·103	101·5	5·18	0·193
142	36·50	0·028	121·5	9·53	0·105	101	5·12	0·195
141·5	34·29	0·029	121	9·35	0·107	100·5	5·06	0·198
141	32·33	0·031	120·5	9·17	0·109	100	5·00	0·200
140·5	30·58	0·033	120	9·00	0·111	99·5	4·94	0·202
140	29·00	0·035	119·5	8·84	0·113	99	4·88	0·205
139·5	27·57	0·036	119	8·68	0·115	98·5	4·82	0·207
139	26·27	0·038	118·5	8·52	0·117	98	4·77	0·209
138·5	25·09	0·040	118	8·37	0·119	97·5	4·71	0·212
138	24·00	0·042	117·5	8·23	0·121	97	4·66	0·215
137·5	23·00	0·044	117	8·09	0·123	96·5	4·61	0·217
137	22·08	0·045	116·5	7·96	0·126	96	4·55	0·220
136·5	21·22	0·047	116	7·82	0·128	95·5	4·50	0·222
136	20·43	0·049	115·5	7·69	0·130	95	4·45	0·224
135·5	19·69	0·051	115	7·57	0·132	94·5	4·40	0·227
135	19·00	0·052	114·5	7·45	0·134	94	4·36	0·230
134·5	18·35	0·054	114	7·33	0·136	93·5	4·31	0·232
134	17·75	0·056	113·5	7·22	0·139	93	4·26	0·235
133·5	17·18	0·058	113	7·11	0·141	92·5	4·22	0·237
133	16·65	0·060	112·5	7·00	0·143	92	4·17	0·240
132·5	16·14	0·062	112	6·89	0·145	91·5	4·13	0·242
132	15·67	0·064	111 5	6·79	0·147	91	4·08	0·245
131·5	15·22	0·066	111	6·69	0·150	90·5	4·04	0·247
131	14·79	0·068	110·5	6·59	0·152	90	4·00	0·250
130·5	14·38	0·070	110	6·50	0·154	89·5	3·96	0·253
130	14·00	0·071	109·5	6·41	0·156	89	3·92	0·255
129·5	13·63	0·073	109	6·32	0·158	88·5	3·88	0·258
129	13·28	0·075	108·5	6·23	0·160	88	3·84	0·260
128·5	12·95	0·077	108	6·14	0·163	87·5	3·80	0·263
128	12·64	0·079	107·5	6·06	0·165	87	3·76	0·266
127·5	12·33	0·081	107	5·97	0·168	86·5	3·72	0·269
127	12·04	0·083	106·5	5·89	0·170	86	3·69	0·271
126·5	11·76	0·085	106	5·82	0·172	85·5	3·65	0·274
126	11·50	0·087	105·5	5·74	0·174	85	3·62	0·276
125·5	11·24	0·089	105	5·67	0·176	84·5	3·58	0·279
125	11·00	0·091	104·5	5·59	0·179	84	3·54	0·282

* See page 92.

TABLE—*continued.*

Arc.	A 150 + α	B 150 − α	Arc.	A 150 + α	B 150 − α	Arc.	A 150 + α	B 150 − α
α	150 − α	150 + α	α	150 − α	150 + α	α	150 − α	150 + α
83·5	3·51	0·285	61	2·370	0·422	38·5	1·690	0·592
83	3·48	0·288	60·5	2·352	0·425	38	1·679	0·596
82·5	3·44	0·290	60	2·333	0·429	37·5	1·667	0·600
82	3·41	0·293	59·5	2·315	0·432	37	1·655	0·604
81·5	3·38	0·296	59	2·296	0·435	36·5	1·643	0·609
81	3·35	0·299	58·5	2·278	0·439	36	1·631	0·613
80·5	3·31	0·302	58	2·261	0·442	35·5	1·620	0·617
80	3·28	0·304	57·5	2·243	0·446	35	1·608	0·622
79·5	3·25	0·307	57	2·226	0·449	34·5	1·597	0·626
79	3·22	0·310	56·5	2·208	0·453	34	1·586	0·630
78·5	3·19	0·313	56	2·191	0·456	33·5	1·575	0·635
78	3·17	0·316	55·5	2·174	0·460	33	1·564	0·639
77·5	3·14	0·319	55	2·158	0·463	32·5	1·553	0·644
77	3·11	0·322	54·5	2·141	0·467	32	1·542	0·648
76·5	3·08	0·325	54	2·125	0·471	31·5	1·531	0·653
76	3·05	0·327	53·5	2·109	0·474	31	1·521	0·657
75·5	3·03	0·330	53	2·093	0·478	30·5	1·510	0·662
75	3·00	0·333	52·5	2·077	0·481	30	1·500	0·667
74·5	2·973	0·336	52	2·061	0·485	29·5	1·489	0·671
74	2·947	0·339	51·5	2·045	0·489	29	1·479	0·676
73·5	2·921	0·342	51	2·030	0·492	28·5	1·469	0·681
73	2·896	0·345	50·5	2·015	0·496	28	1·459	0·685
72·5	2·871	0·348	50	2·000	0·500	27·5	1·449	0·690
72	2·846	0·351	49·5	1·985	0·504	27	1·439	0·695
71·5	2·822	0·354	49	1·970	0·508	26·5	1·429	0·700
71	2·797	0·357	48·5	1·955	0·511	26	1·419	0·705
70·5	2·773	0·360	48	1·941	0·515	25·5	1·409	0·709
70	2·750	0·364	47·5	1·926	0·519	25	1·400	0·714
69·5	2·726	0·367	47	1·913	0·523	24·5	1·390	0·719
69	2·703	0·370	46·5	1·898	0·527	24	1·380	0·724
68·5	2·680	0·373	46	1·884	0·531	23·5	1·371	0·729
68	2·658	0·376	45·5	1·870	0·535	23	1·362	0·734
67·5	2·636	0·379	45	1·857	0·538	22·5	1·352	0·739
67	2·614	0·382	44·5	1·843	0·542	22	1·343	0·744
66·5	2·592	0·386	44	1·830	0·546	21·5	1·334	0·749
66	2·571	0·389	43·5	1·816	0·550	21	1·325	0·754
65·5	2·550	0·392	43	1·803	0·554	20·5	1·316	0·760
65	2·529	0·395	42·5	1·790	0·558	20	1·307	0·765
64·5	2·509	0·398	42	1·777	0·562	19·5	1·298	0·770
64	2·488	0·402	41·5	1·765	0·567	19	1·290	0·775
63·5	2·468	0·405	41	1·752	0·571	18·5	1·281	0·780
63	2·448	0·408	40·5	1·739	0·575	18	1·272	0·786
62·5	2·428	0·412	40	1·727	0·579	17·5	1·264	0·791
62	2·409	0·415	39·5	1·714	0·583	17	1·255	0·796
61·5	2·389	0·418	39	1·702	0·587	16·5	1·247	0·802

TABLE—*continued.*

Arc.	A 150 + a	B 150 − a	Arc.	A 150 + a	B 150 − a	Arc.	A 150 + a	B 150 − a
a	150 − a	150 + a	a	150 − a	150 + a	a	150 − a	150 + a
16	1·238	0·807	10·5	1·150	0·869	5	1·068	0·935
15·5	1·230	0·813	10	1·143	0·875	4·5	1·061	0·942
15	1·222	0·818	9·5	1·135	0·881	4	1·054	0·948
14·5	1·214	0·823	9	1·127	0·887	3·5	1·047	0·954
14	1·206	0·829	8·5	1·120	0·893	3	1·040	0·960
13·5	1·198	0·835	8	1·112	0·899	2·5	1·033	0·967
13	1·189	0·841	7·5	1·105	0·905	2	1·027	0·974
12·5	1·181	0·847	7	1·097	0·911	1·5	1·020	0·980
12	1·173	0·852	6·5	1·090	0·917	1	1·013	0·987
11·5	1·166	0·858	6	1·083	0·923	0·5	1·006	0·993
11	1·158	0·863	5·5	1·076	0·929			

A SYNOPSIS OF THE PRINCIPAL EVENTS THAT HAVE OCCURRED IN CONNECTION WITH THE HISTORY OF THE TORPEDO.

Date.	Operator, &c.	Event.	Place.	Remarks.
1585.	Italian Engineer, Zambelli.	Attack on a bridge formed over the Scheldt.	Antwerp.	Bridge completely destroyed. Vessels, each carrying a heavily charged magazine, fired by clockwork, were carried by the stream against the bridge.
1775.	Captain D. Bushnell.	Numerous small experiments with gunpowder charges.	America.	By which he proved that a charge of gunpowder could be fired under water.
1776.	"	Attack on the English frigate H.M.S. *Eagle* by his submarine torpedo boat.	New York.	Attack managed by Sergeant E. Lee. Attack failed, owing to his inexperience in manipulating this novel kind of craft.
1777.	"	Attack on the English man-of-war H.M.S. *Cerberus* by his drifting torpedoes.	New London.	Drifting torpedoes employed. Crew of a prize schooner astern of the *Cerberus* hauled one of the torpedoes on board, which exploded, killing 3 men and destroying a boat.
1777.	"	Attack on English ships by numerous floating torpedoes. Known by the name of "Battle of Kegs."	..	This failed, owing to the ships having previously hauled into dock to avoid the ice, but it created a great amount of confusion and alarm among the crews of the vessels.
1797.	R. Fulton.	Experiments with torpedoes on the Seine.	France.	These first attempts were generally failures.
July 3, 1801.	"	Experiments with his submarine boat named the *Nautilus*.	Brest, France.	These experiments were successful in so far as proving that with such a boat he could descend to any given depth and reascend to the surface at will, and that he could remain below for a considerable time.
August 1801.	"	Attempted to sink a small vessel by means of one of his torpedoes.	"	Completely successful. This is the first vessel known to be destroyed by means of a torpedo. Charge of submarine mine 20 lbs. gunpowder.

Date	Name	Event	Place	Result
1801.	"	Attempted to destroy one of the English channel fleet by means of his drifting torpedoes.	Off Boulogne, France.	Owing to the ship altering her position at the moment of setting the torpedo adrift, this attack failed.
Oct. 3, 1804.	"	Catamarran expedition under Lord Keith to destroy the French fleet.	Boulogne, France.	Failed, owing to a mistake in the construction of the torpedoes. The mines exploded, but did no damage to the French ships.
Oct. 1805.	"	Similar expedition.	"	Similar failure, owing to causes above mentioned.
Oct. 15, 1805.	"	Attempted to destroy a brig Dorothea with his drifting torpedoes.	Dover, England.	The brig was completely demolished. Two torpedoes employed, each charged with 180 lbs. gunpowder and fired by clockwork.
July 20, 1807.	"	Experiment on a large lulk brig.	New York, America.	Finally successful, several attempts being necessary, owing to faulty construction.
Oct. 1810.	"	Attack on the U.S. sloop Argus for finally testing the efficacy of his torpedo schemes.	New York.	Failed, owing to the very ingenious though elaborate defence of the vessel, carried out under the directions of Commodore Rodgers.
1812.	Mr. Mix.	Attack on the English frigate H.M.S. Plantagenet with his drifting torpedoes.	Lynn, Haven Bay, America.	Complete failure, though six different attempts were made.
June 15, 1813.	"	Attack on H.M.S. Ramilies by blowing up a schooner alongside.	New York.	An utter failure.
1820.	Captain Johnson.	Experiment with a submarine boat carrying a torpedo on its back.	Moulsford, Berks, England.	Idea was to fasten the torpedo by means of screws to the bottom of the hostile vessel. Trial proved successful, but the English government refused to sanction the project as being too diabolical.
July 4, 1829.	Colonel Samuel Colt.	Experiment on a raft with his submarine battery.	Ware Pond, America.	Successful.
1839.	General Paisley, R.E.	Destruction of the wreck of the Royal George by submarine mines.	Portsmouth, England.	He is stated to have employed galvanic firing to explode the mines.
1840.	Captain Warner.	Experiment on the John O'Gaunt.	England.	Successful. Details not known.
June 4, 1842.	Colonel S. Colt.	Experiment to explode a submarine mine by electricity.	New York.	Successful. The operator was at a great distance from the torpedo.
July 4, 1842.	"	Experiment on the U.S. gunboat Boxer with electric submarine mines.	Castle Garden, New York.	Successful. The operator was on board U.S. man-of-war at some distance from the place where the explosion occurred.

A SYNOPSIS OF THE PRINCIPAL EVENTS THAT HAVE OCCURRED IN CONNECTION WITH THE HISTORY OF THE TORPEDO—continued.

Date.	Operator, &c.	Event.	Place.	Remarks.
Aug. 20, 1842.	Colonel S. Colt.	Similar experiment on a schooner.	Potomac River, America.	Successful, the operator being stationed at a distance of 5 miles from where the mine was placed.
Oct. 18, 1842.	,,	Similar experiment on the brig *Volta*, 300 tons.	New York.	Successful. The operator being on board the revenue cutter *Ewing*, at a considerable distance from the scene of the explosion.
April 13, 1843.	,,	Experiment to destroy a vessel of 500 tons *under weigh* by electric submarine mines.	Potomac River, America.	Successful. The vessel was, at the time of the explosion, sailing at the rate of 5 knots per hour, and to prevent the possibility of any collusion between the operator and crew, they left the ship a few moments before the catastrophe. Operator 5 miles distant. Probably several mines were placed in the form of a circle.
July, 1844.	Captain Warner.	Experiment with his invisible shell, on a barque of 450 tons.	Brighton, England.	The vessel completely destroyed.
Jan. 1, 1845.	Colonel S. Colt.	Experiment with an electric submarine mine.	New York.	Successful. The operator being at a distance of 40 miles from where the explosion took place.
1846.	Professor Schonbein.	Discovered the explosive agent "gun-cotton."	..	Brought into use for military purposes about 1863, by Professor Abel.
1846.	Sobrero.	Discovered the explosive agent nitro-glycerine.	..	Brought into use about 1863, for blasting purposes by M. Alfred Nobel, a Swede.
1854.	Russians.	Attempted destruction of the English men-of-war *Merlin* and *Firefly*, by stationary submarine mines.	Cronstadt.	Several torpedoes were exploded near these ships, but with no other results than a wetting to some of their men.
Feb. 18, 1862.	Confederates.	Federal gunboats attempting to force the Savannah river.	America.	Considerably delayed, caused by the submarine mines, but no actual damage done. This was their first appearance in a practical form during the civil war.

Date		Event	Location	Remarks
Dec. 13, 1862.	.	Destruction of the Federal ironclad *Cairo*, by stationary torpedoes.	Yazoo River, America.	Two torpedoes exploded under her; vessel much shattered, and sunk in 12 minutes. First vessel destroyed in this war.
Feb. 28, 1863.	.	The Federal monitor *Montauk*, severely damaged by a submarine mine.	Ogeechee River, Georgia.	She was saved from sinking by being run on the mud, thus enabling the hole to be temporarily closed, and the vessel taken to Port Royal.
July 22, 1863.	„	The Federal ironclad gunboat *Baron de Kalb*, sunk by a submarine mine.	Yazoo River.	The vessel went down in 15 minutes. As she was sinking a second torpedo exploded under her stern. No lives were lost.
Aug. 8, 1863.	„	The Federal gunboat *Commodore Barney* severely damaged.	James River.	The ship was, at the time of the explosion, steaming 9 knots, and ran into it, losing 20 men, and being somewhat severely damaged. It was an electric submarine mine charged with 1750 lbs. gunpowder.
Oct. 5, 1863.	„	Boat torpedo attack on the Federal ship *Ironsides*.	Charleston.	Failed. It was made by a boat armed with a spar torpedo with 60 lbs. gunpowder.
1863.	„	Confederate steamers *Marion* and *Ettiva* destroyed by their own mines.	"	Owing to the shifting of the position of barrel torpedoes.
1863.	„	Confederate flag of truce boat *Shultz*.	James River.	The same cause.
Feb. 17, 1864.	„	Boat torpedo attack on the Federal frigate *Housatonic*.	Charleston.	Successful, the ship being sunk. A submarine boat was employed on this occasion, and owing to her running into the hole made by her torpedo, went down with the ship.
March 6, 1864.	„	Boat torpedo attack on the Federal ship *Memphis*.	North Edisto River, South Carolina.	Failed, owing to the torpedo spar being broken by the vessel's screw.
April 1, 1864.	„	Destruction of the Federal transport *Maple Leaf*.	St. John's River, Florida.	This was effected by a floating torpedo.
April 9, 1864.	„	Boat torpedo attack on the Federal ship *Minnesota*.	James River.	The ship was severely damaged, but not sunk. Spar torpedo, charge 53 lbs. gunpowder.
April 19, 1864.	„	Boat torpedo attack on the Federal frigate *Wabash*.	Charleston.	Failed, owing to the boat being discovered.
May 6, 1864.	„	Loss of the *Commodore Jones*.	James River.	Completely demolished by an electric torpedo, 1750 lbs. gunpowder. This part of the river having been carefully dragged.

A Synopsis of the Principal Events that have Occurred in Connection with the History of the Torpedo—continued.

Date.	Operator, &c.	Event.	Place.	Remarks.
Aug. 5, 1864.	Confederates.	Loss of the Federal monitor *Tecumseh*.	Mobile Bay.	This occurred during the Federal attack on the defences of Mobile Bay, the ship disappearing almost instantaneously. The captain and 70 of the crew were killed.
Oct. 27, 1864.	Federals.	Boat torpedo attack on the Confederate ironclad *Albemarle*.	Near Plymouth, America.	The only Federal torpedo success during the war. The boat was armed with the Wood and Lay disconnecting spar torpedo. The ship was sunk.
Dec. 9, 1864.	Confederates.	Loss of the Federal steamers *Otsego* and *Bazeley*.	Roanoke River.	The latter vessel was proceeding to the assistance of the former. Both were totally destroyed.
1864.	M. A. Nobel.	Introduction of dynamite.	..	A modified form of the explosive nitro-glycerine.
1864.	Captain Luppis and Mr. Whitehead.	First series of experiments with the fish torpedo.	Fiume, Austria.	The idea of such a weapon previously known, but not acted on.
Jan. 15, 1865.	Confederates.	Loss of the Federal monitor *Patapsco*.	Charleston.	Completely destroyed by a barrel torpedo, sinking in a few minutes. Sixty-two officers and men drowned.
March 1, 1865.	„	Loss of the Federal steamer *Harvest Moon*.	Near Georgetown.	The place where this catastrophe occurred had been previously swept for torpedoes.
March 30 to April 19, 1865.	„	Loss of two Federal monitors, and three gunboats.	Mobile Bay.	These losses occurred in the final attack on Mobile, at the close of the war.
Sept. 2, 1866.	Paraguayans.	Loss of the Brazilian war steamer *Rio Janeiro*.	Currupaity. Paraguay.	Completely destroyed by a stationary torpedo at the bombardment of Currupaity by the Brazilian fleet.
1874.	England.	Adoption of the electric light in the Navy.	..	
May 29, 1877.	English.	Torpedo attack by H.M.S. *Shah* on the Peruvian ironclad *Huascar*.	..	This is the first Whitehead fish torpedo ever fired against an hostile ship. It failed, owing to the *Huascar* being at too great a distance.

Date		Event	Location	Result
May 12, 1877.	Russians.	Russian torpedo boat attack on several Turkish ships.	Batoum.	Failed. A Turkish ship was struck by a towing torpedo, but it failed to explode.
May 26, 1877.	,,	Russian torpedo boat attack on the Turkish ships *Fettu Islam, Duba Saife,* and *Kilidj Ali.*	Matchines, River Danube.	Successful. A Turkish monitor, *Duba Saife,* was sunk.
June 9, 1877.	,,	Russian torpedo boat attack on the Turkish ironclads *Feteh Bulend, Moocardemikhair,* and *Idglalieh.*	Sulina, mouth of the Danube.	Failed. The Russian torpedo boat No. 1 was sunk, and her commander, Lieutenant Poutsohin, with his crew, taken prisoner. The attack was made by six boats.
June 20, 1877.	,,	Turkish monitor attacked by the Russian spar torpedo boat *Choutka.*	Rutschuk, on the Danube.	Failed. The officer in command of the boat being severely wounded, and the torpedo wires cut. This attack was made in the daytime.
June 23, 1877.	,,	Two Russian torpedo boats attacked a Turkish monitor.	Mouth of the Aluta, Danube.	Failed, owing to the spirited defence on the part of the Turks. Another day affair.
Aug. 22, 1877.	,,	The Turkish ironclad *Assari Shefket* attacked by four Russian torpedo boats.	Soukoum Kaleh.	Failed. The captain of the *Assari Shefket* had placed guard boats in advance of his ship, by which he was warned of the approach of the torpedo boats, and so enabled to foil the attack by a well-directed, hot fire.
Oct. 10, 1877.	,,	Loss of Turkish gunboat *Suna* at the Russian attack on Sulina.	Sulina.	The gunboat was sunk by striking an electro-contact mine, placed by the Russians about ¾ mile above the Turkish defences. About fifteen officers and men killed and wounded.
Dec. 27, 1877.	,,	Turkish squadron attacked by four Russian torpedo boats, two being armed with the Whitehead fish torpedo.	Batoum.	Failed. The Russians fired two Whitehead fish torpedoes (the first attack of this nature during the war), both of which were picked up by the Turks.
Jan. 25, 1878.	,,	Attack on Turkish ships by two Russian torpedo boats, armed with the Whitehead fish torpedo.	Batoum.	Successful. A Turkish revenue steamer on guard being sunk. Final torpedo attack made in the Russo-Turkish war (1877–78).

INDEX.

GRIFFIN AND CO.,
PUBLISHERS BY APPOINTMENT TO H.R.H. THE DUKE OF EDINBURGH,
2, THE HARD, PORTSMOUTH.

CAPTAIN COLOMB'S NAVAL TACTICS
In Preparation.

QUEEN'S REGULATIONS AND ADMIRALTY
INSTRUCTIONS—*New Edition*, 1879. 2s. 6d.

MANUAL OF GUNNERY,
Corrected to 1880.

THE SHIPS OF THE ROYAL NAVY
3rd Edition.

Portraits of 24 Ships, beautifully Lithographed in Colors from Original Drawings. Demy 4to. blue cloth, extra gilt, 30s. ; Best Morocco, £3 3s. ; Russia, £3 13s. 6d.

> '*Among illustrated works, none has appeared of greater interest than this upon the Royal Navy.'—Times.*
> '*As an illustrated gift-book, independent of its historic interest,* "The Royal Navy," *from the truthfulness of its illustrations, cannot but recommend itself, not only to the Royal Service, but also to the public.'—United Service Gazette.*
> '*This beautiful work does credit to all concerned in its production.'—Pall Mall Gazette.*

THE WAR SHIPS OF EUROPE
Crown 8vo. Illustrated. 10s. 6d.

By Chief-Engineer KING, U.S.A. Descriptions of the Construction, Armour and Fighting Power of the Ironclads of England and other European Powers of the present day. Revised and Corrected throughout, and with additional Notes by an English Naval Architect.

> "A valuable and interesting contribution to maritime literature . . . interesting to the public . . . . and instructive to the Naval Executive generally."—*United Service Gazette.*
> "The book is invaluable as a brief but accurate description of the fighting powers of the Ironclads of England and other European powers of the present day."—*Broad Arrow.*
> "The whole volume possesses a deep interest. Its details are trustworthy."—*John Bull.*

THE ARMIES OF EUROPE AND ASIA
Demy 8vo. Illustrated. 14s.

By Major-General UPTON, U.S.A. Embracing Official Reports on the Armies of Japan, China, India, Persia, Italy, Russia, Austria, Germany, France, and England. Accompanied by Letters descriptive of a Journey from Japan to the Caucasus.

> " His sketch of travel, though most unpretentious in manner, is highly interesting as a preliminary introduction to the very important results of this military tour. The value of this work, particularly as a book of reference, may be estimated from the fact that it contains the results of a lengthened and searching inquiry into matters connected with the great armies of the world, which was conducted by officers of proved ability and enjoying exceptional advantages. . . . . . It abounds in useful information, and may be studied with no little advantage by those who wish to improve their knowledge of the art of modern war."—*United Service Gazette.*

Griffin & Co., Publishers, 2, The Hard, Portsmouth.

2

THE SAILOR'S POCKET BOOK

3rd Edition. 7s. 6d.

By Captain F. G. D. BEDFORD, R.N. A Collection of Practical Rules, Notes, and Tables, for the use of the Royal Navy, the Mercantile Marine, and Yacht Squadrons. With Colored Signal Flags, Charts, and Illustrations. Bound in leather, 500 pages, and carefully compiled Index.

"A Nautical Cyclopædia."—*Liverpool Albion.*
"The most perfect and complete of any publication of the kind."—*U.S. Gazette.*
"A valuable addition to a yachtsman's library."—*Land and Water.*
"Valuable and excellently arranged little work."—*Pall Mall Gazette.*
"A volume quite indispensable."—*The Graphic.*
"An admirable and much wanted little book."—*Edinburgh Review.*

CAPT. SIR GEORGE S. NARES' SEAMANSHIP

5th Edition. Demy 8vo. 21s.

400 beautifully engraved Woodcuts, and Plates of Flags, accurately Colored.

' *It is the best work on Seamanship we have.*'—*Standard.*
' *Is a book for the instruction of young officers, and of reference for older ones it cannot be excelled, many most valuable additions are made in this edition. The book should be the officers' vade mecum.*'—*United Service Gazette.*
' *Every necessary particular is given so fully and completely as to leave nothing to be desired.*'—*Shipping Gazette.*

CAPTAIN ALSTON'S "SEAMANSHIP"

2nd Edition. Crown 8vo. Cloth, 12s. 6d.

Contains 200 Illustrations of Rigging, Sails, Masts, &c. ; with Instructions for Officers of the Merchant Service, by W. H. ROSSER ; forming a complete Manual of Practical Seamanship.

"The illustrations, of which there are 200, are well executed, and the reviser has brought down to the present day all changes in the rig and build of ships of war. The frontispiece gives sectional views of the screw steamship *Russia* of the Cunard line, and H.M.S. *Monarch*."—*Shipping Gazette.*
"It has been revised and enlarged by Commander R. H. Harris, R.N., and includes a treatise on nautical surveying by Staff-Commander May, and also some useful instructions for officers of the merchant service. The book seems well adapted for junior officers of the navy, and the sound advice and high moral tone of its introduction give it an additional recommendation." — *Liverpool Mercury.*

THE RIGGER'S GUIDE.

10th Thousand. New Edition.

Revised and enlarged. Cloth, 3s.

By CHARLES BUSHELL. Fully Illustrated. Being the best and only complete book on the Rigging of Ships.

"This is a valuable little book, adapted to suit every class of ship, whether steam or sailing vessel, and should form part of the kit of every youngster adopting the profession of the sea. Many oldsters will also find it valuable, from the general information it contains. The present is the sixth edition, which has been carefully revised and corrected."—*U. S. Gazette.*

Griffin & Co., Publishers, 2, The Hard, Portsmouth.

THE NAVY OF TO-DAY;

Its Moral and Intellectual Condition.

Crown 8vo. Sewed, 2s ; Cloth, 2s. 6d.

"In the Navy of To-Day, we have a number of thoughtfully written essays which deserve to obtain the widest publicity."—*Broad Arrow*.

"A little work which all should peruse who have the interests of the Navy at heart."—*Christian World*.

"We can with confidence recommend the Navy of To-Day as a book well worthy of attentive reading. We recommend chap. v. more particularly to the earnest consideration of Naval Officers."—*U.S. Gazette*.

SEA TERMS AND PHRASES.

ENGLISH AND FRENCH. By Lieut. E. PORNAIN, French Navy. For the use of Officers of Royal and Mercantile Navies, Engineers, Shipbuilders, Ship Owners, Merchants, Ship Brokers. Crown 8vo. 4s.

"A copy should be possessed by everyone whose profession, occupation, or interests bring them into relationship with a seafaring life.—*British Mercantile Review*.

"A Nautical Phrase Book in two languages . . . . a completeness which leaves nothing to be desired."—*Hampshire Telegraph*.

THE ACTIVE LIST

Of ADMIRALS and CAPTAINS.

By Capt. WILLIAM ARTHUR, R.N. Demy 8vo.

With particulars exhibiting the progress, &c., of Officers, of the Royal Navy, from their entry into the Service to Jan. 1st, 1879.

THE ACTIVE LIST

Of all COMMANDERS and LIEUTENANTS:

Corrected to July 1st, 1878.

By Lieut. M. R. HAYES, R.N. Demy 8vo. 3s. 6d.

Showing Dates of Entry, and Commissions, AGES, AND AMOUNT OF SEA TIME, Causes of Special Promotions, Special Acquirements, Comparative Progress with other Officers, List of all Officers now on the Active List who were promoted to the rank of Commander from Flag-Lieut. or Her Majesty's Yacht, the Age and Sea Time of Commanders, and other interesting particulars.

HARVEY'S SEA TORPEDOES.

With 12 Plates, 2s. 6d.

Griffin & Co., Publishers, 2, The Hard, Portsmouth.

4

NAUTICAL SURVEYING.

By Commander MAY, R.N., F.R.G.S.

Reprinted from "Alston's Seamanship." With Charts. 2s. 6d.

"The treatise is simple and clear in arrangement, and written with the especial object of instructing the officers of the Naval Service in general, and only deals with the use of such instruments as are found on board of every man-of-war. We have never met with any treatise on nautical surveying by any means so well calculated to answer the purpose for which it was written."—*Naval Science.*

THE MANUAL OF THE HYDROMETER.

2nd Edition. Illustrated. Cloth. 3s. 6d.

By LIONEL SWIFT, R.N.

' . . . Has been treated in the clear and simple manner which has been already manifested by Mr. Swift, in his accurate description of the history and philosophy of the Hydrometer.'—*Army and Navy Gazette.*

Will be found of considerable interest to Engineers and all those who are interested in the safe and economical working of Steam Engines.'— *Shipping and Mercantile Gazette.*

By Authority of the Lords of the Admiralty.

QUESTIONS & ANSWERS ON THE AMMUNITION INSTRUCTION.

For Officers passing through H.M. Gunnery Establishments.

Paper 1s. ; Cloth, 1s. 6d.

By J. KITE, Instructing Gunner, H.M.S. "Excellent."

"This book is a valuable *multum in parvo.* All the multifarious details connected with Ammunition Instruction, are dealt with ably and concisely."— *Portsmouth Times.*

TRAVERSE TABLES
Cloth, 5s. 6d.

With simple and brief method of Correcting Compass Courses.

By Commander R. E. EDWIN, R.N.

"Lieutenant Edwin has been at great pains and trouble, and he will probably save many hundreds of persons from calculations which are frequently 'wearisome to the flesh."—*Broad Arrow.*

DEFINITIONS IN NAVIGATION AND NAUTICAL ASTRONOMY.

(FROM VARIOUS AUTHORITIES.)

New Edition. With Diagrams. Demy 8vo. Cloth, 2s. 6d.

For the use of the Naval Cadets, H.M.S. "Britannia."

Griffin & Co., Publishers, 2, The Hard, Portsmouth.

8

ENGINEER OFFICER'S
WATCH, STATION, QUARTER, & FIRE BILLS.
By WILLIAM J. J. SPRY, R.N.   3s. 6d.

A complete *vade mecum* for Engineer Officers in Her Majesty's Navy.

TABLE FOR CORRECTION OF LONGITUDE
WHERE ERROR ARISES FROM INCORRECT LATITUDE.
2nd Edition.   1s.
By GILBERT T. KEY, Commander, R.N.

THE PILOT'S HANDBOOK FOR THE ENGLISH CHANNEL.
7th Edition.   7s.
Illustrated with 17 plates.   By Staff-Commander KING, R.N.

Manual for the use of the Boatmen preparing for Examination in
COAST GUARD SERVICE.
Published by Authority.   With Chart.   Demy 8vo.   1s. 6d.

MESS WINE BOOKS
With Cash Book and Ledger, complete in One Volume.
For 24 Members, 15s. ; For 12 Members, 12s. 6d.
Rough Daily Wine Book, 8s. 6d.

PROGRESS BOOK
FOR THE USE OF NAVAL INSTRUCTORS.
12s. 6d.

WATCH, QUARTER, STATION, AND FIRE BILL.
Admiralty Form, No. 2, 2s. 6d.   No. 3, 2s.

THE ADMIRALTY MANUAL OF SCIENTIFIC
ENQUIRY. 4th Edition. 3s. 3d.

JOURNAL BOOKS.

One Year, 6s.6d ; Two Years, 8s.6d. ; Three Years, 10s.6d.

Four Years, 12s. 6d.

LOG BOOKS (RULED).

Two quires, 8s.   Three quires, 10s. 6d.

CERTIFICATE CASES. Half roan, 2s. 6d.

TEXT BOOK ON THE CONSTRUCTION AND MANUFACTURE OF ORDNANCE.

Printed by Order of the Secretary of State for War.   Second
Edition.   Colored Illustrations.   Cloth Boards.   1879.
Abridged Edition.   9s.

Handbook of the Manufacture and Proof of Gunpowder.

By Capt. F. M. SMITH, Royal Artillery.   8vo., cloth boards.
With Plates and Diagrams.   5s.

Text Book on the
THEORY OF THE MOTION OF PROJECTILES,
the History, Manufacture, and Explosive Force of Gunpowder ; and the History of Small Arms.

Published by Authority.   With Diagrams.   Cloth Boards.
2s. ; interleaved, 2s. 6d.

RIFLE AND FIELD EXERCISES AND MUSKETRY INSTRUCTION FOR HER MAJESTY'S FLEET, 1878. 1s. 6d.

MANUAL AND FIRING EXERCISES FOR THE MARTINI-HENRY RIFLE.

For the use of the Navy.   By Authority.   Threepence.

FIELD EXERCISE. 1877. 1s.

Griffin & Co., Publishers, 2, The Hard, Portsmouth.

**RIFLE EXERCISE AND MUSKETRY
INSTRUCTION**—1879. 1s.

CHRONOMETER JOURNAL—With Diagrams. 12s. 6d.

NOSOLOGICAL JOURNAL—9s.

CLOTHES AND SLOP LIST—5s. and 8s. 6d.

CLOTHES LIST—New Pattern. 4s. 6d. and 7s. 6d.

THE SICK LIST—4s. 6d. and 7s. 6d.
WITH ALPHABET—5s. AND 8s.

NIGHT ORDER BOOK—5s. 6d.

WASHING BOOK FOR NAVAL OFFICERS—6d.

**ANNUAL OF THE ROYAL SCHOOL OF NAVAL
ARCHITECTURE & MARINE ENGINEERING.**
Parts 1 to 4—2s. 6d. each.

Parts 1 and 4 contain particulars of English and Foreign
Ironclads.

TREATISE ON AMMUNITION—6s.

MANUAL OF FIELD FORTIFICATION—3s.

NOTES ON AMMUNITION.

Published by Authority. Corrected to July, 1877. With Diagrams.
cloth boards, 2s. 6d.

BATTALION WORDS OF COMMAND—3d.

THE SAPPERS' MANUAL—Part 1.—2s.

Griffin & Co., Publishers, 2, The Hard,

11

PAMPHLETS.

Remarks on Naval Warfare and on the Navy.
By a Naval Officer. One Shilling.

The Admiralty.
By a Flag Officer. Second Edition. One Shilling.

A Naval Reserve of the Future.
By Commander Arthur H. Gilmore, R.N. One Shilling.

Imperial Defence.
By Captain P. C. Colomb. Two Shillings.

The Loss of the Captain.
By an Officer of H.M.S. "Minotaur." Sixpence.

The Church in the Navy, its Communicants and Bible Classes.—6d.

On the Holy Communion in the Navy.
By a Commander, R.N. Demy 16mo. Sixpence.

Some Remarks on Naval Education.
By Captain A. Gardner, R.N. Sixpence.

Life-Saving at Sea,
BY CORK LIFE-BELTS OR MATTRESSES, &c.,
By Vice-Admiral A. P. Ryder. Second Edition. Demy 8vo.
One Shilling.

SEAMEN'S PRAYERS.

For the use of the Royal Navy; and also Merchant Service.

84th THOUSAND; on Card, 2s. per 100. Per post, 2s. 6d.

Griffin & Co., Publishers, 2, The Hard, Portsmouth.

NAVAL PROFESSIONAL BOOKS.

SOLD BY MESSRS. GRIFFIN & CO.

ON MODERN ARTILLERY; Its Principles and Practice. By Lieut-Col. C. H. Owen. 15s.

THE PHYSICAL GEOGRAPHY OF THE SEA AND ITS METEOROLOGY. 15th Edition. By M. F. Maury, LL.D. 5s.

ON THE LAWS OF STORMS. Considered practically. By W. H. Rosser. 5s.

THE SAILOR'S HORN-BOOK FOR THE LAW OF STORMS: Being a Practical Exposition of the Theory of the Law of Storms. By H. Piddington. 5th Edition. 10s. 6d.

ON THE STEAM ENGINE. By W. Ewers. 3s.

LIGHTS AND TIDES OF THE WORLD. 4th Edition. 1s.

NAVAL ARCHITECTURE. By W. H. White. 24s.

NAVAL ARCHITECTURE. By Samuel J. P. Thearle. With Volume of Plates. (Practical) 7s. 6d. (Theoretical) 10s. 6d. 2 Vols.

WEATHER CHARTS AND STORM WARNINGS. By Robert H. Scott, M.A., F.R.S. 3s. 6d.

A TREATISE ON THE CRIMINAL LAW OF THE NAVY. By Theodore Thring. 8s. 6d.

HANDBOOK OF THE LAWS OF STORMS. By William Radcliffe Birt. 5s.

A NAVAL AND MILITARY TECHNICAL DICTIONARY OF THE FRENCH LANGUAGE. By Colonel Burn, R.A. 5th Edition. 15s.

NAVIGATION AND NAUTICAL ASTRONOMY. By the Rev. R. M. Inskip, C.B. 6s. 6d.

NORIE'S COMPLETE EPITOME OF PRACTICAL NAVIGATION. Illustrated by several Engravings. 20th Edition. 16s.

HOW TO FIND THE STARS, AND THEIR USE IN DETERMIN-ING LATITUDE, LONGITUDE, and THE ERROR of the COMPASS; Illustrated with Woodcuts, and four large Maps of the Stars. By W. H. Rosser. 7s. 6d.

GANOT'S ELEMENTARY TREATISE ON PHYSICS. Illustrated by 4 Colored Plates and 758 woodcuts, 15s.

GANOT'S NATURAL PHILOSOPHY. 7s. 6d.

Griffin & Co., Publishers, 2, The Hard, Portsmouth.

NAVAL PROFESSIONAL BOOKS.

(Continued.)

THE HEAVENS. An Illustrated Handbook of Popular Astronomy. By Amedèe Guillemin. 12s.

THE FORCES OF NATURE, By Amedèe GUILLEMIN. Illustrated by 11 colored plates and 455 woodcuts. £1 1s.

DESCHANEL'S NATURAL PHILOSOPHY. By Professor Everett. 18s.

PHYSICAL GEOGRAPHY IN ITS RELATION TO THE WINDS & CURRENTS. By J. K. Laughton, M.A. 10s. 6d.

JEANS' NAVIGATION & NAUTICAL ASTRONOMY. Price 14s.
PART I.—Containing Rules and Examples. 7s. 6d.
PART II.—Investigations and Proofs of Rules. 7s. 6d.

REGULATIONS FOR PREVENTING COLLISIONS AT SEA. 1s.

THE UNIVERSAL CODE OF SIGNALS of the Mercantile Marine of all Nations. By G. B. Richardson. 12s.

CONTRIBUTIONS TO SOLAR PHYSICS. By Norman Lockyer, F.R.S. 31s. 6d.

JEANS' HANDBOOK OF THE STARS. 4s. 6d.

HALF HOURS WITH THE STARS. By Proctor. 5s.

AINSLEY'S GUIDE to the Examinations of the Local Marine Board. 6s.

SAILS AND SAIL MAKING, WITH DRAUGHTING, &C. By Robert Kipping, 2s. 6d.

EVANS' ELEMENTARY MANUAL for the Deviation of the Compass in Iron Ships. 4s. 6d.

THE MARINE STEAM ENGINE. By Maine and Brown. 12s. 6d.

SPON'S TABLES AND MEMORANDA for Engineers. 1s.

MOLESWORTH'S ENGINEER'S POCKET BOOK. 6s.

PROCTOR'S POCKET BOOK FOR MARINE ENGINEERS. 4s.

THE NAUTICAL ALMANAC. 3s.

MASTING, MAST-MAKING, and RIGGING OF SHIPS, with Tables of Spars, &c. By Robert Kipping. 2s.

Griffin & Co., Publishers, 2, The Hard, Portsmouth.

www.ingramcontent.com/pod-product-compliance
Lightning Source LLC
Chambersburg PA
CBHW020449100426
42813CB00026B/3008